Contents

Quaker Crosscurrents

FRIENDS' BRICK MEETING HOUSE AT NINE PARTNERS.

Nine Partners Meeting House and School, 1820, by Alex. H. Coffin.
Courtesy Friends Historical Library, Swarthmore College.

Quaker Crosscurrents

Three Hundred Years of Friends in the New York Yearly Meetings

Edited by
HUGH BARBOUR, CHRISTOPHER DENSMORE,
ELIZABETH H. MOGER, NANCY C. SOREL,
ALSON D. VAN WAGNER, AND ARTHUR J. WORRALL

With a Foreword by
MARTIN E. MARTY

SYRACUSE UNIVERSITY PRESS

First Edition 1995
95 96 97 98 99 00   6 5 4 3 2 1

The paper used in this publication meets the minimum requirements of American National Standard for Information Sciences—Permanence of Paper for Printed Library Materials, ANSI Z39.48-1984. ∞™

Library of Congress Cataloging-in-Publication Data

Quaker crosscurrents : three hundred years of Friends in the New York
    Yearly Meetings / edited by Hugh Barbour . . . [et al.] ; with a
    foreword by Martin E. Marty.
        p.   cm.
    Includes bibliographical references and index.
    ISBN 0-8156-2651-7 (alk. paper) ISBN 0-8156-2664-9 (pbk.: alk. paper)
    1. New York Yearly Meeting of the Religious Society of Friends—
History. 2. Society of Friends—New York—History. 3. New York
(State)—Church history. I. Barbour, Hugh.
BX7607.N5Q34   1995
289.6'747—dc20   94-48761

Manufactured in the United States of America

Illustrations

Maps

Table

Foreword

BY MARTIN E. MARTY

Almost always when historians touch on religious bodies and then mention the Society of Friends, they say something like, "The Quakers, influential far beyond their numbers . . . ." A dozen such bodies in Great Britain and scores in the United States have always had and still have far more members than do the Friends. Yet the Friends have made their mark, and even those who are barely literate in things religious and historical have some impression of Quakers. This was as true of Quakers of old, when modes of speech and dress made them audibly and visibly very different, as it is in the twentieth century, when their peace witness, albeit ambiguous, has set them apart.

To notice this small group, as the company of historians in this book has done, is not remarkable. To locate them, however, is more difficult in these years when numerous analysts like to contrast "mainstream" with "marginal" religious movements, even as they note a progressive blurring of the line between the two. At least in the United States, getting into the mainstream is like buying a ticket on a slow train to Decline; being in the margin is likely to anticipate the group's being lured toward the mainstream. The mainstream groups have low boundaries and considerable openness to culture. Their marks are tolerance, a readiness to see development in religion, an unwillingness to claim that they alone have all the truth. The marginal groups have thick and high walls and tend to be closed off, sectarian, in "cognitive minority" situations (to use sociologist Peter Berger's words). They are often exclusivist, absolutist about doctrine and prescribed behavior and practice. The Friends always create a problem for those who do such classifying, and *Quaker Crosscurrents,* by focusing on the story of the movement in one place, although in many times, will further trouble

xvii

those who like things neat. Of course, there are the out-and-out liberal Quakers, the left side of the Hicksite movement, the quasi-Unitarian and humanist sorts. Anyone with a taste for irony may find that they were often more focused and even rigid (about and against ortho-doxy!) than were the highly defined conservative groups. Yet for pres-ent purposes one can join the authors in the book, who see open-mindedness and antisectarianism in the liberal impulse.

Again, of course, there are clearly and simply intransigent Quakers, the right side of the evangelical movements, the quasi-fundamentalist sorts. Anyone with a taste for irony will find that they also made their compromises with culture and were capable of picking up very worldly religious elements from the secular world around them.

Those extremes aside, however, the great Quaker middle confuses those who classify for the sake of analyzing and telling stories as his-torians and social scientists do. Friends would have satisfied Ernst Troeltsch's terms for being categorized a "sect" or Berger's for being a "cognitive minority." If they were only that, this would be a book about exotic, arcane idiosyncratic, people. That is precisely what it does not turn out to be.

Mainstream religion tends to have a history, a public place. As a Lutheran who writes about five hundred years of American religion, I find it difficult to find and place my Protestant body, the third largest with its eight million American members, on the map where one lo-cates the great public events. They have a rich worship life, thriving congregations, and histories of local import. Yet until the late twentieth century, they, like so many Catholic ethnic groups, were bland, white, Protestant, and like segregated African-American churches seemed more acted upon than acting.

Not so with the Quakers. Some of us who write about power in the culture and its religion, about the flow of the mainstream, would de-fine one of the criteria for getting into the mainstream this way. It helps, especially in having "influence beyond your numbers," to be in-volved if not positively, then at least not negatively, with the turning-point events and crucial phenomena of the larger culture. Quakers were involved in exploration, settlement, colonial development, inde-pendence, constitution making, evangelizing, facing up to slavery, re-forming, working for temperance, having attitudes toward war and peace, "being in" on urbanization, fighting over issues beyond the boundary of one's own sect, dealing with the sexual revolution, and more. That sequence (with which most cultural historians would feel at home) all but maps and parallels the outline for this book. If there are what Vernon Parrington called "main currents in American thought," there are Quaker crosscurrents, which are currents too, part of the larger historical flow.

No religious cluster with the savor of its salt will be content only to be acted upon, responsive to an agenda set by secular and religious mainstream sources and impulses. As the authors of this book make clear, the Quakers had a history driven by forces from within, innate and instinctive outpourings of the central impulses of the movement. This is particularly true of the most dramatic and pathetic incident in American Quaker history in general and New York history in particular: the Hicksite schism of 1828. Yet even that division is a localized expression of trends that marked and afflicted non-Quaker history. The Hicksite schism, for instance, anticipated by one hundred years the Protestant evangelical-fundamentalist to-dos of the 1920s and again of recent decades. Quakers had to take attitudes toward the Civil War, the two World Wars, and the conflicts in our own times, and their plot is webbed into this war plot more inextricably and vividly than are the attitudes of some bodies fifty times their size.

In every case, however, there was a Quaker twist or spin on the general story. Why bother to tell the story if the Quakers were really like everyone else of their generations? They had special reservations about war and luxury; they found themselves proving their patriotism within the system and had to admit that their once-beleaguered people often prospered beyond their dreams. So they had to use Quaker legitimations for their economic practices.

One could cite abolition and feminism as two other causes that quite naturally involved Quakers alongside non-Quakers yet without obliterating the Friends' distinctives. I confess to having read this book with pleasure "despite the manifold pain that marks many chapters." To come across in New York Quakerism so many names with which even the casual historian is familiar must be a pleasure. Here is Elias Hicks, as famed a schismatic as American religion in that time of fissiparation knew; here are Susan B. Anthony and Mary Calderone and even Sojourner Truth, E. A. Burtt, and Kenneth Morgan. They are not all household names, but they are familiar to historians of religion. They appear alongside Quaker scholars and mystics I have known. Alongside them are some I am not the only one not to have known; there were Norwegian Quakers on the New York frontier in the nineteenth century.

To my taste, the editors have webbed their stories convincingly; I would call them "consensus historians," which sounds like such a

Quaker thing to be—"not referring to a historical school." They are historians who can find a good story and spin out its plot. Although historians do not in the main believe that there were "good old days," there were "pretty good days" before the schism of 1828 and some good things came of Quakerism in New York after the disruption. It may seem to other first-time readers that Quakers migrated and worked and split out of group conviction. After they became virtually two groups, some of the passion was gone. One hundred and thirty years after the great schism they came to each other to reconcile. The authors of this book, taking the long view, can foresee that in the growing pluralism of New York State and the United States in general, trends broadly sketched in this book will develop with immediacy and with demand for comparison. *Quaker Crosscurrents* at least prepares people who must observe, classify, and project the stories of groups they discuss by giving the main plot in a crucial and large locale. Reading it often suggests that one is reading "current events." In many cases, one is.

Preface

Despite considerable scholarly interest in Quakerism and its impact on American society, there has never been a history of New York Yearly Meeting. This volume is the first to treat comprehensively the history of New York Yearly Meeting of the Religious Society of Friends and the activities of Quakers within that region.

The task of the writers and editors was to cover more than three hundred years of history in as many pages. Many topics could be touched upon only briefly, and undoubtedly other individuals and issues could have been included. Although our first objective was to produce a scholarly and readable history of New York Yearly Meeting that can stand on its own merits, our secondary goal was to provide a framework for further research and study and to suggest topics of potential interest. This should not be the last word on New York Yearly Meeting but a new beginning for scholarship.

The limits of cultural regions posed problems for defining the boundaries of the Quaker units of association and discipline called yearly meetings because of their annual gatherings. New York Yearly Meeting at one time or another included all Friends meetings in Connecticut and Massachusetts west of the Connecticut River and in Vermont. In the late eighteenth and early nineteenth century, as a result of migration, it included meetings in Quebec, Ontario, and Michigan. After the separation of 1828, some Hicksite meetings in northern New Jersey moved their affiliations from Philadelphia to New York.

Friends in New York have been neither the shapers of culture, as they were in Philadelphia and the Delaware valley, nor largely a counterculture, as in North Carolina or in New England outside of Rhode Island. It is a crucial region in which to study the relationships of Friends to the surrounding culture, for the New York Quaker community in each period has combined urban and rural ways of life, and interactive and prophetic approaches to non-Quaker mores. Many New York Friends prepared the way for the reforming role favored by most modern Quakers as leaders and pioneers in peace and social service programs and in prison and mental hospital reform. Clashes between New York Friends' ideals of witnessing as "the plain people" versus those of building "the Holy Experiment" were as vital as those over doctrine in the great Separation of "Orthodox" and "Hicksite" Friends, which lasted from 1828 to 1955. New York Quakers neither dominated local movements of social reform nor simply echoed them. After the colonial era, some of them participated in educational and welfare associations and programs on an interchurch basis. New York Friends, becoming more fully immersed in the lives they shared with non-Quaker neighbors, were also influenced more than other east coast Friends by non-Quaker religious revivals and secular movements of thought. Yet they were less fully dominated by any single Quaker faction. As a microcosm of American Quakerism, they were aware of contrasts between their own rural and urban communities, between their older and newer meetings, between quietists, evangelicals, and liberals in doctrine, and later between pastoral and silent worship. They did not avoid divisions caused by these crosscurrents but overcame them more readily than did most Friends elsewhere.

The committee preparing for the tercentenary of the united New York Yearly Meeting faced the diversity of issues and materials needing inclusion in a scholarly history. The full scope was beyond the range of any single historian, and so, in Quaker style, a committee was constituted to draw on the wealth of knowledge about Friends in specific regions and periods. The product was designed to be a mosaic rather than the homogenized work none of us felt competent to write. The original editorial team of Hugh Barbour, Christopher Densmore, and Elizabeth H. Moger early and readily grew to include our chair, Alson Van Wagner, historian Arthur Worrall from Colorado, recorder Mary Ellen Singsen, literary stylist Cheshire Frager, computer specialist Beth Ann Adcock, and oral historian Nancy Sorel, at whose Carmel, New York, home we spent many weekend working sessions. The editorial team solicited additional contributions by specialists on many topics. In addition to those already mentioned, Nancy Hewitt and Mary Finn took major responsibilities for the chapters on women and education. The names of all contributors are listed. John Brush drew our maps and Carol Holmes read proof.

This book would also not have been possible without the early encouragement of Syracuse University Press and financial support from New York Yearly Meeting, the Chase Fund, and the Louisville Institute for the Study of Protestantism and American Culture.

Introductory Summary

The Quaker movement began in England in the 1650s, and its prophetic messengers felt called of God to land in New York within that decade. They convinced some of the English settlers already living along Long Island Sound and the Narragansett and Chesapeake bays to become the first American Quakers. The internal story of Quakerism in the New York region has been briefly told by earlier Quaker historians, but the mutual crosscurrents between the Quaker movement and the wider regional culture or cultures have been much less studied. Major turning points in the region, however, were shaped by that interaction, both events within the Society of Friends, such as the Hicksite-Orthodox Separation of 1828 and the Reunion of 1955, and those within the social institutions of New York City and State from the founding in 1790–1830 of schools, prisons, mental hospitals, and campaigns against slavery to the peace movements of the 1960s.

New York has always been a diverse, multicultural society. Yet from the 1650s to the American Revolution, the autonomous Quaker communities mainly lived and worshipped independently of non-Friends, migrating by stages up the Hudson and westward in parallel with other groups but into their own new, largely rural settlements. They had already taken up stands, or testimonies, against slavery and war but expected and suffered social isolation and persecution for doing so.

After independence, New York City began to grow dramatically, and Quakers were often leaders both in trade and in the philanthropic committees that responded to problems of epidemics, immigrants, the urban poor, and slavery in the nation as a whole. New York Friends turned from founding schools for Quaker children to experiment with schools for African- and Native Americans and public schools for the poor. Later, they similarly moved out from the original equality of women with men within Quaker worship and business meetings to campaign for women's rights in general. Quakers dominated the New York Manumission Society, the New York Free School Society, and the first institution for juvenile delinquents and were a major factor at the Seneca Falls Women's Rights Convention in 1848.

Meanwhile, however, although eighteenth- and nineteenth-century Friends were perceived by themselves and the world as a distinct population, they were influenced by evangelical liberal and rationalist currents in the broader society. These clashes, and the current between urban and rural Friends' relationships to their neighbors, led to the conflict within the Quaker community between the often authoritarian Friends who linked their Quakerism with "Orthodox" Protestant beliefs and those who, like Elias Hicks, were mainly rural, suspicious of creeds and central control, and later became increasingly liberal in doctrine. The resulting division into two regionwide New York Yearly Meetings, "Orthodox" and "Hicksite," and the consequent splits within all the local and monthly meetings, led to a serious decline in Quaker self-assurance, numbers, and influence. The Quaker travelers, whose spirit-led ministry in local meetings had knit Friends together, often served to divide them during and after the clash. Quakers who joined non-Friends in campaigns for women's rights or against slavery became suspect, whether their allies were Unitarians, evangelical Protestants, or secular reformers. To young men in both Quaker branches the American Civil War brought the tragic dilemma between Quaker pacifism and the Northern cause of slavery abolition. Unease over the lost members by the ban on marrying non-Quakers led to a parallel rethinking of Quaker discipline and isolation.

Anxiety over moral compromise turned some of the Hicksites, dwindling after the Civil War, to causes such as peace societies, temperance, and women's purity. It pushed some Orthodox Friends into the Protestant revival movements whose hymns and exhortations produced conversions and experiences of holiness. Orthodox Friends who had been informal traveling ministers thereby turned into full-time revivalists, pastors, and missionaries. Fear that Friends would surrender even their traditional rejection of outward sacraments led New York Orthodox Friends to join in 1887 with others in the first national Quaker bodies and a uniform book of discipline. Hicksite yearly meetings also joined in a series of cooperative conferences.

Late in the century American Protestantism was challenged intellectually by scientific discoveries and scholars' exploration of the origins and historical settings of their doctrines and the Bible. Both evangelical and liberal Quakers, both pastors and college graduates, were helped in dealing with these issues by the Quaker belief, central from the beginning, that the Spirit of God works in every human being, and is the inward—Rufus Jones said "the mystical"—essence of Quaker worship experience. Similarly, the Protestant "Social Gospel," which challenged the economic and structural sources of social evils and war, revived among Friends their testimonies for justice and peace, particularly in the two World Wars and the Great Depression between, so that even the American Friends Service Committee turned its emphasis from relief to social change.

The common programs that Friends designed to meet these shared challenges were among the sources of the movement for unity between the Hicksite and Orthodox branches of Quakerism, which led to the reunion of the New York Yearly Meetings in 1955. In the same postwar decade New York Friends found themselves in a central place within the national crises over civil liberties, racial equality, and antinuclear and antiwar protest, and in response some became leaders throughout America for nonviolent social change. New York Quakers initiated programs to resolve conflict and reduce violence in prisons and schools. These Quaker stands during and since World War II drew many educated new members into urban and suburban unprogrammed meetings at the same time that other social forces caused the shrinking of rural and pastoral meetings and changes in the traditional patterns of the Quaker family, neighborhood, and Sunday School. In the culture of the late twentieth century, Friends are pulled apart by clashing moral commitments and the individualism of private "leadings," which each person feels as God's call, yet they find their unity in their common heritage and in the depth of shared worship.

Chapter Editors

Hugh Barbour (4,6–7,12–14,17), professor emeritus, Earlham College

Christopher Densmore (5,8–9,11), University Archives, State University of New York at Buffalo

Mary Finn (9), Buffalo Friends Meeting

Thomas D. Hamm (12), Department of History, Earlham College

Nancy A. Hewitt (10), Department of History, Duke University

Nancy C. Sorel (16), New York Yearly Meeting

Alson D. Van Wagner (15), New York Yearly Meeting

Arthur J. Worrall (1–3), Department of History, Colorado State University

Quaker Crosscurrents

1

Quaker Beginnings in England and New York

ARTHUR WORRALL
and
HUGH BARBOUR

English Beginnings of the Quaker Movement

The first Friends who came to New York in 1657 were English men and women en route to New England who had recently become convinced Quakers during the heady years of the Puritan Revolution. This was one of the greatest eras of social ferment and religious hope in British history. The civil war between Puritans and Parliamentarians on the one hand and the forces of Charles I on the other had left thousands dissatisfied with both the Anglican establishment and Presbyterian Puritanism. Among those dissatisfied was George Fox, who was to emerge as the Quaker leader. Fox was a shepherd and shoemaker from a Puritan parish in midland Leicestershire. He had gone through struggles as a youth against temptation and despair during which no Anglican, Puritan, or separatist pastor seemed able to help him. It was "opened" to him that their Oxford and Cambridge studies had not fitted them to be "ministers of Christ," but he noted also that their pastoral tenderness with him failed to cover the breach between his longing for moral purity and the conduct of most professing Christians. He felt kinship with Jesus, who had overcome similar suffering and so could "speak to his condition," and he experienced a climactic "opening" that showed that both an "ocean of darkness" and "an ocean of light" were within himself as well as in all people. Facing his own inner motives ended his five years of struggles over temptation and despair and led to triumphant moments when he "was come up in

1

spirit through the flaming sword into the paradise of God" and the sinlessness of Adam, and "all the creation gave another smell unto me than before."[1] Beginning in 1647, Fox revisited the friends among whom he had wandered for five years in the small "Separatist" congregations and the English parish churches from which they had come out to call every person to submit to the Light of Christ within them that could show them their own hearts and guide them to purity.[2]

Most English parish churches were by then in Puritan hands. From 1558 to 1641 several generations of Puritan pastors, trained in the Bible and Calvinist churchmanship and doctrine, had waited in vain to be invited to complete the Reformation of the national Church of England, which they believed had only been begun by Henry VIII's episcopal system, Edward VI's and Queen Elizabeth I's prayer books, and James I's Bible. Meanwhile, university-trained Puritans had taken over the often untended pulpits of the parish churches throughout southern and eastern England. They had centered worship upon sermons and free prayers, replaced candle-lit altars with communion tables, and embroidered vestments with Geneva gowns. They brought Bible reading and daily family prayers into thousands of homes.

When Charles I was crowned in 1625, one year after Fox's birth, he had made clear that he would enforce the episcopal system exclusively. During his father's reign, a few Puritan congregations had separated from parish churches. Facing persecution, some of these separatists had escaped to Holland and later, in 1620, had crossed the Atlantic to found Plymouth Colony. In 1629, a larger group of Puritan pastors, gentry, and farmers, alarmed at Charles's policies, set out on an "errand into the wilderness."[3] They secured a charter for the Massachusetts Bay Company that they used as a basis to establish a civil and religious commonwealth and as a model for a misguided England. Meanwhile, Charles elicited so much resistance in Ireland to military rule, in Scotland to his efforts to establish an episcopal church, and in England to taxes and his efforts to rule without Parliament that all three kingdoms rose in rebellion. After losing a civil war in England, Charles tried to renew the struggle and lost his kingdoms and his head. Triumphant Puritans removed bishops and prayer book, took over parish churches, and purified Parliament even of some of their own. Yet Oliver Cromwell, the Puritan military leader who took control of the British Isles in the 1650s, realized that his volunteer "Ironside" regiments contained many separatists who did not accept a centralized national church or even the baptism of unconverted infants. Like Fox, these separatists considered Puritan pastors too gentle with sinning parishioners and the reforms that Cromwell and his army had achieved imperfect. Such separatists, Baptists, and Quakers felt called by God to witness for the completion of the Puritan dream of a kingdom of God on earth where Jesus would truly reign. These radical groups were strongest among city artisans and rural working folk, whom modern Marxist historians identify as proletarian. Opposing both the Presbyterian and independent (Congregational) wings of English Puritanism, these radicals polarized churches and politics in England in the 1650s. After the Civil War, Oliver Cromwell needed his army to balance factions ranging from radical separatists and reforming levelers, on the one hand, to Presbyterian and Royalist country gentry, on the other. The growth and energy of the early Quakers threatened this balance.

In England, separatists and Quakers became especially strong in areas where parish pastors had been inactive and Puritans few. In one such area, the Lake District moorlands of northwest England, George Fox in 1652 stirred up a regional religious awakening in which thousands met outdoors and dozens met in farmsteads, for exhortation or in silence, to remake their lives under the probing "Light of Christ within" them. Unlike the largely emotional revivalists in later centuries, the earliest Quakers often went through months or even years of mutually supported self-searching, inner struggle, and outward quaking as they faced the Light and yielded to its guidance. At Swarthmoor Hall, Margaret Fell's[4] country house that overlooked the sea in Furness, more than sixty of these men and women organized themselves to spread throughout Britain and Europe the challenge that had changed their lives. Jesus Christ had come to teach his people himself by the inner "leadings" of conscience that taught ethical norms, which Friends call "testimonies": truth and honesty in all speech and business dealing; simplicity in dress and life; equality that humbled all classes and both sexes equally; and the emerging Peace Testimony. Friends thought violence was the wrong way to overcome evil (the Devil's trick to divert humans into destroying the physical creation rather than the evil within). Such basic standards all had roots in local customs, in the Bible, and in radical Puritan ethical teachings, for instance, the refusal to call months after Mars and Juno or days after Thor or Woden. But there was a central element that Friends called "Truth" in all these norms, refusing oaths and insisting that *thee* and *thou* were correct grammar, whereas *you* and *your,* like individual titles, were only used to flatter social pride.

Friends lived these testimonies to bring others to the Light. The Quakers' simple speech and dress, their fixed price for each object bought or sold in the marketplace, and their refusal of "hat honor" (removing their hats) in drawing rooms and courtrooms, were expected to be inherently convincing to proud or thoughtless opponents. Like later feminists and black militants, early Friends understood their hearers' anger as evidence that they had reached "the witness of truth," "that of God" within other people. As Friends broke down their own and their hearers' pride, they used military symbols for inward struggle, such as "the Lamb's War." Their movement had a cosmic dimension. The Spirit's conquest of the world became the metaphor as thousands of English people in new areas were swept into the movement. By 1656, when Friends first came to the American colonies, there were perhaps twenty thousand Quakers in England, and the vision of Paul's Epistles and the Book of Acts seemed finally about to be fulfilled.

In 1656, the Quakers extended their mission to Holland and America partly to express that dream. Yet at home in England their way had become harder. Roving Quaker preachers felt divine leadings to converge on any area where their message was fiercely resisted, notably Cornwall, Ireland, and Massachusetts. Yet Englishmen felt a conservative backlash from 1656 to Cromwell's death in 1658, culminating after two years of growing chaos in the Restoration in 1660 of Charles II, son of the executed king, and the return to power of the nobility and the bishops. More crucial for Quakers was the control of Parliament after 1660 by Anglican gentry who restored prayer book rituals conducted by parish priests in parish churches. Parliamentary enactments, despite Charles's promise of toleration, led to the persecution of any who would not conform to the state church, especially those like Friends who would not hide their meetings.

Convincement, Silent Worship, Ministry, Leadings

In the seventeenth century women and men became Quakers after a direct challenge by a traveling Quaker in a mass meeting or in their own homes, churches, or marketplaces. The goal was their convincement, or conviction (in both senses), by the power of the Light of God or Christ, which showed a person's pride and dark motives and which set aside or overcame them. In the end came joy and inner peace, but only after weeks or months of painful struggle on lonely walks or in the company of a group of other Friends. Sudden conversion experiences were neither common nor expected, and convincement was likely to be a lifelong process as new barriers were found and overcome and as new insights arose in carrying out the leadings already received. The early meetings for worship, normally in private homes, included much personal prayer but began as silent waiting as each person tried to set aside her or his own thoughts and will. The Light increasingly was allowed to lead and to show the truth that began as self-knowledge as well. In the silent meeting a traveling Friend or any other member of the local group might feel led to speak, to guide, or reassure the often desperate newcomers into the movement or might in biblical fashion read aloud an epistle from Fox or other weighty Friends. Robert Barclay and others recorded how they felt the moving of the Spirit in the group as a whole, by which

> each made it their work to retire inwardly to the Measure of Grace in themselves, not being only Silent as to Words, but even abstaining from all their own Thoughts, Imaginations and Desires . . . meeting together not only outwardly in one place but thus inwardly in One Spirit . . . they come thereby to enjoy and feel the arisings of this Life, which as it prevails in each . . . becomes as a Flood of Refreshment, and overspreads the whole Meeting. . . . And when they are through the breaking forth of this Power, constrained to utter a Sentence of Exhortation or Praise, or breathe to the Lord in Prayer, then all are sensible of it, for the same Life in them answers to it. . . . Thus [Barclay] found Evil weakening in me and the Good raised up.[5]

Unlike the methodical Wesley, early Friends did not set up a hierarchy or even appoint local leaders.

Until 1660 Quakers in London and a few other cities hired a hall such as the one at The Bull & Mouth Tavern for the public proclamation of the new way, or a smaller hall for silent worship like the Gracious Street (Grace Church Street) meeting house, before which Penn was arrested in 1670. Most of these were closed or confiscated in the twenty-five years of persecution that followed. Few surviving meeting houses in either England or America predate the coming of toleration in 1689. Yet regular meetings for worship on First Days (Sundays) had become more crucial than informal gatherings in homes as Friends committed to maintaining the Lamb's War needed each other's support and shared worship as they faced imprisonment. Those whose spoken ministry was given repeatedly and was found helpful began to be spoken of by Friends as ministers.

Because there are few early descriptions of Quaker worship in New York meetings except in records by and about visiting Friends from elsewhere, one must generalize from the witness of more literary Friends like Barclay. Although silent prayer and self-examination filled much of the silence and a wordless sharing of love, joy, power, and the presence of God or Christ was the essence of a "gathered meeting," direct messages from the "Witness of God" within were expected to come to some Friends present. Fox and others often spoke for an hour at a time and did not tell the extent to which each word came by divine leading. On principle they wrote nothing down beforehand, and only after 1689 were shorthand notes taken by listeners. Early Quakers distinguished firmly between God and human nature, unlike those modern Friends for whom the boundary between human and divine is at best uncertain. The first Friends often equated Satan with the human ego without fearing him as an ultimate rival to God's power. Because Friends felt that to speak or even offer prayer out of impulses of a human will was an intrusion during Quaker meetings for worship, every flash of insight or moral concern was increasingly tested and screened inwardly before a person spoke in a meeting. Early Quaker journals record experiences of women and men who went through such testing and came to a sense of liberation when a message that seemed divinely given to them was delivered.[6]

Leadings to act and speak in daily life as well are described in journals like John Woolman's, involving similar screening and struggle. Friends were more likely to act on any unwelcome impulse contrary to their pride or desires, so a call to journey to Massachusetts or to greater austerity in dress or furnishing was likely to be heeded. Time was taken for careful testing. Friends verified that a leading was consistent with the Bible because the inner Spirit was assumed to be self-consistent. A Friend would usually test a leading against the "sense of the meeting" as a whole or of its elders and ministers. Because any such testing process might be slow and painful, Friends found it increasingly easy to accept as given the distinctive standards in morality, dress, and speech to which previous Friends had felt corporately led. By the mid-eighteenth century the daily lives of Quakers were increasingly divided into three distinct domains: personal calls to speak or travel in the ministry were expected to come to individuals; human relations were ruled by shared standards such as the testimonies; daily work or craftsmanship and other areas of life in the world were left to normal human intelligence and God's oversight of the creation unless a special call came to act or refuse to act. Personal inner calls to visit distant Friends or tackle social evil often came in the setting of silent group worship, which in itself restrained mere subjectivity. Friends' journals tell little of leadings in daily work, at which even frequent travelers like John Woolman and Elias Hicks spent ten or eleven months each year. Thus, most

Friends who did not minister felt freed to express their general awareness of divine involvement in their lives by a personal immersion in
science or the world of business. Their workaday achievements were
measured by human standards of success, but their frugality limited
their luxuries. Their business ethic implied strict honesty and social
responsibility.[7]

First Friends in New York

New Netherland was something of a seventeenth-century oddity. It
was supposed to help its founding and controlling entity, the Dutch
West Indies Company, turn a profit, but for most of its history New
Netherland did not reward its parent company handsomely. Nonethe-
less, the company still had to be concerned about making its colony
sufficiently attractive to entice those settlers who might just make the
colony a rewarding business venture. So it resorted to much the same
practice largely followed in the United Netherlands—to tolerate dissenters if they did not cause trouble. That was good business practice.
The company still had to face governmental restrictions on religious
practice; like the United Netherlands itself, New Netherland had the
established Dutch Reformed Church, so no matter how tolerant the
company might be for business reasons, it still had to follow the lead of
the church in matters religious. Dutch Reformed ministers wanted no
disturbing competition, so they saw to it that Lutheran and other opponents were hustled out of the colony. Still, they could not always have
their way, for the company needed settlers, found relatively few Dutch
willing to come out (for good reason, because Holland was the most
prosperous part of Europe), and so had to accept settlers from among
dissenters elsewhere. Among these settlers were New England English
who sought new and good land in Long Island settlements such as
Flushing and Hempstead. That many of them were dissenters from the
Standing Order in Massachusetts meant an almost certain challenge to
New Netherland's religious orthodoxy, however uncertainly it might
have been enforced.[8]

As part of this polyglot colony English settlers supplied numbers
and a good deal of trouble for Dutch authorities. The English were not
subservient like the Brazilian Jews happy to escape the Inquisition when
the Dutch were driven from Brazil in 1654. Nor were they conquered
as Swedish Lutherans in the Delaware had been. Usually, the English
had moved more than once, first across the Atlantic to Massachusetts
or another New England colony and, perhaps, another move or two

before coming to Dutch Long Island. They were drawn to the Dutch domains because of the rather lax administration and good land and were pushed from New England colonies, which they did not find congenial. Many of these migrants were religious dissenters; some were incipient Baptists in Lynn. Like many later immigrants, a few had had brushes with the law. Whether they moved for essentially religious or economic reasons, many English settlers had already confronted authorities and would be prepared to do so again.

Flushing proved to be a particular thorn in the side of Dutch authorities. Flushing residents had been without a clergyman for some time when Quaker missionaries first appeared, and they were not conspicuously orthodox when they had one. Flushing had resisted authority in more than just matters religious. In an early instance in 1653 Flushing joined three other English and four Dutch towns in sending a remonstrance or petition to Governor Peter Stuyvesant. The petitioners asserted their rights as a covenanted, not a conquered, people, and among those rights, they argued, was that of participating in lawmaking. They opposed a government "directed and controlled according to the pleasure and caprice of . . . Stuyvesant or one or two of his Sycophants."[9] Government officials should be chosen by the people, the petitioners contended. The petitioners were unsuccessful; Stuyvesant would not and probably could not yield the authority that he derived from the Company. But given the extent of English political assertiveness at this time compared to the Dutch, English residents such as Tobias Feake, the *schout,* or sheriff, of Flushing and one of the signers of the remonstrance, would have stood out. After this challenge to his authority, the governor would almost certainly deal harshly with any town willing to challenge him by itself.

That opportunity soon arose when in 1657 the first Quaker missionaries arrived in New Netherland and quickly attracted supporters in the English towns of Flushing, Hempstead, Newtown, and Gravesend. Just outside the bounds of New Netherland, residents of Oyster Bay also found the Quaker message attractive. These were impressive beginnings among folk essentially unchurched. As in Rhode Island to the north, most conversions went unnoted. Unlike in Massachusetts, confrontations were infrequent and abuse of Friends less serious. In New Amsterdam and Flushing, however, confrontation was immediate and sometimes violent.

The arrival of Friends in Robert Fowler's ship *Woodhouse* was the occasion for considerable excitement. The passengers all seem to have intended to go to New England, but two of them, Mary Weatherhead and Dorothy Waugh, preached in the streets to startled residents of New Amsterdam. Arrested, they were banished from the colony, and, joined by two other *Woodhouse* passengers, Sarah Gibbons and Richard Dowdney, set out for Boston probably via Rhode Island and Plymouth. Although they had not had great success, another Quaker missionary, Robert Hodgson, stayed behind to minister to potential converts in the English towns and apparently had considerable success doing so. Apprehended in Hempstead, he was taken to New Amsterdam. There he was taken before Governor Stuyvesant. When Hodgson refused to doff his hat, a practice that Friends refused to honor, Stuyvesant ordered him imprisoned at hard labor. Hodgson refused to cooperate and for his refusal received such a savage series of beatings that it seemed unlikely that he would survive. But survive he did and he was ultimately expelled from the colony.

Meantime, Stuyvesant and his council had passed an anti-Quaker law. Under it, any resident who entertained Friends was to be fined fifty pounds. Generally, the residents who kept their beliefs to themselves were safe, but not Henry Townsend, who tested the law by entertaining English Friends. Arrested and fined, Townsend soon had the support of his fellow townspeople. Edward Hart, the town clerk, wrote a remonstrance that was signed by thirty-one residents, including Hart, Feake, and magistrates Edward Farrington and William Noble. It turned out that Feake had talked Hart into writing this petition that argued appropriately and correctly that Flushing residents were free to worship. Under pressure from the governor, all leaders except Feake apologized. Aside from the sharpness of the petition, which has come down to subsequent generations as the Flushing Remonstrance, no immediate further action resulted from either the petition or the fact that many residents within New Netherland and Oyster Bay immediately outside it had become Quakers.

Quite unlike in Massachusetts, which endured an escalating struggle between Friends and authorities in these years, after this initial confrontation authorities and Friends left each other alone. One can surmise that resident Friends had their meetings for worship, Friends from abroad visited, and authorities exhibited the good sense, found in Holland, of leaving dissenters alone if they caused no trouble, whether Dutch Reformed clergy liked it or not. English Friends like John Taylor managed to reach New Netherland en route to the much more tempting target of Massachusetts; indeed, English visitors were numerous in the first two decades of the Quaker presence on Long Island. The Quaker enclave in Rhode Island, probably as numerous as on Long

Island, would have transmitted religious information and received it, in turn, because much personal and business information passed between the English in the two colonies. No doubt, Friends at Shelter Island sent an occasional emissary to western Long Island. Although this kind of activity almost certainly went on, strictures against Friends continued in effect in New Netherland.

Late in the summer of 1662, this happy situation changed when magistrates in Jamaica complained about a Quaker meeting in their community and another in the house of John Bowne in Flushing. The formal complaint must have forced Peter Stuyvesant's hand. No doubt, the apprehensions of Dutch Reformed clergy did too. Acting on orders of the colony council, Resolved Waldron, the schout (sheriff) of the colony, arrested Bowne. Despite the fact that Bowne's wife Hannah had recently given birth, Waldron took Bowne to Stuyvesant in New Amsterdam for a hearing. Before Bowne really had a chance to refuse to take off his hat, Stuyvesant had Waldron take it off for him. Fined for his Quaker activities, Bowne refused to pay and was imprisoned. Offered release if he would promise to leave the colony, Bowne refused and remained in prison throughout the fall. Finally, in December, Bowne was released to appeal his case to the Dutch West Indies Company in Amsterdam. His appeal was successful, and in 1663 the directors informed Stuyvesant that he was to leave Friends and others free to worship provided their conduct was otherwise proper. Dutch good sense and Bowne had won.

The decision soon was rendered moot, however, for in 1664 English forces of James Duke of York took New Netherland from the Dutch. It would now be New York, named for the duke. For Friends the change meant little, unlike for the Dutch Reformed church, which now had the freedom to minister to its own members but not to attempt to force its ways on others. The colony expanded under English control, now comprising all of Long Island, Martha's Vineyard, and Nantucket. The expansion affected Friends little, for with the exception of the addition of the Sylvesters on Shelter Island, no Friends came with the expansion of colony bounds at this date. Any difficulties would now emanate from English authorities, especially in wartime when Friends refused to fight, or from Anglican clergy intent on expanding their denomination's influence.

Some Friends had escaped the attentions of New Netherland authorities because they lived just across the boundary with Connecticut in Oyster Bay. In 1650 Connecticut and New Netherland had agreed to set their boundary on Long Island at Oyster Bay, giving Connecticut control over that community. Whether Connecticut authorities were aware of the Quaker presence or not, Friends resident in Oyster Bay were effectively beyond the jurisdiction of Peter Stuyvesant. One can assume that Connecticut under the wise leadership of John Winthrop, Junior, opted not to intrude in a community that was, at best, marginally significant for that colony anyway. Conspicuous sensibility was not to be found in the other Connecticut colony, New Haven. That colony would not brook a Quaker presence no matter how far from its centers of population, as visiting and resident Friends in Southold soon found out.

Eventually, both Southold and nearby Shelter Island at the eastern end of Long Island came to be part of New York. During the Dutch period (when the first Quaker missionaries appeared), Southold and, potentially, Shelter Island came under the jurisdiction of New Haven Colony, which then had settlements on both sides of Long Island Sound. The English conquest of New Netherland in 1664 had terminated claims that Connecticut (which had absorbed New Haven in 1663) might have had to Long Island and any of the islands in the immediate vicinity. It is by this historical accident that Southold and Shelter Island appear in a study of New York Friends.

Southold was one of several towns not served by clergy that were receptive to early Friends. The first Quaker missionary to appear there was Humphrey Norton, recently banished from Plymouth. Norton probably went to Southold after stopping en route at Shelter Island, whose proprietor, Nathaniel Sylvester, may have already begun his merciful practice of letting Friends stay there and who apparently became a Friend in this period. Norton was arrested, tried, and sentenced to be whipped, branded, and fined. He left the colony, perhaps returning to Shelter Island. Now uncomfortably aware that the dreaded Quaker menace was in their midst, New Haven legislators enacted an ex post facto law that served to make legitimate future punishment like that just handed to Norton, who had broken no law.

Shortly after came the first recorded instances in which Friends found refuge in nearby Shelter Island. Nathaniel Sylvester owned the island and permitted an unknown number of Friends to go there. Lawrence and Cassandra Southwick, refugees from Salem, Massachusetts, spent the last two years of their lives there. Mary Dyer went there after her reprieve from the gallows in Boston. Her husband William later indicated that she had joined Friends there rather than return to him in Rhode Island. John Taylor, a visiting English Quaker, later wrote about Friends on Shelter Island in this period, further confirming that in the early 1660s a group of Friends lived there.

Difficulties for New Haven Colony were not over. Southold resident

Arthur Smith came before the General Court to defend his views that were supportive of Quakerism. With remarkable restraint, the court bound him over on good behavior unless he left the colony. Apparently he did. Further annoyances awaited the General Court. In 1660 Nathaniel Sylvester had gone to Southold and defended Friends. Subsequently, he wrote the General Court in much the same vein. Accepting his challenge and assuming a jurisdiction that it may not have had, the General Court fined him one hundred pounds. There is no record that he paid. He remained proprietor, however, after the English took control of Long Island. In 1666, two years after New York gained control of Eastern Long Island, Governor Richard Nichols confirmed Sylvester's title. Sylvester himself continued his affiliation with the Society. He and his wife remained on Shelter Island although the rest of the many Quakers who had taken refuge there in Quakerism's first decade moved on. Sylvester's island attracted Quaker visitors from abroad as long as he lived there, for example, George Fox and Irish Friend William Edmundson in 1672 and Edmundson again in 1675. After the Sylvesters died, the Quaker presence on the island disappeared not to reappear until the twentieth century.

Conflicts Internal and External

As initial Quaker enthusiasm began to cool and the leadership focusing on George Fox in England took control, contention with those who attacked Friends took different forms. After George Fox and his associates brought the business meeting structure to New York in 1672, resistance developed to this orderly way of managing the Society that was unlike the relative freedom that had obtained in Quakerism's early years. Most doctrinal contention appears to have come from within Quakerism or from those once considered Quakers by Friends themselves.

Newtown resident Thomas Case seemed an unlikely person to cause difficulty at first. Numbered among the upper half economically of that town's residents, he and his wife, Mary, were not at first controversial in or out of town. That the Cases were Friends caused no comment; so were others. By 1674, however, they attracted unfavorable notice when William Smith charged that Thomas and Mary Case had detained his wife. The Cases were ordered to cease. Next Mary went to the local meeting house and denounced the minister. But the Cases went well beyond merely challenging the parson in church: their meetings lasted for upward of two weeks; Case announced that three days after his death he would rise to life again; the meetings were disorderly affairs of shaking, shouting, dancing, and singing; one young Friend claimed that he had caught the French pox at their revels; and, most seriously to the community, these affairs had endangered the economic well-being of families when people devoted themselves more to these meetings than to supporting themselves. Case was brought before the Court of Assizes, fined, bound over on good behavior late in 1675, and early in the next year imprisoned at least part of the time in solitary confinement for defiance of court orders. Apparently, shortly after Case's release from prison, the visiting Irish minister, William Edmundson, tangled with him. New York Friends needed help.[10]

The Case group continued, although presumably in a somewhat less disreputable fashion after 1676 as far as the civil community was concerned. Still, Friends had to deal with them, with successor groups after Case's death in 1692, or with groups very much like them for a number of years. They were generally labeled ranters, whatever their source of inspiration, and they caused many problems for Friends. Joan Vokins, a visiting English Friend, tangled with Case and supporters in 1681. They continued to cause trouble in meetings late in the seventeenth century as visiting Friend Thomas Chalkley reported. And they or people inspired by them spread beyond the confines of New York Yearly Meeting, disrupting meetings in New England. By the early eighteenth century these troublesome folk had ceased to bother New York Friends and soon after that ceased to cause difficulties in New England as well. Chances are that after Thomas Case passed to his reward, the group declined, lacking the forceful leadership that he had provided.[11]

A new challenge came to Friends early in the eighteenth century, a challenge partly caused by a new and difficult New York governor, Edward Hyde, Lord Cornbury, and partly by Anglican missionary efforts, especially those of George Keith, a onetime Friend, now Anglican minister. Cornbury, cousin of Queen Anne, became governor in 1702. A difficult man at best, he succeeded in uniting hitherto bitter political enemies by drawing their animosity to him. At first Friends made a show of support for the man, but not for long. In a drive to expand the Anglican Church within his colony Cornbury set about encouraging the restriction of both Quakers and Presbyterians. It was at this juncture that George Keith came to New York intent on attacking Friends and winning them over to the Anglican Church.[12]

Keith had already moved through New England attempting to undermine Friends, much to the obvious delight of the Boston Congregational minister Cotton Mather. Local Friends answered him, assisted by a Quaker truth squad of visiting English Public Friends. He passed on to New York, probably in 1703, appearing during the meeting for worship in Flushing and attempting to speak. During this period, Friends Samuel Bownas, John Richardson, and Thomas Story appeared in New York, setting out Quaker views and speaking critically of Anglican definitions of sacraments. Printer William Bradford, who had supported Keith while he was still a Quaker in Pennsylvania, appeared at one of Bownas's meetings, taking notes that appear to have been the basis for an arrest warrant. Bownas was arrested and charged, but Flushing grand juries twice refused to indict him. Bownas and other Friends thought Keith was behind the arrest; a recent study points to Lord Cornbury. As long as the disreputable Cornbury was governor, outspoken visiting Friends like Patrick Henderson from Ireland and Presbyterians like Francis Makemie were at risk. That the Toleration Act passed by Parliament in 1689 could and should have supported their right to speak did not prevent the likes of a Cornbury from prosecuting them, however unsuccessfully, although one should note that the less-outspoken members of the truth squad, Richardson and Story, did not face prosecution.

There would be other debates between Anglicans and Friends, but no more arrests. The Society for the Propagation of the Gospel (SPG), the Anglican missionary society founded to convert native Americans and African-Americans, sent to the colonies clergy whose major activities focused on converting English colonists. These missionaries complained about Quakers effectively preventing conversion to the Church of England. As a rule these complaints remained in the correspondence of the SPG and may have served partly as a rationale for their failure to convert more colonists. The only debate of any substance came well after the unfortunate Cornbury had left New York and originated with SPG missionary Jared Wetmore.

Wetmore, once of Yale College and now a minister in the vicinity of Rye, had all the enthusiasm of a recent convert. It was his decision to attack Friends, and he wrote two pamphlets assailing them. The first, *A Letter from a Minister of the Church of England to His Dissenting Parishioners*, was a broad attack on all dissenters. He made exclusive claims for Anglican authority. In a brief reference to Friends, he challenged their claims to inspiration by the Holy Spirit. Friend James Mott responded in *The Great Work of Christ's Spirit* that, no doubt, asserted the Quaker claim to that inspiration although the pamphlet is not extant.[13]

Wetmore replied in 1731 in a direct attack on Friends, *Quakerism: A Judicial Infatuation*. The pamphlet is a dialogue between a potential convert to Quakerism appropriately enough named Tremulus and a defender of the Church of England, Eusebius. It consists of a series of outrageous charges concerning Friends, namely, that they were debauched, lewd, and dishonest. To Wetmore, the height of their debauchery consisted of a denial of the sacraments of baptism and communion. If Wetmore sought to impress SPG authorities in England, he was soon disabused of the notion. They informed him that they wanted no public debates with Friends. English church authorities knew the power of the dissenting deputies in Parliament under Robert Walpole's government and the important role that leading Friends played in establishing that power base. If Wetmore was unaware of that power, the SPG was not.

2

Building Traditions and Testimonies

Arthur Worrall
and
Hugh Barbour

Reinterpreting the Testimonies

In ethics as in worship, New York Friends, like those elsewhere, expected to share common experiences and standards, even many generations after their convincement. Local variants grew so strong between countries and regions, however, that traveling English ministers found colonials unruly pupils.[1] Quaker norms of speech, dress, and conduct had begun as commitments to live in truth, simplicity, equality, and peace, and by acts and words had challenged non-Friends to the same universal standard. For instance, Quaker customs demonstrating social equality were meant to be true to fact as when Friends refused to say "your servant, Sir" to strangers or "your excellency" to unworthy rulers. The norms were also testimonies, weapons in the Lamb's War. To keep one's hat on before a noble or a judge was a direct confrontation of pride and a challenge of repentance. Friends refused to use titles as a challenge to human pride. In England "thee" and "thou" were by 1650 used only to servants, children, and lovers and also by tradition to God. The French *tu* and the German *Du* have kept the same specialized uses until the present day. To use them attacks social inequality.[2] At first a Quaker needed courage to use "thee" in polite society whether in Flushing, Boston, Providence, the Chesapeake, or London.

After the first fifty years, however, the Lamb's War of Friends had been replaced by a truce. By the late seventeenth century, Friends in New York, like Friends elsewhere, had achieved a measure of toleration; it was no longer unsafe to worship. As their militancy declined, the Children of Light were thankful to be accepted as a peaceable people. Friends no longer expected the Spirit's power, working through them, to sweep the world. As a result, many Quaker testimonies became acts done less out of personal conviction than out of loyalty to the Quaker community. As badges of God's own peculiar people, they set off Friends from non-Friends rather than winning outsiders to Truth. In short, they became ends in themselves, occasionally with negative consequences.

Thus, the four basic testimonies underwent a sea change in the early eighteenth century both in America and England. Truth itself became a nickname for the Quaker way of life: "How does Truth prosper among you" came to mean the spiritual vitality or even the vital statistics of each monthly meeting. In England Quaker merchants' fixed or single prices and refusal to bargain in the marketplace no longer made them a "dread and terror to the unjust . . . which lets everyone see all deeds and actions they have done amiss"[3] by dishonest palaver to buy cheap and sell dear. Friends stated an object's faults and virtues and what seemed a fair price and stuck to it. But in Fox's lifetime Friends' reputation for honesty began to make their merchants rich and their craftsmen into bankers. Quaker plain language became familiar and merely characteristic of the sect.

The earliest Peace Testimony had described early Friends' aggressive but nonviolent Lamb's War. After 1660, Quaker nonviolence was adopted as one basis of their pleas for toleration in England.[4] After toleration English dissenters were valued as loyal opposition to the established government, dissent in that instance being a necessary ingredient of representative government. In the colonies the Peace Testimony became the basis for Friends' conscientious objection to bearing arms and militia duty.

The Quaker testimony for equality made women and men equal at home and their speaking equally welcome within meetings. Once Quaker women preachers returned from journeys, however, notably after 1660, this testimony did little to change their lives in the home. Quaker women ran the household and kept the books. They also acted for their husbands in their absence. There was little change in their status early in the eighteenth century although American Quaker women could benefit from some marginal improvements that women in general had achieved in New York and New England in areas like divorce compared to their sisters in England. Toward women and even toward slaves, George Fox's attitude was centered on human and paternalistic responsibility rather than on justice.[5] Early Quaker concerns that education be practical, studying "things good and useful in the creation" rather than lascivious Latin classics, made it easier, however, for Quaker schools to give nearly equal education to girls and boys.

Quaker simplicity, despite an objection by Margaret Fell, tended increasingly to encourage uniformity in dress. The testimony of simplicity in speech and dress was at first mainly a protest against the flattery, laces, velvets, and other luxuries of court styles that cost so much in human labor and resources. The mainspring of Quaker dress codes was concern for the poor. Penn wrote from the Tower of London to Charles II's courtiers:

> When People have first learned to fear and obey their Creator . . . to alleviate and abate their oppressed Tennants . . . when the pale faces are more commiserated, the grip'd Bellies reliev'd, and naked backs cloath'd; when famish'd Poor, the distress'd Widow, and helpless Orphant . . . are provided for; then . . . it will be early enough for you to plead the Indifference of your pleasures.[6]

The resulting Quaker costume, Puritan style with a working-class accent, was probably close enough to the styles already current in the early Long Island communities that no great changes were expected of newly convinced Friends there. By the eighteenth century Quaker dress had become stereotyped into a series of distinctive patterns that were expected of all members on pain of being "eldered," that is, being disciplined by senior Friends.[7]

There were more specific ways in which the tides of history left Friends holding to outdated or withered testimonies. Thee and thou became increasingly obsolete and by the late nineteenth century were only used in North America between Quakers. Fox had insisted that oaths were forbidden by Jesus but that a Quaker's affirmation and all his or her statements must be as truthful as oaths. Yet once they were so accepted in law courts, affirming became simply a Quaker privilege. As Quaker simple dress became standardized it became increasingly identified with outdated or conservative fashions. Quakers' aprons remained green, like those of schoolteachers, when white became fashionable, turning white only when it went out of style.[8] Most early Quaker women, like working women, wore tall "witches' hats" outdoors, but, after the French Revolution, Quaker women began to wear over their white indoor caps outdoor over-bonnets of cloth simplified from Paris styles. Women's dresses, although stripped of ribbons and embroidery, by the nineteenth century followed contemporary outlines in the cut of their sleeves and bustles. Quaker men's plain coats lacked collars and cuffs to save cloth and appear plain, but they were cut according to shapes not long out of style.[9]

However staunchly Friends kept their common standards of dress, speech, and conduct, the relationship of the Quaker testimonies to the discipline of the evolving Quaker meetings had changed since the Lamb's War of the 1650s. Crises within Quakerism between 1656 and 1681 had centered on individuals whose acts had made English Friends conspicuous in ways most Quakers disapproved. In each case teams of weighty Friends had tried in vain to persuade the offenders to renounce their acts publicly, to clear "the reputation of Truth" and the public image of Quakers. But the needs of family worship and the guidance of children also drove meetings to disown those who "married out" with a non-Quaker spouse or married through the ministrations of a parson.

In the American colonies the Quaker situation had always been somewhat different from that in England. Even the Dutch knew that Quakers refused oaths and that Quaker ships would not fire salutes. But in early New York, where the Earl of Bellomont and Lord Cornbury were almost the only nobility, the need to use gestures and language as weapons to confront social inequality was minimal. Other testimonies became more important. The Quaker refusal to pay church taxes was of greater significance than other offenses in New York and New England early in the eighteenth century. Happily, there were instances when local authorities connived at the nonenforcement of these measures.[10]

The Peace Testimony also turned out to be more important in North America than in England. In the northern colonies military training and service in militias was, for a time, expected of most males. When there was enforcement, Friends could be expected to suffer.[11]

Meetings for Business and the Discipline

At first Friends in New York and elsewhere had no formal organizational structure; visiting ministers, hortatory letters from prominent English Quakers, and conversations between accepted local leaders at meetings for worship sufficed to manage the affairs of the Society. By 1667 George Fox, victor in struggles to control the Society in England, organized a structure of meetings for business in England, headed by the London Yearly Meeting, with constituent meetings scattered throughout the country. The meeting structure served several needs: it provided control of the unruly and potentially scandalous among Friends; it provided an organizational structure to help resist persecution from established churches; and it served as an organization in which Friends could support each other in times of material and spiritual need.[12]

Once meetings had been established in England and persecution of Friends seemed to diminish, Fox turned to the colonies in 1672 to install meetings for business there too. In 1671, before Fox himself crossed the Atlantic, Irish Friend John Burnyeat came as an emissary to set up business meetings. Burnyeat faced serious opposition, for many early New York Friends, like Friends elsewhere, resisted formal organization. In 1671 at Oyster Bay where Burnyeat labored, the principal opponents were George Dennis and his wife. Despite their opposition, he seems to have succeeded in setting up Flushing Monthly Meeting, the first monthly meeting in the northern colonies. When Fox arrived the next year, opposition collapsed; the Dennises attempted to blame others. From New York Fox went on to the New England colonies, where he had Friends set up monthly meetings and a yearly meeting that eventually came to be called New England Yearly Meeting.

Initially, Flushing Monthly Meeting was a constituent part of this yearly meeting. Fox and most leaders in the colonies probably found it useful to have one yearly meeting for the north with its center in Rhode Island where Friends dominated the government and could, thus, provide a measure of support for Friends in potentially hostile locales elsewhere. Early minutes of New England Yearly Meeting indicate that representatives came from "Oister bay" as the minute identified New York Friends. Nor could the journey to Rhode Island have provided any more of an obstacle than the journey for those Friends who lived in Dover and Salem well to the north of Rhode Island. Contacts had been frequent between New England residents in Long Island and Rhode Island. It need not surprise that Oyster Bay representatives participated actively in yearly meeting affairs. Although the minutes are fragmentary for the early years, one New York initiative survives. In 1686 Oyster Bay representatives encouraged Friends generally not to use tobacco immoderately and distributed their paper on the subject to all the Yearly Meeting's constituent meetings.

Nine years later New England Yearly Meeting set off Friends in New York as a separate meeting. The minutes establishing the new yearly meeting made clear its limited extent: "It is agreed that the meeting at Long Island shall Bee from this time A yearely meeting."[13]

There was only one constituent monthly meeting—Flushing—although one should note that Rhode Island and Flushing Monthly Meetings were about equal in numbers.

Why New York Friends would separate is far from clear. Perhaps, like other constituent monthly meetings in New England Yearly Meeting, a persistent localism continued without a compelling need to stay linked to Friends in other colonies to the north. New York had a half-year's meeting for both business and worship implicitly paralleling the quasi-independent status that kind of meeting gave Irish Friends in that period. Still a half year's meeting did not necessarily imply separate status: both Scituate and Sandwich had them in Massachusetts without becoming yearly meetings. Events external to the formal workings of Quaker meetings may have influenced the establishment of the new yearly meeting. With the overthrow of the Dominion of New England in 1689, New York Friends could have opted to separate from New England. No evidence survives as to why New York Friends should want to separate; indeed, their sparse numbers and relative isolation gave a very good reason not to. Because evidence is lacking, conclusions are entirely speculative.

Initially adopted to provide both support for and control of members of the Society, over time New York meetings for business developed policies and procedures roughly paralleling those of meetings elsewhere in the Society, but until reform of the Society got underway in the 1750s, New York meetings were able to go their separate ways in key matters. Although the basic organizational structure existed from the outset, the initial small extent of New York Yearly Meeting permitted a small and generally congenial group of Friends (at first in Flushing Monthly Meeting, later joined by Westbury Monthly Meeting) to act as the monthly, quarterly, and yearly meetings. Reinforcing this situation was the creation of a select meeting of ministers and elders in 1704 and a select preparative meeting in 1706. The meeting structure came to be dominated by a small group of weighty Friends. Under this basically benign, self-perpetuating group, New York Friends prospered early in the eighteenth century.

The business meeting for most Friends was the monthly meeting and its preparative meeting or meetings. To these meetings Friends would apply for permission to marry, to move away from the meeting, for relief if they were in difficult circumstances, and for any projects or concerns that they had. Requests for a school or a poor house would go before this meeting to be referred to superior meetings. Friends also looked to their monthly meeting to find support for their testimonies, including refusals to take oaths, pay church taxes, and participate in military service.

In addition to the assistance given members, the monthly meeting also was responsible for enforcing Quaker rules—the Discipline. Those Friends who married outside the care of the meeting, who did not marry a Friend, or who had a child too soon after marriage could expect to come under "dealing" for violating the Discipline. Approximately one-half the rule violations were in this category. Other offenses that resulted in dealing included drunkenness, military activity, failure to pay debts, dishonesty (especially in business), and fighting. Frequently, more than one offense was included in the charges. Friends taken under dealing had a chance to acknowledge offenses in writing and publicly in a meeting. Before 1750 New York monthly meetings were charitably inclined toward miscreants and permitted most of them to acknowledge their misdeeds. A small minority, however, either refused or were unable to make an acceptable acknowledgment and were disowned, that is, they were formally removed from the membership of the Society. Not only were few removed, but, based on statements from Flushing Monthly Meeting in 1734 and Westbury Monthly Meeting the next year about marriages outside the care of the meetings, many offenses may have not resulted in dealings at all. Perhaps only scandalous or unlucky offenders were taken under dealing.

New York's Discipline was informal, carried by tradition and local precedent before 1755: the Yearly Meeting had no formal written discipline until then. Even then, New York Friends in their monthly meetings resisted what was essentially a British form. Indeed, the absence of detailed rules collected in a book and enforced had helped Friends' numbers grow in New York. The experience in the British Isles had been quite different. There, rigorous enforcement of rules had already stopped the growth of Quaker numbers and begun the precipitous numerical decline that would only be arrested in the next century.

As visiting public Friends reported in great detail, Quaker meetings in the northern colonies prospered. Indeed, by the middle of the eighteenth century Friends' numbers were growing at an especially rapid pace in New York because of natural increase, high membership retention because of few disownments, and growing immigration from New England. In the first half of the eighteenth century many visiting English Friends reported that Truth prospered in New York.

The English Friend with the highest opinion of New York was Mary Weston, who visited Friends in the American colonies between 1750 and 1752. When she visited New York, she was entertained by the leading older Friends: John Bowne, Benjamin Ferris, and Walter Franklin. She was impressed by them, and she apparently made quite an impression in her own right. Wherever she went, she attracted large throngs. Apparently, she and leading Friends took pleasure at the large numbers, and she and others must have compared these large crowds to those attracted by Great Awakening preachers; Friends could do as well as revivalists.

The enthusiasm about the great numerical growth among American Friends was short-lived, however. Just two years after the departure of Mary Weston came Mary Peisley from Ireland in 1754 and Samuel Fothergill from England, leading a large group in 1755. What they observed was declension among American Friends and what they prescribed was reform. Fothergill, too, attracted large throngs. Wherever he went, he encouraged yearly meetings to tighten rules. Like George Fox in the 1670s, he urged the adoption of British practices but with a much different thrust and result. And like Fox he met resistance, but unlike Fox it was not from schismatics like John Perrot or ranters like Thomas Case, rather it was apparently from some of the same leading Friends who had so impressed Mary Weston just three years earlier. As Fothergill put it in a letter to Israel Pemberton after a meeting in Flushing: "the lamentable defection of those who would be thought the head but are the tail—I mean the more advanced in years, profession, and station amongst the people gives painful prospect. And as it is hard to lift up a hand against gray hairs, my progress has been more difficult and afflicting than I can express."[14]

As Fothergill's letter indicated, acceptance of his reform proposals was not unanimous. In fact, several New York meetings resisted reform for several years. By 1760 New York Yearly Meeting had decided to require of constituent quarterly and monthly meetings detailed answers to queries. Before the period of reform, the yearly meeting had accepted general answers. That practice, reformers thought, had permitted lax observance of Quaker practices. Many meetings resisted. Westbury was the first to refuse to answer in detail from 1761 through 1767. Newtown Preparative Meeting, a part of Flushing Monthly Meeting, joined from 1763 through 1766. The overseers, who would have to gather the detailed evidence to support the answers, did not think it would work. After resistance collapsed in Westbury, Oblong Monthly Meeting took up the cause in 1771, although not for long, as open opposition disappeared after a visit from a yearly meeting committee in 1773. Meanwhile, in 1763 New York Yearly Meeting adopted the Lon-

don Yearly Meeting Discipline, the first to have been established for
New York.

Also given attention for the first time was the question of membership. The issue first arose over the need to identify Friends to secure
exemption under the militia law of 1754. Although New York Friends
ultimately chose not to comply with the act, initially they had to determine who was a Friend, something they had not formally done before.
The yearly meeting decided that a Friend was a person who applied
successfully for membership or one whose name appeared in Quaker
records. That did not go far enough, however, for in 1772 the yearly
meeting tightened the definition of birthright members to stipulate
that both parents of a child must be Friends, otherwise a parent would
have to make formal application.

The effect of reform was soon apparent. Numbers of Friends taken
under dealing rose throughout the yearly meeting after 1755 so that
for the years 1770 through 1774 those taken under dealing were triple
the number during the period twenty years earlier. And the numbers
continued to grow during the War for Independence. Of greater importance was the rise in disownments compared to acknowledgments.
After 1770 disownments substantially outnumbered acknowledgments.
The effect was especially significant for those young people who married out of meeting, most of whom were disowned and were lost to
Friends. For New York the effect was not as drastic as in other yearly
meetings because New York did not handle disciplinary cases as severely as did older New England meetings, nor were most meetings
into which Quaker migrants moved as severe with miscreants. Despite
the rise in enforcement during this period, the New York Quaker population actually increased. Real loss of members in New York followed
the 1828 Orthodox-Hicksite Separation although some damage had begun as a result of reform.

There were positive sides to the reform discussed elsewhere in this
book. Friends undertook to end slavery and the slave trade within
Quakerism and then to eliminate both from society at large. They also
developed a heightened sense of ministering to all unfortunate people,
especially those victimized by the ravages of war. A new concern arose
over the plight of native Americans. While Friends were purifying their
ranks, they also sought to improve the world in which they lived.

3

New York Quaker Settlements and Immigrants

ARTHUR WORRALL
and
THOMAS BASSETT, CHRISTOPHER DENSMORE,
MARY ELLEN SINGSEN, ALSON D. VAN WAGNER

During the late seventeenth century the northeastern Quakers whose descendants would settle in the Hudson River valley and beyond lived in coastal towns such as Flushing, Oyster Bay, and Westbury in New York and Dartmouth in Massachusetts. In the seventeenth century their residents either had not been forced to move because of land short-ages or had mercantile occupations. Nor had that situation changed early in the eighteenth century. After the first decade, gradually in-creasing population pressure forced Friends in Quaker settlements in the southern parts of New York and New England to contemplate mov-ing. When it came time to move, Friends faced constraints not faced by most. As a matter of conscience, they could not move into communities that required payment toward the building of another denomination's church any more than they could pay taxes to support a minister of that church. For that reason most new communities in New England were closed to them. Settlement along the Hudson in Dutchess County provided available lands without church disabilities. And so in the eigh-teenth century Friends from Long Island were joined by Friends from New England, especially southeastern Massachusetts and Rhode Island, in settling the mainland of Long Island Sound and the lower Hudson valley. What began as a modest influx early in the century turned into a major migration by the 1740s. From then through the first three decades of the nineteenth century, the Hudson valley and, later, cen-tral and western New York became probably the major areas for

25

numerical growth and geographical expansion among Quakers in North America.

From Long Island and New England to the Main

For their first twenty years in New York, most Friends lived in or near the original Quaker centers of Flushing, Gravesend, Newtown, Oyster Bay, and Westbury. Friends in this area were numerous, as numerous as those in Rhode Island Monthly Meeting. Enough land seems to have been available for almost three generations after the first appearance of Friends in this area, so Quakers did not move to the mainland in large numbers.

Some English had moved to Westchester County, but there were few of them in the first generation. George Fox sent two of his number to Rye in 1672, where they had an amicable meeting, although it is unlikely that a Quaker presence continued in this part of "Winthrop's government," as Fox referred to it, in the seventeenth century. The decision by Flushing Quarterly Meeting to establish a preparative meeting at Westchester in 1684 provides the first substantial evidence of a strong Quaker presence in the village of Westchester, a presence that continued because representatives continued to represent Westchester at Flushing Monthly Meeting. Still, the numbers cannot have been great, and there may have been followers of Thomas Case in Westchester, thereby limiting numbers even further, although the evidence of the Case group's presence is thin. There is also a possibility of seventeenth-century Quaker settlement at Mamaroneck on land controlled by the Richbells, descendants of smuggler and land speculator John Richbell.

Unsettled land titles and the continued presence of Indians delayed English settlement in the rest of Westchester County until early in the eighteenth century. In the 1690s the venal Governor Benjamin Fletcher and his cronies of the anti-Leislerian faction had promoted a land grab that was partially reined in by the Earl of Bellomont at the turn of the century. Land titles remained in some confusion for at least another decade. Furthermore, with intermittent war in the region between 1689 and 1713, few settlers wanted to leave the comfortable confines of Long Island for the uncertainties of the mainland until after war and land titles could be cleared. Eventually, the need for land led a few Friends to move to the mainland and thereby expand Quaker numbers. Earlier, John Harrison, a Flushing Friend, had helped lead the way when in 1695 he and four partners purchased land from In-

1. Flushing Meeting House, built 1694. Photograph by John Cox, Jr., 1894.
Courtesy Haviland Records Room, New York Yearly Meeting.

dians in the area subsequently called Purchase (or Harrison's Purchase). Chances are that it was not until after 1715 that Long Island Friends began to move in large numbers to new settlements outside the village of Westchester. Enough Friends had moved by 1725 for the yearly meeting to establish Purchase Monthly Meeting in 1725. When first established, Purchase Monthly Meeting comprised Friends who lived in Mamaroneck, Rye, and Purchase itself. The initial monthly meeting record indicated two preparative meetings in Mamaroneck and Rye, and Westchester.[1]

The major migration into Westchester County started in the 1720s and continued to centers of Quaker settlement like Scarsdale in the 1730s. By the end of that decade most expansion had occurred and the next new area for Friends to settle was in Dutchess County. Remaining in Westchester were lands to be filled with relatively little migration. Settlement was extensive enough by 1745 for Chappaqua to receive preparative meeting status some five years before the first recognized meeting for worship in Amawalk. Amawalk became a preparative meeting in 1772, and in 1785, when Chappaqua received monthly meeting status, the northern branch of Westchester Friends finally achieved separate standing. Settlement in the county was finished, and contiguous expansion would have to follow river valleys to the northeast when major expansion had gone well up the Hudson to the Champlain River valley in the north and had turned west to the central part of the state.

A final topic remains in this brief survey of expansion in Westchester—the only significant entry into the political fray by Friends in the colonial period. That it centered on Quakers was accidental, for they had little to do with the issue when it was raised. They happened to have expanded into the political bailiwick of the leading New York politician Lewis Morris just as he confronted Governor William Cosby's effort to control New York politics. Details of this affair are irrelevant for Friends. The issue that caught Quakers was their increased presence in Westchester just as Cosby sought to defeat his opponent and their ally Morris in the 1733 election for the assembly seat. One means used by the Cosby camp was to challenge Quaker voters and require that they take an oath, a revival of past practices, although for most of the eighteenth century New York had given Friends the franchise. The tactic backfired for Cosby in two ways: Morris won the election without the temporarily disfranchised Quakers' votes, and in 1735 the shame-faced Cosby sent to Britain an act permitting Quakers to vote as they were able to do elsewhere in the American colonies. No doubt there was also belated recognition on his part of the political strength of English Friends with the government of Robert Walpole through the faction that they supported—the Dissenting Deputies. With this brief exception, Quaker political activity drops from view in this part of New York until Friends turned to pursue antislavery and to deal with war-related measures, topics covered in chapter 5.[2]

Hudson Valley Quakers

Most Friends who moved to Purchase and the Hudson Valley before 1740 were from New York. Increasingly after that date Friends came from Rhode Island and southeastern Massachusetts although a substantial number still came from Long Island. The New England Quakers had faced a bleak prospect: they were running out of land at home, and New York presented the only viable alternative to staying at home in declining fortunes. By moving to New York they avoided compromising their testimony against a paid ministry in Massachusetts by contributing to the building of a meeting house for the local Congregational parson. Thus, they moved into Purchase and from there into the Oblong to the north in the first stage of their settlement in Dutchess County. But even before settlements in Dutchess County began, some people in New Milford, Connecticut, had asked Purchase Monthly Meeting to recognize a meeting for worship. Purchase complied in about 1729.

Settlement in the Oblong itself began two years later, in 1731, when New York and Connecticut settled their boundary dispute, giving East Greenwich to Connecticut and a strip of land one and three-quarters mile wide (an oblong) north of East Greenwich to the Massachusetts border with New York. The Oblong Patent was attractive to New Englanders who initially would have found the leaseholding arrangements on large estates in the Hudson Valley unattractive. In the Oblong residents could hold land in fee simple, like land in most of New England, so that Friends could now obtain title to their own land without the religious disabilities that frustrated them in Massachusetts. In about 1735 Nathaniel Birdsall and Benjamin Ferris and their families moved into the Oblong. Many New England Friends soon joined them and went well beyond Oblong into the Beekman Patent and the Great Nine Partners Tract. Their numbers enabled them to ask for and obtain a preparative meeting from Purchase Monthly Meeting and in 1744 to become Oblong and Nine Partners Monthly Meeting, a status granted by the yearly meeting, which even went so far as to name the first clerk of the new Purchase Quarterly Meeting. By this stage, settlement in Nine Partners was already about six years old, and Friends there had a preparative meeting. A period of consolidation of settlement followed for these monthly meetings as Friends poured in to settle on their own land in the Oblong or to take up favorable leases in Beekman and Nine Partners lands, now having overcome their reluctance on that score. Quaker settlers in Oblong and Nine Partners numbered in the hundreds in 1760. Reflecting that growth was the creation of ten new preparative meetings before 1800. Of greater importance was the decision to make Nine Partners a monthly meeting in 1769. Most of the remaining meetings in New York and Vermont derived from this monthly meeting.[3]

The steady migration in the middle of the century into Dutchess County led to violence among some latecomers without land, but Friends escaped that conflict. They were unable, however, to avoid the effects of the War for Independence, ranging from combat in the southern part of the county to occasional attacks on them as potential Loyalists. The war and independence indirectly caused a substantial rise in Quaker migration. Some Friends moved to the Hudson River valley to escape war elsewhere. Eighty Friends facing an economic catastrophe left Dartmouth Monthly Meeting for Nine Partners in 1775, and roughly half that number left the next year. Nantucket saw the near collapse of the whale fishery. This was the last straw for many folk on this overcrowded island. As soon as they could, they moved, taking their memberships to Nine Partners Monthly Meeting but frequently settling north of Dutchess County. Some from Nantucket went farther up river to Hudson in the attempt to establish a whale fishery. They had sufficient numbers by 1793 to become a monthly meeting. And there were refugees from older settled areas of New York on Long Island and New York wishing to escape British occupation. Among these was Tiddeman Hull, a city merchant who moved his family to Westchester, then to Danbury, Connecticut, and, finally, in 1777 to Stanford in the northern reaches of Dutchess County Quaker settlement.

Expansion continued around the original Quaker centers and to the north as the century wore on. Like migrants elsewhere in this century, many Friends moved more than once. In Dutchess County the continued influx led to the creation of Stanford Preparative Meeting in 1795; it became a monthly meeting in 1803, appropriately enough because Stanford already was a quarterly meeting. And settlement continued on the west side of the Hudson to the point that Cornwall Quarterly Meeting was set off by Nine Partners in 1816. To the north near Albany, Duanesburgh Quarterly Meeting became the center of Quaker activity in 1813 with constituent monthly meetings in Duanesburgh and Coeymans, joined by the new Rensselaerville Monthly Meeting in 1814.

Meanwhile, many Friends had moved north and east of Albany as part of the next wave of settlement after Dutchess County filled. Beginning in the 1760s, they settled in East Hoosac and nearby communities, many of them from Smithfield Monthly Meeting in Rhode Island, in such numbers that East Hoosac Monthly Meeting was created in 1783. To the north Friends moved to Saratoga (later called Easton). They settled there before the War for Independence began, carving out fields from the forests in time to be caught by John Burgoyne's invasion in 1777. By this date Friends were no longer limiting themselves to careful expansion like that in Dutchess County. Native Americans and French had been removed from the path of English-American expansion so that settlement now leapfrogged to the north and west.

Migration of Friends to the Upper Hudson
and Champlain Valleys

Movements of Friends north of Albany and Rensselaer counties differed from their previous migrations in four ways. First, more of the land than in the narrow strip of the Oblong and the holdings of the Nine Partners and the Rensselaers was available for outright purchase;

it did not have to be leased. Second, most of those who bought land in the northern wilderness, especially in what was known then as the New Hampshire Grants and later became Vermont, bought titles which were even more uncertain (and, therefore, cheaper) than any previous frontier purchases. Third, no one had to pay church taxes until 1783, and after that it was easier in Vermont than in frontier New Hampshire or Massachusetts (including Maine) to avoid paying for the support of preaching and for the building of meeting houses. Most Vermont towns had no church taxes because few ministers were hired or meeting houses built until Vermont canceled the requirement in 1807. Even if one did not make the necessary written statement of dissent to the town clerk, the law was apparently not enforced in areas Friends settled. Fourth, for the half-century after the fall of New France in 1760 the unsettled backcountry was nearly always peaceful, whereas the frontier elsewhere was often a dark and bloody ground.

The Quakers, like other Europeans, assumed they were moving into a woodland with Indian title extinguished. Quakers in northern New England, like other settlers in the wake of the imperial and Indian wars, were beneficiaries of this convenient attitude. Consequently, they made no ritual cessions such as Roger Williams and William Penn had honestly agreed upon in the seventeenth century. Western Abenaki, with the remnants of southern New England refugees, either moved out of the valley or effaced themselves out of whites' peripheral vision. Friends in these parts, to avoid the force and fraud of the world, seemed to follow a similar strategy of withdrawal from commercial centers to quiet country places.

Actually, the region most free from church taxes became Saratoga and Washington counties, New York, first entered before the War for Independence. Nathaniel Starbuck and family came from Nantucket to North Easton in 1763, and as the first in the area, his log house served as a tavern for wayfarers. A 1773 census of Charlotte County, covering what became western Vermont and all of New York north of the Saratoga Patent, showed three thousand inhabitants, a few of whom were Friends. Rufus Hall, a young Dutchess County farmer with Rhode Island roots, bought land in Easton in the fall of 1773. The following year Easton Friends numbered one hundred in three places of worship. This included those scattered in White Creek, Greenwich, and other towns to the north. By the time Burgoyne invaded in August–September 1777 some dozen Quaker families from his former home and southeastern Massachusetts had joined Hall. Hall's matter-of-fact journal recorded: "One day the Indians came to our meeting just as it was breaking up, but they offered no violence: their warlike appearance was very shocking, being equipped with their guns, tomahawks and scalping knives: they had a prisoner and one green scalp taken . . . but a few hours before." Hall continued, when the intruders "understood that Friends were at a Religious Meeting, they went to one of their Houses, got some victuals, of which a prisoner with them partook, and they quietly departed." Friends lost much property that summer, he continued, but none were injured and only a few were briefly imprisoned as suspected Loyalists.[4] Because Friends were at worship and probably weaponless in the war zone, it is easy to imagine the Indians assuming by their peaceful body language that Friends were on their side. How could they conceive of Quakers as disengaged from the conflict? The rebels also assumed they were Loyalists. Legend has it that Robert Nisbet of East Hoosac Meeting, forty miles away in Adams, Massachusetts, was visiting when a raiding party encountered Friends, and helped with his knowledge of French and Indian tongues.

Quakers were concerned with the north country first as speculators and then as settlers. As speculators in touch through Quaker merchants in the seaport of New York, capital of the Province of New York, they must have known that in 1764 the Privy Council had confirmed New York's claim, based on its royal grant of 1664, to the land west of the Connecticut River. They also knew that Governor Benning Wentworth of New Hampshire had chartered 131 towns west of the Connecticut River, especially after the Seven Year's War. We know of no Quaker comment on the dispute between New Hampshire and New York about which province had a legitimate title. Agents for New England proprietors of New Hampshire grants, or those who had bought surveyed land for quick sale, crossed the New York-Connecticut border to hawk their lands among Quakers and others with capital for investment or with younger sons ready to move. Even as late as 1789, when the town of Sheldon was chartered by the independent state of Vermont, Connecticut Friend Uriah Field disposed of lands to the Sheldon family and for twenty years collected installments or rents in beef cattle, which he drove to the New York market.[5]

On the whole, Friends were not original proprietors, but sixteen days after the French surrender of Canada at Montreal in September 1760, a group of land speculators met in Nine Partners, Dutchess County, New York, and appointed a representative to negotiate charters to New Hampshire towns. Less than one year later Governor Wentworth chartered Danby, and Quakers were the most numerous of its first settlers. Proprietors made way for the organization of the town in

1769 with Friend Timothy Bull moderator and his son Crispin Bull a selectman. Town and meeting grew for a quarter-century, and Saratoga Quarter set off Danby Friends from Easton as a monthly meeting in 1795. By then the tide was turning; Friends were leaving for the Holland Purchase in western New York and beyond. Farmington, Collins, and Eden meetings received infusions from Danby.

Did Quaker settlement follow a pattern different from those of others going into the wild back country? Recent studies of Friends moving into other frontier woodlands before the Separation emphasize the similarities between the Quakers and others looking for more cheap land for themselves and their children. As far as we know, Friends destroyed the forest as effectively as their non-Quaker neighbors, used the same farming methods, exhausted the soil as much, and had as many children to provide for.[6] There were proportionally more Quaker merchants, millers, and artisans, and almost no professionals, except, perhaps, a stray doctor.

Certainly, they were active as speculators, not only Uriah Field but also Timothy Rogers, who operated out of Ferrisburgh until he led a flock of Friends to Upper Canada in 1801. Rogers also surveyed in towns like Sheldon, taking pay in land and protecting the rights of other Friends against tax sales. Born in Lyme, Connecticut, in 1756, Timothy was raised by his mother's relatives and others until his uncle found him in an abusive family and took him to Nine Partners where he fell among Baptists and was eventually attracted to Quakers. Married at nineteen, he came to Danby early in the war, "hired" money to buy land, "working out" for others, taking pay in grain that he carried on his back to the mill. Soon we find him in the Saratoga-Easton area, then back in Danby, and then in Ferrisburgh before the end of hostilities. He traded in Quebec City and in 1789 entered a partnership with New York City Quakers, Richard Bowne, James Pearsall, and Richard Burling, to develop the great falls of the Otter at Vergennes. They erected mills and established a store, but creditors descended on him, whereupon the restless Rogers sold off land and horses to cover his debts and withdrew from his commercial-industrial venture.[7]

Friends were as mobile as others. Although the flow appears strongest from Dutchess County, every Quaker region in the Northeast had representatives in the Champlain valley. Many had moved there more than once before they came from the Piscataqua basin in New Hampshire, the area of Plymouth Colony in Massachusetts, Rhode Island, Long Island, and the neighborhood of New York. The process of buying land from the proprietors (more land than they settled on), clearing, burning, stump pulling, cropping, and moving on was often repeated. Mount Holly, Shoreham, Weybridge, Ferrisburgh, Charlotte, Monkton, Lincoln, all with "allowed" or regular meetings for worship, were settled mainly in the twenty years after the Declaration of Independence. From Addison County Quakers fanned out northeastward to Montpelier, Sharon, Strafford, Barton, and Derby, northward to Grand Isle and Farnham in the eastern townships of Lower Canada (Quebec), and across Lake Champlain to Peru, New York. All these places had allowed worship, too, in Friends' cabins. At least ten grew large enough to build log meeting houses, sometimes replace them with frame structures, and conduct their own church business. The old practice of settling Quaker communities was approximated in Danby until the Revolution, but instead of reinforcing that nucleus, later comers preferred prime wild land to clear instead of leftovers in a town only second rate for farming. There is evidence of isolated Friends living in a score of Vermont towns without even the benefit of regular worship or visits from traveling ministers. In Strafford Timothy Blake, a disillusioned revolutionary veteran of the Quebec campaign, gathered likeminded spirits and began worship before he had any contact with Quakers. Moses Brown visited them in 1786 and Timothy Rogers with David Hoag in 1789.

At the Separation in 1828 each side counted the sheep and the goats with slightly different proportions of Hicksites and Orthodox, but nearly the same totals: 1,075 Friends in Vermont by one count. In addition, there were 255 Friends across Lake Champlain around Keeseville, two-thirds Orthodox, 134 in Granville, New York, evenly divided and linked as a preparative meeting with Danby, then much larger (226) and overwhelmingly Hicksite, and 127 entirely Orthodox in Farnham. The side they chose seemed to depend on the influence of the leaders. The 505 Friends in five preparative meetings of Starksboro Monthly Meeting (Lincoln, South Lincoln, South Starksboro [Creek], Starksboro, and Montpelier) were all Orthodox, probably because of the presence of Clark Stevens of Montpelier, Huldah and Joseph Hoag and their large tribe, and other ministers.

What caused this large number to evaporate so that by the end of the nineteenth century only remnants of Ferrisburgh, South Starksboro, and Monkton were left? Some say disownment was the most disastrous policy, but the disaster was being swallowed and digested by the surrounding non-Quaker society. Disownment was not judgment upon evildoers, but like a divorce decree, sad recognition of a fact that a person no longer treasured the spirit of the testimonies, that is, was no

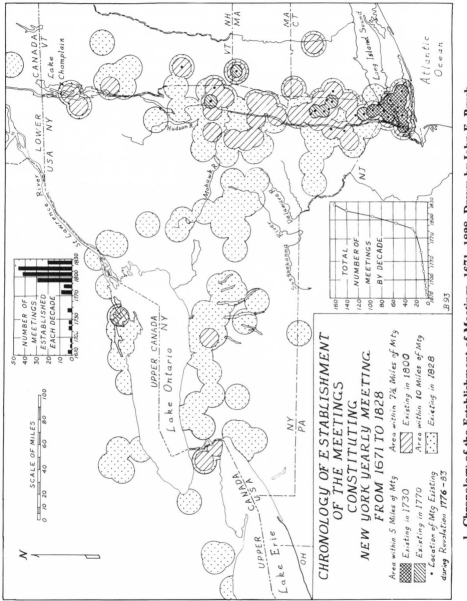

1. **Chronology of the Establishment of Meetings, 1671–1828. Drawn by John E. Brush.**

longer a Friend. Others say that the Separation left each side too weak to function and too bitter to focus on their proper Quaker mission. Departure to New York, Ontario, or elsewhere would not have damaged a healthy body of Friends. But many itinerant Quaker ministers reported a "low state," a lukewarm condition. Those who stayed home lacked the vitality to survive as a people with principles different from those of the surrounding society. Many solid devout individuals continued as patterns and examples to those around them, but as a group the Quakers had lost the enthusiasm that their competitors, especially the Baptists, Methodists, and Universalists, had in abundance. Friends kept the shells of peculiarity, in dress and address, in aversion to the world, without the meat of the testimonies.

Western New York

Between 1760 and 1790 New York Yearly Meeting continued its already considerable expansion north along the Hudson River, east into Massachusetts and Vermont. Although little movement to the west along the Mohawk occurred for more than thirty years, the continued expansion in areas north and east of Albany help identify this as a thriving yearly meeting.

In 1789 a group of Quakers from East Hoosac Monthly Meeting near North Adams, Massachusetts, took up new lands in the Genesee country two hundred miles west of the Hudson, farther from established centers of Quakerism than Friends had gone before in New York. Although most of the Friends moved under the care of their monthly meeting, several did not and were disowned for their avoidance of established rules. Still, the disowned continued their Quaker ways, for when William Savery traveled among them, he found them still wearing Quaker garb and observing Quaker customs. Despite difficult circumstances observed by Savery, they and their fellows, who had escaped being disciplined, built a meetinghouse in 1796 or 1797 and obtained formal recognition as a meeting for worship from Saratoga Monthly Meeting some two hundred miles away in 1799. They became Farmington Preparative Meeting in 1800 and Farmington Monthly Meeting in 1808. Eventually, the disowned Friends were restored to membership in this rapidly growing new center of Quakerism that eventually had nine monthly meetings and two quarterly meetings (Farmington in 1810 and Scipio in 1825). Geographically, this area extended from DeRuyter in Madison County in the east to Eden in Erie County to the west.[8] Norwegian Quaker immigrants represented another group moving to this area in the 1820s. They were refugees from persecution by the established church at home and were the first of their nationality to move to North America in the nineteenth century. Numbering fifty-two individuals, they settled in the town of Kendall in Orleans County.[9]

Shortly after Friends moved to Genesee country, settlement exploded into central and western New York following the Mohawk Valley west to Oneida, Otsego, and Madison counties and from the headwaters of the Mohawk north and west. North of Syracuse and Utica near Watertown, LeRay became a monthly meeting with preparative meetings ranging from Lowville to the south to Chaumont and Indian River. Sufficiently numerous to establish four monthly meetings, Friends in these new regions strained the institutional resources of the Society.[10]

Greatest stress came from the great distances between meetings. When Elias Hicks visited Duanesburgh Monthly Meeting in 1806, he noted that one meeting for worship was ninety miles from the place where the monthly meeting met. Hicks worried that the scattering of Friends in the new country made it difficult for younger Friends to attend meetings for discipline "which I have often considered as schools of very profitable instruction to well minded youth."[11] Scipio Monthly Meeting was so spread out that six of its constituent meetings were separated by at least twenty miles from other meetings. The most extreme case was that of Deerfield Preparative Meeting in Tioga County, Pennsylvania, one hundred miles from the site of its monthly meeting, Farmington, to the north. Like most of the rest of the yearly meeting, Friends in these newly settled areas lived in the country.

A study of migration into Scipio Monthly Meeting suggests that approximately 60 percent of the migrating Friends to these new areas came from eastern New York and some 30 percent came from Rhode Island and southeastern Massachusetts, especially Dartmouth and New Bedford, thereby continuing a long-established migrant pattern. The migration was usually by stages with some families moving more than once. Similar patterns would continue beyond New York to Canada and Michigan in the next generation.[12]

Most of the membership of the new meetings derived from Friends who came from meetings to the east and who were members, had been members, or had family who were members when they moved. Happily, in the newly settled areas Friends attracted new members, in some meetings perhaps as many as half joined the Society as adults. Elias Hicks noted the growth and hoped it would continue "in the Lord's time . . . and fill the whole earth." His optimism before the schism was

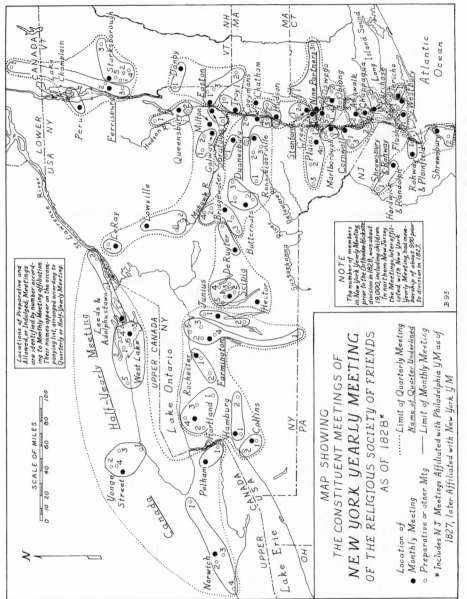

2. Constituent Meetings of New York Yearly Meeting, 1828. Drawn by John E. Brush.

TABLE

Status of Meetings in 1828 with Date of Founding

Canada Half Yearly Meeting: Upper Canada (Ontario)
Leeds and Adolphustown 1798 (1825)
  1 Kingston (Cataraqui) 1801
  2 Leeds 1818
Norwich 1816 (1819)
  1 Ancaster 1816
  2 Malahide 1822
  3 Pine Street 1801
Pelham 1799 (1799)
  1 Black Creek 1799
West Lake (Bloomfield) 1803 (1821)
  1 Ameliasburg [Hillier] 1824
  2 Cold Creek 1825
  3 East Lake 182?
  4 Green Point 1811
  5 Haldimand 1827
  6 Hillier [Wellington] 1817
Yonge Street [Newmarket] 1804 (1806)
  1 Pickering 1819
  2 Queen Street (Sharon) 1810
  3 Uxbridge 1810
  4 Whitechurch 1811

Cornwall Quarterly Meeting
Cornwall 1777 (1788)
  1 Blooming Grove (Upper Clove) 1812
  2 Kakiat [Haverstraw] 1809
  3 Smith's Clove 1803
Plains (Tillson) 1813 (1813)
  1 Esopus 1813
  2 Greenfield (Grahamsville) 1809
  3 Neversink 18?
  4 Paltz (Butterville) 1801
Marlborough (Milton) 1777 (1804)
  1 Newburgh Valley (Plattekill) 1799
  2 Plattekill (Clintondale) 1807

Duanesburg Quarterly Meeting
Coeymans 1793 (1799)
  1 Berne 179?
  2 Bethlehem 180?
  3 Coxsackie 180?
  4 New Baltimore 1814
Bridgewater 1817 (1817)
  1 Brookfield 1811
  2 New Hartford 1810
  3 Smyrna 1812
  4 Westmoreland 1826
Butternuts 1810 (1810)
  1 Burlington 1806
  2 Laurens 1811
  3 Middlefield 1818
Duanesburg (Quaker Street) 1800 (1806)
  1 Charleston 1815
Rensselaerville 1799 (1814)
  1 Harpersfield 1820
  2 Middleburg 1810
  3 Oak Hill 1804

Easton Quarterly Meeting
Danby, Vermont 1781 (1795)
  1 Granville 1802
Easton (First Saratoga) 1778 (1778)
  1 Cambridge 1813
  2 East Hoosac, Massachusetts 1774
  3 White Creek 1783
Troy 1804 (1813)
  1 Pittstown 1796

Farmington Quarterly Meeting
Collins (Concord) 1813 (1820)
  1 Clear Creek 1820
  2 Evans 1827
Farmington 1800 (1803)
  1 Deerfield [Knoxville], Pennsylvania 1815
  2 Macedon 1827
  3 Palmyra 1812

TABLE *Continued*

4 South Farmington 1819
5 Williamson 1826
Hamburg (Orchard Park) 1810
(1814)
1 Eden (Boston) 1813
2 Orangeville 1820
Hartland 1817 (1821)
1 Batavia (Elba) 1818
2 Lockport (Royalton) 1819
3 Shelby 1822
4 Somerset 1826
Junius 1806 (1815)
1 Galen 1814
2 Milo 1827
Rochester 1821 (1825)
1 Henrietta 1825
2 Wheatland 1824

Ferrisburg Quarterly Meeting
Ferrisburg, Vermont 1793 (1801)
1 Farnham, Lower Canada
[Quebec] 1826
2 Monkton, Vermont 1801
3 Weybridge, Vermont 1811
Peru 1796 (1799)
Grand Isle (South Hero),
Vermont 1799
Starksborough, Vermont 1803
(1813)
1 Creek, Vermont 1825
2 Lincoln, Vermont 1801
3 Montpelier, Vermont 1803
4 South Lincoln, Vermont 1815
5 South Starksborough, Vermont
18?

Nine Partners Quarterly Meeting
Nine Partners [Millbrook] 1742
(1769)
1 Canaan, Connecticut 1820
2 Ridge (Chestnut Ridge) 1799
3 West Hartford, Connecticut
1800

Oblong (Quaker Hill) [Pawling]
1742 (1744)
1 Branch (Deuel Hollow)
[Dover] 1783
2 New Milford, Connecticut
1777
3 Valley (Haviland Hollow)
[Patterson] 1785
Oswego (Moores Mill) 1758 (1799)
1 Beekman (Arthursburg) 1810
2 Pleasant Valley 1806
3 Poughkeepsie 1819
4 Poughquaig (Gardner Hollow)
1771
5 West Branch (La Grange)
1800

Purchase Quarterly Meeting
Amawalk 1774 (1798)
1 Croton 1797
2 Peekskill 1816
3 Salem (Bedford) 1792
Chappaqua 1750 (1785)
1 Croton Valley 1804
2 North Castle 1796
Purchase 1725 (1745)
1 Mamaroneck 1716
2 Middlesex [Darien],
Connecticut 1809
3 Westchester [Bronx] 1716

Saratoga Quarterly Meeting
Galway 1797 (1802)
1 Mayfield (Kingsborough) 1804
2 Providence 1801
Milton (Greenfield) 1800 (1818)
Queensbury (Glens Falls) 1797
(1800)
1 Chester 1804
2 Moreau (South Glens Falls)
1827
LeRay (Pleasant Creek) 1814
(1815)

TABLE *Continued*

1 Indian River (Philadelphia) 1810
Lowville 1819 (1825)
  1 Lee 1817
  2 Western (Westernville) 1813
Saratoga 1793 (1794)
  1 Half Moon 1801

Scipio Quarterly Meeting
De Ruyter 1806 (1809)
  1 Madison 1809
Hector 1816 (1822)
Scipio 1804 (1808)
  1 North Street 1819
  2 Salmon Creek 1815
  3 Sempronius 1817
  4 Skaneateles 1821
  5 Union Springs 1816

Stanford Quarterly Meeting
Creek (Clinton Corners) 1776 (1782)
  1 Crum Elbow 1797
Chatham (Rayville) 1794 (1819)
Hudson 1784 (1793)
  1 Athens 1812
  2 Ghent (Klinakill) 1799

Stanford 1795 (1803)
  1 Little Nine Partners 1800
  2 Northeast [Bethel] 1806

Westbury Quarterly Meeting
Flushing 1671
  1 New York [Manhattan] 1682
Jericho 1786 (1789)
  1 Bethpage 1698
Westbury 1671 (1682)
  1 Cowneck (Manhasset) 1704
  2 Matinecock 1671

. . .

Shrewsbury and Rahway Quarterly Meeting
Hardwick and Randolph 1746 (1796)
  1 Hardwick 1756
Rahway and Plainfield 1686 (1704)
  1 Rahway 1742
Shrewsbury c. 1670 (1671)
  1 Squan (Manasquan) c. 1700
  2 Squancome 1778

*The northern New Jersey meetings were affiliated with Philadelphia Yearly Meeting from 1682 until the Orthodox-Hicksite division in 1827. In 1833 the Hicksite meetings of this quarter affiliated with New York Yearly Meeting, Hicksite.

well founded: New York Yearly Meeting had 162 particular meetings in 1821, eight times the number it had had in 1775. Despite the geographical growth in the first three decades of the nineteenth century and the great distances that deprived Friends of mutual support, Friends had every reason to believe that growth would continue.[13]

Friends in Canada

In the early nineteenth century most Canadian Quakers were in Upper Canada (Ontario). Eventually, these Friends came under New York Yearly Meeting's oversight, and, thus, it is appropriate that a study of New York Yearly Meeting includes them. Their migration into Upper Canada was part of the same general movement that began after the Seven Years' War, but with the political imperative after the War for Independence for Loyalists, Friends among them, to leave the United States and retain the imperial connection by moving to the developing province to the north. This migration came in two stages: the first was Loyalist, the second was part of the expansion west that had its counterpart in central and western New York.[14]

Shortly after peace came in 1783 Loyalist Quakers moved to two parts of Upper Canada: the vicinities of Adolphustown on the Bay of Quinte near Kingston and of Pelham on the Niagara peninsula. When Quaker migrants reached both is uncertain, but it appears that the Bay of Quinte settlement came first and, like that at Niagara, occurred without the care of a meeting for business. Settlement apparently came as early as 1784 here with worship meetings held in homes probably from the beginning of settlement. It was not until 1797, however, that there was any contact from an established Friends meeting, in this case, Nine Partners Monthly Meeting. Nine Partners recognized an Adolphustown Preparative Meeting in 1798 and New York Friends made it a monthly meeting in 1800. Meanwhile, Niagara Friends settled within one decade of the Bay of Quinte group with recorded contact with visiting Friends in 1793 and settlement perhaps even earlier. Most Niagara settlers had come from Philadelphia Yearly Meeting shortly after peace in 1783, so when they decided to ask for a meeting for business in 1797 they applied to that meeting. After a visit by a committee, Philadelphia Yearly Meeting established Pelham Monthly Meeting in 1799, placing it directly under the oversight of the Yearly Meeting without the existence of a superior quarterly meeting, a reflection of the awkward distance separating Niagara Friends from Pennsylvania.

The next wave of migration came at the turn of the century, a part of the same movement that saw Friends rapidly settle areas to the west. In this case, the settlement went to Yonge Street, about thirty miles north of York (now Toronto) near the contemporary town of Newmarket. The principal Quaker leader at first was Timothy Rogers, at various times a resident of New York and most recently of Vermont, who moved to Yonge Street in 1801. Most Friends coming to this area were from Philadelphia Yearly Meeting, so it was to that Yearly Meeting that Yonge Street Friends applied and in 1804 received a preparative meeting as part of Pelham Monthly Meeting and, in short order, separate status as Yonge Street Monthly Meeting in 1806.

The rapid creation of three monthly meetings in this province within less than one decade demonstrated a need for an intermediate meeting and reflected strains that migrants almost certainly felt from this sudden expansion. The Yonge Street Friends felt the need most of all and pressed for a meeting the equivalent of a quarterly meeting. Pelham and Adolphustown Friends agreed, and in 1808 the three monthly meetings applied to New York and Philadelphia for such a meeting. A joint committee from the yearly meetings visited in 1809, and in 1810 the New York and Philadelphia Yearly Meetings established the Canada Half-Year's Meeting under New York Yearly Meeting, thereby ending divided authority in the province.

Quaker numbers increased to match institutional growth, reaching as many as twenty-five hundred by 1829. In that year the separations of many of the U.S. yearly meetings caught up with Upper Canada when the Orthodox and Hicksites split, a devastating blow for Canadian Quakers. Most numerous of the resulting group were the Orthodox, who gradually moved toward a separate identity from New York Yearly Meeting, attaining it in 1867, the year of Confederation. In 1834 the less-numerous Hicksites became part of a new Hicksite yearly meeting, Genessee Yearly Meeting, which Canadians soon came to dominate as numbers of Hicksites declined in western New York.[15]

Related Migrations

Quaker expansion into western New York early in the nineteenth century had close parallels in three related groups that, although scarcely Quaker, found some inspiration from Quaker antecedents. Of the three, the Shakers, with tentative Quaker origins, had greatest success in securing converts and expanded well beyond the confines of New York. The followers of Jemima Wilkinson, who called herself the Public Universal Friend, were rather narrowly focused in the western part of the Finger Lakes. The third group, the Children of Peace, were not in New York at all; rather, they were a schismatic group that split from Canadian Friends who, as noted before, belonged to New York Yearly Meeting. All shared with Friends the common ground that at least some of their numbers had moved west from settled regions to the east.[16]

The Shakers are the best known of these groups and became the most successful communitarian society. There were former Quakers among the Shaker founders, but the group was more directly influenced by French Camisards. Under the leadership of Mother Ann Lee (1734–1784), Shakers arrived in New York in 1774 and began missionary activity. Although many aspects of the Shaker life style were compatible with Quakerism (pacifism, plainness, and, notably, the ministry of women), most early Shaker converts came from the ranks of New Light and Free Will Baptists, not Friends. Their chief recruiting grounds were revival meetings from the Second Great Awakening forward, scarcely likely to provide continued Quaker influence. A traveling Quaker minister visited a Shaker settlement near the New York-Massachusetts border in 1795 and was told that Shakers thought that George Fox was a good man "until he mixed with the world; that then he fell away." The visiting Quaker found the Shakers a decent and industrious people but mistaken in their beliefs and "over-confident, in supposing they had witnessed greater attainments than others."[17]

Jemima Wilkinson (1752–1819) was born into a Quaker family in Rhode Island but was disowned in 1776 for joining the New Light Baptists. Later that year Wilkinson became seriously ill and had a religious experience during which she became convinced that the woman Jemima had died and that her body was now inhabited by the spirit of the Public Universal Friend.

For the next twenty years, The Friend preached in New England and Pennsylvania, gaining converts and building meeting houses in Rhode Island and New Milford, Connecticut. Never very numerous, Wilkinson and her followers moved to the Finger Lakes region of New York in the 1780s, ultimately settling in Jerusalem Township, north of Penn Yan. The Friends Society, an unstructured group at best, continued for a number of years after Wilkinson's death. It had all but disappeared by midcentury.[18]

The Friend was an object of considerable Quaker curiosity and hostility during her lifetime. Her detractors considered her a charlatan and impostor. Although it is not clear whether she claimed to be the second coming of Christ and able to work miracles, at least some of her followers believed she had those attributes. Quakers did not credit any of these assertions and went so far, in 1795, as to visit her in an attempt to convince her of the error of her ways. Later, in 1819, another group of Quakers came to her "Jerusalem," as her settlement was called, after she had "left time." One of them asked to see her body, and, after looking at it said, "she was nothing more than flesh and blood, like the rest of us, and is now a mass of inanimate clay as we soon must be."[19]

Unlike the Shakers and The Friends Society, the Children of Peace came directly out of the Society of Friends. In 1811 David Willson, a member of Yonge Street Meeting in Upper Canada (Ontario), felt called to speak in meeting, but his ministry was opposed by a number of the meeting's elders. In the controversy that followed, Willson and a number of other Friends, most from Queen Street Preparative Meeting, were disowned. One of them appealed to New York Yearly Meeting, which upheld his disownment in 1815. Willson and his supporters may have hoped for a reconciliation but soon moved to form a separate society that they called the Children of Peace.[20]

In two important and related aspects the separation of Queen Street Meeting prefigured the Hicksite-Orthodox debates of the 1820s and the Progressive Friends of the 1840s. The theological issue was the nature of Christ, with Willson and his fellows opposing the evangelical understanding of the divinity of Christ. Willson also questioned the right of Quakers to enforce theological conformity and the propriety of having ministers and elders.

At Sharon, northeast of Newmarket, Ontario, the Children of Peace, sometimes known as Davidites, built a remarkable temple filled with allegorical symbols and an organ. The Children of Peace also had some communitarian aspects. Although David Willson did not claim special authority, he was, nevertheless, the dominant figure in the Children of Peace, and the community did not long survive his death in 1866. The outward practices of the Children of Peace sharply diverged from those of Friends. The historian of Canadian Friends, Arthur Dorland, wondered how such a movement could have come out of Quakerism. More recent evaluations of David Willson that focus on his writings have the answer to Dorland's query. They argue that Willson and the quietist and mystical aspects of Quakerism were closely related. The stresses caused by migration and resettlement and the threat of war with the United States may have weakened the internal controls among Yonge Street Friends and, thus, helped bring on the schism.[21]

Meeting House Architecture

George Fox held that "God, who made the world, did not dwell in temples made with hands. . . . His people were His temple, and he dwelt in them." The true church was not a building (Fox referred to the churches of his day as "steeple houses") but "the pillar and ground of truth, made up of living stones, living members, a spiritual household, which Christ was the head of" and not "an old house made of lime, stones and wood."[22]

Quaker meeting houses mirrored the anticeremonial nature of Quaker theology. There was no altar or communion table elevating the sacraments nor a pulpit elevating the ordained ministry. Yet by 1700,

2. Crum Elbow Meeting House, built 1797–1810. Interior, 1920s.
Courtesy Haviland Records Room, New York Yearly Meeting.

Quakers in North America had developed a simple but distinctive architecture that remained the standard until mid-nineteenth century and beyond. The meeting house was a rectangle, generally with the entrances on the long side rather than on the end. The meeting house usually had a porch, extending along the front and sometimes along three sides of the building. Two doors opened into the meeting house, one for men to use and the other for the women. During meeting for worship, men and women sat on opposite sides. During meeting for business, a sliding partition divided the building into two equal halves for the men's and women's meeting.[23]

The interior was fitted with benches. Ministers, elders, and other weighty Friends sat on the "facing benches," raised seating that faced toward the benches occupied by most of the congregation. Although vocal ministry could come from anywhere in the meeting house, it would most often come from the acknowledged ministers.

Many meeting houses had to accommodate not only the members and attenders of the local meeting for worship but the larger assemblies at monthly and quarterly meetings. Meeting houses often had a second-level balcony to accommodate the larger numbers that came to those meetings.

In an era of horse-drawn transportation meeting houses also had carriage sheds, which sometimes functioned as refuges for nonattenders accompanying spouses or other family members to meeting. Most meeting houses also had a nearby cemetery, although tombstones were prohibited by the discipline until 1852. Not all occupants of Quaker cemeteries were Quakers, nor were all Quakers buried in the meeting house cemetery.

Not all meeting houses were alike. The size, proportion, and building materials varied. On Long Island, in Westchester County, and in the Hudson valley, they were of wood frame construction. Nine Partners was of brick; Creek was of stone. Four meeting houses in western New York (Elba, West Shelby, Hartland, and Wheatland) were built of cobblestone. Despite the plainness of the meeting house, or, perhaps, because of it, the buildings often had a pleasing proportion. Like Shaker chairs, the combination of plainness and functionality could be an aesthetic statement.

A number of meeting houses built after 1850 had the doors placed on the short (gable) end rather than the long side, but otherwise kept to the traditional pattern. After 1870 the newer Orthodox meeting houses, reflecting the changes brought about by the evangelical movement and revivalism, came to resemble more closely the simpler Protestant churches. These sometimes had an exterior tower and stained glass windows. The old benches were replaced by pews facing a pulpit. Other additions were rooms created for First Day School and other activities.

4

Wars, Revolutions, and the Peace Testimony

HUGH BARBOUR
and
CHRISTOPHER DENSMORE, ARTHUR MEKEEL,
ARTHUR WORRALL

Sources of the Quaker Peace Testimony

In the twentieth century Friends' ethical stand against violence has been their best-known characteristic, bringing many non-Friends to Quakerism. It has broadened into a wider concern for removing the causes of war and for mediating in conflicts, but it has included as central the refusal to bear arms.

In 1659 as the crumbling of the English Commonwealth threatened to undo the century of struggle for justice and freedom in the Puritan revolution, radical Puritans appealed to Friends to join them. A few did, but most Quakers then recognized that even the free-moving spirit of God is consistent. In 1660/61 the leaders presented to the king a statement that became a classic. "The spirit of Christ, by which we are guided, is not changeable, so as once to command us from a thing as evil and again to move unto it; and we do certainly know, . . . that the spirit of Christ . . . will never move us to fight and war against any man with outward weapons, neither for the kingdom of Christ nor for the kingdoms of this world."[1]

A series of modern historians[2] have challenged Friends' assumptions that the Quakers began as pacifists. These historians' Marxist outlook assumes that a revolution is a class struggle and that radicals turn nonviolent only in despair. They miss the vigor and apocalyptic hope with which early Quakers saw "the Lamb's War" as the conquest of the world by God's spirit within human minds, so that, as Fox quoted Saint

48

Paul, "our weapons are spiritual and not carnal."[3] Many Friends rejected violence from the beginning although certain Friends had, indeed, not resigned from Cromwell's garrisons.

The statement to the king thus shows a second stage of their stand, the basis of the collective, permanent Peace Testimony, reflecting Friends' experience that God consistently works and conquers nonviolently. They spoke of the spirit of Jesus more than of obedience to his commands,[4] but their arguments were biblical, not humanitarian. Even Penn wrote more about the human and economic cost of persecution than of war.

In the third stage the early Quaker Peace Testimony was shown more by shared acts than by statements. Friends made their refusal to bear arms a subject for group discipline, not simply for private conscientious objection. In practice this often reflected the need for Friends' solidarity, both in ethical purity and as a counterculture against established governments. Yet there was always also some tension between Friends' nonviolence and their attitude toward government. Penn, Fox, Barclay, and other early Quaker leaders did not reject the need for police restraint. To this day Friends uneasily combine pacifism (even if God calls only "the powers that be" to be a terror to evildoers [Rom. 13:3] so that true Christians should be neither cops nor robbers)[5] with the Puritan ideal of a Christian commonwealth, which led Friends to accept political responsibility in Rhode Island, West Jersey, and Pennsylvania. In Pennsylvania Penn trusted that a consensus of all citizens would see by the Light the truth in Quaker stands against militias, fortification, oaths, and injustice to Indians. Yet Friends, by refusing militia duty, clashed with fellow citizens during actual wars against the French and Indians in all these colonies.[6]

New York Friends and Wars Before Independence

Although New York was a center for most colonial wars, New York Friends usually escaped the consequences of conflict. First, only rarely did they participate in government, so they did not have to debate over war taxes and compromise their pacifism in relation to war efforts as did Friends in Pennsylvania and Rhode Island. Second, because they lived far from the theater of wars against the French and Indians, they did not have to deal directly with fighting. Unhappily, they did have to face laws that imposed military service.

Before 1750 Friends were harassed about their unwillingness to fight or support military efforts. Although the initial English conquest in 1664 passed without their participation, they were not as lucky during the temporary Dutch reconquest in 1673–74. In 1672 Flushing Quakers protested the building of a fort, and after the conquest in 1675, several Friends were fined for refusing to train with the militia, which probably reflected their recent refusal to help defend the colony or New York City.[7] In East New Jersey under Governor Cornbury heavy fines were laid upon Quakers. New York's moderate fines in 1693 for failure to do military duty continued into the 1720s. Whatever the level of persecution, for the most part Friends escaped major difficulties before 1750. Indeed, New York Quakers may have followed London Yearly Meeting's advice to give thanks for the liberty that they had and not to protest unnecessarily.

With the onset of the American phase of the Seven Years' War in 1754, New York Friends encountered their greatest difficulties in the colonial period. As the colony most involved in the invasion of Quebec, New York was the first to tighten rules for Quaker exemption from military service while appearing to indulge Friends with a way to escape it. Under the militia act of 1755 Friends were to pay fines of no more than twenty shillings for refusal to bear arms and ten shilllings for refusal to stand watch under arms. If there were an invasion, Quakers were to help build fortifications. To ensure that those claiming to be Friends really were members, their meetings were to give them certificates, and they then could register at a cost of one shilling and sixpence. Friends were caught: if they registered to secure this indulgence, they would would have to compromise their Peace Testimony by paying fines; if they did not, they would almost certainly suffer distraints of their property. Initially, some New York City and Dutchess County Friends complied with the law and paid the registration fee. Quakers in Westbury would not compromise. Following Westbury's lead, New York Friends stopped complying with the act and suffered substantial distraints on property between 1756 and 1762. The dangers from French Canada until 1759 led to distraints totaling up to eight hundred pounds a year. By then the drive to reform the Society of Friends led to a stronger Peace Testimony.[8]

As the colonial period drew to a close, New York Friends could be proud that they had maintained their principles by refusing military service and complicity in other war-related matters. Like Friends elsewhere in the colonies and England in this period, they may have paid taxes in which war expenses were mixed with ordinary costs of government. If so, it was the limit of inconsistency at that time, and this pacifist principle was not generally recognized by Friends until later.

The American Revolution: New York Divided

The period of the American Revolution, when Britain's North American colonies resisted imperial policies and in 1775 began a war to obtain their independence, brought upon the Quakers more trials than they had experienced since the seventeenth century.[9] Until war broke out, the colonists attempted to pressure the British government to change its policies by using economic measures such as nonimportation agreements and boycotts of British goods, sponsored and conducted by the colonial merchants. Because most New York Friends outside of Manhattan were not engaged in mercantile activities, they were not caught up in the tide of events until 1774.

In the fall of 1774 the First Continental Congress met in Philadelphia to devise concerted action to protest Britain's policies. The Congress adopted the Continental Association, providing for the nonimportation of British goods and the eventual nonexportation of American goods to Britain. Enforcement of these measures was to be the responsibility of locally chosen committees. In November the colonial patriots in New York City elected a Committee of Sixty, including two Quaker merchants, Lindley Murray and Lancaster Burling. After a similar committee in Philadelphia had led to violent proceedings, Philadelphia Meeting for Sufferings wrote to the New York Friends urging Friends there to avoid becoming involved. New York Meeting for Sufferings thereupon appointed a committee to deal with the Friends serving on the Committee of Sixty. The committee later reported that all Friends except Lindley Murray and Lancaster Burling had heeded its advice and ceased such activities.

In May 1775, after the battles of Lexington and Concord, the problem of Friends serving on patriot committees arose again. A new Committee of One Hundred replaced the Committee of Sixty. Not only were Lindley Murray and Lancaster Burling members but Quaker merchant Walter Franklin, a member of the Meeting for Sufferings, was also named. Franklin was also subsequently elected as a delegate to the newly established New York Provincial Congress. The Meeting for Sufferings remonstrated with Franklin, who thereupon did not attend the sessions of the Congress, and later refused to subscribe to the Continental Association. He was not again elected to the Provincial Congress. Franklin and Murray attended the Committee of One Hundred less than half the time and dropped out in July. Only Lancaster Burling persisted in serving; he was later disowned. These occurrences were referred to the yearly meeting, which approved the actions taken by the Meeting for Sufferings. It further advised the constituent monthly meetings to appoint committees to aid the overseers in dealing with such cases. Friends were heavily concentrated in Queens County at the western end of Long Island and Suffolk at the eastern end, significantly influencing the lack of support for the revolutionary movement in that area. Friends in the towns of Islip and Huntington in Suffolk County refused to sign the Continental Association, and a meeting of the freeholders at Islip refused to send a deputy to the Provincial Congress. They declared that because some of them were "of the People called Quakers," they meant to act no further "than is consistent with our Religious Principles." Several towns in Queens County also refused to send delegates to the Congress, obviously believing that it was the instrument of the colonial patriots to take over the government from the established authorities. In April 1775 Hempstead had passed a resolution reaffirming its loyalty to the king, urging that the union with Great Britain be maintained and that the imperial dispute be settled through constitutional means. Among the delegates elected to the Provincial Congress from Queens County appeared the name of Thomas Hicks, a Quaker from Hempstead. Hicks did not attend the Congress and was queried by that body about his failure to attend. He replied that he had been elected without his consent and that several leading citizens of Hempstead whom he had consulted agreed that in view of the town's former resolution he should not serve.

As a result of these events, the feeling against the Quakers was such that in October 1775 Great Neck and Cow Neck petitioned to be set off from Hempstead "as long as the general conduct of the people is inimical to freedom."[10] Because some towns in Queens County opposed colonial resistance measures and refused to elect a delegate to the Provincial Congress, the Congress resolved that all those persons involved in such actions should be haled before a congressional committee. When the persons listed did not appear as ordered, the Congress interdicted all intercourse with them. The following February it directed that certain men of Queens County, among them three Quakers, should be confined until appropriate investigations could be completed.

Several months later, in the fall of 1775, the Committee of Safety in New York City, whose function was to further the colonial measures of resistance, requested the New York Friends to furnish a list of all male Quakers between the ages of sixteen and sixty residing in the County of New York. The Meeting for Sufferings refused to comply with the request, stating that its refusal was not "the effect of an obstinate disposition but . . . of a truly conscientious Scruple" and religious motives.

After the outbreak of the war between Britain and her colonies in the spring of 1775, the Continental Congress established an army, consisting at first largely of volunteers. When the colonies each assumed statehood in 1775, they enacted military draft laws to raise manpower, levied taxes to support the war effort, and introduced affirmations of allegiance to weed out the Tories. The Continental Congress also issued new continental currency to support military requirements. As did Friends throughout the new confederation, New York Friends faced the problem of maintaining their Pacifist Testimony in view of the various new demands. When the legislature was considering a new militia law in 1775, a committee of the Meeting for Sufferings interviewed the Speaker of the House, who promised to use his best endeavors to obtain exemption for Friends from military service, without payment of fines, as under colonial law. The resulting militia law granted exemption from military service to Friends who presented a certificate of membership from their monthly meeting, except in cases of alarm, invasion, or insurrection. A few months later the Provincial Congress, which was set up to replace the former royal legislature, passed a similar law.

When the military campaigns reached New York in the spring and summer of 1776, several Quakers from Flushing and New York City were drafted. Only one of them was taken to the guardhouse for refusing to serve, hire a substitute, or pay a fine, but he was soon released. When the military authorities issued a general order requiring all inhabitants of the combat zone to give bond that they would not allow their cattle to fall into the hands of the British, there is no record of any Friends being prosecuted for failure to comply.

When New York State adopted a new constitution in the spring of 1777, the section on the militia provided an exemption for Quakers on condition of a money payment. An amendment soon afterward provided that in future drafts all persons subject to military service, exempts included, should be enrolled by the captain in whose beat they resided. Those exempted were to be assessed in proportion to the value of that service and their estates. Subsequent acts to raise additional forces incorporated similar provisions.

A new militia law, passed in April 1778, exempted from personal military service all males between the ages of sixteen and fifty-five "who in judgement of the law are or shall be of the people called Quaker." In return for this exemption, such persons were to pay ten pounds annually when the militia would be called into service. Separate tax lists were to be made for the special levies to be collected from Quakers, to be taken by distraint if not paid. In default of goods or chattels, the offender was to be lodged in the county jail until payment was made. In 1779 these fines were increased fivefold, and in 1780 eightfold. From 1782 the fines returned to the original ten pounds.

As the war progressed, many people came to resent the Quakers' military exemptions, believing that they should bear some part of the responsibility for the common defense. In the winter of 1777–78 the Committee of Safety of Westchester County asked the legislature to levy an assessment on Friends which would be "adequate to the Burthens that Other Members of the State bear in maintaining their Rights." According to the tax lists of Westchester County for the winter of 1778–79, the total assessed sums were: manor of Phillipsburgh, 1,680 pounds; town of Bedford 300 pounds; town of Salem 240 pounds; town of Newcastle, 1,980 pounds. Subsequently, only one instance of imprisonment for refusing military service was reported. Early in 1779 Purchase Monthly Meeting learned that several of its younger members had been imprisoned for refusal to do military service. The meeting supplied the prisoners with certificates of membership, whereupon they were released.

The problem of affirmations of allegiance was especially onerous in Westchester County because of the proximity of the British lines and the presence of a number of British sympathizers. In December 1776 the Provincial Congress directed that all males in the county sixteen years and older should be tendered an oath or affirmation of allegiance. A visiting Friend from Oblong Monthly Meeting took the affirmation after first refusing but later apologized to his monthly meeting for having done so. The monthly meeting reported the matter to the yearly meeting, which declared that any Friends taking such an affirmation should be disowned "except they manifest unfeigned repentance."[11]

In June 1778 the commissioners for Detecting and Defeating Conspiracies were empowered to tender the oath of allegiance to the new state government to any person believed "to have influence sufficient to do mischief."[12] Anyone declining to comply with this requirement was to be sent into enemy territory. Subsequently, several Friends refused to take the affirmation of allegiance, and some of them, despite petitions in their behalf, suffered the penalty. Not until 1784 was the Meeting for Sufferings successful in persuading the legislature to allow two of the men who had been exiled to Long Island to return home. After the war ended in 1783, the question again arose when some Friends took an affirmation of allegiance in view of the conclusion of the war with Britain. The yearly meeting then issued a statement repeating its earlier caution to all members to avoid taking such affirmation because they could "give no greater security to any government than by a peaceable demeanor."[13]

The circulation of the continental currency, first issued in 1775 to finance the war, presented Friends with another test of their Peace Testimony. William Rickman, clerk of the Meeting for Sufferings, after hearing the position taken by some Philadelphia Friends, wrote to his friend John Pemberton that he "came to believe that he would not be easy in accepting it."[14] In December 1776 a committee of the Provincial Congress ordered Jacob Deane, Solomon Haight, and John Hallock of Dutchess County to be sent out of state for refusing to accept the continental currency. The first two were exiled to Exeter, New Hampshire. When New England Meeting for Sufferings intervened on behalf of the prisoners at Exeter, it was informed that they could be released only on orders from those who had committed them. The Meeting for Sufferings told Nine Partners Monthly Meeting, where the accused men were members, of the situation. The monthly meeting then petitioned the authorities for orders to release the exiles.

When the British took New York City in 1776, it became the center of their military and naval activities in America until the end of the war. The area under their control extended over western Long Island and southern Westchester County. The Quakers in New York State, therefore, lived under two opposing governments, and their dealings with the respective authorities tested the genuineness of their neutrality and pacifism. Because Britain had sent to America a fully equipped army supported by the imperial treasury, there was no military conscription or levying of war taxes in the British controlled areas. Consequently, the Quakers living there faced a situation quite different from that confronting Quakers on the American side. Because the city Friends lived under a military occupation, they had to contend with military orders and requisitions. Those demands did not prove to be very onerous. Thus, Friends on the British side of the lines fared noticeably better than their brethren governed by the American authorities.

The first encounter with the British administration occurred in January 1777. Governor Tryon, displeased with the participation of several Friends in revolutionary activities, proposed that Quakers raise a sum of money to furnish British troops with clothing. In reply the Meeting for Sufferings presented an address to the governor, explaining that the Friends cited had acted contrary to the principles and advice of the Society. Moreover, the meeting must reject his request because compliance would be a denial of Friends' religious testimony against war and fightings.

The chief source of difficulty for Friends was the occupation of the meeting houses by elements of the British army. Soon after their arrival in 1776, the king's forces requisitioned the Flushing meeting house for the storage of military supplies and the housing of soldiers. In May 1778 the Meeting for Sufferings petitioned the British authorities in New York and obtained its return. Six months later the conversion of the new meeting house on Pearl Street in New York into a military depot began a long controversy. The Friends in charge of the property accepted rent, which the Meeting for Sufferings considered inconsistent with Quaker principles. It directed the return of the money, but the Friends responsible refused to comply and the matter was laid before the yearly meeting. A deputation, of which Elias Hicks was a member, was sent to Philadelphia in 1779 to obtain the advice of Pennsylvania Friends. Philadelphia Yearly Meeting advised that the money should be returned and cautioned Friends in general not to rent their meeting houses for any military purposes whatsoever. New York Yearly Meeting then appointed a committee to return the money to the commissary office of the British army. When the refund was rejected, an address was sent to the commissary general, explaining that accepting the rent had infringed upon "the Testimony We as a People believe ourselves called to bear to the World against Wars and Fighting." It requested him to "undo the Matter if it can be done in such a manner as to give Relief to our Minds."[15] The commissary general was unable to grant the petition because the accounts and receipts for the date of the transaction had already been sent to England. The yearly meeting then appealed to London Meeting for Sufferings for its assistance. After some negotiations with the appropriate ministry in London, the Exchequer finally accepted the money, and the Meeting for Sufferings received a "Tally" with the following inscription: "Paid by the Society of the People Called Quaker, of New York in America, by the Hand of Daniel Mildred, being the money they had received for Rent of their Meeting House, which had been appropriated for the use of the Army, as such they could not retain it Consistently with their Religious Testimony against War."[16]

In 1781 and 1782 the meeting houses in New York and at Flushing and Cow Neck on Long Island were requisitioned by the British army. Despite a request to the commander-in-chief and to Governor Robertson, the authorities refused to return the houses, declaring that they were being used in the public service. Soon afterward the Cow Neck meeting house was relinquished, but the other two were retained until the British departure in 1783.

Friends were also very careful to refrain from assisting the British army directly or indirectly. In July 1778 the Meeting for Sufferings issued an epistle to the constituent meetings cautioning Friends against allowing any army horses to be quartered on them, receiving pay for forage taken from them, or carting military supplies. In November 1779 Westbury Friends learned that some members had disobeyed this injunction by carting supplies for the British army. Further difficulties arose again in July 1780 when Governor Robertson issued a general order that Long Island should furnish wood for winter fuel to the barrack yards in New York. Queens County was to furnish forty-five hundred cords of wood, and teams were requisitioned to cart it. Those persons giving two-thirds of their hay to the army would receive certificates for the hay and its cartage, the remaining one-third to be free of all military claims. Westbury Quarterly Meeting of Sufferings advised both Flushing and Westbury Meetings that Friends could neither obey such orders nor receive pay for articles requisitioned.

Toward the end of the war the British demanded that Quakers perform some military services. In January 1780 the military authorities ordered all male citizens of the city between the ages of seventeen and sixty to be enrolled by districts. Quakers and firemen were exempted, although they were directed to "exert themselves in case of emergency." Shortly afterward, the male Friends in the city were asked to form five groups and assume responsibility for the city watch together with the Firemen's Marine Society. The Meeting for Sufferings advised New York Monthly Meeting that "Friends complying therewith or aiding in or doing something in lieu of Military Service" were not supporting their testimony against war.[17]

Because of the division of the state into two warring camps, religious visitations and attendance at yearly and quarterly meetings often necessitated passage through the lines of both contestants. Quakers' journeys were constantly subject to suspicion because of their neutral position. The yearly meeting of 1777 was the first to be held after British occupation of New York City and Long Island, and Friends from the mainland had to pass through the lines to attend. On their return from New York, six Quakers from Dutchess County were arrested by the Commissioners for Detecting and Defeating Conspiracies at Poughkeepsie. At the direction of the Committee of Safety, they were confined at the Fleet Prison at Esopus Creek at their own expense until further orders. A petition and several letters, one from Melancthon Smith, a former member of the Provincial Congress, finally persuaded the Committee of Safety to order their release on condition that they take an affirmation of allegiance to the state and pay all fees. Although the prisoners informed the committee that they could not comply with these conditions, they were soon allowed to return home. Throughout the remainder of the war, Patriot authorities kept a watchful eye on the activities of the Friends. In January 1781 General Heath ordered that only those Friends be allowed to attend the Purchase Quarterly Meeting who had recommendations from Captain Honeywel, who was in charge of the Westchester County area. Several months later, some Friends who crossed the lines to attend the yearly meeting of 1781 in New York were accused of carrying political papers and of escorting some people through the lines under a "plain cloak." When both Oblong and Nine Partners Monthly Meetings investigated the charges and found them false, the Quakers who had been imprisoned on that report were soon released. Toward the end of the war several Friends in New York City, through the mediation of Purchase Quarterly Meeting, requested permission from American authorities to pass through the lines to make a religious visit to the mainland. Although the request was refused, four Friends made the journey as far north as Hoosack in northwest Massachusetts. On their return journey they were arrested at Pines Bridge in Westchester County, and General Heath sent the prisoners to Governor Clinton with an accompanying letter declaring that the Quakers "alwaies express much inoffensiveness—and that they do not meddle with Politicks but I have known some of them to collect very good Intelligence; if they will do it on our side they will on the other." Governor Clinton turned the suspected Quakers over to the Commissioners for Detecting and Defeating Conspiracies and replied to General Heath: "The Quakers have already given us so much trouble & have it in their Power to do us so much in Mischief under auspicious Cloaks of Religion that some Means must be fallen upon to prevent their Intercourse with the Enemy."[18]

In the areas of military action Quakers generally refused to leave their homes and continued to attend their meetings for worship as usual. The visit at Easton meeting house of the Indian allies of the British in their "fierce feathers," moving to fight Gates's patriots during Burgoyne's 1777 invasion, was told in chapter 3.[19]

Despite their own difficulties during the war, Friends in New York were not unmindful of the distress caused their neighbors. Already in September 1775 the Meeting for Sufferings called upon the monthly meetings to raise funds for the distress likely to befall many people. In November 1776 Purchase Monthly Meeting initiated two funds, one for Friends and one for non-Friends, netting sixty-one pounds and fifty-seven pounds, respectively. In December 1777 a similar subscription for non-Friends amounted to seventy-one pounds, and, in addition, Chappaqua Monthly Meeting contributed 21 bushels of wheat, 168 pounds of pork, and 80 pounds of beef. A third collection was undertaken in the winter of 1778–79. Early in 1777 Friends in New York City received part of the New England relief fund from Philadelphia Meeting for Sufferings. At the same time, Flushing Monthly Meeting raised thirty-one pounds and Westbury, thirty-four pounds.

The conduct of the Friends in New York State gives convincing evidence of the non-Loyalist, neutral character of their adherence to the Society's Peace Testimony. For their faithfulness to their religious principles Friends paid a price, the total material sufferings of New York Friends amounting to 13,280 pounds. Losses on the American side totaled 12,282 pounds, largely in the form of distraints for nonpayment of military fines and war taxes. Toward the end of the war one of the chief causes of distraints by the American authorities was the black rate levied under a Retaliating Act. Its purpose was to compensate Americans for goods stolen by the British and their sympathizers, and it was especially onerous in Westchester County because of the depredations by British raiding parties known as cowboys. In the northern part of the state the activities of the armies at the time of Burgoyne's campaign caused extensive losses to Friends there. In the British-controlled area the total was 998 pounds, primarily in the form of exactions for the use of the army since the British neither required military service nor levied war taxes.

Although most Friends remained faithful to their Peace Testimony, there were those whose sympathy for one side or the other was strong enough to carry them into the conflict. One hundred nine Friends deviated from the Peace Testimony and were disciplined, forty-six for supporting the British and sixty-three for supporting the Americans. Seventy-one were eventually disowned, the remainder tendering their regrets to their respective monthly meetings. Forty-six were disowned for military service; fifteen for assisting the war effort, such as carting supplies and collecting blankets for the army, and lesser numbers for taking the test affirmation, paying military fines or taxes, serving in public offices, sailing on privateers, making war materials, and so on. Sympathy for the American cause prompted several Friends to leave New York City and Long Island to join the American army on the mainland.

Although peace returned in 1783, the years immediately following presented a number of issues resulting from the war. Already in 1781, with the cessation of active hostilities, sympathy for the American cause, and the conviction that the new regime was permanent had caused some Friends to believe that they could now participate in public affairs. The official position of the Society, however, had not changed, and in May 1781 Purchase Quarterly Meeting Committee on Sufferings declared that in "the present Commotions of Publick Affairs Friends being in any ways active in Government is inconsistent with our Principles."[20] In August 1784 the Meeting for Sufferings learned that some Friends had accepted governmental appointments and issued an epistle of advice to the constituent monthly meetings that the assumption of such positions might lead into practices inconsistent with the religious principles of the Society. It urged all members to "stand upon their Guard against mixing with the Spirit of this World, which hath a tendency to leaven us into the nature of it."[21] Some time later, when the law requiring an oath of allegiance for holding public office was altered to allow an affirmation, some Friends believed they could accept government positions. In 1787 the Meeting for Sufferings reaffirmed to the monthly meetings its earlier position against taking office.[22]

Another postwar problem concerned the payment of taxes to liquidate the state war debts. In March 1785 the Meeting for Sufferings learned that some Friends were paying such taxes. The matter was subsequently laid before the yearly meeting, which cautioned Friends to "preserve from Complyance with any Tax or requisition inconsistent with their peaceable testimony."[23]

An even more serious question was whether Friends could be concerned in the sale and purchase of lands confiscated from Tory Loyalists. As a result of the war, many estates along the Hudson had been confiscated from Tory owners. In September 1784 Jacob Underhill, John Griffin, Zephaniah Burdsall, William Cornell, and other Friends who had been tenants on the Frederick Phillipse Manor notified the Meeting for Sufferings of a difficult predicament in which they found themselves. The land on which they lived had been confiscated and put up for sale. During the years they had occupied this land, located near Chappaqua, they had invested a considerable sum of money in improvements, and they asked whether they could consistently purchase the rights to these tracts whose value was far less than the improvements. The Meeting replied that because their "Testimony against War [was] nearly concern'd therein,"[24] they could not consistently do so. They were advised to appeal to the authorities, explaining the loss that they would incur if the lands were sold from under them. The date of the sale of the lands was at hand; the Meeting appointed a committee, which obtained a postponement. In the meantime the land was sold. Purchase Monthly and Quarterly Meetings and Amawalk Preparative Meeting were informed that some of their members had been buying confiscated lands. The quarterly meeting declared such action was inconsistent with the Peace Testimony. At the next yearly meeting, in 1785, the problem was discussed and the yearly meeting advised its members that it had observed "with Sorrow" that some Friends in Purchase Quarter had "made purchases of Confiscated Lands, which as it is partaking of the Spoils of War, is an open Violation of our Testimony in that Respect, and demands the care and attention of our Monthly Meetings."[25]

During the decade following the Revolution the impact on the Quaker experience became obvious. A basic change in the relation of Friends to society was evident in their complete withdrawal from any political or governmental activity. The experience of the Society clarified for Friends the relationship between adherence to their peculiar testimonies, on the one hand, and participation in worldly affairs, on the other. It also demonstrated the strength and cohesiveness of the Society and its members. Although the faithfulness of Friends to their religious principles had at times created antagonism against them, there was a surprising tolerance in many quarters for their steadfastness. When the bitterness of the conflict had passed, Friends regained a reputation as exemplary citizens and as a constructive force in their respective communities.

French Revolution, War of 1812, and Mexican War

During the twenty-five years after the Revolution maintaining the Peace Testimony in New York State again involved many of the prewar issues of militia duty,[26] fines, and "war taxes," but issues of politics and theology divided both Quakers and non-Friends in new ways. Tom Paine, although raised as a boy in the meeting in Norfolk, England, always held ideals more political than Quaker. He had acted as agent for the rights of his Sussex fellow-excisemen before emigrating to Philadelphia, with Franklin's encouragement, in 1774. He had accepted revolutionary violence and fought and raised funds for Washington's army before proclaiming his Deism.[27] He had already written to oppose monarchy in England, then traveled on to join the liberal "Girondin" leaders of the French Revolution. The fighting "Free Quakers" and Thomas Jefferson's enlightened circle in America, and now Lafayette and Paine's other friends among the French radicals, were from social strata very different from himself, the Paris mob, or most readers of "Common Sense" in 1776.[28] He went on to write the basically rationalist *Age of Reason* to justify the new religion of France while imprisoned by the Jacobins, but his book kept a Quakerish anticlericalism and an insistence that revelation is an individual religious experience although he denied that he had had any. The link of Deism with the guillotines, rather than his rejection of pacifism, underlay the horror of urban English and Americans at "mad dog Paine" when he resettled in New Rochelle, New York, in his last years from 1802 to 1809.[29] Stephen Grellet and his young friend Mary Roscoe later claimed Paine had returned to faith on his deathbed.

In contrast, "New Light" Quakers in Rhode Island and Ireland stood uncompromisingly for pacifist principles when attacking the claim that God had ever commanded Israel's wars in the Old Testament. The clash erupted around the Shackletons' school in Ballitore, Ireland, where Job Scott of Rhode Island died in 1793 and which Hannah Barnard visited in 1799. During 1798, the year of the great "Uprising," "United Irishmen," both Catholic and Presbyterian, rose against English rule. England and revolutionary France were at war, and a massive French fleet had tried to land an army at Bantry Bay in western Ireland in 1796. The Shackletons refused violent pressure from each side to join the struggle and sheltered the wounded from both sides after battles ravaged the towns around the unarmed Quakers' homes.[30] Most English and Anglo-Irish Friends, although committed to personal pacifism, refused to condemn all violence or to support a traveling minute from London Yearly Meeting for "deist" Hannah Barnard and Elizabeth Coggeshall to visit revolutionary France.

England's struggle with France lasted until 1815 and continued to divide Americans. Jefferson and his "Democratic Republicans" remained loyal to France because of common ideals and French military help in America's War of Independence. New York shipowners were as angry as Virginians that the British navy "impressed" American sailors onto their warships at sea and that the British "Orders in Council" restricted trade, although they suffered equally under Jefferson's 1807 Embargo on all overseas trade.[31] When the resulting War of 1812 aligned America with Napoleon against England, New York Friends, amid financial disaster, found it easier than usual to persuade their young men to refuse military service.[32] The 1812 war was seldom mentioned in the journals of Quaker travelers. Henry Hull learned of it when he landed in New York after a two-year journey through England.[33] In 1814 Philadelphia Yearly Meeting issued a statement to the nation at large explaining Friends' lack of interest in subjects of a political nature.

The exceptions were no source of pride. In 1827 Thomas Shillitoe found in Erie County a "Quaker" traveling minister, probably ex-Baptist Talcutt Patching, who had written a book defending Quaker ideas about the sacraments while he continued to receive a military pension for wounds in the War of 1812. Patching left Friends to found his own sect, moved to Texas, lived through the Mexican War there, and died in 1855.[34]

Vermont Quaker Joseph Hoag traveled in the ministry through the Southern states at the beginning of the War of 1812. Though warned against speaking against either war or slavery in troubled times, he felt led to speak on both subjects in public meetings. At Washington, North Carolina, he denied that Christ would order any of his followers to draw the martial sword. In Knoxville, Tennessee, Hoag encountered a general who complained that Quakers would not serve in the militia to defend themselves against Indian attack. The general asked Hoag if he would not kill an Indian attacking his family to save their lives. Hoag replied that true Christians were fit to live or die, and if he and his family died, he expected to go to heaven. An Indian attacking a defenseless family was in a wicked state, however, and if killed would surely go to hell, but if spared might "feel remorse enough to make him repent, so as to find forgiveness, and get to heaven." After further discussion, the general told Hoag that "if all the world was of your mind, I would turn and follow after" to which Hoag replied, "thou hast a mind to be the last man in the world to be good. I have a mind to be one of the first, and set the rest the example." Two days later in a large public meeting attended by armed soldiers he contrasted the "peaceable kingdom of the Messiah" with the agonies of war.[35]

During the War of 1812 three members of New York Yearly Meeting, John I. Wells, James Mott (grandfather-in-law of Lucretia), and Adna Heaton published pacifist tracts with the aid and approval of the yearly meeting. All three writers addressed their tracts to a general Christian audience, giving examples of antiwar arguments from the New Testament, the Church Fathers, Erasmus and Jonathan Edwards. In *Lawfulness of War for Christians Examined* (1814) Mott also discussed the duties of Christians toward civil magistrates. Christians were to be obedient to magistrates, but when governments attempted to interfere with the religious rights, or bind the consciences of their subjects, "then Christians are to endure any sufferings, rather than by complying with the laws of men, violate their higher and supreme obligation to the eternal God."[36] In *War and Christianity Contrasted* (1816) Adna Heaton decried not only conflict between nations but also slavery and racial prejudice, "as though the colour of a man's skin . . . would deprive him of the benefits which all men, whether white or black, are equally entitled." Heaton's tract ended on an optimistic note, pointing to progress on limiting slavery, religious persecution and capital punishment.[37]

Opposition to the Jeffersonians' war against England aligned Friends with the majority of citizens in New England and New York for the first time since the nonimportation agreements. This was also true a quarter-century later when the slaveholding southern states drove the United States into war with Mexico to annex Texas, California, and the Southwest. Quakers thundered against the war, and abolitionist journals praised Friends.[38]

The slavery crisis ended the isolation of Friends from American politics, a fact that in itself alarmed conservative Hicksite Friends such as George Fox White. It drove radical Quaker abolitionists into alliance with non-Quakers such as William Lloyd Garrison, who preached absolute nonresistance but worked with nonpacifists for peace. Most American Friends, unlike British Quakers such as William Allen, had, therefore, stayed clear of the national Peace Societies rising after 1815 led by New Englanders and New Yorkers such as David Low Dodge.[39]

The invitation of Friends to Canada after the American War of Independence had included Lord Simcoe's promise of exemption from military service although Parliament attached to this an annual fee which Quakers refused to pay, resulting in the same distraints as in the States. Friends took no part however, even in the battle around their meeting house at Lundy's Lane. David Willson's "Children of Peace" at Sharon, however, shared their neighboring farmers' anger with the Tory government in Toronto, and some joined William Lyon Mackenzie's luckless rebellion in 1837. The Friends of Sparta Meeting in western Ontario sympathized with Charles Duncombe's similar rebellion although only Joshua Doan was executed for taking part.[40]

5

Slavery and Abolition to 1830

CHRISTOPHER DENSMORE
and
HUGH BARBOUR, THOMAS BASSETT, ARTHUR WORRALL

Early Voices: Quakers and Slavery to 1775

Although Quakers avoided some of the worst problems associated with other religious groups, they, too, shared in the consequences of the unthinking decision made essentially to solve a labor shortage. Whereas they avoided horrors like the Bishop of London's declaration that slaves could be converted and still be enslaved, even Quaker leaders such as George Fox had temporized when pressured by authorities and had not attacked the institution directly. Not all of Fox's contemporaries were as discreet, for there were several seventeenth-century Friends ranging from the weighty to mere members who protested Quaker ownership of slaves. Irish Friend William Edmundson pointed out the inconsistency of opposing the enslavement of Indian prisoners captured in King Philip's War while owning persons of African origin. Furthermore, Edmundson noted, Friends ought to consider how they would fare if they were enslaved, a point that later critics of the peculiar institution would point out: the institution promoted the inferiority of its victims. Unhappily, critics such as Edmundson were not heeded, and many Friends purchased and traded slaves, thereby creating conflict between their property rights, on the one hand, and their religious profession, on the other. The consequences of owning human property were not clear to them.

Unlike Friends in some other colonies, New York Quakers did not own large numbers of slaves. Farmers on Long Island and in the Hudson River valley held slaves, but not in the numbers to be found in

Newport, Philadelphia, or the West Indies. Thus, the moral dilemma of having slaves and the financial impact of freeing them was less in New York than in many centers of slaveholding. Nor do New York Quaker merchants seem to have been major participants in the slave trade. For example, merchants Edward and James Burling had imported slaves on their ships by twos and threes, slaves who had been acquired during trading ventures whose major missions were not the slave trade. Friends in this yearly meeting were thus less likely to have an interest in defending slavery.

Opposition to slavery arose early in the eighteenth century. Coming at the same time as agitation in New England monthly meetings, it shared many of the same principals from Philadelphia and overseas. Horsman Mullenix was the first New York Friend to raise the issue in 1716 at the quarterly and yearly meeting levels (at this stage essentially the same body). Visiting English Friend John Farmer joined him at the yearly meeting, but their efforts to obtain an antislavery decision were frustrated by the meeting waiting until the next year to take action. Farmer went on to press his case at New England Yearly Meeting and to be disowned by it for refusal to submit to its authority. Next year the issue stayed alive in New York where Richard Burling wrote a paper against slavery and, no doubt, circulated it among supporters then and later. Not published at this time, it was still available for Benjamin Lay to include in his *All Slavekeepers* in 1737. In it Burling repeated Edmundson's assertions. Although his paper was not published at first, his and his supporters' pleas were sufficient for the yearly meeting to refer the matter to London Yearly Meeting. London's 1719 reply, received in 1720, was a model of fence straddling and indecision. According to the epistle, Friends were to do unto others as they would want to have done to them. Both sides could take comfort in advice like that: slaveowners because they fed, gave shelter, and employed their slaves; antislavery Friends because no reasonable person would want to be enslaved. The issue dropped temporarily from the purview of Quaker business meetings after 1720 (as far as one can tell) although the less well-to-do rural meetings such as Oblong and Purchase may have continued to raise the objections as did similar meetings in New England. Unhappily, records for these meetings for many years before 1760 are lost.

By the late 1750s New York, like other yearly meetings was ready to act against slavery. In 1759 one year ahead of New England, the Yearly Meeting decided that Friends could not import slaves. This was scarcely a major issue because no Friends were active in the trade and few had imported slaves recently. That some could come under this minute became evident six years later, in 1765, when Samuel Underhill was taken under dealing for importing Africans. After 1770 the pace of antislavery reform quickened, but not fast enough for Oblong Monthly Meeting, which had in 1767 argued for an end to the institution among Friends. In 1771 the yearly meeting ordered its members not to sell their slaves. Finally, in 1774, at the behest of Purchase Monthly and Quarterly Meetings, the yearly meeting minuted that all slaves had majority.

For most of the eighteenth century Shrewsbury Monthly Meeting was part of Philadelphia Yearly Meeting. At the time of the Orthodox-Hicksite Separation, it would return to its roots in New York Yearly Meeting; hence, it is appropriate to include its activities in this period, especially because it played a prominent role in the decision to end slavery in Philadelphia Yearly Meeting. Taking an independent course in 1757, Shrewsbury Quarterly Meeting decided that the monthly meeting could disown Friend John Wardell for buying a slave. This was a remarkably independent gesture. In 1758 Philadelphia Yearly Meeting merely denied the right of participation and financial contributions to slaveowners; it did not stipulate disownment. Nor was this an isolated instance, for this activist monthly meeting continued in the 1760s to act against those who had purchased or sold slaves. Furthermore, when Philadelphia Yearly Meeting decided members had to free their slaves, Shrewsbury Monthly Meeting was in the vanguard in treating with its few members who still held slaves.

The End of Slave Owning in New York Yearly Meeting

The final disentanglement of Quakers took time. In 1824 Elias Hicks recalled his experiences one-half century before. Some of the Quakers he visited argued that earlier Friends, considered good men, had held slaves. "Shall we think to be better than they?" Hicks responded that each generation has its work to do, and that although earlier Friends had done their work faithfully, there was still more to be done.[1] Committees appointed by the monthly meetings preferred to "labor with" such reluctant Friends, to convince them of the errors of slavery, rather than to move quickly to disownment. One Quaker amateur historian of the nineteenth century examined the records and claimed that slavery was ended in New York Yearly Meeting without a single disownment.[2]

There was another major problem in ending slavery within a slave-owning society: Who would be responsible for the welfare of those for-

mer slaves who were too old, too young, or too infirm to support themselves? Why should a local community bear the responsibility for caring
for a superannuated slave freed by a Quaker who had developed scru-
ples against slave ownership? Quakers became responsible for training
for some useful trade those who were, or had been, in their possession
and for the continued support of those unable to care for themselves.

At Nine Partners, nearly all adult slaves were freed in 1775 and
1776 with the last manumission occurring in 1782. Children's ages
were recorded, followed by an agreement to free females at the age of
eighteen and males at twenty-one, the same terms commonly used for
indentured white children. At Westbury Monthly Meeting, the process
took longer. About one-third of all slaves were freed, or indentured, if
children, in 1775–77; most were freed by 1783, but some manumissions were recorded as late as 1798. Some of the later manumissions
probably represent slaves inherited by Friends from non-Quaker relatives.[3] In 1798 New York passed a law recognizing the legality of the
Quaker manumissions.

The responsibility of former Quaker slaveholders to their former
slaves became a generalized concern of the Society of Friends toward
the African-American community. In New York City this concern was
formalized in the work of the Quaker-supported Manumission Society,
the African Free School, the Clarkson Association, the New York Society for Educating Colored Male Adults, and other organizations.[4] On
Long Island, members of Jericho and Westbury Monthly Meetings
formed the Charity Society in 1794 to provide relief for former slaves
and their children. The Charity Society provided education for black
children on Long Island until 1868, when the public schools took over
the responsibility, and later supported schools for African-Americans in
the south. The fund, established in 1794, is currently used to support
scholarships for minority children.[5] The free black community, called
Guinea Town, near Old Westbury, on Long Island, and the local New
Light Baptist Church, had ties with the local Friends.[6] In Westchester
County an African-American community known as "The Hills" had similar ties with Friends.[7] More research is needed to assess the extent of the
rural African-American communities in New York after emancipation
and the relationship between those communities and their neighbors.

The End of Slave Owning in New York State

The slavery abolition issue was raised in the New York State Constitutional Convention of 1777. In 1785 the legislature came close to passing an emancipation act, but the bill foundered on the assembly's

opposition to giving full citizenship rights to former slaves. New York prohibited the importation of slaves for sale in 1785. In 1788 it prohibited the import and export of slaves and permitted owners to manumit their slaves without posting a bond. Finally, a gradual abolition act was passed in 1799; this freed all slave children born after July 4, 1799, at the age of twenty-eight for males and twenty-five for females. The final act came in 1817 when all slaves born before the July 4, 1799, date were to receive their freedom in 1827.[8]

Abolition proceeded much faster in the other regions of New York Yearly Meeting. Vermont, at that time a separate republic, abolished slavery in 1777. Connecticut passed a gradual emancipation law in 1783. In Upper Canada a court case in 1793 had the effect of abolishing slavery although it was not finally terminated in the British Empire until 1834.

Quakers and the New York Manumission Society

In 1785 a group of eighteen men, twelve of them Quakers, met in a New York tavern to found the New York Society for Promoting the Manumission of Slaves. The Manumission Society's activities can be divided into four basic areas: securing legislation to end slavery in New York; monitoring compliance with the laws, particularly those against exporting slaves; educating "people of color"; and, after 1792, cooperating with other abolition societies in the American Convention.[9]

The gradual abolition of slavery in New York, but its continued existence elsewhere, placed New York's black population in danger. Despite legislation in 1785 and later to discourage the export of slaves, there were some instances in which slaves could be legally exported. Some owners sought to take advantage of these loopholes rather than see their "property" become valueless. Less-scrupulous owners and slave traders attempted to export slaves illegally or kidnap freed blacks for sale in the south. The practical work of monitoring the law fell to the Manumission Society's Standing Committee. The work could become exciting. On the night of May 25, 1806, the members of the Standing Committee discovered that a brig was preparing to sail at daybreak for Georgia with "slaves" aboard. Obtaining a writ, the members of the Standing Committee and their allies took the supposed slaves off the ship. One was a kidnapped freedman, another a slave who was being exported illegally, and the third was claimed by an owner who stated that he was unaware of the attempted exportation. The following day, the Standing Committee waited on the mayor, who had issued an export license. When the Standing Committee proved that the license had been obtained by fraud, a writ was obtained against the captain of the brig, who immediately left the city to avoid prosecution. The slave who was being illegally exported was freed under the law.[10]

The other emphasis of the Manumission Society was on the education of freed blacks, particularly through the New York African Free School begun in 1787. This school, actually several neighborhood schools, operated under the care of the Manumission Society. It began receiving public funds to partially support its work in 1798 and was turned over to the Public School Society in 1834, ultimately becoming part of the New York Public School system.

Quakers were heavily involved in the operations of the Manumission Society, particularly in the governance of the African Free School and on the Standing Committee, but the president of the Manumission Society was generally a prominent, non-Quaker politician, such as Alexander Hamilton, John Jay, or Cadwallader Colden. The extent of Quaker involvement in the actual workings of the Manumission Society is striking. At the 1829 annual meeting, ten of the thirteen members in attendance can also be found on the membership lists of New York or Mamaroneck (Purchase) Monthly Meetings. Two of the others, both named Cornell, probably had Quaker connections if they were not also members. That leaves only one non-Quaker, the federalist politician and historian William L. Stone. Six of the known Friends were Hicksites; four were Orthodox.

With the near end of slavery in New York in 1828, the passage of laws to protect free African-Americans, and the transfer of the African Free School to the Public School Society in 1834, the Manumission Society had achieved most of its original objectives. In its final years the Manumission Society provided financial support for education and for the Colored Orphan Asylum founded in 1837. When the Manumission Society dissolved in 1849, its assets were transferred to the Orphan Asylum. There appears to have been little continuity between the leadership of the old Manumission Society and the new, more radical, abolitionist organizations of the 1830s, discussed in chapter 11.

Of the 454 members of the Manumission Society during its first forty years, at least 251 were Friends, including multiple members of families active in commerce, but in few other philanthropies: Bowne, Burling, Cock, Hicks, Hull, Keese, Lawrence, Mott, Seaman, Thorne, and Underhill. Some probably never left their rural Long Island homesteads, but the two main programs of the Society were centered in the city. They achieved the liberation by purchase or persuasion of 429 slaves between 1791 and 1814, averaging 35 a year in the last decade, which led up to the New York law of 1817 that abolished slavery within the state. They also began and supported the African Free School, which averaged 80 children a year, with an average of two teachers (paid about three hundred dollars each), from 1788 through to the war and depression year 1815. In 1823 the state school superintendent reported 866 black children aged five to fifteen in various African Free Schools; 760 of these may have been girls.[11]

Colonization

The objectives of the Manumission Society and of New York Friends assumed a permanent African-American presence in New York. Some, however, envisioned a place for freed slaves beyond the boundaries of the United States. Paul Cuffee (1759–1817), an African-American Quaker from New England, promoted Sierra Leone as a haven for African-Americans, with some support from New York Friends. Thomas Eddy worked with a representative of the Haitian government in the 1820s in an ill-fated attempt to encourage African-American migration to Haiti.[12] The work of former slave Solomon Bayley in Liberia was supported by New York Friends in the 1820s and 1830s. New York Friends also provided aid to free black communities in Canada.

Although there was some initial interest on the part of New York Friends in the American Colonization Society (founded 1817)—John Griscom was a member of the Board of Managers of the New York Auxiliary of the Colonization Society—most Quakers came to reject its plans for massive resettlement of American blacks. Thomas Eddy considered the Colonization Society a scheme on the part of slaveowners to perpetuate slavery.[13] New York Friends were willing to support African-American initiatives for resettlement in Africa, the West Indies, or Canada, but not the plans of the white-dominated Colonization Society to solve the problem of race relations through migration rather than emancipation.

Quakers and Fugitive Slaves

In May 1795 Timothy Rogers of Vermont was at Yearly Meeting in New York City, where Isaac Leggett told him he thought manumission was legal and asked Rogers if he wanted to hire any freedmen. Timothy said he would hire a couple on Leggett's recommendation. When he got back to Danby, he was overtaken by two runaways, whom Leggett had told to find Rogers in Ferrisburgh. As they traveled together northward, a handbill or newspaper advertisement caused a magistrate to stop them, but Rogers arranged to let the slaves come with him until their masters should arrive. When they did, Rogers was away, and the slaves fled into the woods. Three days later, when he came home, he tried to settle with the angry masters in Vergennes, looked up the new fugitive slave law of 1793, and found that he was accessory to the crime of aiding a slave to escape. So while the masters' suit for one thousand dollars dragged on, he settled out of court for seven hundred dollars and made a deal with the blacks to work for him six years. After that term of service he gave them their freedom.[14]

Rowland T. Robinson, one-half century later, did the same thing, but he had developed a new scruple. When a black refugee reached his homestead in North Ferrisburgh, he wrote his master that the slave himself had earned money to buy his freedom but that Robinson could not implicate himself in the slave system by paying the balance. He would, nevertheless, transmit the money if it was acceptable to the master. The master replied that he was worth much more with the result that the black stayed on the Robinson farm as a hired hand, and the master got nothing.

In the Manumission Society and as individuals Quakers worked within the existing laws to prevent African-Americans from being illegally sold or kidnapped into slavery. These activities are relatively well documented in the records of the Manumission Society and in the pages of the abolitionist press. What is less documented is the work of the "Underground Railroad," which aided the escape of fugitive slaves in clear violation of the existing laws. The extent of organization of the Underground Railway is a matter of historical debate with scanty evidence.

Individual Quakers aided fugitive slaves. Family stories about Benjamin Baker of East Hamburg (now Orchard Park), New York, tell of conveying slaves in winter across the frozen Niagara River to Canada.[15] One documented Quaker route ran from New York City to the house of Joseph Carpenter at New Rochelle, continuing north through Westchester County, stopping at the homes of Joseph Pierce at Pleasantville and John Jay at Bedford, and ending at the house of David Irish at Quaker Hill, Dutchess County.[16] Isaac Hopper in New York City, no stranger to using the legal system whenever possible, also proclaimed his willingness to assist anyone escaping from slavery, "be the laws what they may."[17]

Fugitives sometimes lived more or less openly. In 1857 Caroline Putnam was taken by Emily Howland to visit a family of fugitive slaves living near the Howland family in Cayuga County, New York. The family owned their own home and worked in the neighborhood. Fearing the Fugitive Slave Law, they had once taken refuge in Canada but had later returned to New York State. What seems more remarkable was that Putnam's account of these fugitives was published quite openly in the abolitionist newspaper, the *Liberator*.[18]

Antislavery Thought among Friends

By 1775 Friends had reached consensus against owning slaves as well as against buying or importing them. Slaveowners in every yearly meeting could expect to be visited by the elders of their meeting and made to choose between giving up their slaves or their Quakerism. In practice, grace periods, particularly for young slaves who could be considered apprentices, let many wait until 1775–85 before freeing, or "manumitting," their slaves. A recent study of how and when six Quaker communities of New Jersey and Pennsylvania freed their slaves has tried to show how Quakers held two distinct motives: the good of the slaves, often achieved by gradual liberation, and the purity of life and conscience of Friends themselves, the theme of John Woolman.[19] It has often been averred that, by the time of the Orthodox-Hicksite Separation, most of the evangelical or "Orthodox" Friends had become gradualists regarding the liberation of slaves, whereas many Hicksite leaders were radical abolitionists.[20] Yet from 1774, when New England Yearly Meeting as a whole lobbied the Rhode Island Legislature for a law banning the importation of any more slaves, to 1787–1807, when Philadelphia Yearly Meeting's pressure on the Federal Convention and the new Congress led southern Congressmen to equate Quakers with slave revolts, Friends acted—or failed to act—largely together. Quakers of varied theologies united with non-Friends such as John Jay and De-Witt Clinton in the Manumission Society.[21]

In 1811 Elias Hicks published his only tract for both Quakers and non-Friends: *Observations on the Slavery of Africans and Their Descendants.* The nineteen queries left no room for compromise:

> Scripture, consonant with right reason, not only proves that every man is to bear his own iniquity, but fully establishes man's free agency; and, of course, proves that every moral agent, let the conduct and situation of his or her parents have been what they may, is nevertheless born free.
>
> 1st Query. Were not the people of Africa, at the time when the Europeans first visited their coast, as free . . . as the Europeans them-

selves? And were they not possessed of the same unalienable rights of life, liberty, and the pursuit of happiness?

Answer. I think it is self evident. . . . The slavery of the Africans is the product of mere power, without any possible plea of right. . . . Every child of an African, born in America or elsewhere . . . is born free, and therefore suffers the same cruel force of fraud and power.

2nd Query. Are there not some people who profess to believe that Africans are an inferior and different species of rational beings from those of other nations?

Answer. That there are some such persons we cannot doubt; . . . [but different species, like horses & donkeys, cannot interbreed].

3rd Query. Under what name . . . are the slaves to be considered?

Answer. Slaves, being taken by violence . . . are taken prisoners of war, prize goods.

4th Query. What is the chief inducement for making slaves?

Answer. An avaricious thirst after gain. . . .

5th Query. Is not the produce of the slave's labour likewise prize goods?

6th Query. Does the highway robber, that meets his fellow citizen on the way and robs him of all his property . . . and then leaves him at liberty . . . commit as high an act of felony, as he that steals or buys or takes a man by violence and reduces him to a slave for life?

7th Query. Does it lessen the . . . wickedness of reducing our fellow creatures to . . . slaves . . . because the practice is tolerated by the laws of the country we live in?

8th Query. Would it be right and consistent with justice . . . for the Legislatures of the several States . . . to make laws entirely to abolish slavery?

Answer. . . . Nothing can exculpate them from blood-guiltiness short of so doing. . . .

12th Query. By what class of the people is the slavery of the Africans and their descendants supported and encouraged?

Answer. By the purchasers and consumers of the produce of the slaves' labour.[22]

Hicks's characterization of slaves and the produce of slave labor as "prize goods" links the testimony against slavery to the Quaker testimony against war. Prize goods were those seized from foreign ships in time of war and then sold, often at reduced cost. Because Quakers rejected war, Quaker merchants could not conscientiously deal in goods taken by violence.

Hicks then went on to spell out the economic impact of a boycott and to imagine a mirror-image situation in which a foreign fleet invaded the Hudson and Delaware and carried off the American women and children to conditions like those on the slave ships. Hicks himself refused to use cotton cloth even on his deathbed.

African-Americans and Friends

In 1824 Elias Hicks delivered a sermon that explicitly decried racial prejudice: "We are on a level with all the rest of God's creatures. We are not better for being white, than others for being black; and we have no more right to oppress the blacks because they are black, than they have to oppress us because we are white. . . . Can God oppress? Can he look upon a coloured man as mean, because he is not the same colour as others? Has he not as good a right to look upon whites as inferior as we have to look upon the blacks? Oh, that we might rise out of this state of torpor and superstition. Oh! that we might rise above it."[23]

Hicks's efforts were recognized by the black community in the naming of the "New York African Hicks Society" in 1830 and in a memorial service held by the "African Benevolent Societies" in New York City after his death.[24] Another Quaker abolitionist was memorialized in the name of the "Brooklyn African Woolman Society" founded in 1824.[25]

African-American membership in New York Yearly Meeting was negligible, however. Members of Paul Cuffee's family were part of Friends meetings in New York City and at Scipio in Cayuga County, but African-Americans were generally seen as the objects of benevolence, and occasionally as co-workers in benevolent projects. There is, however, little evidence of African-Americans as members of the Society of Friends in New York Yearly Meeting.

6

City Philanthropists and Social Concerns, 1787–1857

HUGH BARBOUR
and
CHRISTOPHER DENSMORE, ROBERT WINTERNITZ,
PETER WOSH

Wealthy City Friends

New York's story of social and ethnic integration early included Friends. The first Quaker settlers in New York City, even fifty years after the end of Dutch rule, were not prominent, although Quaker families on Long Island had from their first settlement traded through New Amsterdam by boat down the Sound and the East River or by wagon to the Brooklyn ferry. The meeting house on Crown (later to be Liberty) Street was considered adequate from 1746 to 1774 when it was replaced by one on Queen (soon Pearl) Street, which, in turn, was replaced by Rose Street in 1823. A second, on Hester Street, dated from 1819.[1] The city's population, 21,863 in 1771, had only grown at 2.1 percent per year from 1695, whereas Dutchess County grew at 7.1 percent. Friends never dominated New York commerce as they did trade in Philadelphia, but they were as central as those in Pennsylvania in the city's service institutions and philanthropies. A list of twenty New York City Quaker men claiming exemption from militia duty in 1755, which includes five Franklins, three Burlings, two Pearsalls, and Robert Murray, calls seven of them shopkeepers and six merchants. The seventeen New York Friends who in 1782 signed a refusal to stand watch under the British occupation included many of the same men.[2]

Under the British army's occupation, conservative city councillors were freed from their fear of the "patriot" crowds aroused by the Sons of Liberty and Committee of Correspondence, many of whom then left. The "loyal" citizens who stayed on prospered by feeding the British. About fifteen thousand of these Loyalists left New York in 1783 after the war, leaving only twelve thousand.

The War of Independence made New York City the center of the nation. It was politically the capital from the ratification of the Constitution in 1789 until June 1790. The population grew to 33,131 by 1790, overtaking Philadelphia; it was up to 60,515 in 1800, to 96,373 in 1810, and to 166,086 in 1825. By then, the area built up with houses had grown from the nucleus south of City Hall up to the edge of Greenwich Village. Both numbers and rates of growth increased to 515,000 in 1850 and 815,000 in 1860.[3] By then Quakers and the old commercial elite had been displaced by newcomers to America and to wealth.[4] After 1865 the influx of Irish and German immigrants gave way to the flood from southern Europe.

The confusions of the War of Independence freed some Friends to move into or out of the city and new careers. Robert Murray (1721–1786), whose parents had brought him from Scotland in 1732 and who had married the "celebrated Quaker belle" Mary Lindley in 1744, had owned a flour mill in Pennsylvania. After an attempt in commerce in Carolina failed, he moved about 1754 to New York City where he prospered by trade to the West Indies. Weak health and trade took Murray and his family to England for five years in the transatlantic Quaker style. He returned to New York in 1775, was one of the tea merchants whose cargoes were dumped overboard to protest British taxes, but eventually made Murray, Sansom and Co. the biggest shipping firm of the era. His country home outside the city later gave its name to Murray Hill above the East River. Here Mary Murray's hospitality became legendary.[5] Robert was outlived by his older brother John Murray (1720–1808), also a wealthy merchant and president of the New York Chamber of Commerce from 1798 to 1806.

Two of Robert Murray's sons became equally prominent by the end of the century. Lindley Murray seems to have been weakened all his life by a neurological disease but led a normal life as a Philadelphia schoolboy and an apprentice in Philadelphia and then in his father's New York counting house until, after a few months of escape from his father's strictness, he persuaded his father to let him train in law. He prospered in both vocations and married Hannah Dobson, a New York Quaker. He spent one year helping his father trade and convalesce in England. Lindley later left British-occupied New York to try to distill salt on Long Island and returned to find his trading flourishing. His country estate, Bellevue, three miles from New York, later became the city mental hospital, prison, and almshouse. His lifelong pilgrimage to find a healthier place settled him back in England in 1784 where he supported himself by a business partnership with his much younger brother in New York. Increasingly disabled, in 1787 he wrote *The Power of Religion on the Mind*. Then he wrote a series of English grammars, teachers' guides, and books of readings for the Quaker schools of York (see chap. 9).

John Murray, Jr. (1758–1819), was also sent to the Friends Grammar School in Philadelphia, but rather than join his father's firm he became a partner with Moses Rogers in another, profitably enough to let him largely retire about 1785 to give his time to New York Monthly Meeting, to be clerk of the yearly meeting and to serve on charitable committees.[6] These activities included the New-York Hospital from 1782, helping to found the Society for Promoting the Manumission of Slaves and its Free School for blacks from 1785, the Quaker visit to the Brotherton, Oneida, Stockbridge, and Onondaga Indians in 1795, the Society for the Prevention of Pauperism (and its offshoot, the Savings Bank), a major reform of the New York penal laws and Murray's service on the state Board of Inspectors of prisons, and the New York Free School Society (see chap. 9). During a midwinter lobbying trip to Albany in 1812 he fell on an icy street and never fully recovered. Nevertheless, he attended in 1816 the national convention of local Bible society representatives out of which came the American Bible Society, serving briefly as one of the four Friends on its board. Most of the same Quaker names occur on the boards of all these voluntary societies and also on a project that neatly combined Friends' skills in finance and philanthropy, the New-York Savings Bank,[7] spun off from the Society for the Prevention of Pauperism, from which also grew the House of Refuge for juvenile delinquents, and the New York Friends' ongoing concern for prisons. Quakers shared leadership in all these committees with non-Friends with whom they dealt in business and government, such as Mayor Cadwallader Colden, General Philip Schuyler, and Governor DeWitt Clinton.

The turn from business to philanthropy by John Murray, Jr., was, evidently, an example to other Friends. Both the life and the account books of Isaac Hicks (1767–1820), cousin of Edward the painter and of Elias Hicks, have been more carefully studied than any other early New York City Quaker's.[8] He was raised at Westbury, Long Island; his mother was Phebe Seaman and his farmer father was already eldered in 1768 for selling a slave to a fellow Quaker. He and, later, two younger brothers moved to Manhattan. He opened a store to sell spices, hardware, and dry goods immediately on arrival in 1789. He married a city Friend, Sarah Doughty, within a year. His partners and business associates were mostly other Friends, and many, such as Willet Seaman, also Westbury kinsfolk. Of these, John Alsop moved to the town of Hudson, just founded by Nantucket Quaker whalers and the home of Hicks's captain, William Bunker. Hicks worked also with Henry Hull. His shipping and commission business was secured by the mutual trust of Quakers in cities such as Liverpool and (London-)Derry, Samuel and Miers Fisher of Philadelphia, Robert Bolton of Savannah, and the Rotches, Macys, and Coffins of Nantucket. Hicks rarely owned a ship of his own and sought out the Nantucket whalers to become their agents to sell whale oil. He found cargoes for their ships when whaling languished and chartered ships for his own venture cargoes of American products to France, Ireland, and Russia.[9] He tried in vain to arrange the ships he chartered on a fixed sailing schedule for their passengers' sake. This was done after 1819 by the Quaker owners of the Black Ball and Red Star "packet" ships. In an era before banks and fixed currency exchanges made it easy to finance international trade Hicks spent many of his business hours negotiating bills of exchange on London, Philadelphia, and New York firms. At the age of only thirty-eight he left most of his business affairs in the hands of his brothers and partners and retired with his sick wife and newborn daughter to a farm he had bought in Westbury. In 1813 he volunteered to be his cousin Elias Hicks's companion and "armour-bearer" on the first of four visits together in ministry to Quaker meetings throughout eastern America. Isaac Hicks read mainly Quaker books and had sent his ships unarmed to a Europe at war; he had always been active in his local meeting. Now he became equally active in the New York Manumission Society and its Free School. Elias Hicks was present when he died of a heart attack at home.

Thomas Eddy

Eddy (1758–1827) was born in Philadelphia, the son of Irish Friends convinced in Dublin. His father, James Eddy, was himself a businessman who pursued mercantile business, mostly in shipping. His "pious and valuable" wife, Mary, bore him sixteen children and ran his business after his death. Small and lively, Thomas at age thirteen was apprenticed to a tanner for two years. Between the ages of sixteen and twenty, he formed a friendship with William Savery, who was to become

3. Thomas Eddy (1758–1829). Etching from Samuel Knapp,
Life of Thomas Eddy.
Courtesy Haviland Records Room, New York Yearly Meeting.

an important Quaker minister, and was to be an important factor in
Elizabeth Gurney Fry's commitment to Quakerism. Eddy and Savery,
together with a third friend, Charles Mifflin, were "all fond of such
subjects and pursuits as were most likely to promote mirth and pleasan-
try," but also held "opinions and sentiments that have been instructive
and useful to me throughout life." Eddy grew up to be a man "about
five feet six inches in height, of a muscular, compact frame, capable of
bearing great fatigue. . . . His head was large and well shaped. . . . The
elevation of his eyebrows gave the whole countenance an air of profound meditation. He dressed with great uniformity and neatness."[10]

   In 1779, at the age of twenty-one, Thomas Eddy went to New York
for the first time. Looking back on the social and emotional upheaval
and political crisis of the times, Eddy believed that "it would have been

more wise and consistent with the principles of Friends, if they had more carefully avoided the intemperate political zeal, then manifested by all parties." A Tory until after the war, Thomas was incarcerated in a Monmouth County, New Jersey, prison after his capture by "patriot" troops as a suspected spy in 1781. In Eddy's first year in New York he bought goods at auctions and resold them to merchants at a slender profit. This was Eddy's first introduction to the world of business. Later, he formed a partnership with his brother Charles and Benjamin Sykes, a New York merchant, to sell goods Charles had brought back from Ireland and later other goods from England. Eddy married Hannah Hartshorne in 1782. He left New York briefly in 1783 before the British evacuation of New York, in fear of the hostile reaction of supporters of the revolution returning to New York against people who had stayed there during the occupation. Eddy refused, however, to follow the ex- amples of his in-laws, the Hartshornes, and flee to Nova Scotia. Through his younger brother George, then only eighteen, Thomas Eddy arranged with General Washington to be the sole supplier of money from the British officers occupying New York City to their men held prisoners in Pennsylvania. Eddy's firm, by a 4 percent commission on the funds delivered, made a lot of money. In 1784, through his brother George in London, Eddy formed a new connection "purchas- ing and making shipments of tobacco." Large shipments of tobacco to England on credit led to a tobacco glut so that in 1786–88 Eddy and his brother lost a lot of money. Eddy moved back to New York City in 1791 and soon became inventive in the insurance business. He specu- lated in "Continental" bonds and public funds, and "in this business I made a good deal of money." He was elected a director of the Mutual Insurance Company, Treasurer of the Western Inland Lock Navigation Company, and "being in easy circumstances" Eddy "had leisure to turn his attention to some of those charities that are of permanent benefit to mankind."[11]

Prison reform had been a major issue in Pennsylvania where Quakers had initiated the reforms at the Walnut Street jail in 1790. In 1796 Eddy traveled to Philadelphia with his friend General Philip John Schuyler (1733–1804), who had been a leader in the War of Independ- ence and was a New York state senator at this time. Schuyler and Eddy met with the Philadelphia Society for Alleviating the Miseries of Public Prisons, visited the Walnut Street Jail, and collected pamphlets from the Philadelphia Society to distribute them to the New York State Legis- lature. With the political support of Governor Jay of New York, a bill drawn up by Eddy and Schuyler was presented to the legislature and passed. It called for the reduction of the list of capital crimes to murder and treason, the substitution of imprisonment for corporal punishment for noncapital crimes, and provision for the erection of two state prisons, one at Albany and one in New York City.[12] This bill, which was enacted on March 26, 1796, marked a major change in penal policy for New York State. Before this date, prisoners convicted of noncapital crimes faced mutilation, such as having the ears cropped or being branded. The stocks were used to humiliate criminals by the public abuse of the local population. Time in a penitentiary became an alternative for such cruelty. Eddy had been influenced by the activities of Quakers in Philadelphia, by the English prison reformer John Howard, and by the progressive thought of Beccaria and Montesquieu. As a direct result of the 1796 law, only one prison, Newgate Prison in Greenwich Village, was built. Eddy found an architect and hired workers to build the prison. The design of the prison, opened for the reception of inmates on November 28, 1797, was influenced by the Walnut Street Jail in Philadelphia, but all types of convicts were housed together where hardened criminals could corrupt newcomers to crime, and it rapidly became overcrowded. Each year nearly as many convicts were pardoned as were admitted in order to keep the prison population down to a number that could be housed.

In 1801 Thomas Eddy wrote an important document in the history of prison reform, *An Account of the State Prison or Penitentiary House in the City of New York*. Eddy states that the "end of human punishment is the prevention of crimes; the amendment of the offender; the deterring of others by his example; reparation to society and the party injured."[13] Eddy was uncomfortable with the death penalty because it made any amendment of the accused's behavior impossible. Eddy preferred that prisoners be fed well and be kept in sanitary conditions where they were to be put to work making practical items such as shoes that could be sold to the public. Schooling of the prisoners was allowed. A room in Newgate prison capable of seating six hundred both on the floor and in a gallery was provided for nonsectarian religious instruction. Among causes of crime he considered the wide availability of alcohol and gambling at horse races. He complained that there was no way of separating the more violent from the less violent criminals and recommended that a special building composed of sixty individual cells be constructed to isolate these convicts. Eddy believed that "police magistrates" should have the right to try these individuals and that their sentences of thirty to ninety days in solitary confinement on a minimal diet should lead to contemplation of the crime committed and subsequent remorse. Eddy campaigned unsuccessfully for a prison within the city of New York to house in single cells inmates of this description. Eddy wrote a paper in 1796, proposing evening classes in reading, writing, and arithmetic, weekly worship, and the need for separating first offenders from "repeaters," and for state prisons to take the load from county jails. Later, he admitted his major mistake lay in not insisting on single cells for all prisoners at night although not by day. When construction for the state prison at Auburn was authorized in 1816, Eddy again called for single cells, but they were used only at night and abandoned as solitary confinement.

In 1793 Thomas Eddy was elected one of the governors of the New York Hospital. His involvement with the Free School Society helped to bring about public education in New York State. In February 1805 it was proposed to Eddy that he along with other Quakers form an association to establish a free school. Eddy thought that it would be impossible to raise the amount of money needed with only Quaker support and "proposed to call to his aid a number of respectable citizens, of different religious denominations."[14] Eddy, along with Quaker educator and scientist John Griscom and Episcopalian banker John Pintard (1759–1844), made up the leadership of the Society for the Prevention of Pauperism between 1817 and 1823.

Between his early involvement in the Manumission Society, the state prison and the hospital, and his later roles in the 1820s in the Bloomingdale asylum, the Society for the Prevention of Pauperism, and the House of Refuge for juvenile delinquents, Eddy's greatest concern was the Erie Canal. A canal westward from the Hudson, an early vision of Gouverneur Morris, became a practical ideal when Christopher Colles surveyed the Mohawk valley in 1785. Eddy, when he visited the Brotherton and New Stockbridge Indians in the Utica area in 1793 with John Murray, Jr., had toured the Mohawk River with Philip Schuyler, and he encouraged the general to draw up the articles of incorporation for the Western and Northern Inland Lock Navigation companies, chartered in 1794. The Northern company went broke; the Western had Eddy as treasurer from 1797. When private funds proved incapable of building the canal beyond five major locks at Little Falls, Eddy vigorously lobbied the New York State legislature to make itself the major stockholder in 1795 and, fifteen years later, to assume entire responsibility for the project. In 1796 he traveled to Cayuga Lake with surveyor Weston. When DeWitt Clinton, mayor of New York, took up the cause in 1810 and sailed up to Albany with Eddy on the first steamboat, the state appointed Eddy as the only Quaker among the six canal commissioners. These men had to tackle the difficult decisions that stalled progress until after the War of 1812: Could the canal be built without locks? (no); Should the canal begin on Lake Ontario, serving Canada, or at Buffalo on Lake Erie to serve Ohio and the west? Wartime politics and the interests of land companies urged the latter. Late in 1815 Eddy was influential in organizing a crucial public meeting and petition drive, rallying New York City's leading citizens to the canal cause, and pressuring the state to appropriate funds.[15] In Albany in 1817 when Clinton was newly elected governor, the legislature approved. Eddy had spent the previous winter lobbying for both the canal and New York's mental hospital. The same year Eddy lost his only son, John H. Eddy, deaf, but a skilled botanist, geographer, and artist. In 1825 Eddy welcomed Clinton as he came in the first canal boat from Buffalo to New York.

Thomas Eddy typified the generation of antebellum urban elites who developed perhaps the most extraordinary array of reform institutions in American history. His work as architect of New York State's penitentiary system and the Bloomingdale Asylum for the Insane masks the essential urbanity of Eddy's benevolent career. As Cadwallader Colden observed in 1833, "There is no benevolent or charitable institution founded of which [Eddy] was not the serious promoter."[16] Temperamentally and socially, Eddy shared many common bonds with the patricians who dominated the governing boards of these public philanthropies through the mid-1830s.[17] Eddy's early mercantile career centered around his handling consignments of goods from England and Ireland, but his global orientation was not limited to commercial affairs. Throughout his entire life Thomas Eddy looked to things British for models and inspiration. His enthusiastic endorsement of solitary cells for the Newgate prison was based on penal experiments in England. When he turned his attention to lunatic asylums, he diligently studied precedents in England and Wales. He influenced the Free School Society to conduct its classes according to the system developed by Joseph Lancaster in England. Contemporaries dubbed Eddy "the Howard of America," acknowledging his debt to the British Howard. Upon Eddy's death the *New York Daily Advertiser* noted that "an extensive correspondence with persons of distinction in Europe, and particularly in Great Britain, rendered . . . his character familiar to many of the great philanthropists of the age."[18]

Family occupied a central place in young Thomas Eddy's life. Like the Murrays and Hicks, he made his brothers business partners. One of Eddy's sisters married David Hosack, the New York City physician who dominated medical affairs in the metropolis during the early years of the nineteenth century. Eddy's philanthropic support of medical institutions owed much to his marital connection. Close kinship ties bound the business community.[19]

One theme consistently recurs in the biographical tributes for Eddy and the other members of New York City's early nineteenth century elite—the concept of "public service." Eddy himself observed that "from early life, all improvement of a public nature, that tended to benefit the country, or in like manner to promote the happiness or welfare of mankind, were considered by me as highly important." Chancellor James Kent agreed that "sound judgment, purity of principle, and . . . uncommon zeal for the promotion of all kinds of public improvement" characterized Eddy's life. Cadwallader Colden noted especially Eddy's work for penal reform. During Eddy's voluntary service as superintendent of the State Prison at Newgate, said Colden, "good order, comfort, cleanliness, industry and devotion" prevailed. Colden contrasted Eddy's role with the situation after 1800, which placed the prison in the hands of the Jeffersonians. A deterioration in penal administration ensued, and Colden drew the moral lesson. Men such as Colden and Eddy viewed Jacksonianism and Jeffersonianism as two sides of the same coin—a capitulation to the pressures of party, faction, and disorder, and a retreat from the disinterested public service from which a republic draws its strength.[20]

The concepts of public service, civic advancement, and republican genius coalesced in the technological achievement of the Erie Canal, completed in 1825. Truly a "public work" on an unprecedented scale, the canal illustrated the manner in which a patrician-directed government could advance common social and economic interests. In the canal's construction social harmony and public commitment to common social goals, patrician interests, and public interests appeared one.[21] The institutions begun by Eddy and his friends in federal New York City stand as tributes to the broadly public vision, cosmopolitan urbanity, and intense devotion to family of his generation.

Hospitals, the Insane, Paupers, and Juvenile Delinquents

The pioneer House of Refuge for juvenile delinquents was one fruit of the cluster of New York Quaker business people and doctors centering on Thomas Eddy and John Griscom between 1787 and 1827. Their involvement in both the Quaker meeting network and the non-Quaker city commercial fraternity, an unusual combination for Friends in other regions and periods, shaped urban Quaker attitudes toward social responsibility and reform down to the present. In Philadelphia and New Bedford, Quakers made up the commercial elite community into the nineteenth century. Around Boston, Baltimore, and the Virginia tidewater, Friends were never among the leaders. The world-traveling New York City Quakers seemed closer in role and outlook to English urban Friends than any other American Quaker community. Individual Friends' human compassion reinforced the "voluntaryism" that was England's and America's official philosophy in the 1780s. Yet these Quaker knickerbockers kept their rural roots, both by their inter-marriages in the first generation and often by retiring to farms or small Quaker towns. The New York Manumission Society, begun in 1787, was indeed their first large-scale public involvement. Their next enterprises drew more widely on the city community's concerns, using London models.[22] English non-Friends got Quaker support for Wilberforce's anti-slavery campaign, Robert Raikes's Sunday Schools, Hannah More's tract societies, the British Bible Society, the foreign missionary societies, and the prison work of Howard and Fry.

By 1780 Eddy had persuaded General Schuyler to lobby with him in Albany for a revised penal code. Mayor Cadwallader Colden admitted that "the laws for establishing our state prison owed their origin to the part taken by the Society of Friends," who made up most of the prison board of governors. As late as 1826, he drew Governor John Jay into a trip up the Hudson to visit Sing-Sing Prison, built partly because of Eddy's renewed lobbying, to improve the revised penal laws and graded classification of prisoners and add a new prison.[23]

Behind the concern for the penal code lay the experience of the Humane Society of New York City since 1787, which gave relief to the families of imprisoned debtors. From about 100 families a year from 1787 to 1796 and about 150 from 1797 to 1806, it increased to between 200 and 1,100 in the embargo and war years 1807–1818. It was not begun by Friends although John Murray, Jr., soon enlisted. Eddy supported a short-lived charity to provide cheap firewood. In 1791 the group opened a soup kitchen that by 1820 was giving out 70,000 quarts a year.[24] In 1805 the city itself began outdoor food relief, using volunteers. By 1815 they fed 16,400 people at a cost of $25,485 for home relief alone.

The City Dispensary program that the Humane Society opened in 1791 had clinics open day and night, volunteer visiting doctors in every ward, and a rescue program for those drowning. This effort was in addition to the city-subsidized medical visitors to the almshouses. The reopening and staffing of the New York Hospital, earlier privately funded, was only possible with state aid. Since 1793 Eddy had been one of the governors of the hospital, founded in 1771. It had been taken over by troops, but reopened in 1791. Eddy was president of its board from 1812 until his death fifteen years later.[25] At best they could scarcely cope with the yellow fever epidemics of 1795, 1798, 1803, and 1805 in which 750 to 2,000 died each year, including some 450 paupers. Because of these, Eddy helped the city lease and then buy the former Murray estate of Bellevue and fill it with almshouses and hospital buildings.

Friends' special concern, however, was for mental patients, first in a wing of the old hospital of 1797, then in a new building on its grounds in 1808, and finally in a building that they set up as a branch of the new New York Hospital on Bloomingdale Avenue in 1821. It was influenced by the Friends Hospital in Philadelphia (1817) but also reflected the model of the British Friends' York Retreat as described in Samuel Tuke's *Description of the Retreat* (1813) and in letters from Lindley Murray. These stressed the importance of careful floor and room design to prevent disturbance of patients by each other or outsiders (even by their own families). Above all they planned a kindly care of patients in an environment that would lead to their cure, although the Tukes rejected the idea that insanity resulted from the tensions of city culture. Their confidence in being able to transform humans by education and environment was an outlook shared by Friends with many kinds of perfectionists. Eddy, like the Tukes, forbade all violent response, even to violent patients, abolishing the older customs of simply restraining the insane in fetters and dark dungeons like Bedlam (= Bethlehem) Hospital in London.

The hospital in New York differed from that of the Tukes in being government supported, although privately managed, and in accepting all kinds of patients, especially the poor. "Eddy possessed a knack for extracting money from the New York State Legislature. During the winter months of 1816 he virtually lived in the halls of the senate."[26] Philadelphia Friends Hospital, influenced by Benjamin Rush, treated mental patients intensively with cold water shock treatment and bleeding and purging (from which Rush himself, like George Washington, died).[27] Eddy's hospital differed from that in Philadelphia in restoring a balance between "moral influence" (as at York) and medical treatment of insanity. New York's Bloomingdale, although it hired as director Pliny Earle from Philadelphia, used only medicines and passive restraints such as straitjackets. As late as 1885, Hack Tuke, after a circuit of all the American asylums, was still horrified at the frequent use of violent restraint.

Meanwhile, the pressure of the needs of the poor, especially in the depression years 1812, 1815, and 1818–19, were pushing Friends and all charitable New Yorkers in new directions. As early as 1794, the Charity Society of Jericho and Westbury Friends was formed. Their minute book may be a model of what occurred in other small communities. Eddy, John Griscom, John Murray, Jr., and others were already active in most of the groups to aid the poor described here. Yet as both immigration and depression intensified, it was clear that there were more indigent in New York than ever—15,000, said Eddy—while the total institutionalized in almshouses, prisons, and orphan asylums would rise from 2,600 to 3,428 over the decade. It was plain to leading Friends that as much intelligence must be put into finding the causes of poverty as into helping its victims. The Society for the Prevention of Pauperism, which began from a meeting in Eddy's home in December 1817 attended by the usual mix of Friends and non-Quakers, commissioned Dr. John Griscom to draw up a report on the causes of poverty: It listed (1) ignorance; (2) idleness; (3) intemperance; (4) extravagant spending by the poor; (5) imprudent marriages; (6) gambling; (7) pawnbrokers; (8) prostitution; and (9) charities that accustomed the poor to rely on others' benevolence. Morality underlined the cultural contrast between Friends and immigrants, who (1) spoke little English, (2) were often unemployed, and (3) used the pub as their social hall. The pregnant (5) married young. Although most members of the Society for the Prevention of Pauperism had started poor, this highly bourgeois work ethic has led recent commentators to call 1817–19 the era when American humanitarianism turned into moralism.[28] Poverty was considered inevitable but temporary, whereas pauperism often seemed incurable and, indeed, was linked with chronic illness as well as alcoholism. The average consumption of hard liquor in America, said Hamilton, was ten quarts per year for each man, woman, and child. Licensed New York taverns and grog houses had grown from 396 in 1773 to 3,400 in 1810. The Society set up a program for home visits in every ward and an eminently successful Savings Bank for the poor. They read books by—and were soon in vigorous correspondence with—Europeans such as Samuel Tuke, William Roscoe, Thomas Chalmers, and Patrick Colquhoun (and through the latter reached William Pitt and Jeremy Bentham).[29] The better side of these New York Friends' moralism was that it at once flowed into two more concrete channels for actual help to the poor. The Free School program was broadened into the state-supported Public School system. Horror at the growing horde of street urchins, child beggars, and prostitutes led to the first American program for juvenile delinquents.

Immediately after presenting his report, Griscom left for a year in Europe; one purpose of his trip was to visit pioneer social institutions. New York prison chaplain John Stanford had suggested a House of Refuge for juvenile delinquents. So had William Allen of London, who set up an institution in 1824 with Peter Bedford, also a Friend. Griscom's report after his return said the purposes of that penal system was not revenge but reform. It was reinforced by a detailed statistical survey by non-Quaker lawyer Charles Haines on immigrants and homeless children, sixteen of whom were then in the penitentiary with senior criminals. An 1821 report to the Society for the Prevention of Pauperism by their Committee on Juvenile Delinquency, was supported by the prison officials. The society voted to transform itself in 1823 into the Society for the Reformation of Juvenile Delinquents, chaired by Cadwallader Colden. This society lobbied for a House of Refuge where boys would be separated by degrees of depravity and isolated from adult criminals as well. In 1824 they got a law passed in Albany that required prisoners under sixteen to be sent to the refuge, not to the penitentiary, and allowed indeterminate sentences, which gave the managers authority to base the length of stay in the House of Refuge on the children's moral progress.[30] The legislature, however, gave no money until another campaign for it in the winter of 1824–25. The House of Refuge, which had 1,150 children by 1835, outgrew the unused armory it had been given. In 1839, after a fire and new grants from the legislature, it moved out to the growing Bellevue cluster at 23d Street and First Avenue.

The first superintendent, Joseph Curtis, was, perhaps, too much a Quaker. He used only limited physical punishment and restraint; he tried to reason with boys and girls who escaped and then stole; he joined them in sports and evening discussions; and he even tried a jury system of inmates to impose penalties on violators. With the Managers' consent, he developed a program of work and apprenticeship both inside the House of Refuge and after inmates' release outside. Despite some protests from labor unions, this effort was a success. Friends on the board suggested indenture as cabin boys for long voyages on a whaling ship. Curtis encouraged a Ladies' Auxiliary committee to work with the girls. After one year, Curtis resigned and was succeeded by the more tough-minded Nathaniel Hart. The House of Refuge, nevertheless, so impressed a series of visitors from Albany, overseas, and other states that it was soon copied in Baltimore, Philadelphia, and Boston. In 1840 the superintendent was Samuel Wood, a Quaker again, who believed inmates could be transformed, even converted. Finally, from 1851 neglected children were referred to the new New York Juvenile Asylum and separated from those under court sentence who were sent to the huge new reformatory on Randall's Island in the East River, closed only in 1935. "The concept of the Refuge was replaced by the reformatory concept."[31]

Friends' attitudes toward the social problems underlying poverty had, meanwhile, changed despite success with many individual delinquents and with the House of Refuge as a whole. The chaos of 1777–1783 had required a new Poor Law in 1788. By 1824 it seemed that New York State could handle its native-born paupers. But the growing influx of immigrants included more each year who had neither resources nor skills to move beyond the city. Irish families who landed together were broken up in New York by the need for the men to work on the Erie Canal and the railroads. Even if they survived, few returned to their women and children, who without money often became beggars or homeless. The Irish in New York, 30 percent of the population, made up 40 percent of the cholera victims and of children in the House of Refuge and 87 percent of immigrant manual laborers. They also probably made up most of the twelve thousand children, 40 percent of the school age population, who attended no schools.[32] Traditionalists had been brought up on English ideas that paupers were the responsibility of their home parishes, each with its own workhouse, poorhouse, and orphanage. Emma Lazarus's welcome to the "lost, the tempest-tossed, the struggling masses" seemed unfair: "The boast that one country is asylum for the oppressed in other parts of the world is very philanthropic and sentimental, but I fear that we shall . . . derive little comfort from being made the almshouse . . . for the poor of other countries."[33]

The way ahead for Friends divided here, in social action and in theology as well. In 1824 the Free School Society (founded in 1805, and still teaching 5,200 children) and the schools run for the poor by Protestant churches and other groups (enrolling 5,174), combined into the larger Public School Society. This upset the Catholics under Bishop Hughes but united children of all classes. Most urban Orthodox Friends approved.[34] The opposite approach to society appealed to Hicksites, who wanted uncompromising action against one or more specific social evils, such as slavery, liquor, or war. Such Friends turned to strengthen the "guarded education" of Friends, leaving the moral life of the city and the immigrants in Satan's hands.

4. John Griscom (1774–1852). Silhouette by August Edouart, 1842.
Courtesy Friends Historical Library, Swarthmore College.

John Griscom and Other Quaker Doctors and Scientists

The years of New York's blossoming also produced a garland of
Quaker doctors and scientists who participated in many of the same
committees for public welfare. Their creativity and reputation could
not be matched by Quakers after 1850 when the city population mush-
roomed but that of the Friends did not.[35]

John Griscom (1774–1852) was, perhaps, the most original and
wide in his interests. He was the organizing mind behind the theory
and strategy of the Society for the Prevention of Pauperism and its
House of Refuge, and his name will recur in the Education chapter in
this book. Born on a South Jersey farm from one of the first families to
settle in Philadelphia, Griscom survived yellow fever there in the terrible 1793 epidemic as a student at Friends Academy. While teaching for
thirteen years at Burlington, New Jersey, he studied alone in the still
rare field of chemistry. Called by a group of Quaker parents to teach
school in New York in 1807, he began the annual series of public lectures and dramatic demonstrations in chemistry in the city's first Lancasterian school and continued them in his own new school building.[36]

He gave similar public lectures for women only in 1817. His friend David Hosack,[37] Friend Valentine Mott, and the whole faculty of the College of Physicians and Surgeons of Columbia College resigned in 1826 after a conflict with their board. Griscom joined them as professor of chemistry in their short-lived Rutgers University medical faculty. In 1810 he wrote a paper on mineralogy based on a trip up the Hudson Valley and back via the Lebanon, New York, Shakertown. He wrote appreciatively of Shaker lifeways. In 1815 he visited Niagara. In 1816 his wife died of childbed fever after bearing their ninth child. In 1818, to recover from this and a lung infection, he sailed for a one-year vacation in Europe where he studied relief of the poor and visited English Friends such as John Dalton, the pioneer chemist, William Allen, a kindred spirit to Griscom, Elizabeth Fry, and Lindley Murray. At the suggestion of Silliman of Yale,[38] he also visited and held lively dialogues with some of the greatest scientists of his or any age: in London, Sir Joseph Banks, Astronomer Herschel at the Royal Observatory, and Sir Humphrey Davy. He visited the new British Museum, the Bible Society, hospitals, Robert Raikes' Sunday School, and the famous Lancasterian schools. In Paris he made friends of the chemists Cuvier and Gay Lussac, Berzelius the Swedish chemist-ambassador, and Baron von Humboldt,[39] besides old Lafayette. Griscom lived in a great yeast-time of science. Visiting laboratories and museums everywhere, he traveled via Lausanne, Chamonix, Geneva, Milan, Genoa, and Haarlem back to England. There he met the poets Wordsworth and Southey and in Scotland, the Natural Philosophers and Sir Walter Scott.

On returning, Griscom threw himself into the projects for the House of Refuge for juvenile delinquents, for an asylum for mental patients, and more centrally into Lancasterian high schools. He wrote no major monographs but probed eagerly into antiseptic substances, the health danger from city cemeteries, Jonathan Dymond's writings on peace, and the pride of Elias Hicks. He retired in 1836 to Haverford and later to Burlington, New Jersey, his early home, founding there a branch of the American Bible Society. Yet he carefully studied geological strata in the field in several countries and lectured on the huge time span of the earth, recently defined by geologists.[40] He surrendered to it any literal interpretation of Genesis although not his belief in the special creation of Adam and humanity.

Griscom belonged to an era when many outstanding scientists and doctors were working men's sons and had either been themselves apprentices or trained only as doctor's assistants. Science and medicine thus opened easily for alert Friends, who were usually uninterested in classical studies. Believing in the unity of truth, Friends have combined more easily than stricter church members a pragmatic approach to science and an intense ethical and religious concern. New York Quaker families produced no philosophers, but many doctors. Griscom discovered the value of cod-liver oil. Griscom's son, John H. Griscom, was a famous doctor and as city commissioner was a pioneer in public health and sanitation. The first outstanding Quaker doctor in New York may have been John Rodman (1653–1731), who moved from Barbados, via Newport and Flushing into New York City in 1695 and within four years was the third wealthiest man in the city. Dr. Valentine Seaman (1770–1817) from Jericho, after studying under Benjamin Rush in Philadelphia, began clinical lectures and the training of midwives at New York Hospital, and, after his son's death from smallpox, studied vaccination under Edward Jenner in England.

His Quaker cousin and pupil Valentine Mott (1785–1865), whose father was also a doctor, became famous as a swift surgeon at New York Hospital. Trained at Columbia College, Mott was in 1807–8 one of the earliest New Yorkers to study medicine at both the fountainheads in London and Edinburgh. His return visits to Britain and to Paris and the Near East in 1834–41 were written up in a travel volume no doubt inspired by Griscom's, but focused on hospitals.[41] Mott performed one thousand amputations, ligatured major arteries for forty patients, and was the first to cut out cancerous lower jaws. No theorist, his achievements depended on his knowledge of anatomy and ambidextrous manual skill. In that era anaesthetics and antiseptics were still experimental.[42] Mott's essay on using ether and chloroform to replace surgeons' previous dependence on narcotics was printed by the government for Civil War army suregons. Mott noted how anaesthetics prevented not only patients' pain but serious dangers of shock and the collapse of the blood system during operations. Mott published on yellow fever and on the chemistry of Saratoga mineral waters.

Thomas Cock (1782–1869), after interning in the offices of both Quaker Valentines, taught medicine at Queens (Rutgers) College, and became president of the College of Physicians and Surgeons from 1855 to 1858. He was best known for his work and works upon epidemics, yellow fever in 1822 and cholera in 1832, and he served on charitable boards. His wife, Elizabeth Ferris Cock, founded the Lying-In Asylum in 1827.[43] Most of these men had doctor sons who left their Quaker meetings. Only James Rushmore Wood (1813–1882) seems to have died a Friend. In 1848 he turned the city almshouse, prison, and clinics at Bellevue into the famous general hospital it has remained.

Quaker Printers: Isaac Collins, Mahlon Day, and
Samuel Wood

In 1803 Samuel Wood (d. 1844) opened a bookshop in New York City and three years later began publishing books. Wood was noted for his "toy books" for young children and is credited with being the first to introduce series of graded textbooks. Mahlon Day (1790–1844), born in Morristown, New Jersey, began printing books in New York in 1816.[44] Day was noted for primers, children's books, hymn books, almanacs, and tables of tariffs. Most Wood and Day children's books were small and inexpensive, many costing less than one cent each, of a few pages, and didactic and religious or moral in tone, but well illustrated with woodcut prints. Samuel Wood's firm was continued by members of his family and came to specialize in medical books. Day's firm became Baker, Crane, and Day in 1846. Mahlon Day retired the following year and published a few Quaker-related titles in the 1830s. Daniel Cooledge, a Quaker printer from New England, printed a few Quaker titles in New York in the 1830s. His sons followed him in the publishing business, but they had been disowned from the Society of Friends. The imprints of Collins, Wood, and Day may be found not only on books printed on behalf of New York Yearly Meeting but also on the reports and publications of many of the philanthropic organizations, such as the Free School Society, supported by Quakers such as Eddy and Griscom. Daniel Lawrence, a Quaker printer who had previously worked in Philadelphia and New Jersey, moved to the Dutchess County village of Stanford in 1806 where he issued reprints of Quaker journals and other Quaker-related titles until his death in 1811.

Isaac Collins (1746–1817) bridged a multitude of worlds and cultures between the American War of Independence and the Hicksite Separation of 1827–28. He was a printer in Delaware, Virginia, Pennsylvania, New Jersey, and New York, at home in the meeting house, the marketplace, and the political arena. He was born on his father's farm on the Brandywine in Delaware and was locally educated and apprenticed. He was a journeyman under William Goddard in Philadelphia in the heady years 1766–70 when the colonies protested against the Townsend Act's "taxation without representation." He also joined the monthly meeting in Philadelphia and opened a printers' shop there with Joseph Crukshank before setting up his own in Burlington, New Jersey. He moved to Trenton in the midst of the war,[45] and moved to New York only in 1796, staying until 1808. For most of his thirty earlier years within the area of Philadelphia, however, he was more involved in revolutionary politics than in Quaker concerns. He did, indeed, print Richard Davies's journal and Benezet's and Sharp's works against slavery, and reprinted Sewel's *History of the . . . Quakers,* and in the 1790s Lindley Murray's grammars and textbooks, along with New Testaments and many religious works by non-Quaker clergy. But he bid successfully to print the paper money and the militia ordinances and resolutions of the revolutionary New Jersey Provincial Congress and edited and printed their subsidized weekly news-sheet, *The New-Jersey Gazette.* For these, Collins was disowned by Friends in 1778 and only restored by Burlington Meeting in 1787. Against even the New Jersey government, he defended the right of the *Gazette* to integrity and the privacy of its sources, preparing the way for the First Amendment to the U.S. Constitution and also for the precedent that truth is a defense against libel. His main project, however, before and after his move to New York, was the "Collins Bible." It was one of the first two complete bibles published in English in America. In New York Collins raised a subscription to reprint George Fox's and Job Scott's *Journals.* But he was as concerned about printing or importing medical books for the New York Hospital, including Valentine Seaman's textbooks for midwives and about yellow fever, from which his wife had died. Isaac Collins's eleven children were with him in New York, Rebecca marrying Stephen Grellet in 1804. Thomas (1779–1859), his father's successor as a printer, was also a founding member of the American Bible Society and a member of the Manumission Society. Charles was so ardently against slavery that he refused to use even a cotton umbrella. Isaac Collins, Jr., was a member of the American Bible Society managers and of the Society for the Prevention of Pauperism and its House of Refuge for juvenile delinquents. He retired to Philadelphia in 1828, returning to New York in 1857 to address a national festival of leaders of "child-saving" institutions at Randall's Island, by then home of the House of Refuge of whose founders he was almost the last survivor.[46]

A Tract Association of Friends was formed in New York City in 1817, which printed and distributed a series of eight- and twelve-page tracts on moral and religious topics. It published at least thirty-five titles between 1817 and 1835, became inactive for a time, and was revived in 1852. In western New York, members of Farmington and Scipio Quarterly Meetings started a Union Tract Association of Friends in 1818, which published two small magazines for children, edited by Joseph Tallcot, *The Child's Companion* and *The Friendly Visitant.* All of the major Quaker publishers—the Collinses, Talcott, Wood and Day, and the Tract Association and the Murray Fund as well—adhered to the Orthodox branch of New York Yearly Meeting after the Separation. Among the Hicksites, Isaac T. Hopper moved to New York City where he opened a book shop and acted as copublisher with Marcus M. T. C. Gould of *The Friend, or Advocate of Truth.* Hopper later published Quaker and abolitionist titles, most notably the journal of Elias Hicks, and the short-lived *Friends Weekly Intelligencer* (1838–1839). A number of important Quaker titles, such as Elias Hicks's *Observations on African Slavery* and *Journal,* were first published in New York where Friends could also obtain Quaker titles from Philadelphia, Britain, or New England.[47]

New York Friends and Native Americans

Friends in New York, unlike those in Pennsylvania, rarely met native American Indians settled near their own homes until they moved to the Finger Lakes after the Revolution. The Indians' needs and sufferings thus became another philanthropic concern of city Quakers. The initiative for an active policy of Quaker assistance to the Indians of New York State came from Philadelphia Yearly Meeting. Philadelphia had approached New York Yearly Meeting in 1793 about their concern for promoting "peace and friendship" with the Indians and the following year had sent a delegation to act as observers at the Treaty of Canandaigua where they met with members of the Iroquois. New York Yearly Meeting created an Indian Committee in 1795.[48] Thomas Eddy and his botanist son, John, were among the delegation sent to visit the Brotherton and Stockbridge Indians of central New York. The state appointed Eddy and George Embree as superintendents of Brotherton. By 1796 Philadelphia had formed a plan for agricultural and technical education, which it offered to the tribes in New York State and which was accepted by the Oneida.[49]

Between 1796 and 1800 the Philadelphia Yearly Meeting Indian Committee had a written agreement to maintain a farm at Oneida where Indian youths were instructed in agriculture, carpentry, and blacksmithing, and several Indian girls were sent to Pennsylvania to learn weaving and domestic skills. The Philadelphia effort was largely directed toward the Oneida, a tribe of the Iroquois, but also was extended to the adjacent Stockbridge and Brotherton tribes. The Philadelphia Friends withdrew from Oneida in the winter of 1799–1800, and thereafter gave their attention to the Seneca Indians in western

New York and northwestern Pennsylvania. During this period, the work of New York Yearly Meeting was largely to support the effort in Philadelphia, monitor progress, and provide advice and consultation. The Oneida, Brotherton, and Stockbridge continued to seek assistance, particularly in dealing with their white neighbors. As Philadelphia turned to the Seneca, New York filled the gap and sent Quakers to live among the Brotherton and Oneida to teach school, agricultural techniques, spinning, and weaving.[50]

Quakers were less concerned than the missionaries sent by other denominations with the Christianization of the Indians. Their effort was focused on the transfer of skills needed for the economic survival of the Indian tribes. In 1810 a Stockbridge woman, Mary Peters, was trained to teach weaving skills to her own people and later to the Onondagas. Some Quakers hoped that the Indians would ultimately become Christians, but they acknowledged the religious and moral dimensions of the traditional Indian culture and their moral superiority to some white neighbors. The Seneca "prophet," Handsome Lake, stemmed alcoholism among his own people. By 1810 New York Quakers were becoming involved in land ownership questions, lobbying the state government on behalf of the "pagan" faction of the Oneida. Later the Quakers became the allies of the "pagan" faction of the Onondaga and Seneca. By 1816 Quakers in both Philadelphia and New York were concerned with the larger issue of Indian rights to their lands. At this time, some of the Oneida, Brotherton, and Stockbridge tribes were considering a move to new lands in Indiana or Wisconsin. New York Quakers counseled against this move and gave support to those Indians who remained on their New York State lands.[51]

From 1809 the New York Indian Committee also gave assistance and advice to Onondaga Indians by providing a loan for the construction of a sawmill and supplying draft animals and tools. Aden T. Corey and his wife went to live near the Onondaga in 1822 to teach agriculture and weaving. Their model farm continued until at least 1834 when the Onondaga were left to carry on by themselves.[52] The New York Indian Committee occasionally provided assistance to the Seneca and Tuscarora living in western New York, but left them mostly to the Philadelphia Committee, who maintained a presence on the Allegany Reservation. Orthodox Friends kept the school at Tunessassa until 1940.

In New York Yearly Meeting the Indian concern became the concern of the Hicksite branch after the Separation. Its major operation at Onondaga remained under Hicksite control. In the 1830s Aden Corey established a model farm among the Seneca on the Cattaraugus Reservation supported jointly by New York and Genesee Yearly Meetings. This effort evolved into a "Female Manual Labor School," which was turned over in 1849 to the Seneca Nation, who wanted to use the buildings for an orphan asylum. This plan was not realized until 1855 with the establishment of what would become the Thomas Indian School.

In 1838 a treaty was signed at Buffalo Creek whereby the Seneca in western New York were to sell all of their remaining land and move to the west. Many of the Seneca were opposed to the treaty and charged that the signatures on the treaty had been obtained by fraud and did not represent the majority sentiment. A "Joint Committee on the Indian Concern" was formed by the Hicksite yearly meetings of Baltimore, New York, Philadelphia, and Genesee.[53] The Joint Committee worked to mobilize support to revoke the treaty through publicity, petitions, and visits to government officials. The result was a compromise treaty in 1842 by which the Seneca retained the Allegany and Cattaraugus reservations but lost those at Buffalo Creek and Tonawanda. The Tonawanda Band refused to move and regained their lands and reservation status by 1857.

Philip M. Thomas of Baltimore Yearly Meeting was the leading figure in the Quaker effort and for a time served as the ambassador from the Seneca Nation to the United States. After 1842, Thomas and other members of the Joint Committee recommended that the Seneca replace their old government by chiefs with an elective body, which was done in the Seneca Nation constitution adopted in 1845. That constitution and the Treaty of 1842 ended the active involvement of the Hicksite Quakers with the Seneca.

New York (Orthodox) and New England Yearly Meetings sent representatives to study the condition of the Indians living west of the Mississippi. Their report advocated a government policy toward the Indians based on peaceful relations and education. The approach it articulated became part of the "Peace Policy" of the Federal Government in the late 1860s and 1870s. When training Indians in agricultural and technological skills, Quakers naturally thought of their own world of family farms worked by males. Traditional Iroquois agriculture was controlled by females; land was worked collectively. Quakers have been faulted for undermining the Iroquois social structure and the status of women. Such criticisms may be true but must be measured against the Quakers who saw the economic condition of the Indians as disastrous, the aim of Friends to create Indian communities not dependent on whites, and the Quakers' ability to modify their approach in response to the wishes of the Native Americans.

Through the Indian Committee New York Friends acted as a corporate body to bring a Quaker approach to a social issue. Quaker testimonies were not only a matter of individual faithfulness on the part of Friends but matters that could be incorporated into public policy. Increasingly, Quakers from different Yearly Meetings were acting in concert as when they overturned the Buffalo Creek Treaty of 1838.

7

The Orthodox-Hicksite Separation

Hugh Barbour
and
Thomas Bassett, Christopher Densmore,
H. Larry Ingle, Alson D. Van Wagner

Rationalists, Quietists, and Universalists, 1745–1826

The most traumatic event in American Quaker history was the Separation of 1827–28 between Friends who came to be called Orthodox and Hicksite. Its resulting breaches in both beliefs and organizations remain among Friends to the present day although in the New York Yearly Meetings they were largely overcome in the Reunion of 1955. The multiple causes and course of the Separation are the subject of this chapter. Christ-centered, or Orthodox, Friends have blamed the split on the rejection by their opponents of the beliefs held by Fox and the original Friends about the Bible and Christ, especially on Christ's atonement for human sin. Hicksite Quakers insist on the centrality for Friends of obeying the Light of God within each person but have always blamed the division on the dogmatism and authority of the meeting elders. Many cultural and historical factors were also involved. Before turning to Elias Hicks himself, the Long Island farmer whose messages as he traveled constantly to visit meetings throughout America precipitated the Separation, one needs to explore the movements of thought in his day, both among Friends and in the wider culture. One was the language of reason.

The eighteenth century has been called the Age of Reason,[1] but reason was understood in various ways. Different forms of the belief that human reason reflects the divine Law of Nature underlay the philosophies of Plato and the Stoics, the biblical Book of Proverbs, and the

Catholic theology of Aquinas. Even Calvin believed God gave reason to humans as one of many ways the created world could serve God. From rational premises Calvinists challenged Catholic dogmas and established hierarchies in church and state. So also did sects seeking liberty, and individual doubters and creative thinkers. Yet from such rational bases, old doctrines and authorities were also defended.

Early Friends distrusted reasoning or "notions" not based on experience. Yet by the 1670s Penn based his doctrinal tracts point by point on reason and scripture like those of his opponents. He knew that private religious "revelations" were publicly suspect[2] since claims by individual radical Puritans to be divinely guided had led to violent conflicts. Yet even the English bishops who argued for a broad "natural religion" felt an intense concern for lay ethics in England's libertine society. These Anglicans identified the Ten Commandments with universal human nature as well as with divine wisdom. By contrast, Quaker worship turned to Quietism, resisting the temptations of "pure reason" although by 1750 even John Woolman found it natural to use "the divine wisdom" as his name for God. Quietist Friends reminded their meetings to "dig deep" to find the "pure springs" of God's will beneath their busy minds because leadings to act or speak might be muddied by rationalizing or self-will or frosted by persecution. Quietists read Catholic mystics and European Pietists, not philosophers. In meetings for worship they increasingly gave messages in ministry in a special sing-song chant that seemed to distinguish them from human utterances. After 1750 the "Reformation" of American Quakerism, led by Woolman, Benezet, and Churchman, and inherited by Elias Hicks, made Quietist self-renunciation the mark of true faith, and called each Friend to return to purity of conscience, whatever it cost for daily life.[3]

After 1750, moreover, reason itself took on new connotations. Since the 1650s the ideas of Deism had reduced God to an abstract Mind, the founding architect of the universe. (Friends, by contrast, believed in the activity and power of God in human lives.) French Deists now invoked Natural Law to justify a new social order. Voltaire attacked the power of the Catholic church in France and praised both reason and the Quakers, who did not return the compliment. Deism was enshrined by the French Revolution as their new national faith to replace Catholicism. The *Age of Reason* (1794–95), by New Yorker Thomas Paine, attacked the clergy and all dogma by an ultimate form of religious individualism, skeptical about everything but "common sense" and "the rights of man." In New York in 1794 non-Quaker Elihu Palmer led a small "Deistical Society," but when Joseph Priestley, the

English chemist and Unitarian who had been mobbed out of Birmingham for praising the French Revolution, visited New York, the orthodox clergy there closed ranks in alarm.[4] Idealists such as Wordsworth turned against the Revolution and Deism. The Deism of pro-French Thomas Jefferson was a key issue in the election of 1800.[5] French guillotines were the vivid background for the yearly meetings' distrust of the Quaker rationalism of Abraham Shackleton in Ireland. In 1798 Hannah Barnard visited Shackleton, raising issues that later gathered around Hicks.

Hannah Jenkins, of Baptist parentage, was convinced as a Friend at eighteen but was self-taught until adulthood. She married Peter Barnard, a carter and widower with three children, moved with him from Oblong to a frame house in Hudson, New York, and became a recorded minister there. From 1786 Hannah was eight times representative to Nine Partners Quarterly Meeting and in 1793, 1794, and 1796 to New York Yearly Meeting. She served on the Nine Partners Boarding School Committee. An eloquent speaker, she visited western Connecticut in 1793 and was approved to travel in the Genesee, Cherry, and Champlain valleys. In 1794 and 1796 she visited meetings in New England. In the fall of 1796 she asked her meetings for support for a religious visit to Friends in Britain. It took nearly two years for her mission to win approval. She embarked in company with Elizabeth (Hosier) Coggeshall, a young mother whose gift in ministry had recently been recognized in Rhode Island. They landed in July 1798 and visited nearly all the Friends Meetings in England, Scotland, and Ireland. When young Betsy Gurney and her father visited Ackworth School, Hannah deeply impressed her by asking Betsy her own opinion of the students. The American women found British Friends in a "low state" and were uneasy over the control concentrated in the hands of elders in London while itinerant ministry was left largely to women.[6]

Contact with the Shackletons led Hannah Barnard to state more openly the ideas on the Inward Light, war, and the Bible that she had long held. Some Quakers were alarmed at her teaching, including the New York evangelical David Sands, then traveling in Ireland. Yet when the two women left Ireland early in May 1800, their ministry was endorsed by the General Meeting of Irish Friends. In London Yearly Meeting a few weeks later, however, the women's plan to visit southern France and Germany was rejected by the ministers and elders. Hannah raised procedural challenges at every level of appeal and tried to prove that her system of beliefs were "the primitive Christian principles" of Friends. Penn and Fox could be quoted on both sides of every key issue as Hicks's allies and enemies would do again three decades later.[7] Driven to state her beliefs, Hannah Barnard put reason above orthodoxy about sin and Christ.

> Professing my firm belief in one God, . . . I believe Adam's fall consisted in a fall from innocence, . . . the bountiful Creator's free gift to his creatures being . . . "Christ (or the spirit of anointing) within, the hope of glory." . . . [As Jesus was] the Father's most dignified Son and Messenger, the Spirit or divine emanation was poured upon him without measure, and upon us by measure. . . . When I am asked whether I believe in the vicarious sufferings and atonement of Christ, I answer candidly, I do not.[8]

Hannah Barnard was less concerned with theology than with ethics. Her enemies were shocked that she did not believe God commanded Abraham to kill Isaac and that the virgin birth and other miracles were matters for private judgment. After fourteen months of meetings, at each of which she argued her case at length, the weary London Yearly Meeting elders censured her views and asked her to cease her ministry there. They offered her the passage money customarily given to returning American ministers, but she refused it and sailed home in August 1801. She permitted the publication, without the approval of a Friends meeting, of an *Appeal* from the London proceedings, which provoked a pamphlet war. The British committee, expecting deference to elders, rebuked her "cavilling, contentious disposition of mind." A woman in her late forties, with the enormous respect for the written word common to the self-taught, she had ill-concealed contempt for the rich, aristocratic elders who profited by the European war. Copies of the English proceedings and letters exaggerating Hannah Barnard's "infidelity" had already prejudiced her case when she returned to Hudson Monthly Meeting in November. After six long interviews, the meeting silenced her as a minister in January 1802 and later disowned her as did the quarterly meeting to which she appealed. They denied her right to appeal to New York Yearly Meeting. Hannah read interminably from her own transcript of the British trial saying, "I know I am right, . . . for I keep minutes of these things."[9] Hudson Friends, although most of them later became Hicksites, recorded her husband's death in 1830, but not Hannah's in 1825. The decision of New England, New York, and Philadelphia Yearly Meetings not to print Job Scott's *Salvation by Christ* was hardened by her case and his rationalism and death in Ireland.

The Orthodox-Hicksite Separation reflected also the bitterness of the split within the formerly united parish churches of eastern New England between the evangelical Congregationalists and the Unitarians, who had developed Puritan rationalism and ethical earnestness. Unitarians took over many parish churches with no change of name. After 1820 Congregationalists had to build new churches. Quakers had no major contacts in New York with the Unitarians.[10] A New York Unitarian congregation was gathered, plus seven more by the Civil War, but Friends disliked their intellectualism. Early American Unitarians saw Christ as divine, though less than God, and believed in his miracles, whereas Fox and Quaker tradition had emphasized the unity of God as the Christ-spirit within Jesus and the Holy Spirit in humans.

The meetings at Lynn, Salem, and New Bedford were an important exception to this pattern. As early as 1801, Joseph Hoag encountered New England Friends he called Ranters, but who called themselves "New Lights," although they were unrelated to the revival-centered Baptist and Presbyterian "New Lights." In 1816 Mary Newhall and other "New Light" women began speaking during worship at Lynn about a spirituality based on human perfectibility and about the superiority of the Light that spoke within themselves to the authority of the Bible or of the Quaker elders. These ideas were similar to the Unitarianism then establishing itself around Boston, as Ralph Waldo Emerson recognized on reading them. When Newhall was "eldered," young Benjamin Shaw and three other men tried physically to take over the elders' "facing bench" during worship and for this were convicted of disturbing the peace by a court trial. Lynn Meeting and Salem Monthly and Quarterly Meetings, despite previous disunity, then agreed to disown the offenders. In 1823, however, Mary Newhall carried out an eloquent ministry in and around New Bedford Meeting where Benjamin Rodman had already made a gesture like Shaw's. She was supported by many New Bedford Friends, notably Mary Rotch and Elizabeth Rotch Rodman, daughters of William Rotch, who had moved from Nantucket to become the richest whaling shipowner in New Bedford and the world, and by other whaling in-laws such as Charles W. Morgan. Hull Barton from Stanford, New York, and Phebe Johnson, both disowned by their New York meetings, came to join the rebellion. The letter of New Bedford Meeting asking those meetings to recall them became the opening skirmish of the "Old Light" elders' campaign for discipline, which succeeded by 1826 in "disowning" all the New Light Rotches and others, most of whom then joined Unitarian churches. Unlike the Hicksites or Irish New Lights (or conversion-centered Presbyterian ones), those in New England were, like the Unitarians, an elite minority in wealth and social status and increasingly appealed to reason. Their fate and the disciplinary moves of the elders were prototypes of the Hicksite Separation although they inoculated New England Friends against it.[11]

The Universalist churches were another story. Unlike present-day "Universalist Friends," they were solidly Christian although they denied the exclusiveness of Calvinist predestination. They developed the trust of New Englanders in human perfectibility into a belief that a loving God must ultimately save every living creature, perhaps in a purging afterlife. Universalist piety was centered on Christ and the New Testament.[12] They reached out to all hearers. Whereas "Unitarianism arose in Harvard halls,"[13] Universalists were largely a rural movement of the working class and unschooled. Their preachers had mostly been lay Baptist or Methodist. John Murray had immigrated from England. Their best thinker, Hosea Ballou, although a friend of Emerson, was a Baptist. Their churches were mainly in upper New England and New York State, products of the Second Awakening that the Baptists had carried into the woodland villages. Their main literature was hymn- and songbooks. Most of their annual national General Conventions were held in New Hampshire from 1793 through 1820, thereafter mainly in Vermont and the upper Hudson valley, often in towns with Quaker meetings.[14] Few Friends are recorded as transferring to Baptist or Universalist churches, but interactions between rural Friends and Baptist and Universalist neighbors need to be studied more. Universalists shared Quakers' ideas on water baptism, war, oaths, and slavery—also their printer, Isaac Collins. Baptists shared with rural Friends a "comeouter" distrust of city wealth and mores, a concern for their own kind of moral purity.

A journal with some similar ideas, Lyman Spalding's *Plain Truth* appeared in Canandaigua from 1822 to 1824. *Plain Truth* opposed both Calvinists and missionaries. It was revived in 1828–29 by Elihu F. Marshall and Elisha Dean while Spalding published at Lockport *Priestcraft Exposed and Primitive Christianity Defended*. The three men were Hicksites but published not as Friends but as Christian primitivists, part of a network of publications united in opposing all domestic and foreign mission boards and theological schools, Deists as well as Calvinists.

Rationalism, which had affected the vocabulary but not the faith of Woolman and Job Scott, also influenced some Philadelphia area Friends in this era. Benjamin Ferris, later the Hicksite leader in Delaware, praised "the spirit of free inquiry" in a debate of forty-two letters on each side throughout 1821–23 against the Presbyterian minister Eliphalet Gilbert published as the *Letters of Paul and Amicus*.[15] Some wild words flew, and Gilbert labeled as a "Deist" a Friend who rejected the Bible's authority, but most of the careful argument by "Amicus" centered on paid ministers and physical sacraments, and much of "Paul's" on the Bible, the Trinity, and the need for Christ's atoning death, about which Ferris / Amicus rejected the "orthodox" creedal doctrines. He used a style, language, and examples from William Penn's early debate tracts against the Puritans.[16] The new elements in the debate contrasted careful examples from the new fields of foreign missions: Are the Hindus monotheists and honest, or deceitful, idolatrous polytheists? Can they be saved without Christ? By slaveowning missionaries? The issue here, for which Penn had used as examples Socrates and Roman Stoics, was the Quaker teaching that the Inward Light is enough for salvation in every person universally. The clash between Ferris's group and the Philadelphia Quaker elders was the spark for the conflict that became linked with Hicks's name.

Evangelical Movements in England and America, 1734–1810

The second early nineteenth century movement, whose clash with rationalism produced the Hicksite-Orthodox Separation, was Evangelicalism. Martin Luther called *evangelical* the Gospel that human salvation depends on faith alone, on trust in God, not in one's own merits. Although the term fitted the Puritans, it took on a new intensity when Jonathan Edwards from 1734 onward gave an intellectual backbone to local "awakenings" in Congregational churches in the Connecticut valley. By the time of the preaching tours in 1739–46 throughout the colonies by Wesley's English colleague George Whitefield and by locally trained revivalists such as the Presbyterian Tennents, the movement was already called "the Great Awakening."

Two important elements were added to the evangelical Christianity of Luther and Calvin by Wesley's Methodists and by American Puritans. First, *conversion,* preached as a progressive change of heart by the American Puritans, became a condition for individuals' membership in their parish churches. Edwards's treatises *The Religious Affections* and *Freedom of Will* carefully showed how impossible it was for a self by itself to escape from self-centeredness. The "disinterested benevolence" that lets a person "affirm, in being, each other being" can only come when God takes the initiative and frees a burdened self by changing the subject, often by a sudden experience of delight in the glory of God. Edwards left sinners "in the hand of an angry God" precisely so that they would discover that only God had liberated them. For Edwards, this showed a person's dependence on Christ's righteousness, not on his or her own. For John Wesley, such an assurance that "Christ had died for my sins, even mine" was central in both his own conversion experience and his preaching on human atonement by Christ's blood. Wesley was only freed from merely "clinging to the cross," like the Pietists, by sensing the power of the Spirit to infuse perfect love into a converted heart.

The second special mark of American evangelicals has been the resulting *call to accept a convert's need for atonement by Christ's death.* Except among Calvinists, this doctrine led to the belief that an individual's act of will or surrender was needed for conversion. It followed that such "decisions for Christ" could be encouraged by preaching, hymns, and other methods of *evangelism,* a separate issue from *evangelical beliefs.* Unexpected "revivals" of religion, observed in various churches, evolved into the regular, professional practices of revivalism such as townwide, late-night "protracted meetings" and "altar calls" for the repentant and the infection of one town or church by a revival in its neighbors. Such movements rolled through the South and along the American frontier continuously after the American Revolution but seem not to have moved Friends. One result was new congregations made up only of the converted, which led to the early dominance of American religion by Baptist and Methodist denominations limited to such members.

Evangelical ideas and experience, however, had also spread more sedately in England from Wesley through the Baptist and Congregational churches and notably to leaders of the episcopal Church of England, which Wesley claimed never to have left. Home prayers and Bible study were revived as in Puritan times. Hymns of Charles Wesley, Watts, and Cowper were sung everywhere. England owes its foreign missions to William Carey, the Baptist, and Henry Martyn, the Anglican, and the boards they inspired around 1800. This group of evangelical leaders, centered in London, included the pioneers in the social reform programs in prisons, against slavery, the Bible Society, Sunday Schools, and England's Factory Acts to limit child labor. John Griscom, traveling in England, had worshipped and discussed reform methods with such folk.

The American "Second Awakening" dates from two contrasting events of 1801. In the west, frontier revivalists at Cane Ridge gathered fifteen thousand settlers, 10 percent of the total population of Kentucky, for a week-long revival that began a tradition of evangelistic camp meetings with wild outbursts of emotion. In New Haven President Timothy Dwight built upon a sedate but general awakening of 150 western Connecticut churches to reawaken Yale. The fruits, the American Board of Commissioners for Foreign Missions in 1810, the Baptist analog in 1814, and the American Home Missionary Society of 1826, clearly reflected English pioneers. New York City Friends shared, just as Friends did in England, in such voluntary service and philanthropic groups. In the dozen years before the Quaker Separation of 1827–28, New York became the center for national organizations: the American Bible Society in 1816, the American Colonization Society in 1817, and in 1823–26 the American Tract Society, the American Sunday School Union, the American Education Society, and the American Society for the Promotion of Temperance. In their home cities New York and Philadelphia Friends shared with non-Quakers a common religious experience, home worship, Bible study, and scholarly books. Doctrines of human depravity and awareness of human needs for forgiveness were part of the experience of leaders in such groups, who were also usually the families of bankers, merchants, and factory or shipowners aware of moral ambiguity in daily decisions.

As a Quaker banker, Joseph John Gurney, from whom American evangelical Friends are often nicknamed "Gurneyites," held the two halves of his world together. In 1824 he published for his non-Quaker friends his *Observations on the Religious Peculiarities of the Society of Friends* to explain Quaker silent worship, pacifism, costume, and speech. Yet he wrote mainly for Friends his *Essays on the Evidences, Doctrines, and Practical Operation of Christianity* in 1825, in title, reliance on Bible quotations, and doctrines of God, Christ, sin, atonement, and Scripture wholly in line with English evangelicals of other churches. He himself did not travel in America until 1837, after Quakers split, but his books strongly influenced some New York Friends. Except for Henry Tuke's *Principles of Religion* in 1805, few Friends before 1820 expressed these experiences in doctrinal writing. In America they were voiced by such traveling ministers as Stephen Grellet or David Sands.

Traveling Public Friends

A list of "Public Friends that visited Long Island" offers precise documentation of Friends traveling in the ministry in New York. It includes the names and origins of 830 "Public Friends" and their traveling companions who visited Long Island between 1732 and 1827, almost nine each year. The list excludes local Long Island Friends, such as Elias Hicks. Only 151 (18 percent) were from elsewhere in New York Yearly Meeting. One-half (416) were from Philadelphia Yearly Meeting, including John Woolman and other important eighteenth-century Quakers; 110 (13 percent) were from New England, and 76 (9 percent) were from England. Others came from Ireland, North Carolina, Indiana, Canada, Virginia, the West Indies, and Tennessee. About one-third of the visitors were women. Some came repeatedly.[17] A similar list was kept by an Orthodox Friend at Shelby, Orleans County, New York, from 1836 to 1850, after the Separation. This list recorded 113 visitors, 31 of them women. One-half (57) came from within New York Yearly Meeting, 6 from Britain, and the rest from elsewhere in North America.[18]

In the fifty years after 1780, when traveling Quaker ministers flourished throughout America, they gave roots and links to the dozens of new meetings established on every frontier from the southern Piedmont to northern Vermont. The evangelicals among them have been blamed for forcing the Hicksite split,[19] but the impact of such "Public Friends" on New York meetings has not been studied from local minute books and letters. Many small older meetings or home worship groups would not have survived without them. Preparative and monthly meetings were formally "set off" and structured in new settlements within three to five years of the spate of visits.[20]

The end of the War of Independence and the years of political chaos just after it, which had left Quakers socially isolated in both England and America, freed Friends in the 1790s to reaffirm their unique identity by transatlantic visits and travel in ministry. In Woolman's day Samuel Fothergill, James Gough, and Catherine Payton Phillips had visited from England. The leading Quietist reformers who had tightened Quaker structures in the "Reformation" of 1748–83,[21] were not New Yorkers but Philadelphia Friends such as Woolman, Anthony Benezet, John Churchman, John Griffith, and James and John Pemberton. Their main work had been in their own yearly meeting, but they had traveled widely among Friends. That generation had been born in the peaceful times before 1727. The itinerants of the 1790s, born twenty years later, grew up in war times. Those who traveled widely in New York Yearly Meeting were diverse in both theology and class, yet journals in the style of Woolman's were written by Elias Hicks, born in 1748, Rufus Hall (1744–1818), Joseph Hoag (1752–1845), David Sands (1745–1818), and his much younger brother-in-law, Henry Hull (1765–1834), all New York State Friends and farmers, also by William

Savery (1750–1804), a Philadelphia tanner, Job Scott (1751–1793), a Rhode Island teacher, and Isaac Martin, a New Jersey hatter born in 1758. Many of these Friends also traveled in Europe. From England came Martha Routh (1743–1817), a schoolteacher, Deborah Darby of the family of ironmasters, and shoemaker Thomas Shillitoe, both born in 1754.[22] They became part of a network of friendship that included those Friends who were most often their hosts, who preached less but also traveled, such as John Murray, Jr., of New York, both William Rotches of New Bedford, Nicholas Waln of Philadelphia, and, in England, the Gurneys, Peases, and Reynoldses. Because they traveled when possible on Quaker ships, Deborah Darby could sail back to England in 1796 with William Savery and Samuel Emlen as they set out from Philadelphia for the visit that would convince Betsy Gurney to become Elizabeth Fry. Martha Routh sailed home in 1797 with Charity Cook of North Carolina and three other Quaker ministers when huge storms led to intense shipboard Quaker meetings. Amid the Anglo-French war they thanked God also for escapes from privateers.[23]

The itinerants adopted the old pattern of visiting every preparative meeting and worship group within each yearly meeting and often every family within a meeting in their own homes. In three winter weeks in 1800 Isaac Martin, having just crossed the Hudson three times on the ice to attend meetings, visited ninety-five Quaker and ten non-Quaker families around Nine Partners Meeting. Deborah Darby and Rebecca Young in 1793–96 pushed through blackwater swamps and sounds in Carolina, then along the Piedmont into Georgia, across the mountains to Lost Creek, Tennessee, to Redstone on the Monongahela, and north to Vassalboro, Maine. In New York they visited every meeting northward up the Hudson to Monkton, Ferrisburg, and Vergennes near Lake Champlain. Martha Routh in the same years had covered most of the same states and villages, holding sixteen meetings between Rahway and Nine Partners, eleven en route to Grand Isle on the Canadian border, and eleven more returning west of the Hudson, then (detouring to West Hartford) to a dozen meetings on Long Island. The traveling ministers rarely met each other in the wilds but had encounters like Martha Routh's with Deborah Darby in Philadelphia.

Many of the journals themselves describe the "convincement" of these itinerants through the challenge of an earlier traveling Friend. Rufus Hall during his youthful time of inner guilt was convinced by a home visit from Robert Willis, who said, "Young man, see that thou dost not endeavour to get from the sketch of the net." The humbling first call to speak in ministry left Henry Hull "in consternation, . . .

trembling" in his home meeting.[24] Deborah Darby convinced Elizabeth Fry that she might be "a light to the blind; speech to the dumb; and feet to the lame."[25] Two years earlier Deborah Darby won Stephen Grellet. The journals report the calls to undertake lengthy visits in ministry as a struggle between God's command and a selfish desire to remain silent or at least with one's family at home. The travelers spoke constantly of taking up their cross, using Penn's familiar image. They applied it as he had to the social self-sacrifice of living by the Quaker discipline of clothing, speech, honesty, and justice. They felt the personal self-sacrifice of their journeys justified their constantly calling their hearers back to purity and Quaker commitment. Some, like Grellet, left their housebound or chronically weak wives at home for years at a time and wrote of repeated inner struggles whether to continue their mission. Self-denial edged on masochism when a Public Friend such as Isaac Martin, who had already denied himself all slave-made products and war-taxed goods, curtailed his craft and moved out from New York to Rahway, accepted deaths in his family and hardships of winter travel while sick, and struggled alone by canoe or through snowstorms to fulfill a promise to a "called meeting" of Friends, non-Friends, or a "promiscuous company" of both. He felt "many a bitter cup of poverty and suffering, . . . as . . . seasons of probation and refining . . . making known to me what to do and what to leave undone."[26] Yet devout wives, mothers already of many children, may not have protested their husbands' calls. They were usually well cared for, and farmers like Rufus Hall and Elias Hicks, who regularly set out in winter, were freer from household duties in those months. Most journals describe only the author's travels; many Public Friends, like John Woolman, by careful reckoning only averaged a month or two per year away from home.

The language of Quietism, about stilling inner self-will, is not distinct in pre-1800 Quaker journals from words about "making up the sufferings of Christ" through outward discipleship.[27] Rufus Hall, claimed as a Hicksite after he died in 1818, had called each Friend to "study to be quiet, as to thy own wit; . . . as to thyself, without Divine influence, thou art a fool. . . . Thy mind must be quickened and influenced by the life-giving presence of Christ . . . to be rightly informed what to say and when to speak, and when to be silent; . . . where the message is to be delivered and who it is for."[28]

Although Sands and Grellet imported phrases on human depravity from their Presbyterian and Jansenist Catholic backgrounds, Elias Hicks also made no place for innate human goodness: "Self in man, is the son of perdition. . . . Concerning the kingdom of God, . . . nothing short of our coming into a passive state without a will of our own, as a little child, agreeably to the doctrine of our Lord, will ever qualify us."[29] Yet Public Friends respected one another's leadings as well as enjoyed one another's company. Friends who would later clash theologically felt called to travel in ministry together: Grellet and Sands with Elias Hicks and Elizabeth Coggeshall with Martha Routh in England.

David Sands, Stephen Grellet, and Joseph Hoag

Four New York Friends besides Hannah Barnard were centers of controversy and powerful ministers as well. To Elias Hicks this study will return. David Sands (1745–1816), born a Long Island Presbyterian, was convinced at age twenty-one by Samuel Nottingham from England and further by his neighbor Edward Hallock. He married Hallock's daughter, Clementina, after both families had moved to New Marlborough and Cornwall, across the Hudson from the Nine Partners Meeting, which Sands joined. He was recorded as a minister nine years later. Like other Quaker itinerants Sands bore his cross, but he also preached Christ's, saying that "we should live . . . unto Him who died for us . . . through the death of self and selfish motions of the mind" and was led by his sufferings in New England to feel that "my will was almost subject to the will of my Heavenly Father, who has led me through the water. . . . He has never taken his spirit from me." "Self should have no reputation, nor any share, especially in religious performance. The nature of man is activity, which in these [areas] ought to be laid in the dust."[30] Four years after his marriage, he had already felt called to travel in ministry to the Rhode Island meetings and two years later, 1777–79, to travel for more than two years ministering in New England and, also, nearly one year each in 1785 and 1794. There he laid the foundations for the Friends meetings in the Vassalboro and Windham areas of central Maine. Clemmie (Clementina) was literally left to mind the store while it was occupied by fifty patriot troops, although after the war Sands was at home to bring to justice—tempered with mercy—a party of young soldiers from West Point when they pillaged it. Sands went with Elias Hicks to Adolphustown in Canada in 1790 and in 1792 felt called as a prophet to warn Philadelphia of impending disaster one year before the yellow fever epidemic. He went south and admonished the slaveowners.

In 1795, after doubts about his leadings and a harrowing shipwreck off Marblehead, Sands sailed on from Maine to England. His *Journal,* including numerous letters from weighty Friends in New Bedford and

5. Joseph Hoag (1762–1846). Sketch by Marcus Mote, ca. 1840.
Courtesy Friends collection, Earlham College.

Philadelphia and from the Darbys of Coalbrookdale is mainly a trav-
elogue of his next ten years of ministry in England, Ireland, and Ger-
many. After the "United Irish" Rebellion was crushed, he attacked
Deism and Hannah Barnard in Ireland. In Europe Sands went with
Savery and three other Philadelphia Friends to Bremen, Pyrmont, and
Brunswick and on to Paris and the French "Quaker" community at
Congenies near Lyons in 1796–97 in the midst of a war that required
their being landed by smugglers off Margate on returning to England.
After his return to America he traveled in Ohio and Indiana where he
found Friends more cordial to his atonement-centered preaching.

Joseph Hoag (1762–1846) was a stern moralist, the oldest son from
a New England Quaker farm family, raised in the Dutchess County
Quaker communities centered in Oblong and Nine Partners and in

Creek Meeting. His earliest memories were of meetings for worship in homes and barns, but his first visit to a meeting house gave him a vision that he would later preach from the facing bench. He records several later visions, including premonitions of the great Separation and of the Civil War. When his father was jailed all summer for refusing to help patriot rangers, Joseph and the other children brought in the harvests. Abel Thomas, visiting Oblong Meeting, convinced Hoag "that if the manifestations of the Spirit of Christ within are faithfully obeyed, a submission of self to the Lord's disposal in life or in death [he would] go forth and tell what great things the Lord has done for his soul."[31] He spoke in meeting. About the same time he felt trapped when he was with a group of young Friends who danced secretly. He continued alternately depressed and exhorting, despite David Sands's effort to help. His failure on his own farm, a few miles north, he took as divine judgment for failures to warn others. About 1790 he moved to a log house in Vermont. His wife, Huldah, became a minister to struggling settlements on both sides of Lake Champlain. Many of their children became important Public Friends.

Within one year he, too, began a series of thirteen major preaching journeys for up to two years each to New England and Nova Scotia, to upstate New York and Upper Canada, to South Carolina and Tennessee, to Ohio, Indiana, and Iowa. He made shorter trips, notably to his former Dutchess County neighbors, to rebuke laxness in discipline, both individuals' luxury and drunkenness and groups' rebellion against the elders' shared leadings. From 1815 on he denounced the heresies of Elias Hicks about Christ and in 1819 confronted him to his face. Although he helped to reorganize rural New York Orthodox Friends after the Separation, he held ideas more like those of John Wilbur in rural New England and led the group within Ferrisburgh Quarterly Meeting, who came to be called Wilburite after his death.

Stephen Grellet (1773–1855), a highly emotional mystic, was trained as an intellectual but was shocked by unorthodoxy. A keen-faced little man, he had been born into a Catholic family of French nobility. His father was a pioneer in making Limoges porcelain. He was trained at the Lyons College of the ascetic Oratorians and shared in sacramental experiences. During the French Revolution he joined the forces of the luckless Louis XVI and after their rout fled with his brother to Holland, thence to Guiana, and finally to Long Island where Huguenot Colonel Corsa's daughter lent him a copy of William Penn's *No Cross, No Crown*. Soon after, an inner voice warning him of "Eternity, Eternity" and a talk with two traveling English Quakers, fellow guests at

6. Stephen Grellet (1773–1855). By Jane Gurney, Jr., Norwich, England. Courtesy Friends Historical Library, Swarthmore College.

the Corsas's home, Deborah Darby and Rebecca Young, converted him to Christianity and convinced him to live as a plain Quaker. He moved within a year to Philadelphia where he was accepted into membership and spoke in meetings there, taught French, nearly died of yellow fever, and in 1801 moved back to New York. His business partnership there with Robert Pearsall is entirely ignored in his *Memoirs,* but in 1804, after his three brothers (two with American wives) had returned to Europe to rejoin their parents, he married Rebecca, daughter of Isaac Collins the printer. Grellet felt a lifelong call to bring the Gospel of Christ to dark places. He is best known for four long visits of nine, forty-two, twenty-six, and thirty-seven months to Europe between and after the Napoleonic wars when he visited his family and most of the crowned heads of Europe, preaching in every kind of church and to every class in society. His wife, an invalid, never went along. He traveled

equally widely among American Quakers, visiting yearly meetings from
New England and North Carolina to Indiana. A trip that New York
Yearly Meeting asked him to share with Elias Hicks in 1808 to
strengthen the discipline in rural meetings began the theological rift
between them.[32]

The embargo and war between England and the United States cut
off most contact from 1808 through 1816. The kindest of the Public
Friends died and were replaced by harsher English visitors such as
Anna Braithwaite, Elizabeth Robson and her brother Isaac Stephenson,
and George and Ann Jones. In the wake of a war that had aligned
America with the French, they felt led to come in the 1820s no longer
like a "nanny" eager to teach the colonials Quakerism but more like an
uncle desperate to save his family from destruction by Deism. Like New
Yorkers Hull, Hoag, and Martin, Thomas Shillitoe, who belonged to
the older generation and was no maverick as a Quietist, found himself
driven to draw theological lines.

Elias Hicks: Man and Model

Elias Hicks was the most influential of the traveling Public Friends.
He was a Quietist, unlike most modern Hicksites. Phrase patterns in his
Journal show that he modeled his life on John Woolman's. Both men
were raised on family farms, largely self-taught, but constant, quiet
readers of the Bible and other books. Hicks, however, carried on the
most voluminous correspondence of any American Public Friend. His
tall, lean profile supplanted Penn's as the nineteenth-century image of
the Quaker.[33] He kept all his life his father's salt meadows on southern
Long Island on which he had hunted and fished often as a boy and
continued to cut hay with his men. He seldom lived with his father
after his mother's death when he was eleven. He moved back near the
north shore to Jericho in 1770 at age twenty-two, to take over the farm
of his father-in-law, Jonathan Seaman. Jemima had been an only child
although from a clan who had been Friends since the seventeenth
century. They had ten children, but only five reached adulthood.[34] In
1777 Jemima lost both parents and a grandparent in two days from
an unnamed epidemic. Elias Hicks's stern bearing reflected his own
familiarity with suffering. Like Woolman, Hicks had earlier served an
apprenticeship as a craftsman. While traveling between jobs as a carpenter, he had learned to dance, play cards, and race horses and had
wrestled with other youthful temptations. In a moment of crucial decision while dancing, he felt that if he had "withstood at this time the

7. Elias Hicks (1748–1830). Silhouette by Richard Fields, 1829.
Courtesy Friends Historical Library, Swarthmore College.

merciful interposition of divine love, . . . [God] would have withdrawn his light from me, . . . for with long-suffering and much abused mercy he had waited patiently for my return. . . . [Although] dancing masters plead for excuse the example of [dancing] David, we have a . . . higher example than David, Jesus Christ."[35]

After a period of inner conflict and of "watchfulness and deep humiliation" before "light broke forth," he "had many deep openings in the visions of light, greatly strengthening and establishing to my exercised mind." He always admitted his imperfections and need of God's mercy, but he accepted the discipline of Quaker life with a moral certainty that never left him. Like most of the Public Friends, he records in his *Journal* rejecting his first leading to speak in a meeting for worship, great resulting guilt, and a sense of forgiveness when he submitted to his next such leading. He was recorded as a minister in 1778.

Living close to the meeting places of both his monthly and New York Yearly meetings, until the latter moved to New York in 1794, he was soon deeply involved in many committees. The shared Quaker witness against slaveowning may have first moved him to take part in the committee visitations by which the one slave of his father, the three of his father-in-law, and others were set free. Once committed, he carried his testimony all the way, to reject all slave-made products. He believed in radical moral obedience although he felt obedience to leadings of conscience, for example by Catholics over meat in Lent, to be more important than the letter of any law.[36]

When the War of Independence broke out, he sided neither with his two patriot brothers nor with the three who called themselves Loyalists; following the Friends' testimony, he "did not meddle in the controversy."[37] Friends' reputation for nonviolence let him pass six times through the warring lines. His first such trip was in 1779 to ask Philadelphia Friends about the British rent money. Two years later he went to visit the meetings in the area near Saratoga ravaged by the war, worshipping in 15 meetings in as many days. To recover from an illness he made another tour among skeptical non-Friends farther out on Long Island. His 1797 trip to the southern yearly meetings included 143 meetings gathered for worship in 165 days. In 1803 he visited the Friends in Adolphustown, Ontario, who had been driven out of American communities after the War of Independence. In the role of Public Friend he made altogether 38 trips totaling an estimated thirty-five thousand miles, often on exhausted horses.[38]

He did not record what national or Quaker events contributed to his discernment of times and places to travel, but evidently he did not wait for local invitations. In 1782, 1792, 1795, and several other times up to 1808 he visited many meetings within New York Yearly Meeting at the request of its ministers and elders, who were troubled about the moral slackness of local Friends. Yet most of his longer trips began when he felt his mind drawn in "gospel love" to visit Friends in distant areas who faced crises. After delays for certainty, often of some months, he went to his monthly and quarterly meetings for a never-denied "traveling minute." Like Woolman, Hicks may sometimes have had multiple reasons. In November 1807 he and Jemima visited many meetings while they traveled to Nine Partners to attend the board of the new boarding school he had helped found in 1796 and placed there two of their daughters. They had outgrown the local Jericho Meeting School, whose committee Hicks had also "clerked." Except for three shorter trips, Jemima otherwise stayed at home. Elias's love for her stands out in letters to her and in his late sermons: "When we enter into union with a beloved fellow-creature, we love such a one above all others in the earth." Yet he could only let himself write her that he would "return home immediately if I were set at liberty from my religious obligations, but that is not the case." He felt ministry as the cross laid upon him.[39] He bore it often. Most earlier Public Friends had made only one to three visits to any single distant area. Hicks traveled through much of Philadelphia and Baltimore Yearly Meetings in 1797, 1801, 1813, 1817, 1819, 1822, 1824, and 1826. In his messages many themes and phrases of moral exhortation recur regularly. His constantly growing audiences included longtime members of the same meetings who were increasingly exasperated by his message. In his *Journal* Hicks does not mention until 1813 his messages that condemned slavery and totally rejected war and oaths, seldom his central topics, yet he often spoke informally, judging users of slave-made products. But in meetings of ministers and elders he was challenged for his doctrines. In a funeral at Westbury—he often shared in several per week—he

> felt led to open to Friends the three principal requisites to the being, and well-being, of a Christian: . . . a real belief in *God* and *Christ, as one undivided essence,* known and believed in *inwardly* and *spiritually.* The second, a complete passive obedience and submission to the divine will and power inwardly and spiritually manifested, which . . . brings to . . . a crucifixion of the old man, with all his ungodly deeds. The third: for the . . . well-being of a Christian, it is necessary that they often meet and assemble together, for the promotion of love and good works.[40]

The only salvation, he said repeatedly, was by "an obedience to the manifestation of the will of God by his own spirit in the soul." Hicks spoke often and humbly of his own imperfections, but he could be as harsh as early Friends on Quakers who pleaded that pleasures could be ethically neutral or complex. He said every person was reponsible for his or her own acts and would face final judgment for them. People should be "as fearful of evil thinking as they are of evil doing." The Light "if they are open to receive, would find out all their secret lurking places where *self-love* and *self-will* lie shrouded under a mask *of doing good.*" He rejected predestination, saying that even believers in it were not predestined to hate their neighbors.[41]

Like earlier Friends, he contrasted inward and outward aspects of religion, inward and outward authority, inward and outward covenants with God, quoting Jeremiah 31:31, because "God only is light, and he is in us and not without us." Like Robert Barclay and most eighteenth-century Friends, Hicks made a sharp separation between physical and spiritual, body and mind, yet he rarely condemned the physical as evil, saying that "bodies are not accountable. They are passive to the mind. . . . In the soul it is that all sin begins." So although he stressed love of brethren and enemies and attacked greed and passion, he said little about other human emotions. He sometimes spoke of reason in language typical of his day: "Nothing is a recipient for the will of God to man, but the rational soul."[42]

Hicks was a Quietist, not a rationalist. In worship he spoke often of silencing minds as well as bodies and would not speak or even pray without a leading. He deplored and attacked Deism and witchcraft as well, both of which relied on human wills and minds. He insisted that salvation is never by our own strength: "We are not to make our own resolutions in our own will to get rid of any sin." "When we centre down into a state of self-abasement and nothingness————when the . . . temple of the heart is emptied of every thing of self, . . . it can become a fit receptacle for the King of glory to . . . make himself known there." He spoke often of God as his strength when he himself "felt weakness and nothingness." When evangelicals tried to shout him down, he insisted that the meeting "sink down, . . . and be delivered from any attempt arising from the contrivance of the creature." His message in worship was often built on the text from Luke 24:49: "Tarry at Jerusalem—now Jerusalem signifies place of quiet [shalom]—Tarry at Jerusalem till ye shall receive power from on high."[43] Yet Hicks believed that "the Master's Presence" was shared by the whole meeting for worship "to the . . . tendering the hearts of many present." A truly "exercising meeting" climaxed for Hicks when "that . . . vivifying power was felt gradually to arise, by which my mind was quickened and led to minister" so that "life spread over the meeting, tendering many hearts, and we parted under a grateful sense of the Lord's mercies."[44]

He went on to affirm that "Christ formed in us is the sum and substance of the Gospel state, which is the new birth. . . . None are any further Christians, than as they come to experience the self-denial, meekness, humility, and gentleness of Christ, ruling and reigning in them." Hicks held the old Quaker doctrine that there is no "Justification," divine forgiveness, without "Sanctification," the transforming work of God within us. Like early Friends he never possessed a clear intellectual formula as to how a new personality can be created in us and in all other people while still the old self and our cultural limits remain. The new self lives only in its openness to God's spirit, moment by moment. Here Hicks turned to the meaning of the humility and obedience of Jesus, who "had no will of his own," and yet knew temptation.[45]

The debate over Hicks's ideas of Christ was more narrowly focused than modern Friends often notice. To stress the moral example of Jesus seemed to his contemporaries to make Jesus merely human:

> Here now, what a life of righteousness! [Jesus] is our example that we should follow in his steps. But if he had any more power than we have, how could he be an example to us? He had no more power than would enable him to do the will of God, and he had it in its fulness; and this every rational creature has in his proportion. He had more, because he had a much greater work to perform.[46]

At times his dualism of the outward and inward made him imply that, as an outward model, the human Jesus was the savior only of the outwardly directed Jews rather than of later ages. But he never doubted that the spirit within Jesus was the eternal Spirit-Christ and was divine. He totally identified the spirit of God, the spirit within Christ, and the Light within humans, just as Fox, Penn, and Ferris had done. Like the Unitarians of his time, Hicks seems not to have doubted Jesus' miracles or virgin birth.[47] His dualism, however, led him to talk about both the cross and the resurrection of Jesus primarily in spiritual terms, not as historical events shaping our history but as models of the death of self-will and the new birth of Christ within every person. He rejected all doctrines of the atonement by God's forgiveness that depended on anything except what happened within human hearts. He denied "that material blood, made up of the dust of the earth can be considered a satisfactory offering for a spiritual being." "The blood of the covenant is the life of God in the soul." Even heaven and hell are present states of souls.[48]

Hicks's attitude toward the Bible also began from the early Friends' contrast of the Letter and the Spirit. As in the examples cited, Hicks knew, loved, and constantly used the Scriptures, but always for a timeless and usually symbolic meaning. They were inspired, they teach true morality, but humans must turn directly to their source, God's Spirit. They must be interpreted by the Spirit, not by human effort, learning, nor Bible societies.[49]

From 1818 to 1828 Hicks found himself increasingly in arguments with evangelical Quakers over the atonement and the Scriptures. He deliberately set out to visit the four out of the five Philadelphia meet-

ings who called his ideas heresy, and wrote long letters stating his beliefs and encouraging the Friends who shared them. His followers had
no trouble finding quotations from Fox, Barclay, and Penn, distinguishing Friends from Puritans, to parallel everything Hicks said, and his
opponents found in the same writers equally outspoken statements
about Christ and the Bible to contradict Hicks. Each side clutched half
of early Quakerism. He himself, aged more than eighty, visited Philadelphia and Baltimore Yearly Meetings again in 1826 and 1828 and
traveled to Ohio and Indiana Yearly Meetings in 1828. His presence
crystallized the controversy by which American Quakers were perma-
nently divided. He wrote a journal in which he never mentioned the
devastating division and only obliquely distinguished "those called orthodox" from those he called Friends. The newly immigrated,
staunchly evangelical John Butler wrote to his English mother, describing Hicks's entry into Rose Street Meeting House: "Tall and spare [he]
took the second seat in the Ministers' gallery; . . . he had on a very light
suit with very plain round crowned White Hat, his coat was the plainest
. . . without cuffs; . . . though the morning was dry and fine he had on a
heavy pair of boots." Returned from a final trip to the Lake Champlain
meetings in 1829, Hicks died of a stroke on February 27, 1830, content
with his spiritual life as was gratefully recorded in a minute by his meeting, who shared his gratitude for "the unmerited mercy and loving
kindness of our Heavenly Father."[50] He carried to the end his mission
as Public Friend, as concerned for the life of each meeting as for individual faithfulness and truth.

The Separation in New York Yearly Meeting

The division of New York Yearly Meeting from 1828 until 1955 was
part of a much deeper cleavage that still divides American Friends over
doctrine and authority (roughly the contrast of today's Friends General
Conference with the Evangelical Friends International and much of
Friends United Meeting). From the start Friends whose experience was
evangelical called themselves Orthodox in relation to Christian tradition and blamed the split on the "unsound" teaching of Hicks and his
friends. The group that became known as Hicksites, who called themselves the "tolerants," blamed the split on the pride and dogmatism of
the yearly meeting elders. Both groups were right. Hicks made the Bible and the historical life, death, and resurrection of Jesus into symbols of timeless truth that must be known directly through the Light
within each person. Although Hicks never rejected the divinity of

Christ or the inspiration of the Bible, his attitude toward biblical history made human dependence upon atonement by Christ's death unessential. Personally, the elders feared Deism. Hicks was so "innerdirected" that he was unable to hear others' experience.

The elders were indeed authoritarian. Larry Ingle's careful study has shown that Hicks and his reforming friends worked more aggressively than historians used to assume to take power from the elders. "The followers of Hicks nearly always seemed more combative" although they aimed at uniformity in moral behavior, not in doctrine.[51] Friends had always felt called to keep in balance individual guidance with Quaker unity and sharing of truth. Early Quaker individualists, however saintly, had been "eldered:" Nayler by Fox and Keith by Penn. In each yearly meeting a committee of ministers and elders or an administrative Meeting for Sufferings had taken responsibility for supervising the travels of Public Friends and publications on behalf of Friends. In 1825 an evangelical "Demi-Quaker" pointed out tenderly the problem Friends always faced with no creeds or bishops:

> In other societies preachers of the gospel . . . are confined by doctrines and observances to which they are bound. . . . [W]ith the Society of Friends this is not the case: sincerely believing that they are called to the ministry by a . . . divine impulse and speaking without preparation under the same influence, it does require all their care, lest they mistake the operation of other causes for a call of duty. They are but men. . . . Hence arises the necessity of the greatest care in the appointment of your elders, and the most vigilant attention . . . [by these] faithful and friendly monitors.[52]

In 1812 the Philadelphia elders' proposal for a uniform book of discipline for all American Friends (a dream finally realized by the Orthodox only in 1902) was sucessfully opposed by Hicks in New York and Baltimore Yearly Meetings.

The tension had mounted for twenty years between the two Quaker groups and also in the nation from the embargo of 1808 to the presidency of Jackson. In 1808 young Stephen Grellet had become alarmed about the doctrines of Christ that he heard Hicks preach and his attacks on missionary and Bible societies. In 1811 Hicks, who had wrestled in his own yearly meeting over a ban on "prize goods" and slave produce, published his scathing pamphlet on slavery. For the next five years Hicks traveled only in the northeast while "the alarm of war [was] heard in the land." Hicks's carefully arranged southern trip in 1817 was peaceful. Yet his own earnest, brief summary of his beliefs, in reply to letters from his more evangelical Jericho neighbors, Phebe and Thomas Willis, was copied into print and began a decade of massive and bitter tract debate. An evening's chat in 1824 with the English evangelical Public Friend Anna Braithwaite, which she summarized from Liverpool, was also printed "without the knowledge of the parties concerned."[53] These attacks were often answered by Hicks's friends, who felt Hicks's "treatment [was] that which reformers of every age have experienced at the hands of the illiberal and prejudiced," but they conceded that Christ's death and "all that was outward could not possibly be more than types pointing to [the] everlasting Teacher" within. The liberal publishing at this stage was by Philadelphia and Wilmington reformers who reprinted the "Paul and Amicus" letters. Theophilus Gates edited a radical journal, *The Reformer*,[54] and Marcus Gould, the first volumes of transcriptions of the sermons of Elias and Edward Hicks and some of their friends; the Pennsylvanian painter of "the Peaceable Kingdom" was much less gentle in his language than his older cousin. Although meant to pacify Hicks's opponents, these transcripts provided them with quotations usable as further evidence of heresy: "There is a greater number . . . that serve God acceptably among [the heathen] than among those who call themselves Christians." Not only Jesus, but "every child of God has the full . . . divinity of God Almighty."[55]

Events hardened the hostility that ideas had aroused. In 1819 the Unitarians and Congregationalists split; in 1820–24 New England's dominant Quaker elders disciplined the "New Light" Friends in New Bedford. In 1818 Hicks persuaded New York Yearly Meeting not to read into its minutes an epistle from London warning against Deism. In 1819, after a visit to western Friends, Hicks spoke in all the Philadelphia meetings, including the men's and women's meetings for business of Pine Street Meeting. There he returned from a lengthy address to the women to find that evangelical elder Jonathan Evans had persuaded the men to walk out on him. Hicks's next visit to the Philadelphia meetings again drew huge crowds. His request to the liberal Green Street Friends to visit 140 of their families was challenged by elders from the other Philadelphia meetings, whose jurisdiction Hicks denied, but who insisted that "ministers are answerable to the elders." During the same month the elders made a twenty-page compilation of *Extracts from the Writings of Primitive Friends Concerning the Divinity of our Lord and Saviour Jesus Christ* to rebut the ideas of "Amicus." The reformers in the yearly meeting feared a creed and prevented it from being issued, but the elders put the text into the minutes of the Meeting for Sufferings.[56]

New York Yearly Meeting was stirred up in 1822–26 mainly by visits from evangelical English Friends: William Forster, Ann (and George) Jones, Anna (and Isaac) Braithwaite, and Elizabeth Robson. They all denounced Hicks's doctrines in his presence, in large groups, and in private homes and at times tried in vain to keep him from speaking. Last and most uncompromising was Thomas Shillitoe, a Quietist but strictly orthodox in theology, who avoided personal dialogue with Hicks but tried to travel wherever Hicks went. The books of the highly educated English Quaker banker Joseph John Gurney were also influential.

In Philadelphia deadlocks between the city elders and Green Street and Wilmington Meetings moved both sides to bitterness, not consensus. After a tense but inconclusive yearly meeting session in 1826, its elders moved toward setting up a committee to visit every monthly meeting to test the doctrinal soundness of their ministers and elders. The rural meetings' effort to head this off by doubling their representatives at the 1827 yearly meeting led to a deadlock between the evangelical, but not vindictive, clerk Samuel Bettle and the assistant clerk, Quietist schoolteacher John Comly, whom the reformers tried to put into the clerkship. After four days of shouting by both sides, Comly persuaded the liberals to withdraw to an evening gathering at Green Street, which led them to set up the framework of a second, parallel Philadelphia Yearly Meeting. Hicks was not there and was reluctant to consider separation, but in 1828 he visited the newly formed yearly meeting, which by his ideas and dominant spirit became known as "Hicksite."

The Separation, which had been meant to be only temporary and at the level of the yearly meeting, forced each quarterly and monthly meeting to choose which yearly meeting they would recognize and led to what turned out to be a permanent division within almost every meeting. Families and friends were separated for life, and each group refused to recognize the other as Friends, although only the Orthodox went on to disown every member of the opposing groups. A crucial legal case in the Court of Chancery of New Jersey over the school fund of Crosswicks Meeting, argued until 1831, provided detailed descriptions of the doctrines and grievances on both sides. The verdict awarded the property, and thereafter by precedent all other Philadelphia Yearly Meeting Quaker funds and meeting houses, to the Orthodox, forcing the Hicksites in West Chester, Pennsylvania, Moorestown, New Jersey, and many other towns to build a new meeting house as big as the old one and directly across the town square from it.[57]

The need to recognize the rights of visitors and epistles from other meetings now forced every meeting in America to choose between the sides in Philadelphia. London Yearly Meeting, with its powerful elders and evangelical families, North Carolina, and the little Virginia Yearly Meeting kept their own unity by recognizing the Christ-centered Philadelphia Orthodox elders. So did New England Friends, although they would split later. Most of Baltimore Yearly Meeting, although they divided, was Hicksite, most Indiana Friends, Orthodox. With Hicks present, Ohio in 1828 would divide savagely. New York had not been able to dodge the issue.

By 1828 Hicks's eminence was just the reason that others complained about him. Staunchly evangelical Henry Hull complained about his "sorrowful" influence. Hicks's handful of New York enemies resembled the elders in Philadelphia in their distrust of the rank and file rural Quakers who were his natural constituency. These men had for long exercised central power. Samuel Parsons of Flushing had been clerk of the yearly meeting for nearly twenty years. Most lived in or near New York City where Quakers numbered a bit more than 10 percent of the nineteen thousand yearly meeting members. They naturally distrusted majorities, especially if the majority supported Hicks. As hefty John Griscom succinctly explained, "Truth does not go by *bulk* but by *weight*." Proceeding on this basis, when Parsons faced contests, he deferred to weighty members. The elders had embraced evangelicalism, wanted to establish doctrinal conformity and belief in the Bible's infallibility, and supported mixed philanthropic and Bible societies. In the new world of commerce and industry, many had invested their excess funds in roads and canals, which Hicks opposed. They resented Hicks's "severity of expression" in mien and words. Thomas Eddy feared Hicks would prejudice "great men" of the city by "preaching against the clergy and particular popular institutions, such as missionary, Bible Societies, etc."[58]

By the time of the Philadelphia Separation in April 1827, New York Friends were verging on a split too. Hicks's rural supporters used their strength in monthly and quarterly meetings to discipline their opponents. Even in the city, Eddy had been "under dealing." In Cornwall Quarterly Meeting, west of the Hudson, the factions sent up rival responses to the Queries. New York Monthly Meeting divided about a marriage petition from a prospective groom who was a member of the Hicksite Green Street Meeting in Philadelphia. Thomas Shillitoe was appalled at the aggressive actions of Hicks's followers at the yearly meeting in May 1827. They knew their strength and intended to unleash it at the yearly meeting of 1828. Evan Lewis, a journalist and schoolteacher of Westchester, New York, who had lived in Pennsylvania, drew appropriate lessons from the struggle there. He informed the clerk of the secessionist Philadelphia Yearly Meeting that New York's "liberal" majority intended to avoid their mistake; they would see to it that when New York Quakers divided, "the *minority* will leave the *majority* in possession of the field—*and this is as it should be.*"[59] To effect this, some upstate quarters sent increased numbers of representatives and excluded others with evangelical views.

Clerk Parsons and his cohorts recognized the possibility of trouble as they prepared for the 1828 sessions. The skirmishing began on Saturday, May 24, when the evangelicals complained about the presence of unqualified (i.e., Hicksite) visitors from Philadelphia at the meeting of ministers and elders. Parsons took the precaution of writing out some minutes ahead of time, and he also left the minute books and reports from the quarters safely behind when he came to the Hester Street meeting house for the opening session on Monday, May 26. Shillitoe, who recognized Hicksites wherever he looked, initiated the conflict by rising to protest admitting the Philadelphia secessionists. Hicks rose to identify himself with the guests, to explain that he had attended the recent reformist yearly meeting in the City of Brotherly Love, and to announce himself in agreement with it. Two hours of debate later, an evangelical ventured that "the sound part of the meeting" should retire to the basement so that legitimate business could be dealt with. As if on cue, Nicholas Brown, a minister from Canada, alleged that this action pointed to a plot by the minority to separate and suggested that a new clerk, more in tune with the majority, be selected. Voices shouted the name of Samuel Mott, a suggestion Parsons ignored as he stood to read a minute that his opponents feared would adjourn the session. Some yelled, "Don't let him read it," others, "He is not clerk of the Yearly Meeting." Even Hicks could not silence the uproar as umbrellas thumped on the floor. Parsons read his adjournment minute into this din. Meanwhile, Mott was passed bodily over the heads of the audience toward the front. When he got to the ministers' gallery, Hicks reached out his hand to steady his supporter but, his grip slipping, watched helplessly while Mott tumbled into his seat. He then read a minute abolishing the evangelical-dominated Meeting for Sufferings, which had administered the yearly meeting between annual sessions.

The evangelical minority had by this time made their way to the cellar but discovered that the doorkeeper would not surrender his key. In the yard Parsons rose to the occasion and read a minute moving the meeting to a room that Griscom, foreseeing such an outcome, had previously secured at Rutgers Medical College. The evangelicals marched to their new meeting place, their faces so grave that on-lookers thought them part of a funeral procession. Someone then re-membered that they had left the women behind and rushed back to get them, but the gate was locked; not until the next morning did the evangelical women convene at the African Methodist church. Two days later, on Wednesday morning, the two factions met for worship, in their last joint session, at the Rose Street meeting house. Hicks held forth. Shillitoe did not shirk his duty to preach on the historic Christ who died outside Jerusalem, a topic sure to anger the Hicksites. At the rise of the meeting, Shillitoe made his way through the crowd, whispering that they should beware of that man Hicks. The Separation had gone quietly compared to the one in Ohio where they would next meet.

Two separate yearly meetings emerged, each claiming to date back to 1695. Parallel committees were set up, hampered by clerks who had taken the record books home. Locks were changed or newly installed on meeting house doors to keep the other side out. Each yearly meet-ing sent representatives to constituent meetings, causing divisions where there might not have been any. One observer lamented, "This is a hard time for a timid old man."[60] The split undermined a group whose peculiar testimonies had stood as a judgment, an alternative way, against the larger society and opened the way for the more rapid sub-mersion of Quakers into that society. The evangelicals had already made their peace with modern progress. Now the Hicksites, separated from the order and discipline the Orthodox had demanded, started down the same path. The "Great Separation" assured that both sides would struggle with this dilemma separately, less successfully.

The division within monthly meetings was quieter but, except in the few places where the two congregations agreed to share the meet-ing house, was equally final. This did not keep Valentine Willetts, the Willises, and other evangelicals, who eventually formed the Orthodox Monthly Meeting of Westbury and Jericho, from publishing a testimony against Hicks, duly rebutted by Evan Lewis, nor other New Yorkers from writing tracts that quoted early Quakers for and against Hicks's ideas.[61] Respect and love for Hicks, and a two to one majority of Hick-sites among New York's nineteen thousand membership, kept Friends there from the helpless anger with which the Hicksites in Pennsylvania had built new meeting houses. In New York City the two groups agreed to continue to share the burial ground (with some squabbling over gates and keys). The Orthodox did, in fact, build a new meeting house on Henry Street, leaving the Rose Street and Hester Street meeting

houses in Hicksite hands, but committees from both sides made an
effort at compromise so that the Hicksites would buy out the Orthodox
claims. A long series of letters and meetings to arrange a price or set
up arbitration was repeatedly derailed by issues challenging the validity
of the rival Meetings. New York City Friends kept the issues out of
court, despite some threats and the New Jersey precedent. An orthodox headmaster kept the Nine Partners boarding school in Orthodox
hands, although admitting Hicksite children, while a Hicksite Board of
Managers kept the school farm minus its cows.[62]

Friends had principled objections to engaging in legal disputes.
Ownership questions involving meeting houses, burial grounds,
schools, and other properties were resolved at the local level. A case
involving funds, however, was brought to trial and resulted in a decision by the Supreme Court of New York. The Hicksite treasurer of
Purchase Preparative Meeting attempted to collect a debt owed to the
School Fund. The debtor, an Orthodox Friend, felt that he owed it to
the Orthodox meeting. The case was heard in the local circuit court of
Oyer and Terminer in September 1830 with the judge ruling that the
Hicksite as the majority party at the time of the Separation was entitled
to the assets of the Meeting. A jury decision in favor of the Hicksites
was reversed in the New York Supreme Court. In September 1832
Judge Nelson delivered his opinion. He refused to consider claims
made by the Orthodox Friends that the Hicksites had "abandoned the
religious faith of the Society of Friends" because the court could only
be concerned with legal rights, not matters of religious doctrine. The
case had to be judged by the usual and accepted practices of the Society of Friends. He rejected the lower court ruling in favor of the Hicksite majority on the grounds that Friends meetings for business were
not based on majority rule and no votes were taken. The deciding factor was the role of the clerk of the meeting in opening the business
meeting. Nelson, therefore, recognized the meeting at Purchase that
had been opened by the old clerk (the Orthodox meeting) as the legal
successor of the older Purchase Meeting. Nelson set aside the ruling of
the lower court and ordered a new trial. This was held, but the original
verdict for the Hicksites was then reaffirmed in the Court of Chancery
in 1837.[63]

Tales from Philadelphia and unrecorded dialogues among Meeting
representatives at the dividing New York Yearly Meeting in May 1828
may have prepared monthly meetings to act fast. By July 1 division had
occurred in all the monthly meetings up the Hudson: in Purchase,
Nine Partners and Oblong and Stanford Quarters east of the river;

Cornwall on the west; Duanesburgh, Rensselaerville and Coeymans to the north; and Farmington near Rochester. July saw splits in almost all meetings westward to Lake Erie and northward near Saratoga and in Vermont; Easton split in August, four scattered meetings in September.[64]

In Canada the meetings near the Thousand Islands, West Lake, Adolphus, and Leeds / Adolphustown and those west of Niagara, Pelham, Norwich, Yonge Street, and Pickering (Toronto) seem to have divided in 1828. The Ontario meetings, visited by Elias and Edward Hicks and Hugh Judge but also by evangelicals William Forster, Elizabeth Robson, George Withy, Stephen Grellet, and later by Thomas Shillitoe, trusted Quietism, but most were Christ-centered and would not have split but for outside pressure. The Pickering Orthodox disowned the Hicksite clerk, Nicholas Austin, Nicholas Brown, a minister, and fifteen others in September 1828. Hicksite visitors Brown and Hugh Judge and representatives of the New York Orthodox clashed again at West Lake. By 1829 the Canada Half Year's Meeting was itself split, and in 1834 the Hicksite half joined its western New York counterparts in Genesee Yearly Meeting.[65] Not all the often far-flung preparative meetings divided, but many were so weak they had to merge. Flushing's tiny Orthodox meeting only lasted until 1830. All Friends and their meetings were weakened and shamed. The love that had carried Friends through persecution had not overcome their own anger. Their confidence that the infallible inner guidance of God's spirit would guide them to truth as a group had been broken by clashes with other Friends equally confident of different truths.

8

After the Separation

CHRISTOPHER DENSMORE
and
HUGH BARBOUR, SABRON REYNOLDS NEWTON,
ALSON D. VAN WAGNER

New York Yearly Meeting, circa 1830

After the Separation, both the Orthodox and the Hicksite branches of New York Yearly Meeting took a census of the members of the yearly meeting. This was the first time that New York Friends attempted to compile figures on membership. The two branches came up with similar totals for the overall membership of the yearly meeting but significantly different figures for the proportion of Hicksite to Orthodox. By the Hicksite count, there were 19,302 members: Hicksite, 12,532 (65 percent); Orthodox, 5,913 (31 percent); and 857 (4.4 percent), attempting to remain neutral. The Orthodox counted 19,831 members, divided into Hicksite, 10,627 (54 percent); and Orthodox, 9,204 (46 percent).[1]

Starksboro Monthly Meeting in Vermont was entirely Orthodox; all but five of the 320 members of Troy Monthly Meeting were Hicksite. In these cases only one meeting remained after the Separation. Most meetings were more evenly divided, resulting in two meeting houses, one Hicksite and the other Orthodox, where a single united meeting had stood before.

There was considerable disagreement and confusion over who held membership in the Society of Friends and about the affiliation of some Friends who were unwilling or unable to choose sides. The Orthodox counted 291 members in Oblong Monthly Meeting, but the Hicksites counted 330. If we count all people considered by one branch or the other to have been members of New York Yearly Meeting, the total membership for the yearly meeting would probably exceed 22,000.

The era of growth of Quakerism in New York State had ended. The addition of new meetings in Michigan and Canada in the 1830s and after did not offset a decline in New York. In 1869 the Orthodox branch of New York Yearly Meeting and Canada Yearly Meeting (until 1867 part of New York) had a total membership of 6,049, which was 3,000 fewer than they claimed in 1830.[2] Hicksite losses during the same period were probably greater.

The growth of New York Yearly Meeting up to 1830 had been impressive, but it did not match the population growth of New York State nor the success of other denominations. In 1700 Quakers were the third largest religious body in New York State, surpassed only by Congregationalists and the Dutch Reformed Church. In the 1845 New York State census, Quakers were still the seventh largest religious body in the state with 153 meeting houses, a figure that exceeded the number of churches for the Universalists (112), Catholics (104), and Unitarians (65). These denominations, however, were far overshadowed by the Methodists (1,123) and Baptists (782).[3]

Migration Westward to Michigan

In the 1820s New York Friends were migrating westward to Michigan. In 1829 Farmington Quarterly Meeting (Orthodox) turned its attention to these Friends and in 1831 established Adrian Monthly Meeting, which included meetings at Farmington, near Detroit, and in Logan Township, near Adrian, in Lenawee County. Orthodox meetings were later established in Lenawee County at Raisin (1834) and Palmyra (ca. 1840), at Rollin (1840s), and Tecumseh (1851). Adrian Quarterly Meeting was established in 1843.[4]

A joint committee of the Hicksite branches of Scipio and Farmington Monthly Meetings set up Nankin (later called Plymouth, then Livonia) Preparative and Monthly Meeting in 1834. Later, meetings were established at Milton (later Battle Creek) in 1834, Parma, in Jackson County (1840), Logan (later Adrian) and West Unity, Ohio (1859). Michigan Quarterly Meeting was established in 1838 as part of Genesee Yearly Meeting but was discontinued, and the meetings were attached to Pelham Quarterly Meeting in 1848 during the Congregational / Progressive separation.

The affiliation of the Michigan meetings with New York Yearly Meeting (Orthodox) and Genesee Yearly Meeting rather than with

Ohio or Indiana Yearly Meetings reflects the origins of most Michigan Friends. Members of Royalton Preparative Meeting in Niagara County, New York, moved en masse to Michigan in 1833–34, reportedly taking their record books with them, to form Raisin Preparative Meeting.[5] In Cass County, in the southwest corner of Michigan, meetings were organized under Indiana Yearly Meeting in the 1830s and 1840s.

Shrewsbury Quarterly Meeting

In the 1660s Friends moved from Long Island to Shrewsbury and Middletown in what was then known as East Jersey. Meetings were organized as early as 1665, and in 1672 Shrewsbury Quarterly Meeting was set up with the approval of Westbury Quarterly Meeting on Long Island, which was still a part of New England Yearly Meeting. One decade later, in 1682, Shrewsbury Quarter was transferred to the newly formed Philadelphia Yearly Meeting.[6]

Northern New Jersey has natural ties with New York, and in 1833 the Hicksite branch of Shrewsbury Quarter was transferred back to New York Yearly Meeting although the Orthodox meetings remained with Philadelphia. At the time of the Hicksite-Orthodox Separation there were 750 Hicksites and 175 Orthodox in the three monthly meetings of Shrewsbury Quarter: Hardwick and Randolph, Rahway and Plainfield, and Shrewsbury. The current All Friends Regional Meeting of New York Yearly Meeting, with the monthly meetings of Dover-Randolph, Montclair, Ridgewood, and Summit in northern New Jersey and Rockland in New York State, is largely a product of the revitalization of Quakerism, beginning in the early years of the twentieth century. Plainfield and Shrewsbury Half-Yearly Meeting includes the older meetings of Manasquan, Rahway and Plainfield, Shrewsbury, and the newer meetings of New Brunswick and Somerset Hills.

The Formation of Genesee Yearly Meeting

In the early 1820s, before the Separation, Friends in Western New York and Ontario proposed the creation of a new yearly meeting. It was difficult for Quakers from East Hamburg and Collins, not to mention Norwich and Yonge Street in Canada, to make the long trip to New York City to attend the sessions of the yearly meeting. In 1834 the Hicksite Quakers set up Genesee Yearly Meeting, which encompassed Farmington and Scipio Quarterly Meetings in New York State plus Upper Canada and Michigan.[7]

At first the sessions of Genesee Yearly Meeting were held in Farmington, but after 1860, the yearly meeting was held alternately at Farmington and at Bloomfield in Ontario. Genesee Yearly Meeting continued to be a transnational body until its merger with the Orthodox and Conservative branches of Canada Yearly Meeting in 1955, but it became increasingly a Canadian body as the older meetings in Farmington and Scipio Quarters declined in the later nineteenth century.

Congregational Friends

During the 1840s two interrelated issues troubled Hicksite Friends: the role of the meetings of ministers and elders, and the involvement of Friends in political movements, particularly abolitionism. The ministers and elders had special responsibility for the spiritual guidance of the Society, and anyone speaking inappropriately in meeting for worship could expect to be "eldered." Radical Hicksites, however, began to regard the appointment of some individuals to judge the spirituality of others as a practice not in keeping with true Quakerism. Hicksite Friends were split in sentiment between those who regarded the system of acknowledging ministers and the "select" meetings of ministers and elders as a necessity for nurturing spiritual growth and those who saw it as a hindrance, likely to enforce a stale orthodoxy.

The Society was also divided on involvement in the abolitionist movement. Friends were wary of political activity and involvement with worldly activities. Thus, whereas Friends such as Isaac Hopper, Lucretia Mott, and Thomas M'Clintock saw active involvement in the abolitionist movement as the logical extension of Quaker beliefs, others saw it as becoming entangled with the conflicts of the world. Neither side approved slavery, but, as Sunderland P. Gardner stated in 1846, "Wrong may be wrongfully opposed, and war may be opposed in a warlike spirit."[8] The fear of the radical Friends who were actively involved outside the Society in the abolition and temperance movements was that they would be opposed by the conservatives in the select meetings.

The issue came to a head in Genesee Yearly Meeting in 1843 when Michigan Quarter unilaterally laid down its meeting of ministers and elders. For several years the yearly meeting discussed the issue before it finally resolved the issue in 1848 by laying down Michigan Quarterly Meeting and attaching the monthly meetings in Michigan to Pelham Quarterly Meeting in Canada.[9]

The radicals considered this improper and called for a conference the week following the yearly meeting session to discuss actions. At a subsequent conference at Farmington in October, the radicals agreed to set up a new structure, without select meetings and with all power residing in the local congregations, under the title of the Yearly Meeting of Congregational Friends. Michigan Friends set up a similar meeting. Similar splits occurred in Ohio and Indiana Yearly Meetings and somewhat later in Philadelphia Yearly Meeting.

In New York Yearly Meeting (Hicksite) a similar event occurred in 1846 with the laying down of Cornwall Quarterly Meeting. Marlborough Monthly Meeting and Cornwall Monthly Meetings were attached to Westbury Quarterly Meeting at that time, and Plains was attached to Nine Partners Quarter. Marlborough Monthly Meeting was laid down by Westbury Quarter in 1848, but the insurgents kept the books of records and refused to recognize the action. The rapid decline of the Hicksite meetings on Nantucket and in Ferrisburg Quarter (laid down in 1846) may also have been related to these events although neither resulted in an organized body of Congregational or Progressive Friends.

The initial intent of the Progressive Friends was a simplified and egalitarian Quakerism, which would also nourish social action on behalf of abolitionism, peace, temperance, and women's rights. Within a few years, however, the Yearly Meeting of Congregational Friends had become the Friends of Human Progress with the sole function of an annual meeting open to all shades of reform opinion. Although these meetings, which attracted the involvement of non-Quakers such as Frederick Douglass, Samuel May, and Thomas Wentworth Higginson were highly interesting, the organization had ceased to function as a religious body with local meetings for worship. The annual meeting at Waterloo, New York, was held until at least the late 1860s. The annual meeting in Michigan became increasingly identified with Spiritualism as did the Collins Annual Meeting of the Friends of Human Progress, begun about 1856. The Marlborough Progressive Friends continued until the 1940s although apparently only as a burial society in its latter days.

Having precipitated the Separation by laying down Michigan Quarterly Meeting, the Friends of Genesee Yearly Meeting were reluctant to go further. No one seems to have been disowned for involvement in the new movement.

Radical Friends and Early Spiritualism

The modern Spiritualist movement began in March 1848 when the Fox sisters of Hydesville, Wayne County, New York, claimed that they were able to communicate with the spirit of a murdered peddler. The "mysterious noises" attracted the attention of many reformers, including Amy and Isaac Post and Eliab W. Capron, who, after initial skepticism protected and promoted the Fox sisters. The Posts and Capron were former Quakers who had left the Society of Friends in the mid-1840s to become more active in the abolitionist movement.[10] The messages received from the spirits offered the hope of continual and inevitable progress. Isaac Post, acting as a "writing medium," published *Voices from the Spirit World* in 1852 filled with messages from Quakers including George Fox and Elias Hicks. In these messages Elias Hicks apologized for his former sectarianism and over-reliance on the Scriptures and called on all reformers to work together against war, slavery, discord, and intemperance. George Fox warned that "when any association of men so bind themselves, either by rules or usages, that they set bounds to their outward aspirations of the seeking soul, then their God is made subservient to their sectarianism."[11]

The differences between Quaker and Spiritualist sensibilities about the role of women can be seen in an encounter between Susan B. Anthony and Spiritualist Andrew Jackson Davis at the Collins Friends of Human Progress Annual Meeting in September 1857. Both Davis and Anthony agreed on the need for women's rights, but Davis argued that women represented love and men wisdom. Anthony countered that if she accepted Davis's understanding of the nature of women, she would return to her father's house and never again work for women's rights.[12]

The next month, abolitionists, including Andrew Jackson Davis, attending the annual Meeting of the Michigan Friends of Human Progress had hard work to counter the idea that Spiritualism ended the need for working actively for abolition and women's rights.[13] The reformist strain in Spiritualism continued at North Collins, with Susan B. Anthony and Frederick Douglass sharing the platform with mediums at annual meetings in the 1870s and 1880s.

The Hicksite Ministry after the Separation

In the years immediately after the Separation that took place in New York Yearly Meeting in June 1828, almost every local meeting of both the resulting branches carefully recorded which of the persons who were members before the division chose its branch and which "went out" to the other. For this reason we have a rather complete list of the names of all the members of the Society in 1828.[14] No such effort was made to list those members who had been recorded as having a gift in the ministry or who had been appointed as elders. Because such recognition or appointment had been for life, it is extremely difficult to construct a list of ministers and elders before and after the Separation from minutes of the monthly meetings, many volumes of which are missing. It is generally accepted that one of the principal causes of the Separation was dissatisfaction of the faction led by Elias Hicks with the dominance of the ministers and elders in the life of the Society. It would be expected, therefore, that a preponderance of these leaders would have chosen to go with the Orthodox group. The degree of disproportion of members to ministers between the two branches is not certain, but there is ample evidence that the Hicksites were left with relatively fewer ministers than the Orthodox. The situation in any individual meeting could be quite unlike the average. It is difficult for persons acquainted with late twentieth century Quaker unprogrammed meetings for worship, where most of the participants occasionally contribute spoken messages, to realize how devastating the loss of a local recognized ministry after 1828 could be. If no minister was present, there frequently was no message. Fewer visits of traveling ministers to the smaller, rural meetings often resulted in stretches of many weeks with no word spoken. Such a situation was acceptable to older members, but was puzzling and repelling to the youth and to attenders not accustomed to the traditional waiting in silence.

Chief among the ministers left with the Hicksites, of course, was the aging Elias Hicks himself. When he died in 1830, there was no one of his popularity or power to take his place. Among the ministers traveling around the local meetings and prominent at yearly meeting were several women. Elizabeth Newport of Philadelphia was a strong influence. Rachel Hicks of Long Island was beginning her forty-five years of public ministry. Margaret Judge Brown had married Nicholas Brown of Canada, the two traveling in the ministry throughout New York and Genesee Yearly Meetings. Most prominent of the ministers of New York City Friends was George F. White, a very conservative minister most remembered for his role in the disownment of Isaac T. Hopper for joining with non-Friends in antislavery and other reform movements. Less well known, but equally conservative, was Eleazar Haviland of Dutchess County, whose fifty years as an acknowledged minister closed with his death in 1864.

Most of the small number of ministers traveling among the Hicksites after the Separation were little known or not yet acknowledged in 1828. They were about evenly divided between men and women. In addition to John J. Cornell and Sunderland P. Gardner of Genesee

Yearly Meeting, who will be treated at greater length, Elizabeth Haviland of Oswego Meeting and Daniel Griffen of Amawalk Meeting can
be mentioned. Among visitors from outside the two Yearly Meetings
were Rhoda Lamb of Mount Holly, New Jersey, and Joseph Foulke of
Gwynedd Meeting near Philadelphia. Because London Yearly Meeting
did not recognize Hicksites as Friends, there were none of the English
Friends who had been such frequent visitors in the century and a half
before the Separation.

The person from outside who spent the most time in New York
and Genesee was Priscilla Hunt Cadwallader, an acknowledged minister from Indiana. Possibly, her extended sojourns, several years at a
time from 1832 through 1855, during which she is listed in minutes as
a visiting minister to most local meetings, were as much the result of
her unhappy marriage as of calls to minister.

Rachel Hicks, daughter of the leading Long Island Orthodox
Quaker Gideon Seaman and widow of a nephew of Elias Hicks, began
traveling in the ministry in 1836 after the Separation that left her father and herself on opposite sides of the divide. Visitation to yearly
meetings, local meetings, and Friends' families from Long Island to
Iowa and from Vermont to Virginia in earlier years under very difficult
conditions of travel required her absence from the Seaman home
much of the rest of her life, which ended in 1878. During this period
the Society of Friends declined, particularly the Hicksite branch, from
a major religious group in America to one whose survival was in serious
question. But Rachel Hicks remained consistent in her conviction of
the "all-sufficiency" of the Inward Light for salvation, of the evil of a
paid ministry, and of the need for close adherence to the Discipline of
the Society of Friends. If this path led to the diminution or extinction
of the Society, she felt that such must be the will of God. In one of her
letters she wrote, "If the Society of Friends wane away, undoubtedly
another people will be raised up upon the same foundation on which
the living members of the Church of Christ have ever stood—the
'Spirit of Truth' the revealed will, the power and wisdom of God in the
soul of man."[15]

The message of Rachel Hicks was often inward and backward looking, a call for purification of the Society and of the lives of its members. She felt no call for Friends to reform society at large, leaving that
task to God. Nowhere in her memoirs does she directly mention Lucretia Mott, the reform-minded Hicksite minister whose life overlapped
eighty-five years of her own and of whose activities she disapproved.
Particularly in the later years, when attendance at Friends meetings

8. Rachel Hicks (1789–1878). From *Memoir of Rachel Hicks.*
Courtesy Haviland Records Room, New York Yearly Meeting.

had greatly declined, even by members, Rachel Hicks's visits were as much to families as to meetings for worship and business. She died quietly in 1878, assured of having gained an award of eternal life by her faithful discharge of her divinely assigned duties.

A messenger more in tune with the main body of Hicksite Quakerism was Sunderland Pattison Gardner. Born in Rensselaerville, Albany County, in 1802, Gardner moved with his parents to Farmington. Self-educated but a dynamic speaker, he soon became a leader in the new Genesee Yearly Meeting. His gift in the ministry was recognized in 1849 at the time when Hicksite Quakerism in western New York State and Michigan was being rent by defection to the more politically activist Congregational Friends and to the Spiritualists. His travels throughout Genesee Yearly Meeting in 1853 were followed by attendance at the yearly meetings in Ohio, Indiana, and Illinois. Despite obtaining little income other than from his farm, he devoted most of the rest of his life to service to the Society of Friends. By his recollection he participated in more than twenty-three hundred funeral services, mostly in the limits of Genesee and New York Yearly Meetings. In his eighties he made major addresses to both Philadelphia and Baltimore Yearly Meetings.

Gardner's message was close to that of the Universalists in whose churches he was a welcome speaker. Reason was his arbiter when dealing with matters such as the nature of Christ and the Bible. Of Christ he said: "Jesus, however, was the Son of God in the same manner that others may become the sons of God, by being led by the spirit of God; and in this sense they are joint heirs with Jesus Christ. But he did not constitute an equal part in the God-head, he was not omniscient, nor is there any omniscience save that of the One God, the Almighty Father." [16] Of the Bible he said:

> The Bible is indeed a precious book, and its doctrines are pure and holy, yet it is not "the Light," but, like John, points to that Light. If we view it in this manner it is of great use to us, and its study should occupy some of our most serious thoughts, yet we must not forget that it is only the testimony and not the substance of the Spirit; it is consequently a thing to be used, not worshipped; respected for its usefulness, not idolized for its antiquity and origin. [17]

Of a future life he said: "We do not know how it will be with us, or in what manner we shall exist; but we all seem to have hope of a life beyond the grave. We all have a desire for a future state and condition. And this, my friends, is one of the greatest evidences furnished us here." [18]

Gardner's liberalism did not extend to his being caught up in the movements for social reform. On two or more occasions he met Lucretia Mott and expressed admiration for her principles and ability, sharing her beliefs in regard to slavery, war, and temperance, but he felt that these evils were best met by preaching personal reform and that political activity by Friends was divisive of the Society of Friends. Nor did his liberalism extend to willingness to give up the traditional peculiar Quaker garb and language that he regarded as necessary marks of the Society.

John J. Cornell was born in Poughkeepsie and moved as a youth to the Genesee country, where he became a prominent minister in Genesee Yearly Meeting. Largely self-educated, Cornell did have formal education at the elementary level in New York City plus a few months at the Nine Partners Boarding School. In addition to constant reading and reflection Cornell had the benefit of mingling with most of the traveling Friends ministers who often stayed in the home of his father, William Cornell. In time he educated himself to the point where new acquaintances assumed he must have had university or seminary training as Cornell frequently remarks in his autobiography.[19] Less than two years old at the time of the Separation, he missed much of the pain of that event. His acquaintance with the Orthodox at Nine Partners Boarding School left him with mild disdain for their rigid theological views and their Bibliolatry. His felt a call to service in the ministry at age twenty; his assurance of his ability to perceive "conditions" and his confidence in his own talents led to frustration and impatience at not having his call formally recognized by Friends until he was thirty-six years old. Unlike Sunderland Gardner, who had to do most of the labor on his farm, Cornell was the manager of his father's large farm so could easily travel in the ministry without neglecting his business. Therefore, after the long-sought recognition came, he spent much of the rest of his life in that service.

In his theological views Cornell differed little from Gardner even though he was able to express them in more sophisticated language. Like Gardner and Rachel Hicks, his message was largely one of minding the Inner Light and living a moral life based on the Golden Rule. Like them, he sympathized with the movements for abolition of slavery, for peace, and for women's rights, but without becoming involved. He was involved in the temperance movement for twenty years, even running for Congress on the Prohibition party ticket, but he came to the conclusion that this was a mistake and that reform could better be achieved by example and moral suasion.

At the close of his life, after he had moved to Baltimore Yearly Meeting, Cornell had views concerning Quaker ministry that differed from those of Rachel Hicks and Sunderland Gardner and also from those of his own earlier years. "So I believe one of the great needs of the Society is a more cultured ministry, but one that does not depend upon intellectuality for its authority or direction, but only for its manner of expression, and whose dependence for its message and guidance and power upon its close spiritual connection upon the Divine Christ within the soul, a ministry that evidences that it comes not from the head but from the heart."[20]

Cornell had come to be less insistent that a message arise immediately from the silence of worship, allowing that it might arise and be developed before meeting. From his own experience he also had con-

cluded that the ability to perceive "conditions" was not an essential
qualification for a minister. He even came to question the prohibition
of financial support of persons recognized as ministers. In their closing
years the ministries of Hicks, Gardner, and Cornell consisted more of
family visitation than of delivering messages to regular meetings for
worship because of a decline in attendance and in the number of
meetings.

Cornell's views concerning the importance of the ministry also differed from the attitude of liberal and Hicksite Quakers of the twentieth
century as expressed in discontinuance of recognition of gifts in the
ministry. New York Yearly Meeting in the 1907 revision of its Discipline
made the recognition of ministers little different from the appointment and terms of elders. The 1930 Discipline mentions neither ministers nor elders, their counterparts being only members of Meetings for
Ministry and Counsel.

At no time did Genesee and New York Yearly Meetings have a
prominent recognized minister as reform-minded as Lucretia Mott. If
one had arisen before about 1870, it seems likely that minister would
have been disowned. Peace in the Society was deemed more important
than vision. There were a number of ministers other than those mentioned here, but generally they were of lesser ability and served only in
their declining local meetings. Able men and women ceased being
called to a lifetime of preparation for a role with little reward or acceptance by the Society. Had the Society adopted Cornell's goal of a "cultured ministry," would the path of twentieth-century Quakerism been
different?

Orthodox Friends after 1828

The divisions in the North American yearly meetings in 1827–1828
caused a realignment among Friends. Although Hicksites were the majority of New York Yearly Meeting, both New England and North Carolina Yearly Meetings, with the exception of a few Friends in Nantucket,
remained Orthodox. More significantly, London Yearly Meeting recognized only the Orthodox bodies as Friends. This meant that Orthodox
Friends would continue to be visited by Friends from the British Isles
and to be influenced by movements within British Quakerism.

The extent of the division between Orthodox and Hicksites before
the 1860s should not be overemphasized. Although the Orthodox in
particular were reluctant to do anything to recognize the legitimacy of
the Hicksites, individuals on both sides read one another's publica-

tions, occasionally attended one another's meetings, and shared common practices. The Orthodox tended to be more theologically similar, whereas the Hicksites were more theologically diverse.

In 1867 the Canadian meetings belonging to New York Yearly Meeting (Orthodox) were set off to form Canada Yearly Meeting. Orthodox Friends in Adrian Quarterly Meeting considered joining Canada Yearly Meeting but in 1869 decided to join Ohio Yearly Meeting. By these acts the territory of New York Yearly Meeting (Orthodox) was reduced to New York State and Vermont and a few meetings in Massachusetts and Connecticut. As noted, Hicksites in New York State were divided between New York Yearly Meeting (Hicksite) and Genesee Yearly Meeting, which encompassed western New York, Canada, and Michigan.

New Methods and Revivalism

In the thirty-five years before the Civil War, New York State was the center of more kinds of religious ferment than any other part of the country in any era. The revivals of Charles G. Finney and others in 1825–32 gave western New York State the nickname of "the Burned-Over District" and has made the region and period the subject of scholarly studies.[21] The direct impact upon Friends of revivals and of the resulting new ideas of holiness, however, came only after the Civil War.

The revivals changed by human effort the convert's relationship not only to humans but to God. The Great Awakening of 1740 had divided Presbyterians into "Old" and "New Lights," but both had been Calvinists, trusting that every event, but particularly conversions, came only at the times that God willed. The Quaker Quietists' "waiting upon God" was similar in spirit. After 1800, the "New Haven Theology" tried to make more room for human freedom to accept or reject God's grace. But Charles Finney's 1835 *Lectures on Revivals of Religion* treated the "New Methods" as instruments for conversion God placed entirely in human hands.

New forms of radical religious movements in upstate New York emerged after and partly because of the revivals. The forms of perfectionism, which included the utopian communities like Oneida, the Skaneateles Commune, and various Fourieristic communities, were aspects of the nationwide optimisim of early nineteenth century America, undergirded by new ideas of human nature by theologians such as William Ellery Channing and Ralph Waldo Emerson.[22] Sanctification, in

Methodist ideas of human perfectibility, seen as pure love and self-dedication, seems to come suddenly and totally. This "Holiness doctrine" was preached by Finney and Asa Mahan at Oberlin. The impact of this movement upon Friends came mainly after the Civil War, but concern about holiness and human perfection had always been a mark of Quakers.

The Temperance Movement

The ultra phase of the temperance movement drove most pastors and many revival converts to total abstention as individuals. Friends had been warned against drunkenness, against "importing or distilling or selling spirituous liquors" or even "selling grain or produce for the purpose of distillation" by the Disciplines of every yearly meeting although no yearly meeting endorsed Friends joining groups "in the mixture" with non-Friends. More Friends were disowned for intemperance than for any other offense. James Mott of Moreau, near Saratoga, after nearly dying of overdrinking in 1808, founded with his friends the pioneer Union Temperate Society of Moreau. Susan B. Anthony, whose father had run a temperance guesthouse in Battenville, New York, became a founder of the New York State Temperance Association before going on to champion women's rights.

Wilburites in New York Yearly Meeting

Between 1837 and 1840, English Friend Joseph John Gurney (1788–1847) toured North America. Gurney was a learned man and a moderate reformer whose books on Quakerism and the Bible were influential in both England and America. His *Observations on the Distinguishing Views and Practices of the Society of Friends* (1824) was reprinted at least eight times by New York Friends between 1840 and 1886. To conservative Friends, such as John Wilbur (1774–1856) of Rhode Island, Gurney and other English Friends were relying on an intellectual understanding of the Bible rather than the Quaker understanding of the inner workings of the spirit.[23] The theological debate between conservative-Quietists and evangelical Friends in England was continued in the "Beacon Controversy" in the mid-1830s.[24] In 1837 Joseph Hoag of Vermont spoke against those Quakers who would "mingle with the world" and had turned "from the primitive principles of a self-denying, cross-bearing life, to one more in the will and wisdom of the creatures" and predicted another separation.[25]

The result of this controversy was the division of New England Yearly Meeting in 1845 into a "larger body" of Gurneyites and a "smaller body" of Wilburites.[26] London Yearly Meeting and most of the Orthodox yearly meetings in North America recognized the larger body as New England Yearly Meeting, although there was substantial Wilburite support in Ohio and Philadelphia Yearly Meetings. In New York Yearly Meeting a Wilburite minority in Ferrisburg Quarter in Vermont and in Scipio and Farmington Quarters in western New York at first resisted recognition of the New England Gurneyites but finally split from New York Yearly Meeting in 1846–47. In 1853 the Wilburite Quarterly Meetings united to "re-establish on its ancient foundations" New York Yearly Meeting, which would thereafter be held at Poplar Ridge, Cayuga County, New York.[27]

Wilburites were a small minority. A delegation to Scipio Quarter from New York Yearly Meeting in 1848 reported 117 Wilburites of a total of 381 Friends in Scipio Quarter. Adding the Wilburites of Ferrisburg Quarter and a scattering of Wilburites in Farmington Quarter and elsewhere, the total membership of the Wilburite branch of New York Yearly Meeting was probably no more than 300. Their strength was further divided by a separation in 1859 into "Otisite" and "Kingite" Yearly Meetings, in part over the editing of Joseph Hoag's *Journal.* The two factions reunited in 1881 and became part of Canada Yearly Meeting (Conservative) in 1916. The Wilburites did maintain ties with the Fritchley Friends in England, with the Maulite Friends in Ohio, and with Wilburite-minded Friends in Philadelphia Yearly Meeting, particularly those who published *The Friend.*

The fragmentation of the Society of Friends increased in the thirty years after the separation of 1828. Wilburites, now subdivided into Otisites and Kingites had left the Orthodox Yearly Meeting. Radical Friends had left the Hicksite meetings in Marlborough, Waterloo, North Collins, and Michigan to form new meetings of "Progressive" Friends that evolved into all-purpose annual gatherings of reformers. The Society of Friends had also declined in numbers in New York State, probably because of a number of factors, including discouragement over continued conflict and the migration of New York Friends westward. Friends were beginning to wonder if their movement would survive. There were also less-tangible changes, moving both Hicksite and Orthodox Friends toward the mainstream of American society.

9

Quaker Education

MARY FINN
and
CHRISTOPHER DENSMORE

Religiously Guarded Education

In 1690 the London Yearly Meeting epistle urged Friends to establish Quaker schools so that Quaker children could be educated without learning the "corrupt ways, manners, fashions and languages of the world."[1] Although there were Quaker schools and schoolmasters in colonial New York, these have left few records. It was almost one century before New York Yearly Meeting succeeded in establishing schools that had the permanence of what is now Friends Seminary (1786), the oldest continuing Quaker school in the meeting.

The increased educational activity by Quakers that resulted in the founding of Friends Seminary and the Nine Partners Boarding School (1796) may have been related to the Quaker reformation of the mid-eighteenth century. The tightening of the discipline, coupled with birthright membership, made it essential to educate Quaker youth in Friends' customs and manners to ensure their compliance with the Discipline.[2] Yet there was a contradiction because the basic tenet of Friends' testimony, the Light (or Teacher) Within, meant education was unnecessary for salvation.

Some Friends argued that education was unnecessary. George Fox and other early Friends spoke strongly against the prevailing devotion to language studies and the view that one needed to be versed through university training in the scholarly languages, Latin and Greek, to be a minister. Because Quakers had abolished that hireling profession (or rather had abolished the laity by making each member a potential minister), they saw no need for university education.

To William Penn and other Quakers interested in education, the emphasis on classical languages was not the only problem with traditional schooling. The following quotation from Penn's *Some Fruits of Solitude* (1693) typifies an attitude toward education shared by many adherents of the new philosophy of experimental science that arose in England contemporaneously with Quakerism and that contributed eventually to the demise of the classical education of the Renaissance.[3]

> We press their memory too soon, and puzzle, strain and load them with words and rules; to know grammar and rhetoric, and a strange tongue or two, that . . . may never be useful to them; leaving their natural genius to mechanical and physical, or natural knowledge uncultivated and neglected. . . . To be sure, languages are not to be despised or neglected. But things are still to be preferred. Children had rather be making of tools and instruments of play . . . than getting some rules of propriety of speech by heart.[4]

Penn was explicit about the connection between the new science and the appeal to the immediate experience of the Spirit, which is the core of Quakerism. He avowed his loyalty to the experimental method in both the natural and the supernatural worlds, saying that he did not trust his "share in either to other men's judgement, at least without having a finger in the Pye for myself." Developing the intellectual or reasoning capacity through education may not lead to a "saving knowledge of God," but, as Robert Barclay stated, "We do not hereby affirm, as if man had received his Reason to no purpose. . . . We look upon Reason as fit to order and rule Man in all things Natural."[5]

Quakers believed children should be denied nothing "that may be honest and useful for them to know."[6] Believing, however, that "The will is not moved by the intellect but by something higher or lower than the intellect," and that "the forces below are not overcome by thought and reason by forces above," education to most Quakers was primarily moral or religious education. Because Quakers denied the right of any to compel the religious life of another, and because they emphasized direct experience rather than ideas and theological concepts (notions and airy knowledge), they felt that religion could not be taught directly. Children, instead, were to be constantly exposed to religious influence. The river of childhood needed to be confined by the banks of guarded education, one which educated children in civil and useful matters while protecting them from dangerous influences that might cause them not to hear or heed the Divine Guidance of the Teacher Within.[7]

Guarding the child so that the still small voice can be heard, however, requires more than assuring the negative absence of evil; it also requires the positive presence of good. Creating the pedagogical forms of this presence is a difficult task. Early Quakers relied on the religious influence of the meeting, the center of all Quaker schools, to teach the basic Quaker testimonies of community, equality, harmony, and simplicity. Some, however, found this indirect method of education, embodying the lessons in the very structure and process of meetings for worship and business, insufficient, and tensions developed regarding the need for more direct religious instruction.

Friends Seminary

In 1780 New York Yearly Meeting recommended that each meeting establish a school. New York City Friends appointed a committee the same year, and in 1781 they sent to London for a schoolmaster, "a young man, unmarried, a member of our Society, of an exemplary life and conversation, a very good writer, well vers'd in Arithmetic and with a competent knowledge of English Grammar."[8] The new school, located on Pearl Street, was under the care of New York Preparative Meeting as of 1784. In 1794 the school accepted boys aged seven to fifteen and girls to age fourteen.[9]

In 1825 there were approximately four hundred Quaker children in New York City, but Friends Seminary had only sixty students. To reach more students without raising costs the school adopted the "modern plan" of monitorial instruction the following year. But this monitorial system was dropped after a single year. Quakers found its discipline and system of rewards and punishments un-Quakerly. The incentives used in the monitorial system to reward good students— badges, prizes, rewards, and honors—were thought to "kindle a passion for honor and power."[10]

In 1826 the tuition rates for the new enlarged school on Elizabeth Street were paid by the monthly meeting for the children of Quakers. The first class of "abecedarians" were charged $1.50 per quarter as was the second, or spelling, class. The third class studied spelling, reading, writing, and arithmetic and paid $2.50 per quarter. The fourth class added geography for the same fee, but the fifth class included grammar, and the fee went to $3.50. The highest, or eighth, class paid $5.00 per quarter and studied bookkeeping, surveying, navigation, geometry, and algebra.[11]

Quaker teachers attempted to shield the school from corrupting outside influences and were suspicious of classical education. The school day started with Bible readings followed by silence. But after the 1828 Separation, the seminary could no longer afford to be strictly Quaker, and by 1865 only 20 percent of the students were Friends. The school had moved to its present location on Rutherford Place by 1860. Prizes were reinstated, classical and college preparatory courses were offered, and Friends Seminary became a worldly finishing school, separate and unequal, where children were guarded against the poor and socially impure.[12]

Between 1876 and 1885 a new Quaker principal, Ben Smith, adopted Pestalozzian methods, which laid the foundation for progressive education. Lessons were taught, not merely heard. Mechanical recitation was replaced by education for "self-instruction, self-government and self-education." Smith established a core curriculum, and aimed to "combine practical work with development of reasoning faculties." In 1878 a kindergarten, one of the first in New York City, was opened at the seminary, and as early as 1890 manual education was offered, years ahead of other private schools.[13]

Reforms at the turn of the century by Principal Edward Rawson included greater concentration on developing students' thought. But Rawson refused to arm the school during the aroused patriotism of 1916, even ignoring the New York State law that made military drill compulsory for boys over sixteen, which led to his early retirement. His successor was more supportive of the war effort. In the prosperous 1920s the concern in progressive education for assuring optimal development of each individual held sway. Self-expression of the individual, however, needed to be balanced with self-discipline in a Quaker school.[14]

In the post-World War II era Friends Seminary faced issues of race and student activism that only rose to the level of national concern in the 1960s. Prosperity had returned after the war, and weekly meeting for worship was replaced with school assemblies. Only when Principal Ernest Seegers came from the Oakwood School in 1966 was meeting for worship restored to a central place in the life of the school. The swing of the pendulum between the health of the spirit and the development of mind, which had long characterized Friends Seminary, appeared more extreme as critics argued that to be more Quakerly was to be less excellent. The tension between the intellectual and the spiritual, the inward and outward authority, instruction and intuition was finally resolved in the 1970s with the realization that Friends Seminary was an excellent school, not despite being Quaker but because it was Quaker. "To be a Quaker is to be an educator if only of oneself, and to sit in any Meeting is a chance to learn" from the Teacher Within.[15]

Nine Partners Boarding School

Friends Seminary filled the needs of Quakers in New York City, but the desire of Friends elsewhere in the yearly meeting for education beyond the primary level was still unmet. In 1793 an Association of Friends was formed to solicit funds to establish a school in Dutchess County under the direction of Nine Partners Monthly Meeting. When this effort failed, the funds were offered to New York Yearly Meeting to start a boarding school. In 1795 Joseph Tallcot (1768–1853), a leading figure in the earlier effort, met with others in New York City and requested New York Yearly Meeting support of the plan for a boarding school.

John Murray, Jr. (1758–1818), an active member of many Friends educational concerns in New York City, was also on the committee for a Yearly Meeting school. When his brother Lindley, the grammarian, heard of the plan to start a boarding school under the care of New York Yearly Meeting, he wrote John recommending the Ackworth School in England as a model.[16] Ackworth, the first large boarding school founded and supported by London Yearly Meeting (1779), was the culmination of eighteenth-century Friends' thinking about education and served as a precedent for Friends' boarding schools. At Ackworth, all staff from housekeepers and domestics to teachers and all students were Quakers; the school functioned as a large Quaker family.[17] One of the requirements for the first superintendent of the Nine Partners School was that he prove his "suitableness for a member of a large family."[18] Nine Partners was established in 1796 but not without trials and tribulations and financial sacrifice by Tallcot and others. In 1812 Principal James Mott (1742–1823) reported there were 140 students, equally divided by sex, and that "all parts of the house are occupied." They were comfortable, however, as he said they had "a very orderly parcel of scholars." The two male teachers at this time, Jacob Willetts and Goold Brown, both authored textbooks used in the New York City public schools. All the faculty, according to Mott, had literary qualifications for the branches they taught, "and I trust some of them [are] not wholly devoid of a religious sensibility which qualifies for the moral instruction of children." The tuition for reading, writing, and arithmetic, was twenty-six pounds per year. With grammar added, the tuition was twenty-eight pounds.[19] Principal James Mott is not to be confused with his grandson, James Mott (1788–1868), an early student and then teacher at Nine Partners, who married another former Nine Partners student and teacher, Lucretia Coffin.

Nine Partners Boarding School was laid down by New York Yearly Meeting in 1852, but the property was leased and remained in use as a school until 1863. In 1858 New York Yearly Meeting (Orthodox) opened a boarding school at Union Springs, New York, which was originally called Friends Academy or the New York Yearly Meeting Boarding School but was later renamed Oakwood Seminary. In 1920 Oakwood moved to Poughkeepsie, New York, a few miles west of the site of the original Nine Partners School at Millbrook. Despite the brief suspension of 1852–58, Oakwood School represents the continuity of concern for secondary education under the care of New York Yearly Meeting that began with Nine Partners Boarding School in 1796.[20]

Brooklyn Friends School

Brooklyn Friends School was begun as a day school in 1867 in the basement of Brooklyn Friends Meeting House. The proposal to establish the school originated in the Brooklyn Women's Preparative Meeting; after a "conference" with the Men's Meeting, which held the purse strings, a joint committee was founded. The proposal was set before New York Monthly Meeting, which referred it to the trustees of the schools, authorizing them "to open a school should the way open for it after examination."[21]

Mary Haviland was appointed teacher, at a salary of four hundred dollars per year in a classroom fitted for fifty students who were promised a "thorough, practical, and guarded education." During the next year an additional teacher was appointed, and together the two women taught nine classes of reading, seven in arithmetic, three each in spelling, writing, and geography, two in composition, and one each in history, grammar, philosophy, and physiology. Each class was so crowded "it was not possible to give 15 minutes to each recitation."[22]

Women continued to head the school until 1907 when Edward Rawson was assigned to serve as principal of both Friends Seminary and Brooklyn Friends. Many progressive innovations of the times were in evidence; "discussions" were emphasized more than drill and repetition, manual training, art, and gymnastics were increased, and concern for students' health led to fitting the roof of the new school (built in 1902 next to the meeting house) with out-of-door school rooms. Certain elements of self-government were also introduced in the high school, in the form of a "Charter of Friends School" which provided that school rules would be made by the students, subject to the approval of the principal.[23]

Rawson was replaced in 1913, at which time Brooklyn was the larger of the two schools under the care of New York Monthly Meeting. Later principals continued Rawson's innovations, extending the policy of school studying and reciting on the roof and expanding the extracurricular activities, which dovetailed with the school's policy of giving "the children employment in agreement with their whole nature."[24] Brooklyn Friends purchased its present facility (formerly Brooklyn Law School) in 1969. In 1993 approximately 350 students were enrolled in prekindergarten through twelfth grade in a community guided by Quaker ideals of tolerance, compassion, equality, and nonviolence.

Other Friends Schools

The history of nineteenth-century Quakerism is replete with examples of less-permanent efforts to provide the Society's children with a guarded education.

In 1811 Joseph Tallcot opened a Friends' school in Scipio Quarter, where he had moved in 1807. This school was to include the children "of a few of those of our neighbors who are not members, but will be comfortable with the order of the school." In seeking funds for this enterprise he wrote that if only Friends "could realize the numerous . . . children who are growing up without benefit of a Friends' school, whose parents . . . are either new members of Society, or else . . . not very well qualified to train up their offspring in the way they should walk," he was sure Friends would be more generous.[25]

Some Friends apparently tried "to throw in the way discouragements," and James Mott wrote to Tallcot wishing more Friends would contribute to the establishment of schools. "It is not from want of ability," Mott said, that "the guarded education of the precious youth is so neglected . . . [but] the too prevalent, though mistaken idea, that school learning, however guardedly obtained, tends to obstruct religious improvement."[26]

The issue of the routine reading of the Scriptures in school caused controversy. With few new members coming into the Society by convincement, the welfare of Quakerism depended, in Tallcot's view, on "the proper education of the rising generation."[27] Because Quakers were scattered and Quaker schools not always available, Tallcot turned more and more of his attention to encouraging Bible instruction in First-day schools and advocating religious instruction of all children in public schools. He met resistance from those who felt that the Scriptures should not be read unless "a religious impulse lead thereto." Some believe, he reported, that "we must come away from the letter and attend to the spirit and nothing else."[28]

In 1815 Tallcot helped establish a boarding school for girls in Aurora, New York. Again, he faced opposition from Friends and was advised to keep the school "low and small" to "rise over opposition and be patronized and supported by those [influential Friends] who now raise objections." James Mott, who wrote in 1818 to express his pleasure on hearing that the school in Aurora was prospering, questioned the wisdom of including non-Quaker children. "Is it best," he asked, "to mix Friends' children with those of other societies in a boarding school? Is there not danger of their becoming unprofitably attached to some habits and customs which we are endeavoring to guard them against?"[29]

Despite the desire for "select" schools limited to Friends' children, many non-Friends were educated in Quaker schools. In 1846 Nine Partners reported that only one-third of its students were members of the Society of Friends.[30] The "non-Friends" unquestionably included Hicksites attending the Orthodox Nine Partners School. The figure also suggests that many non-Quakers chose a Quaker education for their children. In modern times Quaker students make up only a fraction of the student body at Friends Seminary, Oakwood, Brooklyn Friends, and Friends Academy.

The ideal of a "religiously guarded education" was also difficult to attain. In 1838 a report to New York Yearly Meeting (Orthodox) on education revealed that only 15 percent of Quaker children were being educated in the schools under the direct supervision of Friends' meetings with another 25 percent in schools taught by Friends. The majority of Quaker children were being taught in local district schools (49 percent) or had received no schooling in the previous year (13 percent). The report attributed the lack of meeting schools to the scattered locations of Friends' families, the lack of qualified Quaker teachers, the lack of money, and the low cost of tuition in the public schools.[31]

Several efforts to correct this situation were undertaken by the quarterly meetings. Pickering College at Newmarket, Ontario, a secondary school connected with Canada Yearly Meeting, had its origins as the West Lake Boarding School, which opened near Picton, Ontario, in 1841. In 1837 Farmington Quarterly Meeting (Orthodox) recommended to the yearly meeting the creation of "Manual Labor" schools combining instruction in "classical and scientific study" with physical labor by the students that would both improve the students' health and help support the school.[32] Farmington's attempt was short-lived although the planned institution formed the basis for Macedon Academy. In Michigan, Adrian Quarter successfully opened a manual labor school in the 1850s. Perhaps the most successful manual labor school within the territory of New York Yearly Meeting was the Raisin Valley Institute, notable for its interracial student body, which Quaker Laura Smith Haviland established in 1837. Chappaqua Mountain Institute was established by Purchase Quarterly Meeting (Hicksite) in 1870 and was operated as a boarding school by the quarterly meeting until 1906.

Because most "Quaker" schools were independent rather than under the direct control of a Quaker meeting, it is uncertain how many such schools existed. Quaker letters and diaries of the early nineteenth century mention many schools that otherwise have left little documentary record. Susan B. Anthony was taught in a local school by a graduate of the "Rensselaer Quaker Boarding School" and Anthony later taught at a Quaker school in New Rochelle. Anthony's letters refer to another Quaker boarding school at Tarrytown.[33] In the same period Emily Howland attended Quaker schools taught by Susanna Marriott at Aurora and then the Poplar Ridge Seminary, both Quaker institutions.[34] A tentative listing of Quaker-related schools during the early nineteenth century would also include "The Hive" in Skaneateles, taught by Lydia Mott, and the Henry Street School in New York City, taught by Goold Brown in the 1820s. In the 1850s and 1860s the Hicksite *Friends Intelligencer* carried advertisements for the Union Vale Boarding School at Oswego Village (Dutchess County), Friends Seminary (Easton, Washington County), the Lake School (Oneida County), Genesee Valley Seminary (Monroe County), and the East Hamburg Friends Institute (Erie County).

Friends Academy in Locust Valley, Long Island, was founded in 1877 by Gideon Frost (1798–1880), a Hicksite Friend and member of Matinecock Meeting, for the "children of Friends and others similarly sentimented" to obtain literary and scientific instruction. It operated as a boarding school until 1959 when it became a day school. Although Friends Academy was never under the care of a Friends meeting, its Board of Trustees included a majority of Long Island Friends, and the school continues today as a Quaker-related institution. A 1982 accreditation report lauded the school's "constant and consistent integration of Quaker ideals into a largely non-Quaker constituency."[35]

Not all New York Friends received their education in New York institutions. The 1849 catalog of Friends Boarding School at Providence, Rhode Island, listed a small but significant contingent of New York Yearly Meeting Friends, and the school was then under the supervision of Silas and Sara M. Cornell from Rochester, New York. Friends from other yearly meetings also attended New York schools.

Recently Founded Friends Schools and Programs

Some twentieth-century schools founded in this long tradition include the Westbury Friends' School, begun in 1957 to meet a community need for the kind of education Friends desired for their own children in nursery through sixth grade. At the other geographical end of New York Yearly Meeting, the Rainbow School was begun in 1979 under the care of Fredonia Meeting and the guidance of Faith Woolson for children in kindergarten through eighth grade. Another western New York Quaker school, the Blossom Garden School (kindergarten–twelfth grade), was started by Janice Ninan in 1976 under the care of Collins Meeting. The Mary McDowell Center for Learning, located in the Brooklyn Meeting House, is a Quaker school for children of average or above-average intelligence, ages five to eleven, who have special learning disabilities. Scarsdale, New York, Ridgewood, New Jersey, and Wilton, Connecticut, meetings have long conducted nursery schools in their meeting houses. Friends World College, established in 1965, is described in chapter 16.

Collegiate Instruction

The development of collegiate-level education for Friends was a joint effort between New York, Philadelphia, and Baltimore Friends. In 1815 John Griscom published an open letter to several Friends in Philadelphia, proposing the establishment of a "Barclay College" at some site convenient to Philadelphia.[36] Nothing came of this early effort, but the concern was revived in 1830 in the pages of the *Friend* and by meetings in New York City and Philadelphia, resulting in the establishment of Haverford College, which opened in 1833, west of Philadelphia. Although the majority of the support for Haverford came from members of Philadelphia Yearly Meeting, New York Friends, including John Griscom and Samuel Parsons, were among the founders of the college. Haverford's first graduating class of two in 1836 included one New Yorker and one Philadelphian.[37] Swarthmore College, the Hicksite equivalent of Haverford, came from joint efforts of Baltimore, Philadelphia, and New York Friends, was chartered in 1864, and opened for instruction in 1867.

In 1863 the Young Ladies Collegiate Institute, later known as the Howland School, was founded at Union Springs, New York, with Robert Bowne Howland as superintendent. Students at the school elected a Modern Language, Classical, or Scientific Curriculum. Some students at the Howland School were students from Emily Howland's school for African-American girls at Arcadia, Virginia. Henry Hartshorne of Haverford succeeded Howland as president of the school from 1876 until the school closed in about 1881.[38] M. Carey Thomas, the longtime president of Bryn Mawr College, attended the Howland School in the 1870s before transferring to Cornell. Cornell University itself, opened in 1868, was founded by a former Quaker, Ezra Cornell (1807–1874), born in DeRuyter, New York, who had been disowned in the 1830s for "marrying out" of meeting.

First-day Schools

The earliest Quaker "First-day Schools" in New York were those organized by the Clarkson Association in New York City in 1815 to teach adult slaves and freed blacks to read the Bible. Similar schools were taught by Friends in Flatbush, Brooklyn, incurring the opposition of the slaveowners. A different type of First-day school was organized at Scipio under the supervision of Joseph Tallcot in 1817 and is credited as being the first school for scriptural instruction of Friends' children on First-day (Sunday) in the United States.

Orthodox Friends frequently expressed concern for the scriptural education of their children, but it appears that First-day schools did not become general in New York Yearly Meeting until the 1850s when meetings were supplied with guidelines published by the New York Tract Association of Friends and lessons prepared by New York Friend Mary S. Wood.

Hicksite interest in First-day schools awakened in 1860 as part of their traditional interest in a "guarded education" of their youth. Gideon Frost, in a letter to the *Friends Intelligencer,* advocated First-day schools as a vehicle for teaching the "distinguishing doctrines" of Friends. Fellow New York Yearly Meeting Friend D. E. Gerow dissented. Gerow feared that such schools represented a "mingling with the spirit and friendship of the world" and might "divert the inexperienced and youthful mind from a steadfast reliance upon the saving operation of divine grace, or light of Christ within." Most Hicksites sided with Frost, and First-day schools became a feature of Hicksite meetings by the end of the 1860s.[39]

The difference between Hicksite and Orthodox Friends in midcentury is shown in the curriculum of the First-day schools. The Orthodox schools stressed scriptural instruction and bringing students to the knowledge of Christ. Hicksite schools, although teaching the Bible, also stressed practical morality and an emphasis on distinctive Quaker teachings. Both Orthodox and Hicksite First-day schools reached beyond the membership of the Society of Friends; in 1863 only 610 of the 1,663 scholars enrolled in the Orthodox schools were members of the Society.

Schools for Non-Quaker Children

In the early nineteenth century Friends provided active and effective leadership in developing schools for children of non-Friends, especially in New York City. This work, conducted largely by philanthropists who were not themselves educators, provided elementary schools for poor children whose parents were not attached to any church, which made their children ineligible for existing denominational charity schools. In this effort Quakers worked alongside non-Quaker philanthropists.

The New York African Free School began in 1787 with a bequest of two hundred pounds from Robert Murray to the Manumission Society, which ran the school until it was taken over by the New York Public School Society in 1834.[40]

In 1798 a group of Quaker women met at the home of John Murray and Catharine Bowne Murray to establish the Association for the Relief of the Sick Poor. Catherine was appointed treasurer and served in that position for nineteen years. The "Female Association," as it became known, established several schools for female students for whom no other provision was made. By 1817 there were 600 girls in several schools and by 1825, 750 pupils. These schools were absorbed by the New York Public School Society in 1845.[41]

When John Murray proposed that Quakers establish a free school for non-Quaker children, Thomas Eddy recommended that they also seek the involvement of non-Friends. The subsequent organizational meeting held at Murray's home in 1805 included four Quakers and eight non-Quakers selected by Murray and Eddy. The resulting organization bore the lengthy title, "Society for the education of such poor children as do not belong to, or are not provided for, by any religious

Society," which was later shortened to New York Public School Society (NYPSS). DeWitt Clinton, mayor of New York City and, later, governor of the state, was their first president. Public School No. 1 opened in 1806 with forty-two scholars. This Quaker-initiated NYPSS was the origin of the New York City Public School system.[42]

Public School No. 1 was the first school in the United States to adopt the monitorial system of education popularized by the English Quaker schoolmaster Joseph Lancaster; the African Free School adopted the system in 1809. A controversial figure, Lancaster joined the Society of Friends in London in 1794, and in 1798, at age 20, opened a school in his father's house. Philanthropic Quakers and others (including King George III, who wanted every member of his kingdom to be able to read the Bible) assisted him in clothing and feeding his poorer students.[43]

English Quakers warned their American Friends of Lancaster's difficult personality. Lancaster's fiscal irresponsibility led to his disownment in 1814, but he continued to attend Friends meeting, and Friends continued to support his educational efforts. When Lancaster arrived in the United States in 1818, there were 140 monitorial schools from Nantucket to New Orleans.

The monitorial method, which Lancaster "discovered" in his attempt to educate a large number of pupils with too little income to pay assistant teachers, consisted of having older, better pupils teach the younger ones. It was not a totally new idea, but Lancaster was its systematizer and publicist.[44]

The key features were economy, efficiency, discipline, motivation, and nonsectarianism. Monitorial education was more efficient than the traditional system in which the size of the school was limited to the number of individual pupils' recitations that could be heard each day by one master. Forty to sixty pupils was the usual range of school size under the traditional method. If a second school was desired, it required another master, who heard the same assortment of lessons from beginners learning the alphabet to grammar students. Most large monitorial schools fell into the four to six hundred student range, with one master providing instruction to the monitors, who in turn instructed classes of twelve to twenty students. This system permitted a tenfold increase of the traditional teacher to pupil ratio, allowing a tenfold decrease in cost.

Lessons were learned in front of the monitors, which eliminated the long periods during which the pupils sat waiting for their recitations. Continual activity and participation kept discipline problems to a minimum, and, because a lesson could be heard every ten minutes, more learning occurred.[45]

An elaborate system of rewards kept the system moving along. Students stood in a semicircle in front of a monitor. When one student failed to recite correctly, the next had an opportunity to take his place and literally to move to the head of the class, the reward for which was a chance to wear a badge of honor. Promotion to the next class entitled one to prizes, which Lancaster claimed were useful stimuli. A highly regimented, almost militaristic system of inspections, marches, and commands kept the whole system flowing with a minimum of disorder. Although disobedience was punished when it occurred, no corporal punishment was to be used.[46]

The founders of the NYPSS accepted as necessary the disciplinary and motivational aspects that were so closely interwoven with the features of efficiency and economy. More important, perhaps, and as tightly connected to the whole was the religious and moral instruction made possible by the nondenominational character of the system. For nearly fifty years the NYPSS school included Bible reading and scriptural instruction based primarily on texts written or edited by Quakers.

To the nineteenth-century mind, moral education was inconceivable without religion.[47] But to Quakers, teaching religion is not like teaching spelling. Lessons in morality, or "attempts to make children righteous by the application of moral rules and religious creeds," were the methods of the Calvinists with their emphasis on human depravity through Original Sin.[48] The Quaker view that the child is neither naturally good or evil, simply innocent, means that he or she can choose between good and evil. Among Quakers, the object of moral and religious education was "to give every opportunity for the good principles in the soul to be heard and followed and as little opportunity as possible for evil principles to be heard and followed. . . . Every opportunity is afforded for the voice of goodness to assert itself."[49]

Learning passages from the Bible without indoctrination about their meaning appears to be the way Lancaster and the advocates of the monitorial free school sought to provide children with an opportunity to gain knowledge of God without formal religious instruction.[50] Lancaster stressed the importance of the Scriptures in the education of youth. Deism, he believed, would have fewer converts if more youth had such knowledge. The monitorial instruction manual directed that neither the schoolmaster nor the monitor was to attempt to interpret Scripture, and that if students asked questions, they were to be referred to other passages where the word or phrase in question occurred.[51]

The nondenominational approach to religious instruction was an important step in urban school reform in America because it represented the divorce of denominational religion from charity schooling and, thus, permitted the expansion of charity schooling into the public school system. Lancaster's pan-Protestant solution predated that of Horace Mann by thirty years.

But pan-Protestantism was non-pan-Christianity. The Catholic opposition that arose to this instruction was based on the overwhelmingly Protestant nature of the Bible lessons. This opposition resulted, in 1840, in the removal of several controversial passages from the NYPSS approved textbooks. Friend Samuel Mott was the leader of the compromising party in this controversy. He proposed several alterations in the approved texts, such as eliminating an article on the "Life of Luther" from Lindley Murray's *English Reader*.[52]

Monitorial instruction had waned by the 1840s. A "mixed" method of instruction was adopted, and eventually trained and salaried apprentice teachers replaced monitors entirely. The monitorial system was not overthrown; it was phased out. Joseph Lancaster had died in a carriage accident in 1838, penniless and in the midst of yet another writing project for which he had raised funds.

Some recent historians have seen the monitorial system as a means of "social control." They liken the monitorial methods to those of the factory and contend that socializing future factory workers to obedience and authority was a primary outcome of these schools.[53] Despite its failings, however, the monitorial system accustomed the American public to the idea of providing education at public expense for all children.[54] In 1853 the NYPSS turned all of its schools over to the New York City Board of Education.

Quaker Educators and Authors

Quaker educator John Griscom's (1774–1852) account of his travels in Europe, published in 1821, helped awaken Americans to educational advances in Europe, particularly those of the Swiss educator, Johanne Heinrich Pestalozzi (1746–1827). According to Griscom, Pestalozzi criticized traditional education as too artificial, placing too much stress on memorization while the imagination was neglected. "If the native feelings of the heart," Griscom reported, "are allowed to operate, under the dominion of the native powers of the mind, drawn out and expanded by faith and love, the child is competent of itself to arrive gradually at the most correct and important conclusions in religion and science."[55] Griscom's English translation of Pestalozzi's idea may have been rather broad, but there is some germ in them that appears to be close to the Quaker idea of the Teacher Within. Griscom also reported favorably on the monitorial system used in the Edinburgh High School and on Robert Owen's school in New Lanark, Scotland.[56]

In 1823 Griscom and Dewitt Clinton called a meeting to organize "infant" schools in New York City modeled on Owen's system. They argued that "as soon as the tongue can utter words, and the eye regard objects, the care of society and the boon of public instruction" should be extended to children.[57] This initiative did not bear immediate fruit, but in 1827 a group of women formed the Infant School Society and opened the first infant school that same year. The Infant School Society may have been a continuation of the Quaker-organized Female Association.[58]

On his return from Europe Griscom began planning a high school for New York to teach children from the beginning of their schooling until they were fit to "enter the best college in the country" or "engage in any of the practical pursuits of business." His New York High School, the first monitorial high school in the United States, was based on the model he had seen in Edinburgh. Opposition rose immediately from existing schools, which worried about the competition that would ensue from the lower fees charged in such a school. Griscom and his assistant were even censured by the New York Teachers' Society.[59]

The school opened in March 1825 with Griscom and his assistant responsible for the older students and a Lancasterian teacher obtained from one of the NYPSS schools responsible for the junior department. By May there were 650 scholars, including 270 in the junior department, all taught by the monitorial method. Despite initial optimism, the school closed in 1831.[60] Griscom next served as principal in the Yearly Meeting Boarding School in Providence, Rhode Island (now the Moses Brown School), and finally retired to Burlington, New Jersey, where he served as trustee and superintendent of the public schools.

Since educational historians have often seen Pestalozzi and Lancaster as advocating opposite theories of educational practice, Griscom is particularly interesting as an individual who combined both with ease.

A remarkable number of Quakers wrote or published textbooks in early nineteenth-century New York State. Of all the Quaker authors, Lindley Murray (1745–1826) was best known. Although Murray left New York for England in 1784, he maintained close contact with New York Friends and left a substantial bequest to New York Yearly Meeting, which continues today as the Lindley Murray Fund.[61] Murray's *English Grammar* (1795) and *English Reader* (1799) were standards. The reader was, perhaps, the most widely used school text in the United States before the Civil War, and "Murray" became a synonym for grammar as "Euclid" was for geometry.[62] Murray's *Grammar* required extensive memorization of rules before students could begin the formal study of grammar. Murray did not think that students needed to understand grammar (he did not think they were capable of rational reflection); they just needed to memorize and apply the rules in practice.[63]

The success of the *English Grammar* encouraged Murray to produce the *English Reader* (1799), aimed, he said, "at a chaste and guarded education of young readers."[64] Part of the popularity of Murray's texts was their nondenominational nature. According to one biographer, Murray held a view of Quakerism that was typical of that period. Guarding students against an irreligious world and not against "corruption by tenets and practices of other denominations" was accompanied by the goal of advancing Christianity generally, not Quakerism particularly.[65]

Goold Brown (1791–1857), Griscom's assistant in his first New York City school, later a teacher at Nine Partners, and then head of his own school in New York, criticized the examples of parsing in Murray as "so verbose, awkward, irregular and deficient" that they were of no help to the students. Brown's own *Institutes of English Grammar* was first published by Samuel Wood in 1823.

Brown's Quaker publisher, Samuel Wood, has been credited as the compiler of the first series of graded readers, beginning with the *Young Child's ABC* in 1806 and continuing through the *New York Primer, Preceptor, Spelling Book, Expositor,* and the three levels of the *New-York Reader.* The Lancasterian schools of New York City, with their "well defined levels of reading ability" may have been the first substantial market for Wood's series.[66]

Joseph Tallcot was another prolific Quaker author. Under the aegis of the Western New York Union Tract Association of Friends, he published two small periodicals for children, the *Friendly Visitant* (1817–?) and the *Child's Companion* (1818–?). Later Tallcot issued a second series of the *Friendly Visitant* (1833–37), followed by a second series of the *Child's Companion* (1838–39) and a new monthly periodical, *The Acorn* (1839–40).[67] His *American Practical Catechism* (1821), published by Mahlon Day, was used by the NYPSS and by the Philadelphia Public Schools, which were administered by Friend John Ely.[68]

Tallcot energetically promoted religious education in Quaker families and schools and in the public schools of New York State. He recognized that for most Friends in rural districts the only choice for their children was the common or district school or no school. He encouraged Friends to take responsibility with others in the superintendence of local schools as trustees and inspectors so that they could have a voice in the selection of teachers and an influence in the "order and government" of the schools, as a means of "preserving their own children and at the same time being useful to others."[69]

Other Quaker textbook writers of the early nineteenth century included Jacob Willetts (1785–1860) of Dutchess County, a former teacher at the Nine Partners School, whose most successful works, the *Easy Grammar of Geography* (1815) and *Scholar's Arithmetic* (1816), were published through the 1850s. The spelling books of Rochester Friend Elihu F. Marshall were widely used in New York and New England in the 1820s and 1830s.

A book by Abigail Field Mott (1766–1851), *Biographical Sketches and Interesting Anecdotes of People of Colour,* first published by Mahlon Day in 1826 and reprinted several times, was widely circulated with the support of the Lindley Murray Fund. *Biographical Sketches* extolled the good character and piety of African-Americans and denounced slavery. The work was later revised and expanded by Mary S. Wood as *Narratives of Colored Americans* in 1875 and later reprinted. Abigail Mott also published *Observations on Female Education* (1825).

James Mott (1742–1823), one-time superintendent of the Nine Partners Boarding School, distilled his philosophy in a short pamphlet, *Observations on the Education of Children,* first published in 1815. Although Mott wrote, "The first inclination a child discovers, is the gratification of the will; therefore the first business of education is its subjection," Mott's methods were based on parental reason and judgment and, more importantly, parental love. Parents were to children the "friends most interested in their welfare" and to be treated as companions within the family. "An important step . . . is to make ourselves beloved; and teach our children virtues by example as well as precept. Those who would teach others, should first subdue their own passions." In a letter written in 1797 while he was superintendent at Nine Partners, Mott wrote of the love that desires the good of all. Children should not be made to obey out of fear of punishment, but from love.[70]

Several key leaders in the progressive education movement of the twentieth century, including Rachel Davis DuBois, Carleton Washburne, and Morris Mitchell, were New York Quakers. Many Quaker schools subscribe to the progressive ideals of educating the whole child, providing a democratic and participatory educational environment, promoting social justice and tolerance through celebrating diversity, exploring the relationship and mutuality of responsibility between the group and the individual, and connecting the theoretical to the practical or real world by experiential methods.

Oakwood School at Poughkeepsie

When the Oakwood Seminary moved from Union Springs to Poughkeepsie in 1920, it incorporated under the name of Oakwood School with a Board of Managers appointed by the Orthodox yearly meeting. William J. Reagan was principal several years before the move and continued in that role until 1948. Many boarding students still came from Quakers meetings in upstate and western New York State, for only a year or two, to acquire a higher quality of education than available in their home communities in order to gain entrance to good colleges. Reagan became widely known in educational circles and managed to draw students to Oakwood from all strata of society.

Upon the 1955 reunion of the two New York Yearly Meetings, the school came under the care of the united yearly meeting. Recently the Board of Managers has added alumni and at-large members, but a majority of board members are still drawn from New York Yearly Meeting.

Children's Creative Response to Conflict

A final note about Quakers and education in New York Yearly Meeting concerns the Children's Creative Response to Conflict program developed with the support of New York Yearly Meeting in the 1960s. Training teachers both to use and to teach conflict resolution skills can have a major impact on the learning environment of the classroom and the social environment of the surrounding community as well. The program's curriculum guide, *A Friendly Class-room for a Small Planet* (1968), combines the Quaker goals of spirit uplift with the utility of problem-solving skills. It includes the best of the progressive tradition of individual empowerment and social action and reflects Quaker sensitivity to the nature of the individual and group relationship. Being receptive to the Teacher Within while answering that of God in others is seen as the transforming power that can guide this and other Quaker educational efforts into the next century.

10

Women's Rights and Roles

Nancy A. Hewitt
and
Margaret Hope Bacon, Christopher Densmore,
Thomas D. Hamm, Sabron Reynolds Newton,
Katherine Sorel, Alson D. Van Wagner

Women's Meetings

The preceding chapters provide abundant evidence of the prominent roles played by women in the Society of Friends. From the founding moment of the Society women were recognized as spiritual equals with men, and from the first establishment of the New York Yearly Meeting the Discipline called for the establishment of separate women's meetings. Women helped to formulate Quaker doctrines, disseminate Quaker ideals, and promote Quaker charitable and reform efforts. Women are, thus, incorporated into the entire story of New York Yearly Meeting. Yet they also deserve separate treatment, for it is important to understand not only how Quaker women gained rights within the Society of Friends but also how they expanded their roles in the larger society and thereby increased all women's access to equality.

Beginning in the seventeenth century, the Society of Friends developed a parallel structure of men's and women's meetings for discipline. Meeting houses were customarily equipped with sliding panels that made it possible to divide the building physically into two equal halves during meetings for business. The existence of these separate meetings offered women Friends an autonomy unmatched in any other Christian denomination and unimaginable in the secular world. They served as the primary arena in which a wide range of women's testimonies, ministries, and charitable and reform initiatives were nurtured throughout the eighteenth and nineteenth centuries.

On matters of mutual concern, which could be initiated by either men or women, the two meetings consulted. When necessary, ad hoc joint committees considered proposals for action, such as a change in the Discipline or a request that the Meeting for Sufferings lobby the state government about Indian lands or capital punishment. During the yearly meeting, however, men and women rarely met together unless it was to hear a minister with a religious message.

Men's and women's meetings were not truly equal, however, at least not before the mid-nineteenth century when the first major reforms occurred. Earlier, the Meeting for Sufferings and other committees of the yearly meeting were appointed by and from the men's meeting although they reported on their activities to both meetings. A change in Quaker practice was introduced in 1804 when the Indian Committee recommended and the Society agreed that because Indian women were equally entitled to the sympathy of Friends, the members of the committee should be appointed from both men's and women's yearly meetings. This change came, in part, on the initiative of Stockbridge Indian women, who began addressing communications to their Quaker sisters soon after the Indian Committee was established to minister to the indigenous peoples of central New York State.[1]

In the monthly meetings women were required to obtain the concurrence of the men's meeting when receiving or disowning members or granting removal certificates. The men's meeting had no reciprocal obligation although other matters of mutual concern required the approbation of both meetings. In 1838 Genesee Yearly Meeting altered its Discipline so that "men and women shall stand on the same footing on all matters in which they are equally interested. . . [E]ach branch of a monthly meeting shall obtain the concurrence of the other."[2] During the same year, New York Yearly Meeting (Hicksite) considered a similar proposal and approved it in 1839.[3] The Orthodox branch of New York Yearly Meeting retained the older provisions of the Discipline until 1874 when women's and men's meetings were finally put on an equal footing.[4]

In Genesee Yearly Meeting full implementation of the change in the Discipline came in 1843 when women were appointed to membership in the Meeting for Sufferings. Women's and men's preparative, monthly, quarterly, and yearly meetings, however, remained separate. A more dramatic step was taken by a circle of dissident women and men who left Genesee Yearly Meeting in 1848 to form the Yearly Meeting of Congregational Friends. The "Basis for Religious Association" published by this body specifically acknowledged the equality of women and stipulated that men and women "will meet together and transact business jointly."[5] Interestingly, the "Basis" was signed by the co-clerks of the meeting, one male and one female.

Among the Hicksite and Orthodox Friends the system of separate meetings at the preparative and monthly level began to be replaced by joint meetings in the 1870s. At the yearly meeting level, joint meetings appeared in Genesee and New York (Orthodox) Meetings in 1884 and in New York (Hicksite) in 1894. After a decade of meeting jointly, the New York Hicksites actually merged the men's and women's yearly meetings in 1903. The pace of change in New York stands in sharp contrast to that in Philadelphia where the men's and women's meetings for discipline did not achieve full equality among the Hicksites until 1877, nearly forty years after those in New York and Genesee. The full integration of men and women at the yearly meeting level was not accomplished there until the 1920s.[6]

The status of women and men within the new joint meetings was made explicit in both the Hicksite and Orthodox Disciplines. The Orthodox Discipline of 1890 stated that "the rights and privileges of membership are to be in no way affected because of sex," whereas the New York Hicksites affirmed in their 1893 *Discipline* that "recognizing that all are one in Christ, Friends believe that there shall be no distinction of sex."[7] By 1900 the partitions that once divided Quaker meeting houses had become historical relics.

Women's Ministry

Changes in the Discipline reflected as well as inspired changes in practice. They, thus, provide a useful window into the larger question of how and why women's roles and rights were transformed within the Society of Friends and the wider community. The process of transformation was frequently stimulated by religious upheavals that encouraged particular meetings and factions to enlist actively the assistance of all members, women as well as men. Such upheavals parallel the pattern set during the founding years of the Society of Friends, from roughly 1648 to 1725, when George Fox and his followers eagerly embraced female converts to the faith.[8] In the next century when, according to Quaker historian Rufus M. Jones, the Society became more timid and exclusive, women continued to take full part in the public ministry but failed to gain equality with men in the business affairs of the Society. And by 1783 women and men ministers could no longer travel together "as companions in service, to avoid all occasions of offence thereby."[9] Only with the schisms of the 1820s and 1840s would women again join men as relatively equal partners in defining the meaning of Quakerism.[10]

Throughout the late eighteenth century women like New York Quakers Phebe Willets Mott Dodge, Hannah Davis Taber, Sarah Lundy, Elizabeth Coggeshall, and Hannah Jenkins Barnard sustained the tradition of female preaching. Despite the general quiescence in Quaker ranks in this period, it was the isolated pockets of upheaval that often formed the centers of women's influence. One area of particular trials was Ireland. Sarah Grubb's visit there in the 1790s coincided with a defection that was "destined to be the precursor of still more serious events." The crisis suggested by the Irish controversy "came to light as a result of the European visit of an American Quaker minister named Hannah Barnard." Jones described Barnard as the "leading champion in the first years of the nineteenth century of a freer type of thought in the Society."[11]

From the turn of the century through the 1820s, as tensions within the Society of Friends intensified, the desire for consensus and the need of each side for spiritual and practical support increased the significance of women's participation in Quaker meetings. Thus, women were arrayed on both sides of what became known as the Hicksite controversy. Ann Shipley emigrated to the United States in 1794 and traveled in the ministry while relatives looked after her children. In 1824 Shipley interviewed Elias Hicks in the company of Anna Braithwaite, one of the most outspoken advocates of Orthodoxy. Braithwaite soon penned a commentary on her conversation with Hicks, and "thanks to the rapid circulation of [Braithwaite's] memorandum . . . a barrage of pamphlets became available for anyone who wanted to participate vicariously in the discussion."[12]

Those New York Friends who migrated north and west from Long Island in the 1820s remained well-informed about developments at home. From Jericho, for instance, Mary Kirby Willis wrote to her sisters Hannah Post and Amy Kirby in central New York, detailing Hicks's response to Braithwaite and the local monthly meeting's refusal to sustain a female member's ministry alongside the Orthodox English woman.[13] A constant stream of letters poured forth from Long Island and central New York women, describing and analyzing the latest events in the confrontations between Braithwaite and Hicks, almost all sympathetic to the famous reformer. Such sympathy did not arise, however, from any vaunted sense of male authority, because these same correspondents also applauded the labors of Lucretia Mott and Priscilla Hunt and, later, those of their New York counterparts such as Lydia Mott, Rachel Hicks, Phebe Merritt, and Huldah Case Hoag.[14]

Despite the openings for women produced by the schism, some female Friends regretted the disruptions more than they applauded the opportunities. Hannah Post lamented Braithwaite's visit to the New York Yearly Meeting in 1826, claiming that it would "spoil the pleasure of being there by rousing diversity of sentiment."[15] Others simply wished to continue their ministries to the poor, uneducated, or heathen undisturbed by divisive theological debates. Benjamin and Mary Slocum Howland settled in Cayuga County, New York, in 1798 and built a house in which the first Friends meeting in the area was held the following year; they remained active in the meeting and the community right through the 1820s. In Kendall, New York, a group of Norwegian Quakers arrived in 1825, cleared land, established farms and businesses, and provided lodging to hundreds of Norwegian immigrants on their way west. Martha Larsen, one of the original Kendall settlers, was soon widowed and moved to nearby Rochester where she joined the educational and charitable efforts of a small but growing circle of Orthodox Friends. The ministry of Elizabeth Hannah Hoyland Walker was approved by Purchase Meeting from whence she traveled to New England, Lower Canada, Virginia, North Carolina, and England. Although active during the Hicksite controversies, she focused her attention on ministering and education; before her death in 1827, she preached in the U.S. capitol.

Whether they were anxious to join in the controversies that swept through meeting houses in the 1820s, female Friends seem to have gained a new sense of women's centrality to the Society through the combined upheavals of migration and separation. On a personal level some women lost their fear of condemnation by the meeting. When Amy Kirby and Isaac Post married "out of the order of Society" after the death of Isaac's wife Hannah, who was Amy's older sister, the Jericho Monthly Meeting investigated both the couple and those who attended their wedding. A sympathetic Friend reported that some members of the committee found Amy's responses, in particular, "a little too *tart*."[16] The following year, Amy's sister-in-law reported favorably on the ministry of a woman named Rhoda, noting especially her claim that "many are joined in wedloc [sic] that are not married in the true sense of the things."[17] Some two decades later a woman who started down the Hicksite path in the 1820s concluded that a woman "ought to be better qualified to direct the spiritual life of her own sex than any belov'd disciple or even Jesus himself as a man and a brother."[18]

Still, in the years following the schism, most female members of the New York yearly meetings were more concerned with education, ministries to frontier settlements, temperance, prison reform, and slavery than with women's rights per se. Whether Hicksite or Orthodox, female Friends continued to place these traditional Quaker concerns at the center of their activism until at least the mid-nineteenth century. Four remarkable women from Michigan demonstrate the dedication of Quaker women to a variety of causes during the decades between the Hicksite separation and the end of the Civil War.

Four Remarkable Women from Michigan

Elizabeth Margaret Chandler was born in 1807 and began writing essays and poetry for Benjamin Lundy's abolitionist newspaper, the *Genius of Universal Emancipation,* in 1826. She became the editor of the "Ladies Repository" section of the *Genius* in 1829. During the next year she moved with her brother and an aunt to a farm near Adrian, Michigan, where she was active in the local Quaker community and in the formation of the state's first antislavery society. A major theme of Chandler's essays and poetry was the moral responsibility of women to become active in reform efforts despite the strictures against public speaking. When her writings were published in book form in 1836, two years after her death, the volume included two engravings. One was of Chandler herself, pen in hand, and the other of a kneeling slave woman, bound in fetters. These images echoed sentiments in Chandler's poetry: "When woman's heart is bleeding / Shall woman's voice be hush'd?" And referring specifically to the bound slave, she wrote, "Is it not a sister's form, / On whose limbs these fetters rest?"[19]

Joining Chandler in the abolitionist movement were a number of her Orthodox Quaker neighbors, including Laura Smith Haviland. Haviland was the daughter of a Quaker minister and a Quaker elder, but as a young girl she was drawn to Methodist revivalism. In 1839 she and nineteen others resigned from Adrian Monthly Meeting to protest the insufficiencies of the Friends with regard to both evangelicalism and abolitionism. In so doing, they made common cause with local Wesleyan Methodists, who were also leaving established churches to form antislavery congregations. For the next fifty years Haviland was a tireless worker for abolition and related causes. She rejoined the Society of Friends in 1871, a move that probably reflected the increasing evangelicalism among Orthodox Friends rather than any change of heart on Haviland's part.[20]

Elizabeth Wright, an English-born Quaker widow with a young daughter, arrived in Canada in 1854 and four years later married John T. Comstock, a native of Farmington, New York, who had become a prosperous farmer in Rollin, Michigan. She quickly immersed herself in the activities of the local Quaker community, involving herself in antislavery efforts and aiding fugitive slaves. Having been recorded as a minister in 1861, Comstock expanded her sphere of activity during the Civil War, visiting army hospitals, prisons, and refugee camps. In 1863 alone, she traveled almost six thousand miles, visiting sick and wounded soldiers, prisoners of war, almshouse inmates, refugees, freed people, and "fallen women." In addition, she held religious meetings among Orthodox and Hicksite Friends as well as non-Friends. In 1864 Comstock gained an audience with Abraham Lincoln to plead the cause of newly freed blacks, and in the post-war period, she joined with Quakers in a number of cities to educate and "uplift" the poor. She was also an ardent temperance advocate and an active publicist and fund-raiser on behalf of the "Exodusters"— African-Americans who chose to leave the South and emigrate to Kansas.

Throughout her career in America, Comstock associated with the Gurneyite Friends, the largest and most evangelical of the three Quaker groups that emerged from the schisms of 1827 to 1854. Yet she combined her evangelical beliefs with an appreciation for traditional Quaker practices, and toward the end of her life worked for reconciliation among Hicksite, Orthodox, and Gurneyite Friends. One of the common Quaker values she prized most highly was equality between the sexes: "We profess to be the only pure democracy in the world," she wrote, "men and women being one—on an absolute equality in the Lord Jesus Christ, is one of our fundamental doctrines."[21]

Perhaps a fourth woman should be included among these notable Michigan Quakers. Sojourner Truth, born a slave in New York in the late 1790s, was well known in the mid-nineteenth century for her preaching on behalf of abolition and woman's rights. She is best known today for her "Ar'n't I a Woman?" speech, which she delivered at the 1851 Ohio woman's rights convention in reply to a man who dared to suggest that women were weak. At various points in her career, Truth worked with Quakers, including Laura Smith Haviland who assisted her in her attempt to integrate the streetcars of Washington, D.C., during the Civil War. Truth seemed particularly drawn to the Quaker community in Battle Creek, Michigan, where she made her home after 1856. When the Battle Creek Friends held their first meeting at a newly built meeting house in 1871, Truth rose to speak: "I have always loved the Quakers and would have joined them, only they would not let me sing; so I joined the Methodists." She then asked permission to sing and got it.[22]

Quaker Women and Reform

Like female Friends in Michigan, many in western New York also pursued reform both within the Society of Friends and within society at large during the mid-1800s.[23] Here temperance and abolition served as the entrées to a more explicit advocacy of women's rights. The first Quakers in upstate New York communities joined in the benevolent efforts initiated by non-Quaker Christian women. After the Separation in 1828, Orthodox women in cities such as Rochester continued to pursue charitable and reform activities in company with evangelical Presbyterians and Baptists. Abigail Moore, for instance, was active during the 1830s in the Rochester Orphan Asylum Association and the Female Anti-Slavery Society, both of which were dominated by evangelical Presbyterians.

Abigail Moore's Hicksite neighbors joined her in testifying against slavery. In 1837, for example, Hicksite women, such as Amy Post and her daughter Mary along with their Orthodox sisters, including Abigail Moore and her daughter Ann, signed the massive antislavery petitions to Congress circulated in Rochester at the behest of the Anti-Slavery Convention of American Women. Here they followed the lead of such birthright Quakers as Lucretia Mott and converts Angelina and Sarah Grimke, who were urging women to take a stand against the brutality of slavery.

Yet that very year, Phebe Post Willis of Long Island queried her upstate relatives, "How is it that you tell us nothing about abolition movements in Rochester? I should scarcely suppose you were members of that society by your silence on the subject."[24] And, indeed, those Hicksites who had joined the Genesee Yearly Meeting did seem to be more concerned at the moment with matters internal to the Society of Friends. The Posts, along with their co-worshippers, the Fishes, De-Garmos, and Burtises, supported a resolution introduced to the yearly meeting in 1837, asking that "the discipline be so alter'd that men and women shall stand on the same footing in all matters internal in which they are equally interested." The meeting as a whole, however, found "the way not open" to alter the Rules of Discipline and postponed action to the following year.[25] Even after the Discipline was altered to include the desired wording, the meeting postponed implementation for several more years.[26]

In the meantime, debates over the participation of Quaker women and men in worldly associations became more heated within New York Yearly Meeting, Michigan Quarterly Meeting, and Genesee Yearly Meeting. The Posts, Fishes, DeGarmos, and Burtises, now joined by the Anthony family, began to hold "numerous little abolition meetings" in their homes and to wonder why they should "exclude all who do not happen to be included within the pale of our religious faith."[27] Then in 1842, former Quaker Abby Kelley arrived in Rochester as an agent of the American Anti-Slavery Society, and her visit inspired the formation of the Western New York Anti-Slavery Society. The founding meeting was held at the Bethel Presbyterian Church and attracted the support of numerous Hicksite women and men who soon dominated the association. Among the early officers of the society were Sarah Fish, Sarah Burtis, Sarah Hallowell, and Amy Post.

Yet as the worldly labors of these dissident Quakers increased, so did tensions within Genesee Yearly Meeting and its constituent meetings. Rochester Monthly Meeting noticed, for instance, when Amy Post "left her home for the purpose . . . of Antislavery work" and appointed a committee to advise her "in regard to her duty toward her family" and "her attitude [in] working with the 'world's' people."[28] Amy Post made her contempt for such proceedings clear in a letter to Abby Kelley. Selecting a piece of antislavery stationery embossed with a woman slave fettered in chains, Amy wrote, "The overseers [of the monthly meeting] have taken no further notice of my case, but expect they will have a fresh charge against me soon, as yesterday transcribed some Epistles for the Preparative meetings on such paper as this, and have but little doubt but that imploring image [of a slave in chains] will disturb their quiet."[29]

During the next five years Amy and Isaac Post, their daughter Mary Hallowell and her husband William, along with Lewis and Sarah Burtis, Griffith Cooper, and numerous other antislavery Hicksites were released or withdrew from Genesee Yearly Meeting. They were joined by like-minded Friends from other areas, including Isaac Hopper and Charles Marriott of New York Yearly Meeting. The women, both those who left the Society and those who remained members, dedicated increasing energy to antislavery fairs held in western New York primarily to support the publication of Frederick Douglass's *North Star*. The efforts of Rochester's antislavery Quakers was part of a web of activity that stretched across central and western New York and as far south as Long Island and Philadelphia. Calls for antislavery fairs were often signed jointly by such disaffected Hicksites as Sarah Burtis and Amy Post of Rochester, Mary Ann M'Clintock of Waterloo, Phebe Hathaway of Farmington, Sarah Thayer of Scipio, and Abby Kelley.[30]

The final break between the Hicksites and their critics came at Genesee Yearly Meeting in June 1848 to which Lucretia Mott had been invited as a visiting minister.[31] There, unresolved tensions from the previous year's meeting burst into acrimonious charges and counter-charges among the meeting's participants. Although the issue of women's and men's equality within Genesee Yearly Meeting had been settled on principle in 1838 and finally implemented in 1842–43, other questions relating to the authority of some over others remained. Most importantly, the Michigan Quarterly Meeting had discontinued its separate meeting of ministers and elders in 1843. In 1847 some members of Genesee Yearly Meeting attempted to discipline Michigan Quakers, but not until 1848 did the issue come to a head. Then, when clerks from the men's and women's meetings refused to read reports from the Michigan Quarterly Meeting and the men's clerk accepted reappointment, "everyone understood that this was 'equivalent to recording a separation of the Yearly Meeting.' About two hundred Friends ('something towards half,' according to one observer) walked out."[32]

Taken in conjunction with earlier reluctance on the part of many Hicksites to support the equality of women and men and the continued struggles over the right of members to participate in worldly reform efforts, this crisis over authority within Genesee Yearly Meeting and its subsidiary meetings convinced the dissident faction to establish an entirely new association.

These Congregational (later Progressive) Friends, gathering in October 1848 at the site of Junius Monthly Meeting from which many of the dissidents emerged, crafted a new and radical "Basis of Religious Association." Claiming that "perfect liberty of conscience is the right of every sane and accountable human being," the Congregational Friends eliminated the "subordination of meetings, or the vesting of larger meetings with authority over smaller," and discontinued the meeting of ministers and elders. In addition, "not only will the equality of women be recognized, but so perfectly, that in our meetings, larger and smaller, men and women will meet together and transact business jointly."[33]

Here, the legacy of women's spiritual equality and organizational separation, passed down from the earliest Quaker forebears, bore fruit in the form of both separation and emancipation. Moreover, in 1848 the trajectory of Quaker dissidents intersected with that of legal reformers and political abolitionists in western New York to form the basis for the first woman's rights convention in the world.[34] For Quaker women, the most important aspect of this intersection was the impetus it gave them to join their efforts with those of non-Quakers who were also concerned with advancing the status of their sex. Supported by both their male co-worshippers and kin and by non-Quaker women experienced in legal reform, temperance, and abolition, these feminist Friends would have an impact far greater than numbers alone would suggest. For instance, of the five women who drafted the Declaration of Sentiments for the Seneca Falls conference, Lucretia Mott, Martha Wright, Mary Ann M'Clintock, and Jane Hunt had all attended the June 1848 Genesee Yearly Meeting; only Elizabeth Cady Stanton had not. When it came to signing the final declaration, "at least twenty-three signers were affiliated with this wing of the Friends"—the largest single group among the one hundred known signatories—of whom nineteen came from Junius Monthly Meeting.[35]

Just two weeks later in Rochester, New York, many of those in attendance at Seneca Falls reconvened to continue the discussions regarding the "social, civil, and religious conditions and rights of women." Now, however, with Congregational women Friends as organizers, the agenda was expanded to include the "Rights of Women, Politically, Socially, Religiously, and Industrially," and a woman, Abigail Bush, was selected to preside.[36] At Rochester, the elective franchise, which had received hesitant support at the Seneca Falls convention, topped the agenda. Yet the convention organizers also urged "women no longer to promise obedience in the marriage covenant" and to allow "the strongest will or the superior intellect" to "govern the household." They beseeched women to claim equal authority within their families and "on all subjects that interest the human family." Of particular interest to the convention participants was women's economic and occupational status, and several speeches and resolutions were devoted to promoting women's equality in the workplace, the educational system, and the professions.[37]

The concerns of the participants at the Seneca Falls and Rochester Woman's Rights Conventions were echoed over the next decade in the resolutions and proceedings of the Yearly Meeting of Congregational Friends. But they resonated in wider circles as well, including New York Friends who had not broken with the Orthodox and Hicksite meetings. Quaker women engaged in temperance work or those pursuing entrance into the professions were particularly susceptible to pleas for expanding the political, economic, and educational rights of their sex.

Quaker Women and Temperance

Quakers had long testified against the evils of drink, but only in the mid-nineteenth century did female Friends initiate or join organized campaigns to end alcohol abuse. The original inspiration for much Quaker temperance work was intemperance in their own community. Then in the 1840s with the rise of organizations such as the Washingtonians, an early self-help group for alcoholics, some Quakers began expanding their vision of the cause.[38] When two Washingtonians visited Rochester, New York, in the early 1840s, for instance, Sarah Bills Fish decided to ban wines from her house. Hannah Southwick Jewett and her husband Lester Jewett, a physician, became the mainstays of the temperance cause in their hometown of Seneca, in central New York. Already offering refuge to runaway slaves, the Jewetts now provided "a welcome and lively conversation to passing temperance lecturers," who considered them "uncompromising temperance people."[39]

Susan B. Anthony: From Temperance to Women's Rights

The Anthony family also became ardent temperance advocates. Daniel Anthony of Battenville, New York, left bankrupt by the Panic of 1837, moved his family into an unoccupied tavern from which he served meals to travelers, but no intoxicating drinks. Previously, he had refused to sell rum at his mill store or to furnish gin to employees. Though disowned by Easton Monthly Meeting for opening his upstairs assembly room to dances for young people—to save them from dancing at a nearby saloon—Anthony remained a committed Quaker, at least until his resettlement in Rochester in 1845. After joining the circle of radical Quaker activists in Rochester, Daniel Anthony became more critical of the claims of the Quaker Discipline. Having kept his daughter Susan, who was then teaching school in central New York, informed of the various social issues of the day, he wrote her in July 1848 that "those who had left the 'shriveled up nutshell' of Genesee Yearly Meeting were those 'who take the liberty of holding up to view the wickedness of War—Slavery—Intemperance—Hanging &c" and "who are of the opinion that each individual should have a right to even think as well as act for himself & in his own way to assist in rooling [sic] on the wheel of reform."[40]

Susan B. Anthony had already learned to think for herself by 1848 although she was initially more amused than inspired by news of the Seneca Falls Woman's Rights Convention.[41] Susan's father was a birthright Quaker, but her mother, Lucy Read, was a Baptist. He was disowned for marrying out of the meeting, and only readmitted after making acknowledgment, much to the humiliation of his wife. Susan grew up in a Quaker community in which the emphasis on an Inner Light and, therefore, on the spiritual equality of all persons vied with "the evangelical Protestant ethic of true womanhood which asked women to look into themselves, not for self-reliance, but with piety and humility." For Susan the Quaker message won out; she grew up hearing women speak freely and was encouraged to become self-reliant, educated, and self-supporting.[42]

Although Daniel Anthony was supportive of his daughter's independence, he sent her mixed messages about the application of Quaker principles to daily life and politics. He supported the antislavery Hicksites but continued to profit from the products of slave labor through his cotton factory. He preached self-reliance to his daughters but paid his female employees considerably less than a living wage. And Lucy, Susan, and Mary took on increasing burdens of unpaid domestic work as the number of children and boarders increased during the 1830s.[43]

In 1837 Susan Anthony escaped to Deborah Moulson's Female Seminary, a Quaker boarding school outside of Philadelphia, where a liberal education was combined with training in "the principles of Humility, Morality, and love of Virtue." Here Anthony first heard Lucretia Mott speak and was introduced to her more socially engaged form of Quakerism. Returning home to assist her family after the collapse of her father's business and the loss of all of her mother's property to pay his debts, Susan obtained a teaching position at Eunice Kenyon's Quaker boarding school in 1839. As a teacher in the 1840s, she first came into direct contact with popular movements against alcohol and slavery.

The Anthony family, meanwhile, moved to Rochester, New York, where Daniel joined the Hicksite meeting in 1846 and became enmeshed in abolitionist and temperance activities. By 1847 Susan had also joined Genesee Yearly Meeting and the Daughters of Temperance. Over the next few years as Genesee Yearly Meeting split and the first gatherings focused solely on women's rights were held, Susan concentrated on temperance. She presented a temperance speech at the Canajoharie Daughters of Temperance supper in 1849; she organized a chapter of the Daughters in Rochester in 1851; and she attended the Sons of Temperance convention in 1852. When she tried to speak there, however, she was told, "The sisters were not invited to speak, but to listen and learn."[44]

Anthony, like many female temperance advocates, already saw the fight against alcohol as a woman's issue because it was women and their children who suffered both economic deprivation and physical abuse at the hands of drunkards. But not until Anthony was denied the right to speak at the Sons' convention did she begin to think about the broader implications of women's limited sphere of action. With Lydia Mott, Anthony soon gathered a small circle of women and issued a call for a convention in Rochester in April to form a statewide women's temperance society. At the first meeting of the New York State Women's Temperance Society, Quaker advocates of women's rights made common cause with evangelical reformers and with Elizabeth Cady Stanton. Over the next year Anthony and her coworkers canvassed thirty counties, collected twenty-eight thousand signatures on petitions for a statewide prohibition law, and demanded votes for women so that legislators would have to listen to their female constituents. Still, the fragile coalition could not hold. Evangelical reformers were shocked by the women's rights agenda advocated at the 1853 meeting by Stanton and others while many Quaker radicals found temperance work less compelling in the 1850s than antislavery.[45]

By the mid-1850s not only Anthony but most Quakers ended their affiliations with organized temperance. Although the Good Templars, a temperance organization that recognized the equality of women, attracted a few individual Quakers after its founding in Utica in 1851, no widespread involvement in the cause emerged among female Friends until well after the Civil War. In the meantime, Anthony turned her attention to abolition in the late 1850s, then to the Women's Loyal League during the Civil War, and finally to the long campaign for women's suffrage in the postwar period.

Other female Friends in New York would travel much the same path as Anthony, at least through the Civil War. Teaching and temperance, education and abolition, piety and personal independence would characterize the lives of many Quaker women in this period, particularly those who, like Anthony, remained single.

Emily Howland

One of the most notable of these Quaker women was Emily Howland, a reformer who was passionately committed to the struggle for racial and sexual equality, to education, and to the temperance cause through her participation in the local Good Templars lodge.[46] Born into an Orthodox family in Sherwood, New York, in 1827, Howland was introduced early to the antislavery cause. Later in life she claimed that the antislavery standard had "colored all the texture of thought and principle and swayed the course of my life more than any other influence; it has been 'the University' for me."[47] As a young adult, she renounced marriage, considering it a sacrifice of personal independence and rights for women. She did not feel called to the ministry so instead spent six winters at Mary Robinson's school in Philadelphia where she became part of a group of nine women, all reformer-scholars who were deeply committed to improving the position of both women and blacks in society. As she began teaching at a school for black women in Washington, D.C., Howland became increasingly disenchanted with the meeting—its strictures against music and dancing, its failure to support social activism, and its insistence on pacifism even at the cost of the slaves' fight for freedom. Although retaining her membership in the monthly meeting, she stopped attending and became involved in activities at the Unitarian church instead.

During the Civil War, Howland went to Washington to teach in one of the contraband camps for newly freed slaves. Realizing that meeting basic needs as important as teaching basic skills, Howland began organizing relief and medical efforts and taking on roles denied women under normal circumstances. Returning home to Sherwood in 1865 to nurse her ailing mother, Howland hatched a plan with her father's support to buy a few hundred acres of land in the South and develop a self-sufficient farm for freed blacks. She founded Arcadia as a racially integrated community, opened the Howland School in Virginia for poor blacks and whites, and coordinated programs for freedmen's education at Fort Ethan Allen.

By 1868 Arcadia was self-sufficient, and Howland returned to Sherwood where her father's death left her emotionally devastated but financially independent. She devoted the rest of her life to advancing education for women and promoting women's right to economic and political equality. At the same time, a growing concern with global militarism helped reconcile her to the Society of Friends before her death at age 102.

Quaker Women in the Professions

While women such as Susan B. Anthony and Emily Howland carved out careers for themselves as activists and educators, other New York

Quaker women sought to translate their social concerns and intellectual abilities into professional careers. Often motivated by the same sense of calling as those who entered the ministry and with the advantage of good Quaker educations, these women again broke ground not only for female Friends but for all women seeking entrance into domains long dominated by men.

Quaker women were among the first, for example, to enter the field of medicine and to provide medical education for other women. Dr. Eliza Mosher fits both categories. Born in Cayuga County in 1846, the sixth child of a Quaker farm family, she attended Friends Academy at Union Springs. She then attended New England Hospital for Women and Children, the University of Michigan College of Medicine, graduating from the latter in 1875 and returning to Poughkeepsie, New York, to set up a private practice. In 1877 she accepted a position as resident physician at a new state Reformatory Prison for Women in Sherborn, Massachusetts, where she later served as superintendent and made many reforms in the medical care of inmates. Eventually, she established a medical practice in Brooklyn with another woman physician, and together they shared a position at Vassar for many years.

Another New York professional woman who focused on prison reform was Eliza Wood Farnham who became matron of the women's division of Sing Sing in 1845. While at Sing Sing, she replaced the "silent system" inaugurated by earlier Quaker reformers with a program that included singing, exercise, and education. Although praised by liberals, Eliza was forced to resign in 1848. Farnham then made plans to establish a commune for women in California to help counter uncivilized conditions and became matron of the Stockton Insane Asylum. She also wrote her most significant work in this period, *Woman and Her Era*, a treatise arguing for the natural superiority of women. During the Civil War she returned east, joined the Women's Loyal League, and became a battlefield nurse at Gettysburg, dying of consumption within the year.

Another New York Friend who migrated west was Mary Anne Hallock Foote, an author and illustrator born of Quaker parents in Milton, New York. Despite Quaker concerns about the frivolity of art, she completed a three-year course at Cooper Institute in New York City and found work as an illustrator for *Harpers Weekly* and *Scribners Monthly*. In 1876 she married Arthur De Wint Foote, a civil engineer, and moved with him to California. There she turned to writing fiction and illustrating her own books. Although she did not continue to attend Quaker meeting, Foote retained Quaker speech and dress throughout her life.

More in line with the traditional Quaker testimony in regard to art was Anna Botsford Comstock. Born in Cattaraugus County in 1854, she was the daughter of a Hicksite Quaker mother who loved nature and life. Eager to learn, Anna Botsford enrolled in a zoology course at Cornell taught by John Henry Comstock. In 1878 they married, and she began illustrating her husband's lectures and books on entomology. She returned to Cornell in 1883 and received a degree in natural history. Five years later she was initiated into Sigma Xi, the national honor society for the sciences, one of the first four women to be so honored. Anna Comstock also taught a pioneer course in nature study in the Westchester County schools and was eventually named assistant professor at Cornell, the first woman faculty member appointed at the university. Her major publication was *The Handbook of Nature Study,* published in 1911 and translated into eight languages.

Anna Beach Pratt, a New Yorker who became a Quaker by convincement, made significant contributions to the field of social work. Raised in Elmira, New York, she enrolled in the New York School of Philanthropy in 1906. She soon became the unofficial overseer of the poor in Elmira and secretary of the newly formed Bureau of Associated Relief, a precursor of the United Way. In Elmira, Pratt introduced new social service techniques into local philanthropies, conducted many client interviews, and influenced agencies to coordinate their efforts. After moving to Philadelphia in 1916, Pratt developed a wide-reaching program of school social work, the first such in the country. She lectured and taught graduate classes on the subject of school social work and was named to the Philadelphia Board of Education and to the White House Conference on Children.

Maria Mitchell was equally talented in her chosen field of study, astronomy. Born on Nantucket in 1818, she assisted her astronomer father, and in 1847 discovered a new comet which was named for her. As a result, she received worldwide recognition and was the first woman elected to the American Academy of Arts and Sciences. In 1865 Matthew Vassar invited her to come to his newly founded Female College as a faculty member and to be in charge of the observatory he would build for her. Never having attended college herself, she at first declined but later accepted and became a beloved teacher, influencing many women to enter the sciences. She also founded the Association for the Advancement of Women in 1873, serving as its president in 1875 and 1876. She continued to be widely recognized in the scientific community and in 1869 was elected to the American Philosophical Society, again the first woman to be so honored.

Other New York Quaker women made contributions to a wide array of professions and causes: Abby Hopper Gibbons to prison reform, Gertrude Stanton Kasebier and Rachel Hicks the younger to photography, and Mary Wright Plummer to library science, to name but a few. Stanleyetta Titus Werner was the first woman admitted to the bar in New York State. Like female Friends in early ministries, in antebellum reform movements, and in later women's rights campaigns, these women drew on Quaker traditions and values to expand their horizons and those of the women around them. Often supported by men who shared their belief in women's God-given rights and responsibilities, even those Quaker women who ultimately rejected the faith of their youth benefited from the education, the autonomy, and the egalitarian vision provided in the Society of Friends.

An example of a Quaker woman who found it convenient to further Quaker concerns outside the confines of the dormant Hicksite society was Amanda Halstead Deyo of Creek Meeting in Dutchess County. An organizer, lecturer, and officer in the Universal Peace Union, she represented the union at the Universal Peace Conference in Paris in 1889. She served as a minister in churches of the Universalists in New York State, Pennsylvania, and San Diego, California, founding peace and women's rights societies in every community she served. Upon retirement she rejoined Friends and died on Long Island in 1917.[48]

It was such early socialization and faith that allowed women such as Amy Post, Emily Howland, and Susan B. Anthony to sustain their activist careers over several decades and that assured that Quaker women would remain prominent not only within the Society of Friends but also in movements for racial equality, women's suffrage, temperance, prison reform, and peace throughout the nineteenth and twentieth centuries. When Anthony was once asked, "Do you pray?" she responded, "I pray every second of my life; not on my knees but with my work. My prayer is to lift women to equality with men. Work and worship are one with me."[49] When we consider the life of Anthony and the work of the other New York Quaker women whose lives are documented here as well as that contributed by hundreds of female Friends who joined them in their efforts, we can finally and fully grasp what George Fox meant when he said, "Let your lives speak."

11

Quakers, Slavery, and the Civil War

CHRISTOPHER DENSMORE
and
THOMAS BASSETT

The New Abolitionism

Changes were occurring in the antislavery movement. In 1825 English Quaker Elizabeth Heyrick's pamphlet, *Immediate, Not Gradual Emancipation,* was reprinted in New York, and in 1827 slavery nearly came to an end in New York State. A new era in the antislavery movement began in 1831 with the publication of William Lloyd Garrison's newspaper, *The Liberator,* with its program of immediate emancipation and with the organization the next year of the Massachusetts (later New England) Anti-Slavery Society. The old abolitionist organizations had been small groups of benevolent individuals, working for gradual emancipation through moral suasion and appeals to the government. The new movement would be mass based and militant.

Friends and Abolition Societies

The change in the style of the abolitionist movement in the 1830s presented a problem for Quakers. The Society of Friends was adamantly opposed to slavery. The *Discipline* not only prohibited slaveowning but cautioned Friends to do "no act by which the right of slavery was acknowledged." But what could Friends do when the topic was severely dividing the nation?[1]

Many Quakers in New York Yearly Meeting were active in organizing the local antislavery societies. The first antislavery society in Michigan was organized by Elizabeth Margaret Chandler, the Quaker editor of the women's section of the *Genius of Universal Emancipation,* in a

183

Friends' meeting house.[2] Abolitionist societies, under Quaker leadership, flourished in places such as Farmington, Scipio, Hudson, and Ferrisburg.

All Quakers were opposed to slavery, but many were uneasy about the new abolition movement. Some Friends feared that Quaker principles would be compromised by involvement with non-Friends (many of them clergy) and that the agitation over slavery would draw Friends into the political arena. The question of Quaker involvement in "popular reform" was debated in the pages of the *Friends Intelligencer,* a Quaker periodical published by Isaac T. Hopper in New York City. One Friend wrote that in abolition societies Quakers would be "sometimes reduced to the painful and humiliating condition of passive spectators or tacit supporters of measures [with] which they cannot totally unite." Other Friends were willing to make common cause with non-Friends. "Conformity to the spirit of Truth, and not co-incidence of opinion or practice . . . [is] a higher and more infallible test of propriety," wrote one. "[T]he claims of a party, or of a sect, are nothing to those of truth," wrote another.[3]

Quaker misgivings about the abolitionist movement became a public issue in the 1830s through the issue of the use of meeting houses by agents of the American Anti-Slavery Society (AASS). Some local meetings denied agents the use of their meeting houses either on the grounds that the agents were paid, which violated the Quaker testimony against a "hireling ministry," or that their presence involved the Society in worldly politics, neither of which was appropriate for a Quaker meeting house. Agents (a number of whom were Quakers themselves) who were denied the use of meeting houses charged that the Society of Friends had sadly regressed since the days of John Woolman and Anthony Benezet. On the other side, Friends who were opposed to slavery and conscientiously avoided the use of products of slave labor found themselves characterized as proslavery because of their reluctance to support the new abolitionist movement.

Quakers were not unified in attitude toward the abolitionist movement. Some meetings denied the use of their meeting houses to paid lecturers but allowed unpaid speakers; other meeting houses were always available to agents of the AASS. Aaron M. Powell, a Quaker agent of the AASS, requested the use of the Jericho Meeting House in the 1850s. "[A]ll those present were individually willing, but collectively they were not free to give consent because of some previous action of the Monthly Meeting. . . . It was therefore arranged that we should hold our meeting in a school-house, a mile or two distant. Every Friend

9. Isaac T. Hopper (1771–1852). Silhouette by August Edouart, 1839.
Courtesy Friends Historical Library, Swarthmore College.

in attendance at the meeting in the morning, though the evening
proved dark and stormy, was present at our school house meeting." At
nearby Jerusalem a Friends minister took personal responsibility and
opened the meeting house for Powell.[4]

In 1840 the American Anti-Slavery Society split, in part over the
issue of female participation as equals in the abolitionist movement.
Those who favored the participation of women as equals retained control over the "old organization," whereas those who felt that the abolitionist movement should not become involved in issues unrelated to
the main goal of abolition formed the American and Foreign Anti-
Slavery Society. When the "old organization" selected a new executive
board after the split in 1840, six of the eleven members were Quakers,
and four of those were from New York State: James S. Gibbons (1810–
1892), his father-in-law Isaac T. Hopper (1771–1852), and Charles Marriott (died 1843), all members of New York Yearly Meeting (Hicksite),
and Joseph C. Hathaway (1810–1873), a member of Genesee Yearly
Meeting.

George F. White (1789–1847), a recorded minister of New York Monthly Meeting (Hicksite) was in the habit of frequently speaking against societies for popular reform, a category that included missionary and temperance societies and the abolitionist organizations as well. Oliver Johnson (1809–1889), an abolitionist living with the Isaac T. Hopper family and an attender at Rose Street Meeting, where White frequently spoke, attempted to counter White through correspondence and occasionally in meeting. The issue came to a head with the publication of a highly critical article about White entitled "A Rare Specimen of a Quaker Preacher" in the *National Anti-Slavery Standard,* the organ of the American Anti-Slavery Society, on March 25, 1841. The overseers of the meeting quickly moved to discipline Hopper and Gibbons (and later Charles Marriott, who was out of town at the time) for involvement "in the publication of a paper calculated to excite discord and disunity among Friends."[5] Hopper and Gibbons countered that they were not responsible for the article, and Hopper, at least, seems to have regretted its publication, but neither Hopper nor Gibbons felt that they needed to apologize for an article that was factually accurate. New York Monthly Meeting disowned the three men who appealed the decision to the quarterly and finally to the yearly meeting. Ultimately, New York Yearly Meeting upheld the decision of New York Monthly Meeting, but the committee that heard the case was divided.[6]

Peru Monthly Meeting on the west side of Lake Champlain wrote officially to New York Monthly Meeting to question White's standing among Friends. Friends from Ferrisburg Quarter published an open letter in the *National Anti-Slavery Standard,* endorsing Hopper and criticizing White.[7]

The results were tragic. Hopper was disowned but continued to sit on the facing bench of his local meeting. A few Friends withdrew from membership. Joseph Carpenter of New Rochelle remained a member but would never after attend the yearly meeting session. The disownment of Hopper, perhaps more than any single factor, set the stage for the "Progressive" separations among Hicksite Friends in Marlborough Monthly Meeting and Genesee Yearly Meeting in the later 1840s. It may have also hastened the demise of the Hicksite meetings in Ferrisburg Quarter in Vermont and on Nantucket, both strongholds of Quaker abolitionist sentiment. Undoubtedly, many people, such as Oliver Johnson, who were attracted to Quakerism, were dissuaded from joining after having seen the spectacle of religious schism in the 1820s followed by the Hopper affair in the 1840s.

In the end the Hopper disownments resolved nothing. The Hick-

10. John J. Cornell (1826–1909).
Courtesy Friends Historical Library, Swarthmore College.

site yearly meetings continued to be wary of the abolitionist movement, but even conservative Hicksites were unwilling to go through another trauma. Abolitionist-minded Friends continued to work as before. In the 1850s younger Friends, such as Aaron M. Powell, later editor of the *National Anti-Slavery Standard,* and Susan B. Anthony, became paid lecturers for the American Anti-Slavery Society.

The events of the 1820s and the 1840s forced Friends, Hicksites in particular, to rethink the idea of unity. John J. Cornell, a young Friend living near Mendon, New York, was distressed by the disagreements among those people he had believed were following true leadings and ceased to attend meeting for two months. While plowing in his field, he was "suddenly arrested by a voice speaking to my outer ear. . . . I found I was alone with my God." The message was direct, "Although all men else forsake my law, it will not excuse thee."[8] Cornell later became clerk of Genesee Yearly Meeting, and was one of the best-known Hicksite ministers of the later nineteenth century. What ultimately emerged was a more "modern" attitude, holding that shared religious testimonies do not necessarily result in unity in practice, particularly in the secular activities of Quakers. Modern Friends are more concerned with balancing diversity within a community that has shared religious roots than in enforcing conformity.

The New York Association of Friends

An alternative to joining with non-Quakers in abolitionist organizations was the New York Association of Friends for the Relief of Those Held in Slavery, and the Improvement of the Free People of Color organized by Hicksite Friends in 1839 and probably modeled after a similar association in Philadelphia. The New York Association published pamphlets on slavery, endorsed the free produce movement, and taught evening schools for free Blacks in New York City.

Many of the members of the New York Association were also active in non-Quaker abolition, and when Hopper, Gibbons, and Marriott were disowned in 1842, the New York Association protested the actions of New York Monthly Meeting. The committee appointed in June 1842 to oversee the association's school for colored adults consisted of Charles Marriott, Isaac T. Hopper, Abigail Hopper Gibbons, and Sarah Marshall. The association continued to circa 1846, and one of its last official acts was to publish a memorial, Quaker style, to disowned Friend Charles Marriott.[9]

Vermont Quakers and the Abolitionist Movement

Quaker Rowland T. Robinson of Ferrisburg attended the organization meeting of the Vermont Anti-Slavery Society on May 1, 1834, and four years later he voted against political action. His fifth annual report of the Anti-Slavery Society of Ferrisburgh and Vicinity the previous month still favored "moral suasion" over "legal suasion." By January 1841 the Vermont Anti-Slavery Society voted to secede from the Garrisonian "no-government" national organization with Robinson and Orson S. Murray of Brandon, Vermont, Baptist minister, editor, and communitarian, as the only objectors to this move to work through the Liberty Party. Robinson saw that a one-idea party, bent on ending slavery and ignoring all other social ills connected with it, might win the battle but lose the war for social reform. Both branches of the Society felt that it was un-Quakerly to work with mixed groups that did not infuse their procedures with worship or decide by sense of the meeting. Friends felt that voting and parliamentary procedures were coercive and did not achieve a unity that made for durable decisions. Robinson did not wait to be disowned for joining with non-Friends in a worthy cause but resigned from meeting. This resulted, more or less directly, in the laying-down of Ferrisburg Quarterly Meeting (Hicksite) in 1846.

African-Americans and Quakers

In 1836 Joseph Carpenter (1793–1872), of New Rochelle, Westchester County, became the guardian of three orphaned former-slave children. When the Carpenter family attended the local Friends meeting, one of the elders instructed the black children to sit apart. Carpenter, his wife, and their daughter did not protest verbally but with the children moved from their accustomed place to become a visible reminder that the Society of Friends had fallen short of its egalitarian potential. The criticism was understood, and the Carpenter family, with its African-American members, soon returned to its accustomed seats. Even so, New Rochelle Friends did not entirely heed the lesson. In 1838 Susan B. Anthony, a young teacher in Eunice Kenyon's Quaker boarding school, reported continued prejudice against the colored attenders at meeting and observed that some people had left the meeting on that account rather than associate with the Blacks. Carpenter was later involved with integrating the public schools in New Rochelle. When African-Americans were denied burial in the existing cemeteries, he provided land for a new cemetery where he was buried in his accustomed Quaker garb, his coffin carried by members of the local African-American community.

The Carpenter family was not the only example of African-Americans living with Friends. Harriet Jacobs, author of *Incidents in the Life of a Slave Girl*, lived in the household of Amy and Isaac Post in Rochester in the 1850s. The family of David Thomas in Union Springs, New York, took in a five-year-old freed slave to be raised and educated.[10]

The Free Produce Movement and Compensated Emancipation

Quakers had spoken against using slave-produced goods since the days of John Woolman and Elias Hicks. Genesee Yearly Meeting had incorporated a statement against the use of slave-produced goods in its revised *Discipline* of 1842, and in 1845 New York Yearly Meeting (Orthodox), following the lead of Farmington Quarter, advised members to

use only free goods. A Free Produce Association of Friends of New York
Yearly Meeting, based largely in New York City, was founded in 1846,
and free produce stores were operated in several locations within the
yearly meeting. The "Free Produce Movement" remained a Quaker
concern, however, while the antislavery movement continued to move
in a more activist direction.[11]

The National Compensated Emancipation Society, established in
1856, was a late and unsuccessful effort to resolve the issue of slavery
and avert the coming Civil War. New York City Friend Robert Lindley
Murray served as treasurer, and other Orthodox Friends supported the
movement.[12]

Prophetic Antislavery

In the decade before the Civil War the 1803 "Vision" of Vermont
Quaker Joseph Hoag (1762–1846) circulated widely in manuscript and
printed versions. The first datable appearance was in *Frederick Douglass's
Paper* in 1854, but Friends claimed that it had been circulating in
manuscript for many years.[13] The vision predicted a "dividing spirit"
that would split first the churches and then the nation and cause a civil
war that would end slavery but also establish a "monarchical power"
that would oppress Friends and others.[14] "I was amazed at beholding all
this; and I heard a voice proclaiming: 'This power shall not always
stand; but with it I will chastise my Church, until they return to the
faithfulness of their forefathers. Thou seest what is coming upon thy
native country, for their iniquities and the blood of Africa: the re-
membrance of which has come up before me'."

In 1834 Priscilla Hunt Cadwallader, a well-known Hicksite Friend
from Indiana, delivered a prophecy at the Quaker meeting in Farmington, New York. "I hear the cannons roar, and the beating of drums,
and I see the horse and his rider amid the clash of arms and human
blood. . . . Slavery will go down . . . and I entreat you to wash your
hands in innocency."[15] Although some have seen Hoag's vision as an
actual foretelling of the future, most Quakers would have understood it
as prophetic in the sense of a warning about the consequences of sin.

Quakers and the Civil War: Conscientious Objection

New York Yearly Meeting, at the beginning of June 1863, wrestled
with the problem of paying commutation as an alternative to being
drafted. Set at three hundred dollars, much below the going rates for

substitutes but estimated as equal to the wages of a day laborer for one year, commutation freed from further military service the man whose number was drawn. A large committee considered the question for three days and reported that Friends could not pay "any tax for the specific and exclusive purpose of Military service or the promotion of war, nor any debt . . . contracted by others for such specific purpose." The report, however, sanctioned paying mixed taxes even if part was used for war.[16]

In December 1863 all the Orthodox yearly meetings in Union territory except Philadelphia sent representatives to a conference in Baltimore. They had been negotiating with Edward Stanton, secretary of war, for total exemption. He seemed willing to credit work among the refugee Blacks clustered around Washington and behind Union lines in the West as the equivalent of three hundred dollars commutation, or to earmark that three hundred dollars for a freedmen's fund. Although the conference rejected this proposal, it was incorporated into a February 1864 amendment to the conscription act, effective July 4, 1864, assigning the three-hundred-dollar commutation money to a fund for sick and wounded soldiers and assigning to hospital duty or work with refugees those unwilling to pay commutation. No one has studied what happened to the commutation money under this amendment. As for the conscientious objectors (COs) to commutation, Secretary Stanton ultimately instructed provost marshals of each district to parole COs when they were drafted. Perhaps New England Friends' lobbying contributed to this result.

Cyrus Guernsey Pringle, of Charlotte, Vermont, was one of three Vermont Quakers drafted in July 1863 who would not pay commutation. He had joined Friends in 1859 and married a Quaker minister. He kept a diary, first published in the February 1913 *Atlantic Monthly*, of his experiences in the army when he refused to bear arms.[17] In November 1863 he was paroled from temporary hospital duty with two others from Vermont and two from Massachusetts. He described the higher officers as uniformly courteous with the only troubles coming from sometimes violent noncommissioned officers. An undocumented story has circulated that in his last years as curator of his herbarium at the University of Vermont, Pringle almost threw the pension agent downstairs when the agent told him he was entitled to a pension.

The weighty Friends of Pringle's meeting advised him to pay commutation although that, too, was specifically contrary to the Peace Testimony. Answers to queries on this point did not specify numbers because this was the usual response when drafted. Research has disclosed few pieces in the Quaker press against paying commutation. Gideon Frost, a Matinecock, Long Island, Hicksite, claimed that the elders in both branches urged paying and cited the cases of several young men who refused to pay. These, however, were paroled once they produced "credentials," presumably affidavits of Quaker membership.[18]

"S. C." of East Shelby, Orleans County, New York, was more severe. He attacked those who bought "securities . . . to carry on the war" or voted for "a party, based upon war and pledged to carry it on to victory, by [drafting] . . . innocent, quiet, harmless persons who [want] . . . peace, but have no means of escape." They should follow Paul's advice to the Corinthians and "refuse to do business with the unclean men of the world."[19]

Meeting the first week of June 1865, New York Yearly Meeting summarized the subordinate meetings' answers to the queries at length. To queries about clearness from military activity, two quarterly meetings admitted to exceptions not specified; one, to a case of "advancing money to be used in procuring recruits"; one, to paying commutation and four, that some members paid "the bounty tax"; six had members who furnished substitutes; "several" had members joining the army or "other military organizations," such as home guards. Yet five quarters claimed to be "clear of complying with military requisitions, and of paying any fine or tax instead thereof." The State of Society report omitted any reference to military service by Friends.[20]

The subject of Quakers and the Civil War is a good deal larger than the stories of fighting or pacifist Quakers. How much did they want the Union to win the war? The New York Representative Meeting, soon after Sumter, issued an "Address" to the members of the yearly meeting, reiterating the standard Peace Testimony of Friends, but emphasizing, "We love our country" and are grateful for its "many blessings." The "Address" went on to state no sympathy for the rebels and while declining to help with war preparations or enjoy war profits averred that "We can pray that God will bless our country."[21]

Quaker Military Service

Priscilla Cadwallader told Friends to "wash their hands in innocency," but when the war came, some Friends chose military service. Elizabeth Comstock, a Michigan Quaker involved in relief efforts on behalf of the newly freed slaves, gives an account of a chance meeting of three Union officers in Maryland. One was the son of the clerk of New England Yearly Meeting, another the elder brother of Rufus

11. Sunderland P. Gardner (1802–1893).
Courtesy Friends Historical Library, Swarthmore College.

Jones, and the third, the son of William Henry Chase, a minister in Scipio Monthly Meeting.[22]

We do not have figures for the number of New York Friends who served in the Union Army. A recent study of Indiana Quakers estimated that 21–27 percent of Friends of military age served in the armed forces, compared with 62 percent of the general population. Of the 1,212 Indiana Quakers who joined the army, 238 died in service; among those returning, 220 apologized for their actions and were retained in membership, and 148 were disowned. There is no record of disciplinary action against the remaining 608.[23]

In May 1863 Sunderland P. Gardner of Farmington, New York, preached at the funeral of a young man, a Quaker by birth, who had been killed in battle near Fredericksburg, Virginia. "I fear our testimony against war, as well as some many things, is becoming merely nominal." The following year, he lamented over those that "professing Christianity . . . are still warriors; bearing the name of Christ they follow Moses." Even some "professing to be Friends cannot bear to hear the peaceable gospel of Christ held forth!" During the Civil War Gardner preached at the funerals of at least six men who were killed or had died in military service.[24]

Gardner's words could well apply to the sermon delivered by Unitarian O. B. Frothingham at the burial of Edward Ketcham, a Quaker from Milton, Ulster County, killed at Gettysburg. Ketcham, Frothingham avowed, had not violated the spirit of Quaker testimonies because he fought to eradicate slavery and in the "holy cause of peace."[25]

What had become of the Quaker Peace Testimony? It is likely that in New York, as in Indiana, many Quakers violated the Peace Testimony and joined the army or otherwise supported the war effort. The Society of Friends, however, and those who spoke on its behalf did not waver in their pacifism. What had changed was the ability, or perhaps the desire, of the Society to enforce uniformity of behavior through disciplining or disowning those who violated Quaker testimonies. Upholding the Peace Testimony was becoming a matter of individual conscience.

New York Draft Riots and the Burning of the Colored Orphan Asylum

In the spring of 1863 the United States government introduced conscription. That summer, riots broke out in several northern cities, brought on by dissatisfaction with the government, the war, and the resentment, particularly among working people, toward the draft. Often Blacks and abolitionists were the focus of mob anger. Innocent Blacks were beaten and sometimes killed, and Black businesses and homes were burned. A conservative estimate places the death toll of the New York City riot at seventy-four.

The riot began in New York on July 11. After two days of rioting, at 4:00 P.M. on the 13th, a mob numbering in the hundreds, if not thousands, reached the Colored Orphan Asylum at Fifth Avenue between 43d and 44th streets where 233 children were housed. After breaking down the front door with an ax, the mob looted the building and set several fires. Chief Engineer John Decker of the NYC Fire Department arrived with ten or fifteen men and proceeded to extinguish the fires. He was told if he attempted to do so again, he would be killed. Decker and his men persisted in their efforts for more than one hour but were unable to save the building from the mob. The asylum, a four-story brick building, was totally destroyed. While the firemen confronted the mob, the 233 children and their 8 caretakers, after a silent prayer, quietly left the building and went out into the streets, which were filled with rioters. The group did not know where to seek refuge but finally reached a police station on 35th Street where they remained for three days. Friends of the asylum sent in food to supply the orphans and other Black New Yorkers who had sought refuge in the police station. The refugees, both orphans and adults, were placed under the care of the superintendent of the asylum. When peace was restored in New York, the orphanage was moved to Carmansville, in upper Manhattan.[26]

New York Friends and the Freedmen

In 1861 the federal government denied any intention to interfere with the institution of slavery. Slaves, however, began to take matters into their own hands by escaping into the Union lines. Initially, these fugitives were returned as lawful property but by 1862 were declared "contraband of war." This policy not only deprived the Confederacy of slave labor but aided the Union cause because the contrabands worked for the Union Army as laborers and teamsters or grew food and cotton for the Union cause on confiscated plantations. The result was that hundreds and then thousands of self-emancipated former slaves crowded into the Union lines in Virginia and the portions of the Southern coast held by the Union Army. Many worked and drew wages, but the old, the children, and the sick needed assistance.

In October 1862 a committee from the Meeting for Sufferings of New York Yearly Meeting (Orthodox) toured the contraband camps in Virginia. They found pressing needs, and soon New York Friends were shipping cloth and clothing to the refugee camps. The women in the New York City and Brooklyn meetings assisted in organizing the distribution and in sewing needed garments. The first distributions were made through individuals already working in Virginia, including Emily Howland, a young Orthodox Friend from Cayuga County, New York, who had taught in a black school in Washington before the war, and Abby Hopper Gibbons, the daughter of Isaac T. Hopper. In January 1863 Harriet Jacobs, a former slave, was hired as an agent by the committee, and, later, Harriet's daughter, Louisa Matilda, was also appointed agent.[27]

Whenever possible, it was the policy of Friends to sell rather than to give away clothing if the recipients had the ability to pay. Those who

12. Freedman's School, Camp Todd, Virginia, 1865.
Pencil sketch by Emily Howland.
Courtesy Friends Historical Library, Swarthmore College.

could not, the aged, the sick, and orphaned children were given clothing freely. Later, when Friends became involved in educational efforts, the same policy applied. Refugees built their own schools and, where possible, paid at least part of the teacher's salary. The strategy was to leave, as soon as possible, with local schools for the newly freed slaves built, supported, and taught by local people at least until such time as the public school systems could assume responsibility for the education of all citizens. Given the conditions of the South during the Civil War, there was no discussion of integration although Quaker assistance was sometimes extended to white refugees, particularly Southern unionists displaced by the war. Orthodox Friends were initially most active around Alexandria, Virginia, later extending into other parts of Virginia and the Carolina coast.

New York Hicksites contributed money and supplies to the Freedman's National Relief Association and later to the Friends Association of Philadelphia for the Aid and Elevation of the Freedmen. Notes of New York activities published in the Hicksite *Friends Intelligencer* also spoke approvingly of the efforts of the "other portion of our Society." In 1864 the Hicksites began the New York Friends Freedmen's Association, whose primary work was the support of schools at the government farms near the Patuxent River in St. Mary's County, Maryland.[28]

Although Quaker efforts began as short-term relief to clothe and feed refugees, they soon turned into an educational program. Although the early Quaker schools were not envisioned as permanent institutions, by the later 1860s some Friends were beginning to realize that the solution was to take longer, and New York Quaker support for education of blacks in the South continued into the next century.

Quakers and the World

In the 1840s Friends were unsure about mixing with non-Quakers even in the good cause of abolitionist societies. In the 1860s Quakers from both the Hicksite and Orthodox branches of New York Yearly Meeting were freely working with non-Friends. Quakers taught in schools built by the labor of former slaves from supplies furnished by the army, using books donated by the American Tract Society. Quakers had become willing to be engaged with the world.

12

Evangelicals and Hicksites, 1870–1917

Thomas D. Hamm, Hugh Barbour
and
Elizabeth Moger, Sabron Reynolds Newton,
Marty Walton

From Revival to Modernism: Gurneyite Friends

As the year 1870 dawned, an observer of New York Yearly Meeting of Gurneyite, or Orthodox, Friends would have had little trouble knowing that this group held ties back to the days of Fox, Penn, and Barclay. Outwardly, they preserved all of the evidences of traditional Quakerism. The plain dress was still the rule, especially for women. Meetings for worship were still held based on silence, with songs or Bible readings unknown, the men and women seated separately, the weighty Friends facing them at the front. Meetings for business, from the preparative to the yearly meeting level, were conducted separately as well. Outside the meeting houses, whose architecture changed little over one hundred years, the bare expanses of the burying grounds would be broken by only a few small, plain stones. The names of those who dominated the yearly meeting proceedings—Wood, Underhill, Titus, Chase, Hazard, Murray, Valentine, Haviland, Purdy, Birdsall, Mott, Collins, Taber—would have been familiar to New York Friends a century earlier.[1]

Forty years later, signs of change were everywhere. Men and women now mingled, seated together for worship, meeting jointly for business. Some meetings were still worshipping on the waiting in silence, but others had become almost indistinguishable from those of other Protestants with pastors, choirs, organs, hymns, and all of the other elements of a "program." In some meetings, revivals, complete with altar

calls, occurred annually. The outward marks of traditional Quakerism—plain dress, plain language—were the preserve of the elderly.

These changes were largely the result of a revolution in Gurneyite
Quakerism between 1870 and 1890. At its heart was the interdenominational holiness movement that was causing ferment in almost all of
American Protestantism. It swept away most of the distinguishing marks
of traditional Quakerism. Its effects were not as sweeping in New York
as they were among Friends west of the Appalachians, but they were
profound. Gurneyites moved from being a self-conscious sect to a denomination. This revolution had been long in the making; its roots lay
in the growing acculturation of Friends before the Civil War as they
increasingly read the same books, newspapers, and periodicals as other
evangelical Protestants, joined the same political parties and reform
movements, and formed ties in business and educational enterprises.
New York Yearly Meeting had been the first to acknowledge tacitly a
declining suspicion of "outsiders" when it relaxed the rules on "marriage out of unity" in 1859. Gurneyite theology was also vital. It moved
Friends to think of conversion as definite and instantaneous, to emphasize the authority of Scripture, and to participate actively in Sabbath
Schools and other enterprises of evangelical piety. By the mid-1860s
many New York Friends, such as William H. S. Wood, Robert L. and
Ruth Murray, and Mary H. Thomas, were leaders in the growing renewal movement of young Gurneyites who sought to reform Quakerism by paring away seemingly archaic regulations on dress, speech, and
marriage while preserving fundamental distinctives, such as unprogrammed worship, women's ministry, and a Peace Testimony.[2]

Late in the 1860s, however, this movement was pushed aside by the
advocates of holiness. They drew brilliantly on traditional Quaker language and concepts but used them to work a fundamental change
among Friends. Sanctification, or holiness, was a doctrine with a long
history among Quakers. It meant that humans were, while living, capable of achieving perfection, attaining a state of sinlessness in which
they were freed from any propensity to sin. Traditionally, Friends had
taught that it was inseparable from justification; indeed, that one was
saved by being sanctified. This was a gradual experience, however, usually spread over the course of a lifetime. Joseph John Gurney's influence was critical here also. By leading most Friends to see conversion as
distinct from sanctification, he moved them closer to the evangelical
mainstream of American religion. Gurney, however, always spoke and
wrote of sanctification as a gradual experience subsequent to conversion. In the generation after Gurney's death in 1847 most Orthodox

Friends came to accept his views. The holiness movement, by contrast, taught that sanctification was a second experience, instantaneous, subsequent to conversion, achieved by love released by the power of the atoning blood of Christ. Holiness was a powerful force in American Protestantism from the 1860s to the 1890s. In the 1860s a number of Gurneyite Friends were drawn into the movement. These Friends originally were drawn entirely from Indiana and Ohio Yearly Meetings: David B. Updegraff, Luke Woodard, Jacob Baker, John Henry and Robert Douglas, Nathan and Esther Frame, Caroline Talbot. They used holiness teachings to introduce the trappings of aggressive revivalism to Gurneyite Friends.[3]

The original vehicle for this movement was the general meeting. Indiana Yearly Meeting had set up the first in 1867; they originally were intended to educate Friends about essential Quaker doctrine. They were, in short, teaching meetings. By 1870, however, a change had taken place as the holiness believers came to control the meetings. David B. Updegraff, the Ohio Friend, succinctly summed it up: "I was one of that number and joined with others in imploring that 'the dead' might be left to 'bury the dead,' and that we might unite in preaching the gospel and getting converts to *Jesus.* In the providence of God such counsel prevailed, and then it was that our General Meetings became 'Revival Meetings'."[4]

The stories of both unprecedented evangelizing and large numbers of converts in the "western" general meetings came to the attention of New York Friends by sympathetic accounts in the Philadelphia *Friends' Review* or through relatives in the West. There had also been a movement of Friends from Indiana and Ohio to New York City after the Civil War, pursuing business opportunities. Thomas W. and William H. Ladd, both educated at Haverford, were sons of Benjamin W. Ladd of Smithfield, Ohio, a leading elder and clerk of Ohio Yearly Meeting.[5]

More important, however, would be a procession of traveling ministers from the West. Revivalism was almost never spontaneous; it was the work of ministers, usually traveling in groups. In the 1870s every Orthodox yearly meeting session in New York included at least a dozen visiting ministers, in 1870, eight from Ohio alone, including two prominent advocates of holiness, Caroline Talbot and Updegraff, plus John Henry Douglas of Indiana.[6] The 1870 yearly meeting set the revival in motion by uniting with a proposal from Farmington Quarterly Meeting to copy the western yearly meetings and set up a committee on general meetings. The yearly meeting minuted its hope that they would prove effectual both in increasing knowledge of Quaker principles and as a "return to . . . [the] zeal of [early] Friends . . . in gathering souls to Christ." Thirty-two Friends were named to it, including Robert Lindley Murray, the clerk of the men's yearly meeting, and his wife, Ruth Shearman Murray, William H. and Caroline Ladd, Mary H. Thomas, Augustus Taber, and Friends who would become increasingly prominent as the revival gained strength: Jonathan DeVol of Glens Falls, Alexander M. Purdy of Palmyra, and William H. Chase of Union Springs. It was left, however, to the discretion of the quarters to decide whether they would hold meetings within their bounds with the help of the yearly meeting committee.[7]

Ministers from the west dominated the first general meeting, appropriately at Farmington, in five days of August 1871. Twenty-nine ministers were present, sixteen from within the yearly meeting. Esther Frame later told that "the spirit seemed to be moving someone to engage in vocal service" constantly; "even then some went away without 'relieving their minds'." There was an unbroken service of sermons and prayers from Robert W. Douglas, the Frames, William Wetherald of Canada, Updegraff, Caroline Talbot, Elizabeth Comstock, Luke Woodard, and Sarah F. Smiley of Baltimore. All but Comstock had experienced sanctification. There was no singing and no altar call, but the impassioned preaching emphasized the authority of Scripture and the necessity of conversion through faith in the blood of Christ. A Palmyra newspaper told how the women ministers would "exhort and beg the sinner to come to Jesus. . . . Arguments, appeals, exhortations, are poured forth from the lips . . . like molten lava, and issue from the gurgling fountain of cool water, eyes unused to tears are dimmed, and many a strong frame made to shake."[8]

The critical one of the four other general meetings was in Brooklyn in November. Leading it were the holiness champions from the West: the Frames, Woodard, Updegraff, and Esther Tuttle, along with Smiley and Wetherald. Present also was John Henry Douglas, who was converted to holiness at the meeting. The preaching of sanctification was pronounced, and there were numerous outbursts of unrestrained emotion. A newspaper reported: "The lady preachers are eloquent and . . . work the audience to such a pitch of excitement, that some screech and scream, cry amen, and groan." There was no singing, but that was a last barrier that would soon fall. Some Brooklyn Friends attempted to hand out a pamphlet setting forth the views of the early Friends and were rebuked by the ministers. Notable was the welcome Friends extended to ministers of other denominations. After the meetings at Brooklyn came ones at Glens Falls and Rochester. Alexander M. Purdy noted some Friends came to criticize, like the "scribes and teachers" but ended up on their knees, crying, "Lord, be merciful to *me a sinner.*"[9]

The revival tide continued to build throughout the 1870s. At the 1872 yearly meeting the General Meeting Committee was continued. Some expressed reservations, but most thought that the work was of God. Revival scenes became increasingly common.

> [Glens Falls, 1872.] All rules of church etiquette were made subservient to the salvation of souls. Degraded men were brought from haunts of sin—the blood of Jesus Christ was the one watchword—the name of the Lord Jesus magnified . . . in a glad outburst of love and gratitude.
>
> [Clintondale, 1873.] The power of the Holy Ghost, as of fire, was most wonderfully felt (in some of the meetings) to be as a cleanser, a consumer of the chaff, and as a sanctifier of the wheat which remained; and in the hearts of those thus cleansed imparting a perfect trust for the future.
>
> [West Branch, 1874.] The refined and the cultivated and the uneducated and the dissipated; wives and husbands newly married; and parents and children knelt side by side, and prayed, and wept, and rejoiced together. Cards, whiskey and tobacco were abjured. Wives who had almost become broken-hearted over husbands, sung aloud for joy.[10]

The yearly meeting looked with favor on these scenes. "From every place we received the same testimony of the blessed results of this work," the Committee on General Meetings reported in 1877. "The indifferent have been aroused, the weak and timid encouraged, the wavering settled, all classes of Christians strengthened, and many sinners turned from being aliens to become children of the Lord." A Friend who was otherwise skeptical about the revival admitted its power: "It resembled the earthquake, the whirlwind, and the fire."[11]

Officially, then, the revival was an unmitigated success. By 1880 it had wrought significant change in the yearly meeting. The revival brought a new group into positions of leadership. Ministers from the west continued to play important roles. Luke Woodard from Indiana lived for a time in Rochester and Glens Falls, and winter, the traditional revival season, always brought others from west of the Appalachians to hold meetings. Thomas W. Ladd was the driving force of the General Meeting Committee for most of the decade. A fervent proponent of holiness, he was uncompromising in his evangelical views and commitment to aggressive revivalism. Perhaps the best-known figure to emerge from within the yearly meeting in this decade was Elizabeth

Mallison. Originally a Methodist, she joined Friends after the first general meeting at Glens Falls because the Methodists would not let her preach.[12]

Thomas Kimber embodied the course of New York Gurneyism in these years: born in Philadelphia in 1825, a birthright Friend, educated at Haverford, he finished his education with extensive travels in Europe. By age thirty-five, he was well established at the pinnacle of Philadelphia society: president of a small railroad, head of the Philadelphia Board of Trade, his estate on the Delaware River "the scene of many a notable gathering" of "scholars and men of note." Still, Kimber found something lacking in his life. That changed in 1864 when he experienced conversion. Thereafter, he was at odds with Philadelphia Yearly Meeting's Wilburite leadership so that he resigned his membership. In 1872 Kimber began to devote most of his time to traveling to revivals and general meetings from Maine to Kansas. He became a convert to holiness views. His contributions to the *Christian Worker* and the *Friends' Review* expressed uncompromising evangelicalism and hostility to anything that smacked of Wilburite or Hicksite views. In a series of articles Kimber attacked the Inner Light as an "ignis fatuus," which "leads to bewilder, and dazzles to blind."[13] Kimber was received into membership at his request by New York Monthly Meeting in 1878. Technically, the permission of Philadelphia was required, but in view of Philadelphia's conservatism and Kimber's abilities as a preacher and writer, the Representative Meeting broke with tradition. Soon afterward he was recorded a minister and moved to an estate on Long Island. Until his death in 1890 he was probably the most highly regarded minister in the yearly meeting and certainly was its most prolific author.[14]

The centrality of the ministry to the revival led to a new concern for orthodoxy in preaching. In 1876 the yearly meeting became the first in the world to require subscription to a doctrinal statement by all of its recorded ministers. This test probably grew out of a desire to improve the quality of yearly meeting ministry generally as early as 1873. In the spring of 1875 a conference of ministers and elders, with only one dissenter, decided that all ministers must be saved and be willing to testify to that. William H. Ladd warned ominously that it was not the case with all in the yearly meeting; Luke Woodard said they should require "bold answers" to definite questions. In the spring of 1875 the Yearly Meeting of Ministers and Elders proposed eight uncompromisingly evangelical questions:

1. Dost thou believe in one only wise, omnipotent, and eternal God, the Creator and Upholder of all things?

2. Dost thou believe in the fall of man through disobedience to God by yielding to the temptations of Satan; in the depravity of the human heart resulting therefrom; and that in consequence all men have sinned, and come under condemnations?

3. Dost thou believe in the Deity and Manhood of the Lord Jesus Christ; that His willing sacrifice on the cross at Calvary was a satisfactory offering to God for the sins of the whole world; that He arose from the dead and ascended into heaven, and now sitteth at the right hand of the Father, . . . that man is justified and made acceptable to God through faith in the atoning blood and the mediation of the Lord Jesus Christ; that this salvation is the free gift of God; that it is offered to all, and that all have power to accept or reject it?

4. Dost thou believe in the Holy Spirit, the promise of the Father, whom Christ declared He would send in His name; that He is come, and convicts the world of sin; that He leads to repentance towards God, and . . . to faith in the Lord Jesus Christ; . . . opens to them the truths of the Gospel as set forth in Holy Scripture, . . . guides, sanctifies, comforts, and supports them; that it is by Him the Lord Jesus Christ performs the work of grace in the hearts of men?

5. Dost thou believe that the Holy Scriptures were given by inspiration of God; that they are to be believed and accepted in their entirety; and that whatever doctrine or practice is contrary to them is to be rejected as false?

6. Dost thou believe in the spirituality of worship; that the one Baptism of the Gospel dispensation is that of Christ, who baptizes His people with the Holy Ghost; and that the true communion is a spiritual partaking of the body and blood of Christ by faith?

7. Dost thou believe in the resurrection of the just and of the unjust; in a day of Judgment; . . . everlasting punishment, [and] eternal?

8. Hast thou been born again and thus become a child of God?

Any time anyone was proposed for the stations of minister or elder, affirmative answers were to be required. There was considerable opposition at the yearly meeting session, however, so the Representative Meeting was ordered to take up the matter and report to the next yearly meeting.[15] The proposed queries became the center of a heated controversy. The *Friends' Review,* increasingly skeptical about the revival, labeled the action a dangerous step toward creedalism, a charge echoed by the Wilburite-leaning Philadelphia *Friend* and the *British Friend* in Glasgow. Proponents made it clear that their major concern was assuring doctrinal uniformity. New York Friends had suffered "a great deal of Hicksite influence, wrote John J. Thomas. David B. Updegraff in the *Christian Worker* branded opponents deceivers and latitudinarians. "In this day of unbelief and misbelief, when truth's conflict with error rapidly grows . . . more desperate, indefiniteness on cardinal points of faith [is] criminal."[16]

At the 1876 yearly meeting the queries were approved. A ninth was added, dealing with Christ's headship of the church. In 1880 Westbury Quarter asked for the matter to be reconsidered, but there was little sentiment to do so. Instead, the New York queries became a model for doctrinal tests in other yearly meetings. Not all New York Friends accepted the revival with enthusiasm. Most in New York City never took to it; there were skeptics in Brooklyn and Westbury Meetings. Cornwall Monthly Meeting in Orange County was agitated for years, needing a yearly meeting committee to bring it to order.[17]

The worst troubles, however, were in LeRay Monthly Meeting in Jefferson County and, more generally, throughout Butternuts Quarter. LeRay had been contentious for years; formerly there had been a LeRay Quarterly Meeting, but in 1872 it was laid down because of "irregularities." Conservative Friends apparently had the upper hand and were not afraid to use it. When Luke Woodard held a series of meetings there in the winter of 1874–75, they refused to consider applications from converts. When one convert sang in meeting, they brought him before a magistrate on a charge of disturbing a religious meeting. Warren Gardner, the leader of the revival party, was briefly disowned by the monthly meeting although the yearly meeting reversed that decision as "hasty" and irregular. Happily, the situation was resolved through the division of the meeting property rather than by the wielding of a heavy hand by the yearly meeting as was usually the case. The conservatives built a frame meeting house in which they continued to worship in the old ways. For a time, they remained part of New York Yearly Meeting but eventually joined Canada Yearly Meeting (Conservative) at its formation in 1881. The "progressive" or revivalistic group soon joined Westmoreland Monthly Meeting. By 1910 both meetings had collapsed.[18]

Other Friends in Butternuts Quarter also tried to resist the new departures. In 1878 they presented a long statement to the quarterly meeting, blasting the new Discipline approved in 1876. They judged it utterly inadequate on plainness and all of the traditional peculiarities. They were especially unhappy about its acceptance of music; the early Friends, they claimed, had burned musical instruments, not brought them into meeting houses. Pastoral committees were also unacceptable. Christ would be the pastor over those "truly united with him." The General Meeting Committee earned the worst criticism: "The practice of sending evangelistic committees forth with unlimited power . . . to set aside the judgment of every meeting and overrule all the remonstrances of Friends wherever they go is . . . taking the Lord's work into our own hands and . . . calling many to the service that are not qualified for it." Such protests did not change the course of the yearly meeting.[19] By 1877 the revival's place in New York Yearly Meeting seemed to be beyond challenge. By 1880, however, the holiness forces found themselves thrown into confusion over the issue of the "ordinances," the outward sacraments.

The original controversy centered around Helen Balkwill, an English minister who in 1877 began a two-year tour of the United States. By 1879, however, Balkwill had become convinced that water baptism was commanded by Scripture. English Friends promptly called her home. Balkwill's quandary reflected a growing anxiety among holiness Friends. Indeed, their view of sanctification made acceptance of water baptism almost inevitable. Friends had traditionally justified their views on baptism with the argument that the only true baptism was the baptism of the Holy Ghost. Holiness Friends believed, however, the baptism of the Holy Ghost was that which sanctified, the work of God alone. Because Christ had clearly commanded his disciples to baptize in his name, it seemed apparent that this could not refer to the baptism of the Holy Ghost but only to water baptism.[20] Before Balkwill went back to England, there was a conference of leading holiness Friends at Glens Falls, including Balkwill, Updegraff, Woodard, John Henry Douglas, and Thomas W. Ladd. Ladd claimed that they had met to discuss the promotion of holiness. Others there were sure that their goal was to promote the observance of the ordinances among Friends. All denied this, but subsequent events make it appear likely that it was so.[21]

The events at Glens Falls gave rise to a controversy that would, in New York, drag on for a decade. The "weight" of the yearly meeting, including a number of Friends hitherto favorably inclined toward the revival, was against any toleration of the ordinances. The foremost proponents of toleration were holiness advocates, notably Luke Woodard and Thomas W. Ladd, who died in 1882. Because Woodard's membership was still officially in Indiana, his repeated statements that he was "commanded" to preach toleration of water baptism were especially galling. In the spring of 1881 the Representative Meeting moved against him. Thereafter, Woodard, who had been one of the most active evangelists in New York Yearly Meeting, remained largely in Indiana, and the focus of the debate shifted to Ohio, Updegraff's stronghold. Controversy flared again occasionally: in 1885 New York Yearly

Meeting barred Noah McLean, one of Updegraff's disciples, from preaching in its bounds. Yet in 1889 Glens Falls created a stir by allowing two "waterites" to hold a revival.[22]

The most lasting product of the revival, and the greatest innovation, was the rise of the pastoral system. It was a logical outgrowth of the revival and by 1900 had worked a transformation of ways of worship in many meetings. One of the by-products of the revival was an influx of new members. Between 1872 and 1888 the yearly meeting membership grew from 2,814 to 3,848, modest by the standards of yearly meetings to the west, but still an increase of about one-third. These new members were, for the most part, unfamiliar with traditional Quaker worship. The atmosphere of the revival with its singing and emotion and fervent preaching was very different from the waiting silence of an old-fashioned meeting for worship. Many Friends, in New York and elsewhere, thought that new converts, feeling lost and unwanted, drifted into other denominations or, worse, backslid out of a state of grace. At best they remained in meetings, lukewarm in commitment. All agreed that the solution to this problem was pastoral care—to have older members instruct and guide newer ones, introducing them to the ways and beliefs of Friends. Some argued that this was the natural province of elders and overseers, but they apparently showed little interest in or aptitude for the work. By 1881 there was a growing sentiment that pastoral work should become the concern of ministers. That year the General Meeting Committee called for a "supply of Ministers who shall become pastors over the flock, and be able to preach the Gospel in an intelligent, attractive, and comprehensive manner." Thus began a debate that would last a decade.[23]

Alexander H. Hay, the most careful student of the coming of the pastoral system to New York Yearly Meeting, called it a "slow and careful process" in contrast to its more rapid acceptance to the west. The yearly meeting's leaders, including many whose evangelical commitment was unquestioned and who had supported the revival, were almost unanimous in opposition. Isaac P. Hazard of Poplar Ridge feared that it would end the liberty to speak in meeting. His neighbor, Mary S. Thomas, called it a "one-man system" that would make all members dependent on the pastor. James Wood thought that it would discourage members from developing their gifts. Thomas Kimber labeled the pastoral system both unscriptural and undemocratic: if the pastor was carried away "by any of the modern dogmas, or novelties of the hour," the flock would quickly be infected.[24]

Here, however, other forces proved more powerful. As early as

1875 Luke Woodard had served informally as the pastor at Rochester, and in 1884 he entered into a more formal arrangement at Glens Falls. By 1886 Mary Jane Weaver had assumed the pastorate at Brooklyn. That year the Representative Meeting, although minuting its opposition to "the official employment of a Minister as the official Pastor of any meeting at a fixed salary," did sanction monthly meetings making "sufficient Provision" for ministers who felt "called to a special labor within their bounds." By 1889 there were ten employed, more than in Indiana.[25] By the late 1890s the pastoral system had become an informal fixture in the yearly meeting. In 1893 the yearly meeting set up an Evangelistic and Pastoral Committee with a requirement that quarterly meetings establish their own committees. When John W. Graham, an influential English Friend, visited in 1897, he found pastors to be general, except in New York City, and judged that there was "no notion among the bulk of the membership that anything else is or ever has been Quaker practice." With acerbity he wrote that the yearly meeting was in a state of "degeneration," the roots of which went back to the 1870s. Alexander Purdy agreed that nearly all of the old landmarks had been swept away in the name of evangelism. "It has broken up free expression from the body of the meeting, and silenced worthy, beloved, and able ministers, and has driven from the meetings life-long Friends," he wrote, to "bring in those who know nothing about Friends."[26]

Another fruit of the revival was a growing interest in missionary work both at home and abroad. Although comparisons were always made to the travels of seventeenth-century Quakers, evangelical American Friends were also moved by emulation of the missionary impulse that swept nineteenth-century American Protestantism.[27] New York Friends played a crucial role in the development of Quaker missions. Probably the best-known American Quaker missionary before 1890 was Samuel A. Purdie, a birthright Friend born in Chenango County in 1843. After the Civil War he went to North Carolina to preach and teach. While there he felt led to begin studying Spanish and in 1871 to undertake work in Matamoros, Mexico, under the auspices of Indiana Yearly Meeting. Purdie did not go as a missionary in the conventional sense; his primary interest was promoting peace in a war-torn country. In Matamoros he had within a decade started a newspaper, translated a number of Quaker works into Spanish, and founded two schools. He was joined by other Friends who gave their attention to proselytizing. When Purdie and his wife, Gulielma, came home in 1895, they left behind six hundred Mexican Friends in six monthly meetings.[28]

Few New York Quakers were involved in the Friends Africa Industrial Mission, begun in 1902, from which grew the East Africa Yearly

Meetings, the largest in the Third World, although Edgar Hole returned from Kenya for a period of retirement in Poughkeepsie. But New York Friends played a central role in China through the work of George Fox DeVol, who came from Glens Falls. He was born in 1871 and educated at Earlham College where he met Isabella French, a Friend from Damascus, Ohio. After completing medical school, she joined another Ohio Friend, Esther Butler, and her assistant, Margaret A. Holme, a Brooklyn Quaker, in Nanking. After Isabella and George were married in 1900, they settled at Luho near Nanking. There the DeVols' work grew steadily. Chapels, a hospital, and schools were all built. George DeVol's reputation as a surgeon brought him patients from a wide area. The DeVols gave special attention to warring on the "opium habit." The number of converts grew steadily. Neither of the DeVols was robust: George DeVol died in Luho early in 1917; Isabella at home in Ohio in 1920. Other New York Friends followed them to China.[29]

The main support for these efforts came from women Friends. A women's missionary union for the yearly meeting was formed at the yearly meeting in 1887 and united with similar groups in the other Gurneyite yearly meetings to form the Women's Foreign Missionary Union of Friends in America, later the United Society of Friends Women. By 1900 missionary societies had become a fixture of many meetings, gathering to discuss the reports from the *Friends Missionary Advocate* and to take up collections. In 1904 Macedon's five members collected $10.85 to send to help the DeVols.[30]

The missionary impulse also included the "home field." Friends schools for the poor in New York City and Brooklyn were emphatically evangelistic in their instruction. Robert Lindley Murray, the clerk of the yearly meeting, had gone south after the Civil War to work with Samuel A. Purdie and other Friends. Early on, however, there was resistance to anything that suggested proselytizing.[31] The revival changed this. By 1873 Achsah Hazard of Ferrisburgh, Vermont, was conducting a Bible school for French Canadian children there. In 1878 Glens Falls reported that it was maintaining several mission schools. By 1881 New York Friends were conducting three, an adult mission at the 20th Street Meeting, and separate ones for Armenians and people of color.[32] New York Friends' primary home missionary enterprise was in North Carolina. In 1885 they undertook, in cooperation with North Carolina Yearly Meeting, the operation of a secondary school for blacks in Asheboro. In 1891 it was moved to nearby High Point, which had a much larger black population, and renamed the High Point Normal Industrial Institute. There was a farm to supply provisions, and the education was relentlessly vocational. "Much has been accomplished in dispelling ignorance and encouraging industry and frugality among the colored race," the board of Home and Foreign Missions reported in 1908. "Our students go out as Teachers, Dressmakers, Carpenters, Masons, and Farmers, and in their turn influence and encourage others." Religious observance was a regular part of the instruction for the sixty or so boarders and more than three hundred day students. New York Friends kept charge of the school until it was turned over to the local school board in 1920.[33]

By 1900, then, New York Friends were thoroughly acculturated. Most of the old plain ways were gone—the dress discarded by nearly all, the speech a habit of the elderly or a practice confined to families. Silent worship was the exception rather than the rule. With the pastoral system, complete with organs and hymns, and a complex of mission, evangelism, temperance, and educational boards, New York Yearly Meeting had taken on all of the trappings of a denomination. The process of change had not come to an end, however. In the first quarter of the twentieth century the yearly meeting would make a gradual transition from holiness revivalism to liberal modernism. It would not be a uniform process; some meetings remained much more evangelical than others, and the result seems to have been to normalize and rationalize the pastoral system, rather than weaken it. Still, by 1917 signs of change were apparent: the disappearance of the queries adopted in 1876, the increasing ties with the Hicksite yearly meeting, the lack of concern over modernist "heresies" that so agitated other yearly meetings, the identification of the yearly meeting's leadership with the liberal stalwarts like Rufus M. Jones, Elbert Russell, and Alexander C. Purdy. At the center of these changes was James Wood, clerk of the yearly meeting. Rufus Jones, the Haverford philosopher who became the leader of liberal Quakerism, remembered Wood as "a liberal-evangelical Friend, a genuine sympathizer with the message of Gurney" although "grow[ing] steadily in the direction of modern thought as time went on." Jones's description of Wood is apt for his yearly meeting.[34] By then the transformation of the Gurneyite Friends of New York was completed. Plainness was, fading. Outwardly, these Friends were indistinguishable from their neighbors. The power of the revival was also passing in New York. A new path of transformation had opened.

James Wood and the Five Years Meeting

James Wood (1839–1925), a gentleman farmer from Mt. Kisco and member of Croton Valley Preparative Meeting, had been educated at

13. New York Yearly Meeting (Orthodox) at 20th Street Meeting House, 1914.
Left to right: David Sherman Taber, James Wood, and L. Hollingsworth Wood.
Courtesy Haviland Records Room, New York Yearly Meeting.

Westtown and Haverford, schools of Philadelphia Orthodox Yearly
Meeting. He became active in the yearly meeting in the 1870s. He was
"probably at the time the best-known Friend in the United States," and
fulfilled the "urban" Orthodox Quaker pattern of philanthropy set up
by Eddy and Griscom although, in fact, he was raised and lived on the
same farm already owned by his family for one century.[35]

   He had not needed to serve in the Civil War. As an experimental
farmer he was active in state and local farmers' clubs, and in Bedford
town politics as a Teddy Roosevelt Republican, running in vain for Congress. He later became a manager of Haverford College and head of
the board of managers of Bryn Mawr (he declined its presidency), and
later president of the University of ChengTu in China, of the New York
State Reformatory for Women, for twenty-eight years of the Westchester
Temporary Home for Destitute Children (dissolved in 1909), and of
the American Bible Society, for whose sake he went to the World Missionary Conference in Edinburgh in 1910 and to San Francisco and
Seattle in 1914. In 1891, after a winter in Dresden where he set up
Mark Twain's lecture to support the American church there, he and
his daughter Carolena made a horseback tour of Egypt, Palestine, and

Syria, noting amid the sacred sites of three world religions, "If you can shut your eyes to the misery and simply look at it all as a picture, well for you, but I cannot."[36] In Lebanon he visited Theophilus Waldemeier, "the Abyssinian princess his wife," and their Friends School at Brummana. His lecture on *The Society of Friends and its Mission* to the World's Parliament of Religions in Chicago, September 22, 1893, and a major revision of it for Philadelphia Yearly Meeting in 1898 on *Distinguishing Doctrines of . . . Friends* were his only published works. Like Gurney's *Peculiarities,* they united Christian doctrine and Quaker practice, but Wood added a plea for Christian missions. He served as clerk of New York Yearly Meeting (Orthodox) in 1882, 1892, 1894, and from 1897 to 1925. In 1907 he was clerk of Five Years Meeting.

In 1887 with Augustus Taber of Brooklyn, then clerk of the Orthodox New York Yearly Meeting, he was present at the Richmond Conference. Wood was chosen to chair the gathering. There Joseph Bevan Braithwaite of London presented the strictly orthodox Statement of Faith that validated Friends' use of pastors but dismissed Ohio Friends' desire to discuss and use the sacraments or ordinances. Wood did not violate his clerk's role by speeches, but he brought the conference back at times to a spirit of prayer and helped the effort of the conference to centralize Friends Foreign Missions. He served on the Business Committee, bringing its conclusions to the whole conference. Augustus Taber spoke in favor of broad, nonpastoral ministry; David Lane of Chappaqua and Mary Jane Weaver of Batavia spoke in favor of pastoral ministry but for the sake of bringing out, not replacing the ministry of ordinary members. James Haviland of Poughkeepsie spoke for the special calling of pastors. James Wood guided the conference to a position that accepted pastors but did not "commit any formal arrangement to any one in our meetings for worship."[37] In 1892 and 1897 Wood again took part in Friends Conferences of thirteen or fourteen Orthodox Yearly Meetings, heading the Program Committee (his daughter Carolena Wood was a recording clerk),[38] proposing the conference rules (more parliamentary than Quaker), and speaking strongly in favor of a unified body for all Orthodox Friends, as did Rufus Jones from New England. As Five Years Meeting began to form as a result of these conferences, Rufus Jones spent long hours at James Wood's home, "Braewold," where they drafted together its plans to unite the work of the Orthodox Yearly Meetings in foreign missions, for Indians, and for temperance. Following the death by tuberculosis of Rufus Jones's beloved first wife, Sallie Coutant of Ardonia near Clintondale, whom he had met while they both taught at the Friends Oakwood Seminary at

Union Springs, New York, his sessions with James Wood led to Rufus's engagement to Wood's daughter Ellen, a trained nurse. Within weeks, however, she died of typhoid after nursing a sick sailor on a trip to Denmark with her father. Jones and Wood worked on a Uniform Discipline, which a fourth Gathering in 1902 accepted, thereby turning itself after its first night into the Five Years Meeting. New York Yearly Meeting accepted the Uniform Discipline, but Ohio and Philadelphia did not. Wood later served on the board of the united *American Friend,* Jones becoming its editor. Later, Wood helped Rufus Jones to found the American Friends Service Committee.

Between 1895 and 1917 the Gurneyite yearly meetings in the United States were embroiled in the same controversies between fundamentalists and modernists that the rest of American Protestantism experienced. Quaker modernists such as Jones attempted to "broaden" Quaker thought in a number of ways: viewing the Atonement as an act of love rather than of propitiatory justice; discounting biblical literalism; emphasizing the Social Gospel over evangelism through revivalism; and giving prominence to the Inner Light, a Quaker teaching that had almost been obliterated by the revival. They also gave new attention to Quaker history and reached out to Hicksite Friends. All of these were anathema to the holiness revivalists and their spiritual heirs among Gurneyite Friends, who were especially strong in Ohio, Iowa, Oregon, Kansas, and California yearly meetings. From the local meeting level up to the yearly meeting, in sermons, in pamphlets, and in the pages of the liberal *American Friend* and the holiness *Evangelical Friend,* they fought over the future of Quakerism. After the Gurneyite yearly meetings (Ohio excepted) formed the Five Years Meeting in 1902, it and its boards and bureaucracies became another battleground.[39]

All evidence is that the holiness opponents of modernism were never very strong in New York. Edward Mott, the inflexibly fundamentalist editor of the *Evangelical Friend,* was a native of Moreau, New York, but he spent his career in Bible colleges in Ohio and Oregon. There were some pastors trained at the Cleveland Bible Institute, such as Samuel Hodges and Fred Ryon, who blasted the growth of "infidelity" and its proponents like Elbert Russell. Such currents were especially strong in Clintondale and Glens Falls. A few older Friends disliked the new developments as well. Alexander M. Purdy of Palmyra, a member of the original General Meeting Committee who had broken with the revivalists over pastors, was by 1907 blasting "so-called Friends" who were reframing the Atonement. "I ask where are we drifting?" he wrote to Mott. "May our heavenly father save us from that kind of theology."

Even as late as 1917, many at yearly meeting decamped to hear Billy Sunday at a nearby tent meeting.[40]

Such eruptions were, however, exceptional. Part of it may have been the influence of James Wood and of his son, Hollingsworth, and daughter, Carolena, all sympathetic to Rufus Jones and to liberalism. Part of it may have been the influence of Friends who came as pastors from the West; William J. Reagan, Homer J. Coppock, Murray S. Kenworthy, Levinus K. Painter, and Richard R. Newby (the yearly meeting superintendent) were all, save Newby, Earlham graduates, and modernist Friends. It may partly have been the lack of a college under the yearly meeting's control; such institutions invariably were lightning rods in the yearly meetings where tensions ran high.[41]

Instead, there were signs everywhere of a movement in a more liberal direction. One was the growing rapprochement with the Hicksites: the exchange of epistles, a joint Peace Committee, and the joint "pilgrimage" of the two yearly meetings in 1914. It could be seen in the disappearance of the queries for ministers, apparently without protest, with the adoption of the new Uniform Discipline in 1902. It could be seen in the growing definition of Quakerism as mystical and its central, defining doctrine as the Inner Light. There was an increasing emphasis on the Social Gospel; in 1916 the yearly meeting considered adding a query on "Christian citizenship." And across the yearly meeting, study groups formed to try to reclaim Quaker history.[42]

The Temperance Crusade

After the Civil War, many Friends who had in their early years been radical abolitionists turned with similar idealism to temperance and the "Purity Crusade." Others found here their first chance to join in common cause with non-Friends. Hicksite Friends became leaders in some pre– and post–Civil War temperance societies. Orthodox Friends also gave strong leadership from the 1870s on. Whether Friends of the two branches mixed at the local level, by the end of the century their leaders were attending the same conventions.

A Friend was involved in the formation of the nation's first Temperance Society at Moreau, New York, in 1808. The movement had already played a role in Rochester politics before Charles G. Finney's 1831 revival there. Washingtonian societies in the 1840s, like Alcoholics Anonymous one century later, were largely mutual-help groups for those with drinking problems. Their rapid growth enlarged the temperance movement and turned the emphasis in it and in many Protestant churches toward total abstinence. Susan B. Anthony tried to bring women into leadership in early New York State temperance organizations, but the resistance she met turned her from temperance into the women's rights movement. Some Friends joined the Good Templars, founded in Utica in 1851. Concerned also for peace and brotherhood, it became an organization of total abstainers seeking to influence lawmakers in England, Scandinavia, and America.

The "Women's Crusade" of 1873–74 closed saloons in hundreds of communities across the country, including Brooklyn. As this fervor subsided, the women channeled their energy into organizing the Women's Christian Temperance Union (WCTU). Until they moved to Chicago in 1885, a core of national officers, including Orthodox Quaker Mary Coffin Johnson, made Brooklyn their center. She went to England in 1876 to start the parallel association there, was New York State vice-president, and president of the Brooklyn WCTU founded by her sister, Caroline C. Ladd. Frances Barnes, also a Friend in Brooklyn, spent two decades there heading the national Young Women's work and, after organizing a similar branch in Britain, was named in 1891 to head the equivalent world department. Rhoda Esmond organized a union at Syracuse, and Hannah Underhill of Chappaqua organized a union at Cornell. Sarah W. Collins of Purchase and Emilie Underhill Burgess of Highland between them chaired the state WCTU's Department of Peace and Arbitration from 1888 to 1914. Hannah Bailey, a New York-bred New Englander deeply involved in Orthodox Quaker missions, was the national WCTU Peace Superintendent 1887–1916, and Mary Hallock Bell of Milton, New York, was her Associate Superintendent of Peace around 1910. Mary Jane Weaver, who became pastor at Brooklyn in 1886, was a National Evangelist for the WCTU, covering seven states from Batavia in 1901, and went to the Richmond Conference of 1887, addressing the Five Years Meeting as head of the New York delegation in 1907. At the invitation of the WCTU, Elizabeth Comstock conducted a preaching crusade in Brooklyn. She also did committee work for the national organization.

In the 1880s all three yearly meetings within New York State had temperance organizations. Hicksites worked through the Union for Philanthropic Labor after 1881. Genesee Yearly Meeting appointed a Temperance Committee in 1883. Meanwhile, the Orthodox New York Yearly Meeting had set up a Temperance Committee, forty-eight strong (including seventeen men) in 1884, headed by Mary G. Underhill, also a state WCTU officer.

The Anti-Saloon League, founded in Washington in 1895 by delegates from many temperance organizations, was, by contrast with the WCTU, a single-issue pressure group. With strong ties to the Protestant churches, it focused on the trade, rather than the victims, and unlike the Prohibition Party, it was nonpartisan, although extremely political. The proper Quaker attitude toward the Anti-Saloon League (ASL) was a matter of debate. Some found its acts too drastic. James Wood guided the 1907 Five Years Meeting in adopting a resolution commending both the ASL and the WCTU as "wise and efficient agencies." He had been among those Friends who had tried in 1902 to call an inter-denominational conference on the liquor traffic for 1906, but this had to be dropped because other churches' responses were discouraging. Local Orthodox Friends' groups continued to work after 1900 to shut down saloons and win local option elections.

The most dramatic action came at Clintondale in 1902: a property was sold, and it was rumored that the intention was "to establish a hotel on the premises and . . . sell liquors" for the first time in thirty years. Drawing on a local ordinance requiring the assent of neighboring residents, the WCTU built a house next door in which they installed the Friends ministers Fred and Olive Ryon. The Ryons were harassed from town and their house burned down in retaliation on the fourth attempt; but the WCTU blocked the tavern. As the Prohibition Amendment, which seemed a success as final as emancipation, went into effect in 1920, Friends relaxed but soon saw that the key issue would be enforcement. Smuggling across the Canadian border and bootlegging in the cities remained problems. Friends rebuked the well-financed interests pushing for repeal.[43]

Hicksites and the Friends General Conference, 1865–1902

Comparable as a Hicksite Friend to women supporters of charitable enterprises among the Orthodox Friends was Phebe Anna Thorne. Born in 1828 in Dutchess County, she removed to New York City with her parents in 1830. She was the only surviving daughter of a wealthy family, but at the age of thirty-two she "turned plain," reportedly because of disillusionment with a man in whom she had been interested. She henceforth wore plain dress and eschewed worldly pleasures; she devoted her energies and her wealth to worthy causes, and participated actively in her monthly and quarterly meetings, serving as treasurer of the Women's Yearly Meeting. At her death in 1908, she was recognized as one of America's first women philanthropists. Her name is perpetuated in the Phebe Anna Thorne Scholarship at Swarthmore College.[44]

14. New York Yearly Meeting (Hicksite) at 15th Street Friends Meeting House,
New York City, *Harpers' Bazaar,* May 19, 1888.
Courtesy Friends Historical Library, Swarthmore College.

In the older tradition of benevolence women of 15th St. Hicksite
Meeting in New York set up in 1862 the Women's Association for the
Employment and Relief by Clothing of the Suffering Poor with Phebe
Anna Thorne as director, three buntings among a dozen managers,
and Cutting-Out and Purchasing committees, working at first at "sustaining a proper self-respect by industry" among the "Contraband," that
is, slaves set free by the advancing Union Army. By 1871 they had taken
on providing clothing for Indian children and the Colored Orphan
Asylum, by then moved to Westchester, and had rewritten their constitution and enlarged their board. In 1872 their Minute Book reported
that unsatisfactory work went back to the sewers, who otherwise earned
three dollars a week. The unusually large attendance of fourteen in
1876 closed the season early, the association being short of funds.

Alice Dudley, Gulielma Field, and Mrs. E. C. Field, Hicksite women
close to the spirit of Susan B. Anthony, formed the Ladies Art Association of New York in 1871. A printed appeal in 1879 stated that they had
brought women artists together to paint and exhibit their paintings as,
for instance, in 1876–77 in the Women's Pavilion at 896 Broadway. The
group survived until 1914.

Aaron Powell,[45] whose farming family moved from Dutchess County to Ghent in 1845, when he was thirteen, had been recruited as an abolitionist by George Thompson and Stephen and Abby Kelley Foster in 1851. While in college near Albany he was "consecrated" in a moving gesture by Sojourner Truth. He worked from 1854 to 1860 as a lecturer throughout the country for the American Anti-Slavery Society and became a friend of Lucretia Mott, Garrison, Whittier, and Theodore and Angelina Grimke Weld. Like other radical abolitionists after the Civil War, Powell transferred his moral urgency to other causes: temperance, prison reform, and rights for women and Indians, and commuted to New York from his home in Plainfield, New Jersey, to edit *The National Temperance Advocate* from 1873 to 1894 and, later, *The Philanthropist*. In 1872 he was in a delegation that petitioned Congress to make an inquiry into the liquor traffic. In 1876 he addressed the opening session of the International Temperance Conference in Philadelphia. In 1877 he spoke in Glasgow and attended the organizational meeting of a total abstinence society in Switzerland. In 1878 he helped to convince the New York State Board of Education to adopt a school textbook on the effects of alcohol. His wife, Anna Rice Powell, and he represented Friends and spoke before the Centennial Temperance Conference in Philadelphia in 1885 and the World's Temperance Congress and World's Parliament of Religions in Chicago in 1893.[46] He traveled to San Francisco in 1872 and to Europe in 1873, 1877, 1883, 1886, 1889, 1891, 1894, 1896, and 1898, the latter times often with Anna, to attend international congresses that would advance their central concerns for temperance, prisons, and especially for the emerging American Purity Alliance. He died of a sudden heart attack while addressing the Philadelphia Meeting of Ministers and Elders in 1899.

The Purity Crusade had begun in the 1830s when Presbyterian pastor John McDowall had founded the Magdalen Society to aid prostitutes, but had seen its support erode when wealthy New Yorkers like the Tappans disliked his vivid portrayal of women's conditions in the slums. It was revived after the Civil War when Powell, Abby Hopper Gibbons, and English reformers rejected the compromises implied in the police efforts to control the health of prostitutes. The women in the WCTU, after a period of alliance with the Purity Crusade, went their own way into issues of women's rights and childhood education while the American Medical Association and most doctors promoted regulation and health inspection of prostitutes. Regulationists and absolutists blocked each other's political campaigns in state and national legislatures. Abby Hopper Gibbons set up the Isaac Hopper Home as a halfway house for prostitutes and other women leaving prison. The American Purity Alliance, now led also by Anna Rice Powell and Dr. Emily Blackwell, and supported also by the WCTU, moved on to tackle the "white slave traffic" and the need for matrons in women's prisons and into the political arena by pressing for vice commissions.

A bridge between earlier Hicksite concerns for social reform and the formation of the Friends General Conference that continues today was the Friends Union for Philanthropic Labor. In 1878 the newest Hicksite Yearly Meeting, Illinois, proposed that "once in five years, or oftener, a general conference be held, composed of two representatives of each Monthly Meeting . . . for the consideration of such subjects as lie outside our own membership, for the advancement of morality and righteousness among men; such as our Indian Policy; Arbitration in all its branches; Capital Punishment; Prison Reform; Temperance; Compulsory Education, and cognate subjects."[47] Representatives from the Hicksite Baltimore, Ohio, and Illinois Yearly Meetings appointed a Central Committee in 1881, and in 1882, with Indiana added, formed the Friends Union for Philanthropic Labor. A second conference of five sessions was held in Baltimore in 1883, a third in Ohio in 1884, and a fourth in Philadelphia in 1886, into which all the previous Hicksite yearly meetings plus New York (but not Philadelphia or Genesee) incorporated their various philanthropic programs. Typically, while Orthodox Friends united over doctrine, Hicksites met over social concerns, but it was mainly urban Hicksites who took part. Executive Committee sessions set up the fifth conference, the first to publish its proceedings, in New York in 1888, greeted a British deputation pleading for international arbitration, and assigned New York 40 percent of the three hundred dollar budget. On their home ground all sixteen New York representatives took part, seven out of nineteen appointed from Baltimore, two out of three from Indiana. Each reported on the subcommittees under which they had reorganized the work they were already doing. Ohio Hicksites dropped out. William M. Jackson made a background address, stressing early Friends' protests and Penn's reforms, but most New Yorkers, too, tended to be specialists: Phebe Wright, the yearly meeting's only activist not from New York City, reported on prison work in New Jersey; Joseph Bogardus and John J. Cornell spoke on temperance. Aaron Powell reported on campaigns in Albany to protest licensing prostitutes and in Washington to urge raising the legal age of protection for women from ten to eighteen.

Friends General Conference roots in the late 1800s go back to four Hicksite organizations' biennial conferences: the First-Day School Conference was formed in 1868, the Union for Philanthropic Labor in 1881, the Friends Education Conference in 1894, and the Friends Religious Conference in 1893 at the time of the Parliament of the World's Religions. They combined in 1900 to set up the General Conference, which first met in 1902 at Asbury Park. There two thousand Friends from seven yearly meetings met to hear an array of addresses[48] and to carry out common Quaker concerns that the yearly meetings felt could be addressed more effectively with combined strengths and perspectives. Four main areas of practical interest and cooperation during the early 1900s were carried out by four committees of the General Conference:

1. The Committee for the Advancement of Friends' Principles provided direct service to Friends traveling, outreach to new Friends and new meetings, gave attention to articulating Friends' principles and developed the pamphlet series: "The Friends and . . . " (Over the years it was responsible for arranging for seasoned Friends to travel among the yearly meetings and for the publication of many books and pamphlets describing various aspects of Quakerism).

2. The First-Day School Committee coordinated religious education of Friends and their children about Quaker faith and practice, the Bible, Quaker testimonies, and how God has been known to people in all lands and cultures.[49] It has continued to develop materials for teachers and published lessons and stories for all ages, and sponsored lectures and conferences on religious development.

3. The Committee on Education oversaw Friends' schools and teacher education and training. The interests of the Committee on the Advancement of Friends Principles and the Committee on Education were later carried out by the Friends Council on Education and the Friends Association for Higher Education. In 1948, about the time of the first Assembly of the World Council of Churches, Friends General Conference (FGC) formed the Committee on Christian Unity, later broadened into FGC's Christian and Interfaith Relations Committee.

4. The Committee on Philanthropic Labor gave Quakers representation in larger religious organizations and led activity on social concerns regarding temperance, purity and prostitution, abolishing the death penalty, Indian affairs, demoralizing publications, mission work among women and children, equal rights for women, and education for colored people. Its concerns were taken up more fully by the American Friends Service Committee, founded in 1917, and by the Friends Committee on National Legislation from 1943.

In addition to the four committees, the organization held its General Conference every two years, until 1966 at Cape May on the New Jersey coast, to provide an opportunity for Friends in all the yearly meetings to speak together about topics of immediate concern, as well as world peace, and to establish Young Friend organizations and Friends Work throughout the world.

13

Liberal Pastors and New Intellectual Meetings, 1900–1945

Hugh Barbour
and
George Badgley, Michael Birkel, Elmer H. Brown,
Lewis W. Hoskins, Herbert Kimball,
Gordon Miller, Sabron Reynolds Newton,
Bertha May Nichols, Alson D. Van Wagner

Liberals, Mystics, and Rufus Jones

Many new movements were changing American religious thought during the four decades after the Civil War.[1] While Orthodox Friends pursued concerns that they shared with other evangelical denominations, such as revivals and missions, and the Hicksites focused intensively on ethics, liberals in other Protestant churches read German theologians with roots in Pietism and romanticism in literature, such as Schleiermacher and Rudolf Otto. Harnack taught Americans to consider personal experience as "the essence of Christianity," and justified the concern of Americans such as William James for all the "varieties of religious experience."[2] Such writers rediscovered the classical and medieval mystics although their doctrines moved toward the views already set out by rationalistic liberals and modernists. Conversion experiences were also important for Gurneyite evangelicals whose doctrines changed more slowly. Whether the moral horror of the Civil War led to self-searching in American churches like that after World War I is not clear.

The Social Gospel in Protestant England and America began because the corruption of the "robber barons" of finance, their violent resistance to the rise of labor unions, and the working-class revolts such as the Paris Commune of 1870, when rulers had been shaken, showed the depths of social injustice. Christian social prophets, such as Washington Gladden and Walter Rauschenbusch in the New York slums, drew on the radicals' optimism and utopian ideas. They also drew on such writers in industrial England as Coleridge and Frederick Denison Maurice, who renewed the medieval vision of a wholly Christian society, and on biblical teachings of the Kingdom of God on earth.[3] They attacked specific sins of society and preached Christian socialism. The Social Gospel had pervaded New York Quakerism by 1920 with fruits shown in chapter 14. Underlying social Christianity were the much wider modernist or liberal movements of religious thought about human nature and the natural world.

The name *liberalism* has been used for theories of economics, politics, and society, but one aspect was an openness to new truth and a respect for its evolving disciplines, notably in history and science. Horace Bushnell of Hartford persuaded many American church members that creeds and language are simply human symbols. The discipline of history was often tied to current beliefs about human progress. Scientists convincingly showed that the earth was millions of years old and that all living creatures, including humans, had evolved. Historians showed the evolution of human culture and applied the same insights and the methods learned in studying classical literatures to biblical writings. At a conference at Manchester in 1895 young English Quakers began to share these disciplines of study.

Ideas of basic reality had changed along with ideas of human nature. Some thinkers moved on to positivism or pragmatism, rejecting all truths not measured and verified with instruments. Others reinterpreted the cosmos from new concepts of human character and experience. In the 1820s Channing and the Unitarians had affirmed human perfectibility in morality and mind. Romantic Transcendentalists, such as Emerson and Parker, affirmed also the potential of unselfish human emotions and intuitions. Emerson read Quaker classics and, in turn, had a massive impact on Rufus Jones and twentieth-century Quaker thought. Whereas Spiritualism and the Mormons in the "Burned-over District" affirmed the revelation of particular spiritual truths by specific spirits to discrete individuals, notably women,[4] Emerson's philosophy rested on that of German "idealist" philosophers for whom universal spirit was the final reality. Kant had asserted that conscience and moral reason reach reality. Hegel saw the world as the interaction of ideas in history. The new generation made natural law and God himself immanent within humanity and the natural world.

Rufus Jones's perspective on human nature was shaped by Emerson's Essay on the Oversoul:

> It must be held, I think, . . . that there is "no bar or wall in the soul" separating God and man. We lie open on one side of our nature to God, who is the Oversoul of our souls, the Overmind of our minds, the Overperson of our personal selves. There are deeps in our consciousness which no private plumb line can sound; there are heights in our moral conscience which no ladder of human intelligence can scale . . . a divine Companion who is the real presence of our central being.[5]

As a student at Haverford, Jones had become fascinated with mysticism.

Around the turn of the twentieth century a broad interest in mystical religion arose as evidenced in the writings of the British author Evelyn Underhill. Interest was also growing in the ancient Asian faiths. Moreover, this was the era of the origins of modern psychology and of interest in the psychology of religion. Proponents of mystical religion found a common ground with other faiths and a response to the threats of modern science in the mystic's appeal to personal experience as the basis and authority for the religious life. Unlike later Friends, Rufus Jones wholly ignored Freud and Jung, but his outlook was shaped by the *Principles of Psychology* and *Varieties of Religious Experience* of William James, which became textbooks for his classes in psychology and philosophy at Haverford.

Quakers had spoken approvingly of Catholic mystics at least since Robert Barclay, whose *Apology* mentions Tauler, Bernard of Clairvaux, and Bonaventure. It was only in the late nineteenth century that Friends actually identified themselves as mystical.[6] In 1890 Caroline Stephen[7] referred to the earliest Friends as "assuredly mystics."

Rufus Jones was a farm boy from South China, Maine, nephew of Sibyl and Eli Jones, who had pioneered Quaker mission work in Palestine and Syria. After teaching at Oakwood, he became a professor at Haverford and editor of the *American Friend,* a driving force behind the creation of the American Friends Service Committee (AFSC), an internationally welcomed orator on religious life, and the author of fifty-four books on Quaker history, mysticism, and the life of the spirit. He knew the works of the classical Christian mystics and American and German philosophers,[8] but his experiences were his own. Out of all these he wove a message that reached more non-Friends than any Quaker writer since Woolman and, perhaps, saved unprogrammed Quakerism from fossilization and extinction.

Rufus Jones saw Quakers as heirs to the great stream of mystical religion, the best of Christianity from biblical times, yet with important differences. He contrasted what he called negation mystics with affirmation mystics. The *via negativa* focuses on withdrawal from ideas of God, from thought itself, from the created world and other human beings. God is sought through self-denial, both in physical austerity and in annihilation of one's personality. Its goal is the rare experience of ecstasy, the loss of self by absorption into the vast sea of divinity.

The affirmation mystics, said Jones, "do not make vision the end of life, but rather the beginning." They find the revelation of the infinite in the finite, and so acknowledge the value of the natural world perceived through the senses. Such a mystic "seeks union with God, but not through the loss of personality. . . . The 'I' and the 'thou' are lost only as they are always lost in love."[9] The most striking effect of the sense of contact with God is the immensely heightened quality of personality and the person's spiritual service. The affirmation mystic does not withdraw from the social world but is instead propelled by mystical experience into service of that world as Rufus Jones was through the Service Committee. Rufus Jones thereby democratized and domesticated mysticism. The mystical life was within the reach of all: "The number of persons who are subject to mystical experiences, . . . who feel themselves brought into contact with an environing Presence and supplied with new energy to live by—is much larger than we usually suppose . . . [although] mystical experience varies in degrees of intensity, concentration and conviction."[10] One of Rufus Jones's own peak experiences came while hiking near the French Alps soon after graduating from college when he "felt the walls between the visible and the invisible grow thin" and the eternal seemed to break through into the world, and he felt a sense of concrete mission to "labor in the realm of mystical religion."[11] Another occurred at the time of the death of his beloved son Lowell at the age of eleven although Jones, on shipboard, was not to learn this until days later. He wrote of "a strange sense of trouble and sadness" followed by the experience of being invaded by a Presence and "held by Everlasting Arms. It was the most extraordinary experience I had ever had. . . . I know now, as I look back across the years, that nothing has carried me up into the life of God, . . . more than the fact that love can span this break of separation."[12]

Rufus Jones's emphasis on religious experience was central to the intense interest in Quakerism among non-Friends and an influx of members into unprogrammed meetings throughout the early twentieth century. His historical writings, teaching that Quakers were disciples of the continental mystics, influenced non-Quaker historians. Because from within New York Quaker families, Rufus Jones won no disciples of the stature of Thomas Kelly, Howard and Anna Brinton, or Douglas Steere, who had been drawn by him to Haverford and Pendle Hill, there is, thus, no way to measure Jones's impact on New York Quakers' thinking. Yet his ideas about "the Light within" every person would become the norm for both Hicksite and Orthodox New York Friends. Despite Rufus Jones's relatively unformed doctrine of sin and evil, his faith was centered on Jesus and the Bible. Although he faithfully attended Haverford Meeting and Philadelphia Orthodox Yearly Meeting when he was not ministering elsewhere, he kept his membership life-long in New England Yearly Meeting partly because (unlike Philadelphia Orthodox) it belonged to the Five Years Meeting (later the Friends United Meeting). He took part in its sessions and committees and edited its journal, *The American Friend.* Its basis was the merger of the highly evangelical *Christian Worker* of Chicago and *The Friend* of the Philadelphia Orthodox for which he worked with Walter Malone of Cleveland, founder of a Bible Institute for training Quaker evangelists and missionaries. Because of his huge influence on liberal Quakers, they often forget that Jones was an Orthodox Friend. Rufus Jones, Walter Malone, and James Wood were drawn together by their practical concerns for Quaker unity and service and their reverence for Jesus and the Bible, but Malone and Wood shared also Jones's belief that inward religious experience was the center of Quakerism, whether it took the form of conversion, personal devotion, or mysticism.

After World War I, Jones and Wood worked together to set up the American Friends Service Committee. Neither man intended the Five Years Meeting to be doctrinally narrow. "While truth is eternal, our . . . expression of it changes," wrote Rufus in a statement meant to supersede what he considered Fox's "thin, poor, mediocre expression," the Letter to Barbados.[13] He persuaded the 1912 Five Years Meeting session to call the Richmond Declaration "not a creed" but ten years later agreed to withdraw that statement in a vain effort to maintain unity with Kansas and Oregon Friends. He tried to build friendship with evangelical leaders such as John Henry Douglas, whom he visited in his own home. Only after a generation would Quaker leaders regain his vision of reunifying American Friends.

Liberal Pastors, 1902–1950

Despite the influence of Friends such as James Wood, the smaller meetings of New York Orthodox Yearly Meeting accepted pastors soon after Iowa and others in the Midwest. In the meeting at Glens Falls, for instance, Luke Woodard was called from Toronto to be pastor in 1884.

Woodard had been converted in 1858 and sanctified in 1862 at Adrian, Michigan. He held General Meetings as revivals in Farmington, New York, and Brooklyn in 1871. He claimed that his paid pastorate in Fountain City, Indiana, in 1873, for which he moved two miles, was the first.[14] Early pastors roamed the American Quaker world and gradually became more professional, but such later preachers as Augustus Benedict of West Branch Meeting and Butternuts, Henry Vore at Unadilla, and Martin Thornton at West Brookfield were primarily farmers who felt a call to serve weak meetings for stipends of four or five dollars a week. Benedict attended Bible school and college and became pastor at Glens Falls, which "in the old days . . . was more liberal, [but] there was no silence, not even a pause that refreshes. . . . You would not have known but what you were with the Methodists or Baptists."[15] "A lot of the people . . . had a long line of Quaker ancestry, but they didn't have much Quaker beliefs."[16] The brother revivalists David and John Henry Douglas were early pastors at the Glens Falls Meeting, which records intermittently supporting George DeVol in China, and Mary Haviland, and Thomas Williams, and thirteen other ministers. South Glens Falls welcomed Fred and Olive Ryon after they had been burned out in Clintondale while blocking an un-Friendly effort to open a tavern there. For the whole of the 1920s Jesse Stanfield was pastor at Glens Falls, and David Barton, Mary Haviland, and Mary Knowles were recorded as the ministers at South Glens Falls. Jesse Wilmore from Indiana, in 1904 the first to complete a theological degree at Hartford, served Poplar Ridge, New York, for two years. Many of these pastorates were close enough to Oakwood School for the pastors to feel supported in their liberal outlooks by Will Reagan. For decades Brooklyn's Lafayette Avenue Friends Meeting was the only one in greater New York with a reed organ and a pastor, who in the 1920s was Eldon Mills, studying at Union Seminary.[17]

In the first years of the twentieth century these ministers included a higher proportion of women than later when Protestant patterns overrode Quaker traditions. Mary Jane Weaver was an early pastor at Brooklyn. Hannah Leggett pastored several meetings. Hannah Pratt "felt called to preach at ages 6 and 12 but did not undertake it until 14." For one decade she spoke mainly to Women's Christian Temperance Union gatherings in New Hampshire, Canada, and New York City but held a Vermont pastorate in 1886–88. Jeanette Hadley went from Penn College to Auburn Seminary, while her brother Bruce studied there and was pastor at Poplar Ridge. She went to a ministry in North Carolina, Kenya, and Friends United Meeting, and for thirty years was office manager for the Friends Committee on National Legislation.

15. Elizabeth Lawton Hazard (1889–1968).
Courtesy Haviland Records Room, New York Yearly Meeting.

Rachel Osborn from Economy, Indiana, was prevented by the Depression and a heart ailment from her first dreams as a missionary nurse. She taught at Friends Tunessassa Indian school and at Friends Academy in Tennessee. She was called as pastor to the struggling Detroit Friends Church and stayed five happy years. In 1958 she was called to South Glens Falls, stayed five years, went via congregations of Colorado ranchers and Oklahoma Indians to Unadilla for five more, and came out of a second retirement to pastor again at Glens Falls and South Glens Falls.[18] Elizabeth Lawton Hazard of Poplar Ridge on Cayuga Lake worked while attending Emily Howland's Sherwood Select School. With her carpenter husband she lived near Oakwood Seminary at Union Springs, became Field Secretary for the Orthodox Yearly Meeting in 1929, and built the Junior Yearly Meeting of Young Friends. She worked with and for conscientious objectors in the 1940s and was central in reuniting the yearly meetings.[19]

The new generation of pastors had inherited Quaker concerns for peace and social justice and had studied the Bible and Quakerism at Penn College or Earlham. Yet, unlike most pastors in Quaker churches in the late twentieth century, largely graduates of Bible schools,[20] they had grown up in Quaker homes, and they trained for ministry in seminaries of sturdy academic discipline. These schools made Friends feel at home by their liberal social ethic and churchmanship. At Hartford Theological Seminary were two nationally prominent Quaker professors of the Bible, Moses Bailey and Alexander Purdy. Henry Cadbury similarly drew gifted Quakers to Harvard, and Roland Bainton drew others to Yale. The Friends at these schools, at Colgate Rochester and at Auburn (later merged with Union Seminary in New York) came from all parts of Quakerism, notably from Indiana and Iowa. Between the world wars these students were a group of gifted pastors such as Orthodox Friends had not had before, a nationwide fellowship. New York and New England Yearly Meetings grew by their presence but supported these men by pastorates, later often part-time.

A second generation of liberal pastors, many of them pacifists in World War II, alternated local pastorates with periods on the staff of national Quaker organizations such as AFSC. As in the older generation, many of them continued in New York meetings for some years before moving to bigger roles in midwestern Quaker churches or national organizations. Hartford Seminary was dependent on no church and had one of the best libraries in the country and a school of missions studying in depth the cultures of non-Western lands as well. Many Quaker students from pastoral backgrounds learned from the unprogrammed meetings for worship on Wednesday evenings led by Moses Bailey and Alexander Purdy, a firsthand experience of the "Inner Light," resulting in major life-changing actions. Hartford alumni included Russell Branson, Elmer Brown, Hiram Hilty, Lewis W. Hoskins, Wilbur Kamp, Rachel Osborn, Jesse Stanfield, Furnas Trueblood; Norval Webb, who later served First Friends in Richmond, Indiana, was also clerk of Five Years Meeting and, still later, was Superintendent of Western Yearly Meeting. Furnas Trueblood served West Richmond Meeting, Indiana, for a number of years. In terms of social consciousness, Levinus Painter, pastor at Collins, is the best example. He served as an American Friends Service Committee representative in Appalachia in the Penn Craft project where the AFSC was trying to rebuild as a community an impoverished coal mining village in 1937. He went to the Gaza Strip with others sent by the AFSC to build peace and community in 1948–50. He represented New York Yearly Meeting on the American Friends Board of Missions and in 1963 represented Five Years Meeting at the official opening of East Africa Yearly Meeting as he described in a thoughtful book.[21]

Some of these pastors, like Willard Reynolds (1893–1990), had taken part in Quaker relief work in France. Reynolds returned to finish Penn College, to spend one year at the Southern California School of Religion, to be headmaster of Friends' Southland Institute for freed blacks at Helena, Arkansas, and to serve a long pastorate at Poplar Ridge, New York, and a short one in Clintondale, preaching for "the Star of Peace" even during World War II and later in Iowa and Colorado.[22]

Cecil Pearson, born in Indiana, was a member of the 1929 class at Hartford Seminary. He had previously spent one year in American Friends' reconstruction work in France. Among his Quaker teachers were Levi Pennington at Pacific (now George Fox) College, Rufus Jones at Haverford, and Alexander Purdy at Hartford. His Hartford thesis was "Movements towards Union in the Society of Friends." He served as pastor at Lynn and Swansea in New England, and Clinton Corners, Glens Falls, Fort Edward, and South Glens Falls, New York. His wife, Mary, daughter of Levi Pennington, would sometimes preach. In 1947 he received his doctorate in Old Testament from Boston University. He worked with others to unite the two New York Yearly Meetings.

At Clinton Corners were Herbert Huffman, Sr., Hiram Hilty, Norval Webb, Furnas Trueblood, Yale student T. Canby Jones, and Lewis W. Hoskins, but under Carl Voss and his successors the meeting left the Friends because the members said they did not want to be Quakers, just Christians.

Another theological school that brought Quaker pastors to New York state was Colgate Rochester Divinity School. Herbert Huffman, Jr., was a student pastor at Gasport Meeting while he attended school and later served full-time at Clintondale. In addition to serving First Friends Church later in Indianapolis, he worked for the AFSC's New England office as a fund raiser and then joined the Friends United Meeting staff for social concerns. Of the ministers at Farmington, Charles Lampman became secretary of the Mission Board, Leonard Hall worked for the Five Years Meeting and then raised funds for the Earlham School of Religion. Robert Rumsey went from being pastor at Farmington and Glens Falls to Executive Secretary for Wilmington Yearly Meeting, then to Oregon as Executive Secretary for the Northwest Region of the AFSC, and then to Plainfield, Indiana, as Midwest secretary for the Friends World Committee for Consultation. Stanfield was pastor at Yorktown and Glens Falls and served ten years at Clintondale. Marlin Dawson left Clintondale to become secretary of Baltimore Yearly Meeting.

Other New York Yearly Meeting pastors with a world view included Kent Larrabee and Dick Faux at Farmington; Wilbur Kamp, who was active in peace work, preached at Poughkeepsie, Farmington, and Poplar Ridge and farmed and pastored at North Weare in New Hampshire; Herbert Pettengill, who pastored South Glens Falls and Clintondale and served on the Commission on Aging; Lewis Hoskins, who served Clinton Corners, Glens Falls, and Collins and entered the prison chaplaincy. Herbert Kimball served the Farmington Meeting twice, went to Kenya in 1954 to be principal of the Friends Bible Institute, was Clerk of New York Yearly Meeting Missions Committee, 1973–81, and while serving in the Western Yearly Meeting (1966–70) was clerk of their Peace and Social Concerns Committee and assistant clerk of the FUM Board on Peace and Social Concerns.

The strong social conscience and liberal Christianity of the Hartford and Rochester graduates has been credited by their successors as making possible the 1955 Reunion and saving the small meetings of New York Orthodox Friends from extinction.[23] Thanks to Hazard and Painter, Scipio Quarterly Meeting was united before the yearly meeting. Of all these men, only Painter and Hoskins, who became a therapist in an institution for delinquents, remained within New York Yearly Meeting as did George Badgley, raised on a farm in Dutchess County. While still farming in the 1940s, he was recorded as a minister by Poughkeepsie Meeting while he worked with the Young Friends; he became a clerk for the Orthodox Yearly Meeting in 1948–50 and then its field secretary for twenty years, 1950–70.

Urban Intellectual Friends and College Meetings

The changes that turned the former New York Orthodox Friends in liberal directions were paralleled by even greater changes among the former Hicksites. The major cities of upstate New York and northern New Jersey drew Quaker couples active in business, science, and medicine, and especially in higher education. Many came from silent meeting backgrounds, often from Philadelphia, and they were less eager for pastoral, programmed worship than for the sharing of religious experience and spiritual pilgrimage. Other individuals or families were drawn to join them by the Quaker testimonies for peace, social justice, and racial equality. The resulting meetings had a higher proportion of members who were not birthright Friends than did the meetings sustained by revivals, but a greater insistence on Quaker distinctives. They joined programmed Friends in peace and social service committees and refused to choose between Hicksite and Orthodox affiliations. Many individual new meetings were drawn together during World War II by psychological isolation from nonpacifists and physically by gasoline rationing.[24]

Although reunion of New York Yearly Meeting Friends came only in 1955, it had precursors upstate. There had been Friends in Buffalo in 1810 and from the 1860s through 1898. Local Friends again began meeting informally from 1914 to 1931 and were formally made an executive meeting in 1923. Affiliated with both the New York Orthodox and the Hicksite Genesee Yearly Meetings, they claim to be the first united meeting in New York State. The reorganized Buffalo and Niagara Monthly Meeting joined Scipio Quarter in 1940.[25]

Ithaca Meeting (1918) was early led by Joshua and Edith Cope from Westtown and by Amy Grace Mekeel, who came from Conservative Hector Meeting, had taught at Olney, and taught zoology at Cornell from 1917 to 1947. They organized as a monthly meeting under the Friends Fellowship Council in 1938, joined Scipio, by then a united quarter, in 1952, and met on the Cornell campus. The former home of Edwin and Marjorie Burtt became their center in 1989.

Montclair, which also claims to be the first united meeting, met temporarily in homes until a meeting house was built and was incorporated in 1926 with thirty-five members, some from an older worship group in Newark, notably Caroline Borton Smith, and out of Race Street, Philadelphia, and 15th Street Meetings. They rented a kindergarten until they built their own meeting house in 1932. In order to join simultaneously both New York yearly meetings, they were given permission by both yearly meetings to form All Friends Quarterly Meeting in 1928.[26] They were joined in All Friends Quarter by Ridgewood where Delbert and Ruth Replogle brought together a group out of Montclair Meeting, which became a monthly meeting in 1939, and built their own meeting house in 1958. They hosted Hiroshima Maidens and refugees. Summit was another daughter meeting of Montclair, set off because travel in wartime was difficult. After the war they aided the surgery for Hiroshima victims and completed a handsome meeting house in 1970. Rockland, the other pillar of All Friends Quarter, took the New York county's name, and met in Nyack under the wing of the Fellowship of Reconciliation until they could build in 1964–65. New Brunswick, another meeting with university connections, started as a worship group in 1927 and was recognized as a monthly meeting in 1955 as part of Shrewsbury-Plainfield Half-Yearly Meeting.

The founding of Syracuse Meeting brought equally great changes in upstate New York. It started in 1929 with nine members brought together by Karlin Capper-Johnson from England and Lesley West who met in a series of rooms in downtown Syracuse. Led by Norman Whitney and Horace and Emily Eaton of the Syracuse University English Department, they were accepted as a monthly meeting simultaneously in 1936 by both yearly meetings. At first a lone meeting in its quarter, Syracuse was asked by the Orthodox Scipio Quarter to be a member of a now united quarter. Elizabeth Lawton Hazard, field secretary of the Orthodox Yearly Meeting, a member of Scipio Quarter, had a strong liberal influence. Whitney made Syracuse in World War II a center for conscientious objectors. Kenneth Boulding met his wife Elise Biorn-Hansen there.

Rochester, although an active Quaker center from 1821 through the great revival of 1830 and thereafter for the Posts' Spiritualist group, lost members throughout the century from both its Hicksite and Orthodox meetings, especially to Progressive Friends. There was a cemetery but no meeting from 1915 to 1933, but wartime travel troubles made the worship group there a monthly meeting by 1944, its membership often academics.

Friends in Albany had broken up their earlier meeting about 1920 but were regathered by Thomas and Eleanor Corneilson in 1938, were invited to meet in Eugene Carson Blake's Presbyterian church and later in two others, and had become a monthly meeting by 1942, joining the older Quaker Street Hicksite Quarter. For part of the 1940s they set off a Troy Meeting, later laid down. In 1964 they bought their Friends Center building, used by many committees and outside groups. They have hosted AFSC work in the area and led peace and prison justice programs and protests to state and national governments.[27]

A similar pattern, although of exurbanites more than academics, revived the ancient meetings, reborn from Purchase Meeting: Housatonic, at New Milford, and Wilton, in Fairfield County, Connecticut, in 1942. Friends who could not get to Purchase because of gasoline rationing during World War II began to meet in Scarsdale, New York, in 1944 and Rye in 1958, building anew but reclaiming old buildings as Stamford-Greenwich Meeting did more recently. Scarsdale has grown large and is a regional leader in issues of justice and peace.[28] All these were begun as united meetings, part of both Purchase Quarterly Meetings, which did not become united until 1957 after fifteen years of joint sessions. Without structural changes, the two meetings on Manhattan,

Hicksite 15th Street and Orthodox but nonpastoral 20th Street, agreed to meet for worship jointly at 15th Street in winter and at 20th Street in summer. Later, the 20th Street Meeting House was sold.

The new meetings within what is now Long Island Quarter emerged mainly after the war as Friends newly moving out from New York claimed local Quaker roots after long gaps. Shelter Island, although visited by Fox himself, still has only a handful of members, but the worship groups at Southold, Southampton, and Sag Harbor gathered into Eastern Long Island Executive Meeting after 1988. Conscience Bay Meeting near Stony Brook turned the carriage house of member William Huntington into a meeting house in 1961 and actively opposed the Vietnam War. When neighbors reacted by painting graffiti on the meeting house, accusing Quakers of communism and treason, Friends refused to prosecute and instead rallied two hundred other neighbors, Jewish, Catholic, and Protestant, to repaint their building. Lloyd Harbor Meeting was built up after 1972 by George and Elizabeth Watson and other faculty and students at Friends World College, since departed.[29] In upstate New York, meetings also began on campuses in the 1950s at Hamilton (Colgate University), Alfred, and Elmira and in the 1980s at Binghamton University and near Keuka and Geneva colleges, which affiliated themselves with Farmington or Butternuts Quarterly Meetings. They have, at times, shrunk as well as grown. Yet between them the new unprogrammed meetings have provided a new network of members for the yearly meeting and its committees to replace the rural Hicksites and pastoral Meetings.

Quakers and Non-Christian Religions

Rufus Jones's emphasis on religious experience was central to the dramatic interest in Quakerism among non-Friends throughout the early twentieth century. More new members were drawn into meetings around New York City by ethical concerns and from non-Protestant backgrounds, and fewer by devotional or mystical experience, than in less-metropolitan areas, but Jones's philosophy undergirded New York Friends' universalism. Outstanding teachers of Asian religions became Quakers in New York Yearly Meeting.

Edwin A. ("Ned") Burtt was born in Groton, Massachusetts, in 1892, grandson of a Baptist minister. His father's ministry relied on faith for financing and took his family to China as a missionary. Ned was sent home to the missionaries' favorite Mount Hermon School and to Yale. He went on to seek a more universal understanding by earning a doctorate in metaphysics under John Herman Randall and Morris Cohen at Columbia University and an S.T.M. at Union Seminary in New York: "Metaphysics is the supreme exercise of our power of adventurous searching. It fills the unique role of bringing the wholeness beyond the horizon within the horizon, so far as this can be accomplished by the finite mind of man."[30]

Burtt's thesis became his first major book, *The Metaphysical Foundations of Modern Science* (1925), focused on the implications of the mathematical but empirical world-model of Isaac Newton. The contrasts between this and the organic world view of the Middle Ages, the timeless idea world of Platonism, and modern empiricism and positivism were worked out in his anthology, *English Philosophers from Bacon to Mill* (1939), and *In Search of Philosophical Understanding* (1957). His essays and books of lectures carried out the same teaching methods. Burtt assembles a "bundle of philosophic and religious systems," which collect, assemble, and evaluate a variety of general truths about the universe, awaiting coordination and assignment of their various spheres of validity. In his *Types of Religious Philosophy* (1939) he surveys the alternative theories, both those usually called religious (such as the Catholic) and the agnostic (empiricist), humanist (pragmatist), and modernist (experiential) views linked to science with as much impartiality as he can.[31]

Ned Burtt taught philosophy at Columbia for two years and for nine at Chicago but was at Cornell University from 1932 until he died. In his hospitable home by the waterfall he became a pillar of the Friends meeting and practiced and led meditation. Burtt's years in China as a youth bore fruit in the widely used little anthology, *Teachings of the Compassionate Buddha,* and his systematic text, *Man Seeks the Divine: A Study of the History and Comparison of Religions.* In these books he surveyed the entire literature and beliefs of Buddhism and other faiths. He also tried to understand from within the religious experience of Asians: "We must bring the best in our own religious heritage [and] a sympathetic appreciation of the religious experience of others [for] sympathetic sharing." Burtt studied in India in 1947, 1953, and 1966, took the vows of a Buddhist layman, made a pilgrimage with Buddhists, lived in a Hindu ashram, kept a lifelong discipline of meditation, and applied in practice the experience-centered understanding of religion since Schleiermacher. He tried to catalogue the diverse answers each religion gave to what he saw as universal human questions about ethics, authority, and human and cosmic nature: "What is the nature and destiny of man in relation to the universe in which he lives and dies?"[32] He

recognized the need for the tolerant and the intolerant faiths to understand each other. "The high endeavours of reflective modern man . . .
will be [helped] by the recognition that the world is his home and not
his unseen tyrant."[33]

Kenneth Morgan of Colgate University was even more influential
in the circle of American teachers of world religions. Born in 1908 the
son of a Methodist minister,[34] he completed his graduate study in philosophy at Harvard, studying the problem of evil and the nature of the
good. He studied in India in 1935, spent eight months sharing life in
key religious communities, ashrams based on Vedanta in Bombay, Vrin-
davan, Varanasi, Calcutta, Almora, and Mayamati, and visiting Gandhi
at Wardha and Tagore at Santiniketan. In contrast to Burtt's patterning
of ideas, Morgan's central concern was with the practical ethics, self-
examination, daily meditation,[35] and the awe that evokes selflessness
within different faiths:

> Religious search is a curious and compassionate turning to the world
> outside onself. . . . You don't follow a religious way because of the
> feelings you get, but because you have seen an act that is kind and
> generous [and] people of sensitive awareness who respond to the
> world with wonder and joyous appreciation, for the beauty and diver-
> sity you see. . . . [But] I have learned to be content with truths that are
> open to revision again and again, but are the best known at the
> moment.[36]

Morgan is cautious about using the word God, preferring "Sacred
Reality," but finds it impossible to make statements about it that would
fit all faiths. He personally lays aside "revelation, salvation, soul, existence before birth and after death, heavens and hells," also miracles,
astrology, amulets, and spirits; he does not objectify mantras.[37]

Morgan, a pacifist, served as director of a Civilian Public Service
Camp during World War II but waited formally to join Friends until the
war was over. He had visited many kinds of churches and religious communities, and "I backed into the Society of Friends, because it seemed
to me to be the only religious organization that would allow me to go
on searching."[38] He had returned from India to head the Hazen Foundation's Society for Religion in Higher Education and then the Lane
Hall student center at the University of Michigan, and after World War
II served as chaplain and professor of religion at Colgate University. He
founded Chapel House as a center for religious study, literature, art,
and personal retreats and as the site of the Hamilton Friends Meeting.
He helped to enlarge the National Association of Biblical Instructors

into the American Academy of Religion and to bring Zen master Shib-
ayama to teach sessions on American campuses, and translated his lectures and the Mumonkan into English. Morgan's own most widely used
books, for each of which he traveled for one year in Asia, were also
teaching tools made up of chapters he individually commissioned
Asian scholars to write for American students about the history, practices, and beliefs of their own religions, in whose languages Morgan
himself was never expert.[39] He compiled indexes of American teachers
of Asian religions and counseled many of them. His own writings included bibliographies for them in English. He never separated learning, teaching, and practice: "The person who experiments is part of
the experiment, and is altered by the experiment. There is no way
back."[40]

Other New York Friends have studied Buddhism and practice meditation although no formal group of "Buddhist Quakers" seems to exist.
A student and curator of the religious art of Tibet, John Brzostoski, of
the Riverside Art Museum in New York, has presented from its inner
experience the concepts and terms that underlie the intricate symbols
and often terrifying figures in one of the world's most complex religions. "Its ultimate purpose . . . is pragmatic. . . . What is misun-
derstood can be called mystical. The everyday reasons for this art in
Tibet are the people's everyday beliefs. . . . All dualities are confronted,
and the resulting energy brings a basic serenity."[41]

New York Friends have probably interacted less with Catholicism
than did such Quaker mystics as Douglas Steere and Thomas Kelly.
Writings of medieval mystics had been read by Friends since Isaac Pen-
ington. With Jews, most interactions have been more recent. George
Fox, Margaret Fell, and other early Friends had made contact with the
Jews of Amsterdam, moved partly by the hope that the ninth chapter of
Paul's Letter to the Romans had aroused in all millennial Protestants
that Israel's conversion would be part of the coming of Christ's Kingdom.[42] Friends contrasted the old, outward covenant of the Torah with
Jesus' New Covenant in the heart but respected Jews' faithfulness as
much as that of the Puritans. Thereafter, Friends were largely cut off
from Jews for two centuries. A number of New Yorkers, however, who
were raised in Jewish backgrounds, came to Quakerism for the sake of
its ethics and Peace Testimony. George Rubin, former clerk of New
York Yearly Meeting, flew in the air force in World War II, was shot
down, and became a pacifist as a result of reflection in prison camp
and reading Quaker literature there.[43] Although bar mitzvahed, he and
his wife, Margery, had been agnostics. She persuaded him to attend

with her and in 1953 to join the then pastoral Lafayette Avenue Meeting in Brooklyn. He still calls himself a Christian although he does not expect that of other Friends. Most other New York Friends from Jewish families, of whom thirty gathered recently for a Quaker Jewish weekend at Powell House, the Quaker conference center near Albany, have preferred the liberal outlook of the formerly Hicksite meetings. Few writings have yet appeared exploring the relationships between Jewish and Quaker traditions.

14

Quaker Service and Peacemaking, 1900–1948

HUGH BARBOUR
and
CHRISTOPHER DENSMORE, WALTER HAINES, ALAN PIKE,
MARY ELLEN SINGSEN, JANE R. SMILEY

Environment, Agriculturists, and Landscape Architects

During the early twentieth century many kinds of ferment grew in American churches. Through the Social Gospel, pastors and writers such as Walter Rauschenbusch woke educated and middle-class church-folk to conditions in the slums and factories and to their causes. Society needed conversion or reordering even more than did individuals. New York Friends, and the liberal pastors in particular, read and preached these messages although at first few worked in inner city settings or with labor unions or political parties. New ideas came more slowly to American Friends on the foreign mission fields, most of whom were midwestern evangelicals.[1] But Robert and Margaret Simkin in West China taught under Henry Hodgkin from England, who had shared the vision of college graduates, challenged by the Student Volunteer Movement, that whoever had skills as doctors, nurses, teachers, or scientists would find the needs were greater in mission countries in Asia, Africa, or Latin America than at home. Some set up demonstration farms as others had earlier among native Americans, but Friends called to minister had mostly grown up on farms, and only in the late twentieth century did protecting the environment become an idealistic cause.

City-bred William Penn praised the virtues of retirement and the life of a country squire. Unlike English Friends, however, American nineteenth-century Quakers were a predominantly rural people, and it is not surprising that many turned their attention to the study of agriculture and the natural world. Quakers writing to Quaker publications about agriculture or natural history included Silas Cornell from Rochester and Gideon Frost from Long Island on geology. Various of the Herendeens from Farmington were connected with inventions of agricultural machinery. Friends devoted to science often turned to botany as did Thomas Eddy's son, John, and wrote for non-Friends.

Several New York Quakers made important contributions to American agriculture. Jethro Wood (1774–1834) patented an inexpensive and efficient cast iron plow in 1819, which was widely copied. His Cayuga County neighbor, David Thomas (1776–1859), was a polymath whose *Travels Through the Western Country* (1819) gave a detailed description of the geology of Indiana. He served as chief engineer on the section of the Erie Canal between Rochester and Buffalo. David Thomas was also a prolific writer on agricultural subjects, particularly fruit growing, and is credited with writing more than eight hundred articles and shorter pieces in the first six volumes of *The Genesee Farmer.*

David Thomas's son, John Jacobs Thomas (1810–1895), was also a well-known agricultural writer. His *Fruit Culturist* (1845), revised and expanded into the *American Fruit Culturist* (1847), went through numerous editions. After Thomas's death, it was revised by another New York Quaker, William H. S. Wood, and was kept in print until at least 1920. Thomas also edited and contributed to numerous New York agricultural publications from the 1830s to the 1890s. Both David and John Jacobs Thomas were active members of the Society of Friends and were interested in the cause of abolition. When Thomas crossed by ferry into Ohio, where slavery was illegal, "I stepped on the shore with emotion . . . and I exalted to find one spot of earth where freedom is the legal inheritance of all."[2] John J. Thomas was active in the affairs of New York Yearly Meeting and from 1858 to 1880 was president and managing trustee of the yearly meeting's Oakwood Seminary, then at Union Springs. He knew the aesthetic side of country life. When not writing about farm machinery, drainage, or fruit culture, he was suggesting the benefits of ornamental planting, well-situated gardens and walkways.

Samuel Bowne Parsons (1819–1906), son of the clerk of New York Yearly Meeting (Orthodox), with his brother began a nursery on the family farm at Flushing in 1839. He is credited with introducing into American agriculture new strains of honeybees from Italy, plants from Japan, and Valencia oranges from England. His book, *The Rose,* first published in 1847, was considered the standard work. His son, Samuel

Parsons (1844–1923), was a well-known landscape architect who designed public parks in New York City and Washington, D.C., and published numerous articles and several books. Members of the Hicks family of Westbury were also prominent nurserymen. Until the late twentieth century, however, Friends rarely wrote to protect the environment as such. They taught the moral virtues of farming mainly to Indians. A turning point was the Smiley brothers' project to make a country inn into a retreat and national meeting place.

The Mohonk Conferences on Peace, Indians, and Race Relations

The twin brothers Alfred and Albert Smiley, born in 1828 on a farm in Vassalboro, Maine, were close partners. In 1860 they became administrators of the Friends New England Boarding School in Providence, Rhode Island. In 1868, however, Alfred and his family left Providence to live on a farm near Poughkeepsie, New York. One year later he wrote Albert about discovering a lovely mountain-top lake with a country tavern beside it on top of Shawangunk Ridge above New Paltz. Albert came to see the property, was entranced by its natural beauty, and arranged to buy it although he had to borrow money to do so. He continued to teach and run the school in Providence to pay for his new property. Under Alfred's supervision, the tavern was enlarged and converted to a summer resort, which they named Lake Mohonk Mountain House. The House opened on June 1, 1870. After the first year, Alfred served as general manager while Albert was in summer residence as host to his paying guests. The business succeeded. By 1879 Alfred had opened his own resort a few miles away, Lake Minnewaska Mountain House.

After Alfred's departure, Albert lived year-round at Lake Mohonk. He was fortunate in persuading his half-brother Daniel to come and manage Mohonk Mountain House, which expanded in thirty years to accommodate more than four hundred guests. Widening circles of guests came, accepting the owner's unwritten rules: no alcohol, card playing, or dancing. Daily morning prayers were voluntary. They appreciated the Smileys' improvements, which created trails, carriage roads, gardens, and observatory towers overlooking the splendid vistas of farmland in the valleys and the Catskill Mountains to the north and west.[3]

In 1879 Albert Smiley was appointed to the U.S. Board of Indian Commissioners. The board members were chosen for their high principles; they served without pay. Albert Smiley found that the one-day meetings of the board members in Washington were insufficient for thorough discussion. Accordingly, he invited them along with additional persons concerned with Indian affairs to meet. In October 1883 Albert Smiley and his wife, Eliza, hosted these people for three days. Fruitful discussions were held both in the stated sessions and informally during quiet walks around the beautiful resort. This meeting became the first of thirty-four annual meetings of the Lake Mohonk Conference of Friends of the Indian. The participant list grew to about 140. The attenders were largely from New England and the Middle Atlantic states. They included missionaries, government workers, members of Congress, army officers, academics, judges, writers, editors, and clergy, people who could share the views expressed at the conferences with a wider audience. Attenders included members of the Indian Rights Association, the Women's National Indian Association, and both Orthodox and Hicksite Friends.

Albert Smiley selected the chair of each conference, often a member of the Board of Indian Commissioners. A core group appointed by the host planned the topics and speakers at each conference. The attenders were united in wanting to improve the lot of Native Americans and in believing that the goal should be the assimilation of the Indian into white society through education, Christianization, and individual ownership of land. A few Indians who were on the way to "assimilation" attended the conferences.

By 1900 these conferences had produced a change in the average thoughtful American's way of considering the Indian. Instead of killing off the Indians or segregating them on reservations, predominant opinion now favored education leading to assimilation and citizenship. Reformers and government officials appeared to feel that the way to achieve these goals was largely administrative.

Concomitant with the supposed solution of the native Americans' problems, concern arose for other national and ethnic groups. In the early 1900s discussions at the Lake Mohonk Conference of Friends of the Indian dealt with problems of education and health of Puerto Ricans, Hawaiians, and Filipinos. In 1904 the conference title was modified to include "Other Dependent Peoples" although Indians remained on the agenda.[4]

Former President Rutherford B. Hayes attended the 1889 Indian Conference and expressed the hope "that the day may soon come when that other weaker race, not of a quarter of a million, but of six millions, shall have some such annual assembly as this to consider its condition."[5] Albert Smiley immediately agreed to call a "Conference on the Negro Question" to be held in June 1890 if Hayes would preside. Hayes had a reputation as a "peace president" for having withdrawn post–Civil War military rule from the southern states although the first effect had been state laws denying voting rights to blacks. The conference was held, a bold effort, scarcely twenty-five years after the Civil War. The conference planners could not agree on having blacks represented, and so there were none. Some members of the conference were not ready to hear forthright comments on Southern slaveholding mentality or Northerners' blindness to injustice in their midst. A few specific topics were discussed, such as improved schooling for blacks and rights to private property. After a second conference, it was clear that the divisions of outlook were too sharp for any truly constructive conclusions; this conference was not resumed.[6]

Four years later Albert Smiley's practical idealism led him to convene the Lake Mohonk Conference on International Arbitration. When welcoming his guests, he requested that the discussion not go into "the horrors of war or the doctrine of 'peace at all hazards,' but [turn] to the consideration of the means by which our own country might have all her disputes with foreign lands settled by arbitration and might bring other nations to join her."[7] This purpose was joined by another, eloquently presented by Edward Everett Hale, the establishment of a permanent international tribunal to which governments would submit their disputes with other nations. These two themes ran through the series of twenty-two conferences, the last held in 1916 with William Howard Taft presiding. From thirty-five attendees at the first conference, the participant list grew to nearly two hundred in 1907. Included were clergymen, government officials, diplomats (U.S. and foreign), military leaders, lawyers, journalists, and members of peace organizations such as the American Peace Society, whose secretary was Friend Benjamin F. Trueblood from Indiana, Carolina, and Rhode Island. Numerous other Friends attended. The founding in 1905 of the American Society of International Law resulted from informal discussions between lawyers attending the Mohonk Conference. American businessmen active in international trade were attracted to the cause of peace and joined peace organizations, including the Mohonk Conference.

The conference attenders were encouraged by the 1899 Peace Conference at The Hague where the Permanent Court of Arbitration was set up. In 1902 President Theodore Roosevelt submitted the first case to the Hague Court. In the decade 1901–1910 more than 130 arbitratration treaties were ratified. The impending Second Hague Peace Conference in 1907 led the Mohonk Conference to add periodic international congresses to its goals of arbitration and an international tribunal. Their greatest boost came in 1910 when Andrew Carnegie contributed ten million dollars to establish the Carnegie Endowment for International Peace for which his good friend Albert K. Smiley was named one of twenty-eight founding trustees.

Albert Smiley died in 1912. His half-brother, Daniel, became proprietor of the resort and also assumed responsibility for continuing the conferences with a commitment equal to his brother's. In 1913 he was appointed to the Board of Indian Commissioners. By 1917, with the United States at war, the difficulties of providing staff and supplies to run the Mohonk resort caused the cancellation of the two conferences scheduled for that year. Despite hopes to resume after the war, the Conference on the Indian was only reconvened in 1929 and ended when Daniel Smiley died the following year.

The Mohonk Conferences marked the change from nineteenth-century meetings about peace to long-lasting campaigns like those against slavery and alcohol. Although English Quakers such as John Bright were pillars of the British Peace Society, the older American peace groups attracted few Friends. The Peace Association of (Orthodox) Friends published a *Messenger of Peace* from 1870 to 1894 and 1900 to 1912, and Hannah Bailey published a *Pacific Banner* in Maine. Few other American Quaker leaders "published peace."[8]

New York Friends in World War I

Friends, like most Europeans and Americans, were surprised by "the Great War." American Quakers' role in it has never been studied as intensively as British Friends have studied their war-time anticonscription drive.[9] Quakers were not as detached as the Mennonites, who besides a long tradition of being nonresistants rather than outgoing peacemakers, were in 1914–17 still treated as pro-German. By contrast, Herbert Hoover, a west-coast American Quaker engineer, found himself positioned to organize the evacuation of all Americans caught in England and France when the war broke out and went on to raise nearly one billion dollars through the Committee for Relief in Belgium. He become the leading American integrator of postwar relief and, thereby, U.S. president.[10] Before America entered the war in 1917, many hoped to isolate their country from the struggle, and others tried to mediate in what had became admittedly a competition in attrition, killing the finest young men throughout Europe. Friend Henry Hodgkin, later head of Pendle Hill School, was head of the Fellowship of Reconciliation (FOR) in Britain, doing relief work in France and Belgium. He persuaded Americans, including Quakers Charles Rhoads and Edward Evans, to set up the American branch of FOR, which became "the central organization for religious pacifists for over half a century"[11] with offices in New York and later Nyack. Yet Wellesley professor Emily Greene Balch was the only Friend present when Jane Addams formed a Women's Peace Party in Washington. They called an international Women's Peace Congress at The Hague in April 1915. From it delegates fanned out to visit European heads of state. They crossed from America again on Henry Ford's "Peace Ship," trying in vain to promote a permanent mediation body of neutral nations. Yet out of these efforts grew the Women's International League for Peace and Freedom, which involved Emily Balch, their international secretary, in all the postwar peace conferences.[12]

Once America entered the war in 1917, pro-war sentiment was less disciplined than in England. Like Emily Greene Balch from Wellesley, Henry Cadbury was driven from his professorship at Haverford. He had written an article in which he warned against anti-German hatred. Mary Stone McDowell, from a Jersey City Quaker family, on graduating from Swarthmore in 1896 had been given their Lucretia Mott scholarship for one year at Oxford and returned to finish her master's degree in classics at Columbia. She was dismissed by the New York City School Board from her teaching post in the Queens Manual Training High School for refusing to take an oath of loyalty. Her reinstatement in 1923 was equally publicized, and she gave her time increasingly to peace work for the rest of her life and to refugees in World War II, helping New York Yearly Meeting act upon its Peace Testimony as chair of its Peace and Social Order Committee.[13]

As in past wars, however, the main issue for most Friends in 1917 was conscription. American conscientious objectors (COs) faced brutal bullying in army camp and out. In April Henry Cadbury and Rufus Jones gathered both Orthodox Friends and Hicksites into an American Friends Service Committee to undergird a Haverford Emergency Unit to train COs, mostly Friends and Mennonites, as relief workers alongside English Friends in France.[14] Alhough working in Quaker gray uniforms and under the Red Cross, many had lengthy struggles to obtain furloughs from draft boards that preferred to send them into "noncombatant" construction or medical army units. Willard Reynolds studied about war at Penn College:

> In February of 1918 I registered as a C.O. . . . In July of that year I was drafted and went to Louisville, Kentucky with a group of about 100 men, to a military training camp. I spent about two months there,

refusing combatant and non-combatant service . . . at Camp Taylor, Ky,
before I was transferred to 1st Development Bn. Aug. 16, taught illit-
erates 4 days in YMCA, met Board of Inquiry Aug. 26, 1918, I was
interviewed to see whether I was a real C.O. or not, . . . and fur-
loughed for 1 year with American Friends Reconstruction Unit. [It
was] quite a large work. . . . Help was given to 1,666 French villages
and to over 46,000 families. . . . They planted 25,000 trees, mostly fruit
trees."[15]

Reynolds sailed to Le Havre and worked near Rarecourt, plowing
and supervising German prisoners in rebuilding ruined farms. They
built two maternity hospitals and a tuberculosis center. In a factory at
Dole, Friends built prefabricated units for the houses and hospitals, and
other teams erected them in shelled-out villages. The German 1918
offensive destroyed so many villages that Friends had then to rebuild
again.[16] A list of about 258 men and 40 women then in France, plus 300
more on the way, included 40 from New York State.[17] In the same period 2,810,000 Americans were drafted, 171,000 were termed draft
evaders, 3,989 claimed conscientious exemption upon being inducted
in military camps, 450 American COs were sent to prison (apparently
only 13 Quakers), and more than 700 were kept in camps, who objected even to noncombatant service.[18]

Relief and Peacemaking Between the Wars: Carolena and Hollingsworth Wood

The Service Committee continued the rebuilding programs in
France until 1920, arranging to sort and sell to French farmers building
materials left behind in American army dumps. It then decided carefully to extend the work into ruined Germany. After three years it
found itself administering the feeding of two million German children.[19]
The way for this was opened when the committee sent Carolena Wood,
Jane Addams, and two others to Berlin in May 1919. They convinced
both the AFSC and the Germans. On her return to Europe, Wood was
put in charge of relief in District 6 around Frankfurt-am-Main.[20] Talk-
ing freely with cabinet ministers, local doctors, and aldermen, building
"friendships along the hard road Germany has to go," she heard
Friends called both "practical Christians" and spies. Howard Brinton
overheard two Germans after an address by Carolena Wood: "These
Quakers believe in guidance by the Holy Spirit, but the Holy Spirit
apparently does not understand the genitive case." Carolena Wood's
letters to her father James and brother ("Brudie") Hollingsworth Wood

16. Carolena M. Wood (1871–1936).
Courtesy Wood Family, Mt. Kisco, New York.

carried more news of visits to friends, known from the family's Dresden stay thirty years before, than grim details of the blockade-caused German famine that filled her official reports: "The tuberculosis charts make one sick at heart . . . since the 'turnip year' 3 years ago when they had no potatoes but only turnip marmalade for breakfast, boiled turnip for dinner and turnip soup for supper." A staff conference decided that she and Helen Vail "should run over to Poland . . . to look about for a few days,"[21] leading to yet another massive AFSC feeding program. By 1924 AFSC feeding programs had extended also to Serbia, Bulgaria, and in 1921–25 to Communist Russia despite the uneasiness of both Lenin, then at war with his peasants, and of conservatives like Hoover. Beulah Hurley from Newark led a team, tackling typhus and mass starvation in Buzuluk. Cordial ties that Quaker relief workers left in France and Germany led to the international Quaker centers and Friends meetings in Berlin, Frankfurt, Nuremberg, Paris, Geneva, and Vienna. But Russians were so desperate, and so many of them dead, that no permanent human bonds were left.[22]

Carolena Wood may represent, in this book, many less-known Friends who in the decades 1910–1930 gave their lives and risked their health in service as it became distinct from evangelism. American foreign missions were undergoing general reexamination by under-funded central boards and the Laymen's Missionary Inquiry, which rec-ommended concentrating American efforts on schools, colleges, and hospitals. In 1897 and after, Wood had served as secretary to the meet-ings that led to the Five Years Meeting and wrote articles to prepare for and report on its 1912 sessions. She had visited and reported on its Mexican mission work. She had worked for its education board, stud-ied comparisons with the procedures of the boards of other denomina-tions, and delivered frequent devotional addresses, carefully written and undergirded by up-to-date Bible scholarship. She had also served on the continuing boards of the Colored Orphan Asylum, the Bedford Women's Reformatory and Garden Club, and the first board of AFSC as well. After her AFSC service, however, she turned to more adven-turous efforts for peace. In 1927 she was asked to go with Elbert Russell and John Nevin Sayre of the Fellowship of Reconciliation by coastal steamer and dugout canoe from Panama via Guatemala and El Sal-vador to Nicaragua to try to persuade Sandino to turn from civil war to nonviolent resistance against the U.S. Marines, who were already occu-pying Haiti, Santo Domingo, and Nicaragua and attacked Sandino while they were there. The American peacemakers met Somosa and Sandino's wife, but not Sandino.[23] Ten years later Carolena made a similar trip to Manchuria after Japan had overrun it. Her friends re-member her traveling everywhere with only a pair of durable corduroy suits for all occasions. For Friends, the meaning of "mission" had changed.

Her brother L. Hollingsworth Wood (1874–1956) had, meanwhile, stayed in New York as a trimly dressed lawyer, seemingly closer to the "urban Friends" pattern of interchurch philanthropy. But he threw himself into increasingly radical issues. From 1908 to 1910 he was sec-retary of the New York Colored Mission, whose donors were mostly Friends. For its Negro Fresh Air Fund he negotiated with railroads for reduced fares and with reluctant country guest houses and camps that only rarely admitted flatly that "our houses are only for white people."[24] Out of this concern, Wood served as secretary for 1912–14 of the Na-tional League on Urban Conditions Among Negroes, which became the Urban League, and its twin group, the National League for the Protection of Colored Women. He was among those who founded the National Association for the Advancement of Colored People. He let himself be enlisted by Jesuit Father John LaFarge as a trustee of the Cardinal Gibbons Institute for black youths in Maryland and later of the Booker T. Washington Institute of Liberia and in 1947–52 to the New York Colonization Society's board to oversee the Kakata Institute in Liberia. He was more personally involved in helping Isaiah Montgomery, the founder of the Mound Bayou black community in Mississippi, float a bond issue to support their oil mill and manufacturing cooperative. He worked with President Thomas E. Jones as vice-chairman of the board of Fisk University and was on the board of Haverford College.

Wood's second continuing concern placed him on the Civic League for Immigrants, the International Rescue Mission, and Eleanor Roosevelt's Good Neighbor Committee on the Emigré and may explain his chairing the hearings of the American Commission on Conditions in Ireland in Washington in the early 1920s after "the Troubles."

His third and biggest social concern, world peace, led him to support the Friends Ambulance unit and the Peace Association of Friends and to become treasurer in 1915–16 of the American Union Against Militarism and in the war years for the Fellowship of Reconciliation; he was a board member of AFSC and chairman of the Civil Liberties Bureau (later the American Civil Liberties Union [ACLU]) into which many Friends and other religious pacifists, who had tried in vain to uphold American neutrality and opposition to conscription, now poured their energies.

After the war, Wood followed these New York-based committees into wider campaigns for disarmament, peace, and justice although this was the era of "the Red scare." Major committees and coalitions, such as the Friends Disarmament Council (1921) and the National Council for Prevention of War, under Fred Libby from Maine (1921), lobbied the Washington Naval Conference of 1921. In the 1930s the National Council for the Prevention of War drew half its support from Friends, and a National Peace Conference tried to coordinate a dozen to twenty groups. The Carnegie Institute and supporters of the World Court and League of Nations set up dignified studies and conferences. Pacifist groups, such as the War Resisters League (1924), formed and re-formed while trying to keep their distance from Marxist splinter parties. The leaders of these groups were seldom New York Friends, but their offices were usually in New York City.

Nonviolent Struggle for Social Justice: A. J. Muste

The Fellowship of Reconciliation added to its staff A. J. Muste, who combined pacifism with a life given for religion, labor, civil liberties, and civil rights. He had been born in Holland and raised in Grand Rapids. An Easter experience and Hope College prepared him to be a Dutch Reformed pastor. Moved partly by reading Rufus Jones, he turned down a call to be Hope's history professor to serve a New York church but left it as a liberal in his beliefs and left a Congregational pastorate as a pacifist during World War I. He joined Friends in Providence but came to national attention when in 1919 he led the United Textile Workers to nonviolent victory in a strike in Lawrence, Massachusetts. Becoming head of Brookwood, a training college for young labor leaders in Katonah, New York, he also joined Croton Valley Meeting there at the urging of Hollingsworth Wood. He acted on his beliefs and knew of Stalin's misuse of the Communist party. In a period of intense intellectual infighting among Marxists, he was drawn to the Trotskyites, who, however, stole control of the "Muste-ite" labor unions.

A mystical experience of inner peace in a Paris church brought him back to religion and to pacifism in 1936. After his year as head of the Presbyterians' Labor Temple in New York, he became for the rest of his life the staff leader of the Fellowship of Reconciliation at Nyack, New York. There he trained Bayard Rustin, James Farmer, and other black leaders in the basis as well as the tactics of nonviolence, and from there he went out to guide and strengthen draft refusers and COs in World War II and the Cold War era afterward. He worked with Victor Paschkis, a Quaker refugee from Europe and Columbia University physics professor, to rally his fellow-scientists for social responsibility. Muste took up other issues of civil liberties and "civil defense." He led civil disobedience against nuclear testing in Nevada and organized a peace march from San Francisco to Moscow. When he refused to pay his income tax, he won a partial victory in court, thanks to his Quaker civil liberties lawyer, Harrop Freeman of Ithaca. Muste tried to set up an international Gandhian "Peace Brigade," based in Tanzania and visited the leaders in North Vietnam just before his death in 1967.[25]

The Great Depression of 1929–39 led many Friends and other pacifists to explore varieties of socialism, led by Evan and Norman Thomas, and made justice as vital a testimony as peace. The AFSC, unlike the British Friends Service Council, had not dissolved itself when postwar European relief was completed.[26] In 1917 Philadelphia Yearly Meeting (Orthodox) had already set up a Social Order Commit-

17. Bayard Rustin (1912–1987). Photograph by Walter Naegle.
Courtesy of Bayard Rustin Fund, Inc.

tee with study groups on issues of wealth and property. In 1924 AFSC reorganized itself to include four major sections: Foreign Service, Home Service, Interracial (and Native American), and Peace. In 1922 AFSC had already found itself using its relief techniques to feed the starving families of striking West Virginia miners although it was still trying to remain neutral over the conflicts with mine owners. In 1929 AFSC again stepped in to help strikers in North Carolina and found neutrality difficult to maintain between the textile workers and mill owners. In Pennsylvania Friends helped unemployed miners build their own homes in the Penncraft community. In 1932 AFSC asked William Simkin of Poplar Ridge, New York, with his wife, Ruth, to work under Homer and Edna Morris and Alice Davis, veterans of the feeding program in Buzuluk, Russia, to work in small "company towns" near Morgantown, West Virginia, where the mines had closed. Programs for

rebuilding homes soon developed into a furniture factory, the Moun-
taineer Craftsmen's Cooperative Association, which supported the families for thirty years. Simkin went on to train himself as a professional
mediator for labor-management disputes in the textile industry. Each
summer from 1934 to 1942 the AFSC organized summer volunteer
work-camps for college-age young people in a dozen communities.
These were revived after the war—there were twenty-four in 1951—but
endless conflicts between campers and local communities over race relations, drugs, sex, and alcohol[27] made them harder for the Service
Committee, who facing needs of rival AFSC programs gradually terminated the work-camps. From 1927 to 1936, AFSC also sent high-school
and college young folk on Peace Caravans, which presented international issues to meetings and small towns.

Intense revulsion against the slaughter of World War I and a flood
of scholarly books exposing its causes had turned about half the students in some eastern colleges and pastors in liberal churches into pacifists by 1930. A Brown University poll of 65 colleges and 21,725
students found 8,415 "absolute pacifists"; many took the "Oxford
Union pledge" not to fight. As late as 1937, 95 percent of Americans in
a poll were against all foreign wars.[28] The Fellowship of Reconciliation
turned to race issues, and in 1941 Lee Stern and other New York Young
Friends founded Ahimsa Farm near Cleveland, studying and applying
Gandhian methods to ending segregation and interracial violence:
Rustin, Farmer, and George Hauser went on to form the Congress of
Racial Equality. But campaigners for disarmament or world federalism
were becoming radicalized.

Their protest parades and personal pledges never to bear arms
made deep impacts on governments such as Chamberlain's in England,
despite the fate of Republican Spain and independent Ethiopia under
Fascist attack. A mosaic of socialist groups evoked by the Depression
moved kaleidoscopically in and out of the 1935 National Peace Conference of some forty groups, Quaker Fred Libby's National Council for
the Prevention of War, and the Emergency Peace Campaign. The
AFSC, the only major group not centered in New York or Washington,
belonged to several such alliances.[29] As late as the summer of 1941
many Friends worked to keep America neutral and resisted the impending draft.

Friends in Civilian Public Service During World War II

The Japanese attack on Pearl Harbor and Hitler's ruthlessness
against Poland and Rotterdam and the Jews united most Americans for

war and suddenly separated the Quakers on the east and west coasts, the most liberal and strongly pacifist, from both urban Marxists and Midwestern former isolationists. The AFSC, campaigning against compulsory military service, but hoping to keep its tax-exempt status, set off its political work to form the Friends Committee on National Legislation, skillfully led by Raymond Wilson.

Friends, Mennonites, and Brethren, although not uniformly pacifists,[30] were ready to present to President Roosevelt in the summer of 1940, while the Selective Service draft was still being organized, a detailed plan for a Civilian Public Service (CPS) program whereby conscientious objectors could do "work of national importance" under civilian direction. Under Friend Paul Comly French, the National Service Board for Religious Objectors, which included Methodists and Disciples as well as the "historic Peace Churches," became the official intermediary with the government, accepting the insistence of Congress that conscientious objectors not be paid and the army's insistence on overseeing the actual work projects in the Civilian Public Service camps. In October–November 1941, AFSC sent urgent appeals to the two New York Yearly Meetings, asking $15,000 from the Orthodox and $10,000 from the Hicksites toward a $150,000 Friends fund to support the camps and their unpaid workers for 1942. On November 11, 1941, there were already fourteen New York Orthodox Friends in CPS camps, but only $2,241 had been raised, one-third of it from Poplar Ridge and Poughkeepsie Meetings.[31] The need grew in later years.

Of 385 men from New York State under CPS, 60 identified themselves as Friends. Many Friends accepted registration in the wartime crisis if their draft boards would classify them 4–E as COs.[32] Some Friends who asked for CO status were classified otherwise by draft boards: Jerome Hurd of Clintondale was deferred to do agricultural work. Many of those whose draft boards refused them went to prison; 1,384 COs and 3,488 Jehovah's Witnesses were jailed in the country as a whole, including Friends such as Tom Hall of Short Hills, New Jersey, James Bristol of AFSC, and others who refused to register. Francis Hall from the Newark Ashram, along with David Dellinger and six other Union Theological Seminary students, refused the divinity exemption they could have claimed. In Danbury prison they gave a sense of unity and identity to fellow-inmates by a hunger strike and nonviolent witness against injustices. Lewis Taylor and Stanley Murphy were praised for their hunger strike in the yearly meeting's General Epistle of 1943.[33]

Out of the 151 CPS camps and units, the AFSC took responsibility to direct 15, of which 10 camps and 962 campers remained at the end of 1944, plus 360 men in eight mental hospital units, 90 in five state training schools for the mentally deficient, 77 in other special schools and hospitals, and one dozen or more in each of eight "guinea pig" units who volunteered to undergo malaria, jaundice, and atypical pneumonia for medical experiments, or diets of sea water, odd proteins, or starvation rations.[34] Only the Big Flats soil reclamation camp and the Cooperstown forestry camp, three medical experiment units on Welfare Island, one in New York Hospital, and one in Rochester were actually located in New York State. DDT was first tested on humans as a means to check typhus at a side camp of the Campton CPS unit, known as the "liceum." Thirty-two men wore for three weeks pants to which a patch containing fifty to one hundred lice had been sewed. Those in the control group only got talcum powder. "Smoke-jumpers" who parachuted to put out remote forest fires gave COs good publicity. Yet the years together built up mutual tensions and anger against a government that put COs out of sight of the public. Kenneth Morgan wrote:

> They are individualists to the core, one step from prison, and not afraid to take that step, accepting C.P.S. as long as it permits them to follow their consciences. All are conscientious objectors to war. I do not know a man in camp who could be suspected of fear or evasion. But not all are pacifists, if pacifism is defined as a way of life in which one's actions are guided by active good will, by willingness to suffer rather than inflict suffering. . . . For some their [sole] duty is to protest against the actions of a government which seems to them to be in the wrong. Others . . . wish to act in the present emergency to relieve the suffering caused by war.[35]

At the end of the war AFSC decided it would never again act as agent of a government at war.

In the long run the greatest impact was on the CPS campers themselves and on the nation's mental hospitals, their staffing and ways of working with mental patients. Work as aides or attendants led to great changes at Williamsburg, Virginia, and at Byberry, the Pennsylvania hospital where CPS men founded the National Mental Health Foundation. In July 1991 to prepare for this book twelve members of New York Yearly Meeting who had served in CPS were interviewed at Silver Bay. Only three had been Friends before CPS. Most were engaged in forestry work in CPS, especially in the earliest year of their service, planting or weeding seedlings and cutting trees at Big Flats, New York, working on the Blue Ridge Parkway in Virginia, and reclaiming land in Trenton, North Dakota. When asked, most of the men answered that both their parents and their spouses were supportive, even though as a result of choosing Civilian Public Service, not only the men but their families lost all or much of their financial support for up to four years, except as local meetings acted to fill their needs.[36]

In 1941, as war neared, New York Yearly Meeting's Joint Peace and Service Committee and local meetings demonstrated against conscription in Washington, distributed literature and sponsored speakers on peace, supported their men of draft age and counseled those seeking CO status. In 1943 the yearly meeting thanked Julien Cornell, chairman of the Joint Civilian Public Service Commitee, for legal services he was giving to COs. In New York City three hundred people helped in the work room at 144 East 23 Street, collecting old clothes and making new ones for refugees in France. More than twenty-two thousand articles of clothing came to them from Friends nationwide to be sent on to war zones.

During the war years local meetings suffered some harassment, as did pastors like Willard Reynolds, who preached sermons on peace although Friends were not persecuted as fiercely as pacifists had been in World War I. Later, a Friends Ambulance Unit of draft-exempt men served in China. Syracuse Meeting kept weekly contact with the CPS campers at Big Flats, some of whom thereby became Friends, and supported the Syracuse Peace Council's full-time city center, offering both medical and moral counsel for young men facing choices in response to the draft. Its leader, Norman Whitney, became a father figure to COs as he traveled throughout the system and to the meeting. Jean Young and Graham Leonard "were *quite* surprised to find ourselves doing dishes with him, . . ." the Weighty Bishop "wielding a dish towel in his shirtsleeves, . . . pince-nez perched on the regal nose."[37] In 1946, still teaching at Syracuse University, and again in 1960, Whitney went on behalf of AFSC to encourage British Friends after their war years of hardship. In 1957 he quit teaching to head the National Peace Education Program for AFSC. In the 1950s the AFSC let COs fulfilling Selective Service requirements serve two-year internships at the Syracuse Peace Council, with stipends. In the late 1960s AFSC's Middle Atlantic Region established the Upper New York State Area Committee (UNYSAC), severing its tie to the Peace Council. By 1970 the UNYSAC had funding for and an office in the Syracuse Friends Meeting for office and Peace secretaries. The mid-1970s school situation in Syracuse led the formation of an Ad Hoc Caucus on School Integration, putting a formerly all-white area committee in touch with concerned blacks sympathetic with peace and justice issues. A project on Assertive Conflict Resolution later dealt directly with children and youth in schools. The UNYS Area includes all the counties in New York State outside of the New York City metropolitan area. The Area Committee of twenty-five members includes Friends from upstate meetings. AFSC's Affirmative Action has led to diversity among committee members, staff, and the constituencies served. The momentum that their wartime work had established also led Syracuse Friends to form the Syracuse Friends Housing Committee, which helped black Americans find homes despite efforts of real estate dealers.[38]

New York Friends and Foreign Missions

New York Yearly Meeting (Orthodox), although it had helped to found the Friends Africa Industrial Mission in 1901, for fifty years had limited its mission activity to sending representatives to the Missions Board of Five Years Meeting. But Levinus Painter, long a supporter of missions, took a furlough from his pastorate at Collins to supervise relief feeding of Arabs in Israel for AFSC in 1949 and in 1965 took part in the setting up of East Africa Yearly Meeting in the western Kenya area of the Friends Africa Industrial Mission.[39] Such recognition that former "daughter churches" were ready for equality and independence was aided by the independence of many former African colonies. Such steps in non-Quaker Asian and South American churches had occurred between the wars. Walter Haines, administrator of Friends Hospital in a year of crisis, trained an African administrator to take over his job. His wife, Hazel, meanwhile, taught at Kaimosi. Rodney and Joan Morris led agricultural work in the mission. Herbert and Bea Kimball taught at Friends Bible Institute in Kaimosi. Wilma Wilcox taught at and recorded in text and pictures the Friends Girls School at Ramallah where Shirley Tuttle was later principal and Dean Tuttle an administrator (1974–77). In the 1980s Dale and Karen Dorrell spent three years directing a leadership program in Uganda and returned to minister at Farmington.

15

Reunion

ALSON D. VAN WAGNER
and
HUGH BARBOUR

The dramatic events taking place in nearly every preparative, monthly, and quarterly meeting after the yearly meeting of 1828 left most Friends in a state of shock. Wherever a split had taken place, and this was the case in most meetings, the members of each severed body expected their former associates soon to recognize their erring ways and rejoin them. As months and years went by without this return, the monthly meetings reluctantly disowned those who failed to associate with their branch. Justification and acceptance of the necessity of the separation probably was more difficult for the Hicksite group, which was more tolerant of diverse beliefs than was the Orthodox. In many cases the "neutrals" remained in the larger Hicksite meetings because, although their personal beliefs may have been in accord with the Orthodox, they disapproved of separating.[1]

Because fewer Hicksite Friends accepted the wisdom of Friends' separating and remaining separated, it is not surprising that the proposals for ending the breach should have come from them. An early attempt to initiate such a move was that by Nine Partners Quarterly Meeting when, in its sessions in May 1855, it minuted:

> This meeting after a due and weighty consideration of the disadvantage resulting from the unhappy division that occurred in 1828 in our Yearly Meeting and its subordinates this meeting is united in suggesting to the Yearly meeting the propriety of appointing a committee to confer with a like committee should one be appointed by the other Branch of Society and our yearly meetings giving to theirs this information and extending to them a friendly invitation to do so for the

257

purpose of effecting a reunion of Society the women's meeting uniting therewith.[2]

In the next meeting of the quarter it was reported that the matter was
brought before the yearly meeting, but no action was taken. The time
was not yet ripe, but the hope persisted.

In chapter 12 of this history, it is noted that, after more than forty
years of separation, the two branches strongly resembled each other
and appeared not much different from the Society before the split. In
the following twenty years, however, the gulf widened greatly as the
Gurneyite Orthodox group moved rapidly toward conformity with the
practices and tenets of American evangelical denominations.

Perhaps the evangelistic revival meetings that the Orthodox insti-
tuted after 1870 had some precedent in seventeenth century Quakerism, but they had no later parallels in the Society before this time and
were anathema to the Hicksites. Much more unacceptable to the latter
was the institution of a virtual creedal test for ministers and elders that
was incorporated in the 1877 Orthodox Discipline. Affirmative answers
to nine queries, sometimes called "the Questions," required of Friends
seeking recognition as ministers or appointments as elders, must have
strained the powers of rationalization or consciences of many for the
twenty-five years that the 1877 Discipline was the constitution of Orthodox Yearly Meeting. Adoption of the Uniform Discipline of the Five
Years Meeting in 1902 apparently ended general use of a doctrinal test
among New York Friends and removed an unscalable wall between the
two groups.

Innovations of the Orthodox that arrived slightly later than the
evangelistic methods were the pastoral ministry and programmed worship services. George Fox and his followers through more than two
centuries had maintained that the gift of ministry was a divine bestowal
and could only be perceived, or recognized, by humanity. The pejora-
tive term "hireling ministry" was used in the 1810 Discipline and in the
1839 and 1872 Disciplines of the Hicksites to characterize the salaried
clergy of other Christian bodies whose qualifications for the position
usually included education and training or human appointment. In
the 1859 and later Disciplines the Orthodox continued to maintain
that ministry was a free gift and was to be shared freely, even after many
meetings actually were paying ministers an annual stipend. This latter,
however, was in accord with the advice in the 1877 Discipline: "And
while on the one hand, the Gospel should never be preached for
money, on the other it is the duty of the Church to make such provision that it shall never be hindered for want of it." Such reasoning

never persuaded the Hicksites to pay for the services of their ministers, aside from occasional meager reimbursement for traveling expenses. In the twentieth century, after relations between the two branches became easier, it was not uncommon for the Hicksites to invite salaried Orthodox ministers to speak at their conferences and special events, their own ministry being depleted and generally less trained in public speaking. As a result the Hicksite prejudice against ministers began to erode, particularly as New York pastoral ministers frequently became graduates of liberal seminaries, such as Hartford Theological Seminary, Colgate Theological Seminary at Rochester, and Yale Divinity School, who had not had to give affirmative answers to "the Questions" of the 1877 Discipline.

By the end of the first quarter of the twentieth century few Orthodox members of New York Yearly Meeting, aside from those of 20th Street Meeting in New York City, had any experience with a traditional Friends meeting for worship where there was an hour or more of silence broken, if at all, by spoken messages or prayer. So dependent had they become on the message of the pastor and the program of music and responses arranged by him that a period of five minutes of unbroken silence was burdensome. Reintroduction to the ancient Friends practice came to most Orthodox Quarterly Meetings only when new united meetings became established within the quarters during the second twenty-five years. For the Friends attached to the Hicksite branch, the preaching, music, and formalized prayer of programmed worship was an intrusion on the time when they expected to worship in silence.

Obligatory Common Action

Immediately following the Separation, in many locations, the two groups arranged to use the same meeting house, but such sharing by the hostile factions soon proved too stressful and inconvenient, so the smaller body, usually the Orthodox, built a new meeting house. Less frequently, a new burying ground was established to separate the Friends families in death as in life. Generally, both branches continued to bury their deceased members in the old grounds, even though care of the grounds had passed to the other branch. For some time there had been dissatisfaction with provisions of the Discipline forbidding erection of gravestones. It was logical, if somewhat amusing, that in the same year, 1852, the two yearly meetings modified their provisions to allow gravestones with simple inscriptions but with strict limits to their size. The Hicksites allowed the stones to be a maximum of 5 in. by 16 in. by 8 in. high. The Orthodox allowed the stones to be 6 in. by 16 in.

and 1 ft. high. Even though subsequent size requirements were liber-
alized by both bodies, they never arrived at a consensus until both
ceased specifying exact measurements.

Even the most intransigent of the separated Friends had to con-
cede that the two groups had one thing more in common than their
burial grounds—their history. The record of their history was largely in
the minutes and registers that had fallen into the hands of one or the
other contending party at the Separation and were not conveniently
available to the other when matters of property or genealogical interest
needed attention. By the late 1800s each side despaired of bringing all
these records into its possession, and increasingly the wall of separation
was being ignored in practical recognition that the only access to the
desired information was through communication with those who possessed the records, no matter how illegitimately.

Although many of the local meeting records still remained with the
local meetings, often in the homes of the clerks or recorders, there
had been an effort by both yearly meetings to get the older records,
particularly of discontinued meetings, deposited in New York City by
the end of the century. The Hicksite books were in safes in the 15th
Street Meeting House, and those of the Orthodox were mostly in a
rented vault. A small committee of 15th Street Meeting engaged the
clerk of the committee, John Cox, Jr., to catalog the Hicksite holdings.
In 1897 the Orthodox arranged to have the same Friend catalog their
materials "in Safe [presumably at 20th Street] and at Produce Exchange Safe Deposit Company."[3]

Naturally, many searches led from 15th Street to the holdings of
the Orthodox, located many blocks away and only accessible by special
arrangement. This inconvenient situation led to a proposal in 1904 by
the Hicksite Records Committee to the Orthodox Yearly Meeting that
it appoint some of its members to form a Joint Committee on Records
and locate all the records at the 15th Street Meeting House, rent free.[4]
The proposal was approved. The new committee named John Cox, Jr.,
its clerk, a position in which he remained for the next forty-four years,
remaining on the committee until his death in 1950.

Joint Committee on Peace

Cooperation of the two branches of New York Friends to care for
and access the historical documents that had been scattered at the
time of the Separation and that each needed for information about its
own property, history, and family genealogy, might be viewed as almost
a necessity. The next common effort and formation of a joint commit-

tee by the two meetings entailed no such pressure. The group meeting at 15th Street for its annual sessions in May 1908, proposed that all Friends meetings, worldwide, "appoint special committees, one from each Yearly Meeting, which may confer and co-operate to arrange and formulate measures for the support of the movement for peace, and for the better establishment of the principles of international peace, having also in view the International Conference appointed to meet at the Hague in the year 1915."[5] Not only did the other branch warmly receive the proposal at their meetings at Poughkeepsie the next week; it proposed that the invitation be a joint one from the two meetings. This must be one of the earliest instances in which the bodies torn apart in 1827–28 appeared in common endeavor before all Quakerdom and all the world. The Joint Committee on Peace continued to forward shared peace concerns until 1919 when its Orthodox members were made a subcommittee of the Peace and Arbitration Committee of that branch.

During the World War, and immediately after it, a Joint Service Committee related the two yearly meetings to the work of the American Friends Service Committee in the New York City area.

Joint Committee on Affiliated Service

The next committee, after formation of the Joint Committee on Old Records to which members of the two yearly meetings were appointed, was the Joint Committee for Affiliated Service. When this was set up in 1916, John Cox, Jr., and L. Hollingsworth Wood were selected as co-clerks of the committee. Interestingly, Wood, son of the Orthodox Yearly Meeting clerk, James Wood, had married Hicksite Helen Underhill in the Hicksite Jericho Meeting House in 1915. Hollingsworth's second wife, Martha Speakman, whom he married after Helen's death, was from the Hicksite Philadelphia Meeting.

The Affiliated Committee served as the channel for communication between the two groups until, in 1944,[6] it felt its usefulness had ceased, and it was laid down. The same two men remained as co-clerks for the entire twenty-seven years, Wood also as assistant clerk of the Orthodox Yearly Meeting for ten years and clerk for six.

An immediate task confronting the new joint committee was coordinating expression of Friends concerns relating to the war already in progress in Europe; this ultimately resulted in formation of the American Friends Service Committee. As the war ended, the Quakers' relief efforts often centered in New York. Friends were also concerned that public policy on armaments and international relations should further a lasting peace. Through the Service Committee and by initiative of

New York Friends, a number of open forums to educate the public were organized, some of the events taking place in the New York City and Brooklyn meeting houses.

The tercentenary of the birth of George Fox provided an obvious occasion that could be observed by all Friends. The Joint Committee on Affiliated Service obtained allocations from both yearly meeting budgets, so that in late 1924 the committee arranged a joint celebration of this event in New York City.

Friends were quite conscious and conscience stricken that 1928 marked one hundred years of their unfortunate separation. Few felt that Friends were in any way ready to become a unified body, but at least many felt the centenary could be observed by one joint meeting at which each body conducted its own business. The Joint Committee planned the sessions, which were held in New York City, with morning sessions at 20th Street and afternoon and evening sessions at 15th Street. The London epistle greeted the joint meeting warmly, confessing London Yearly Meeting's partial responsibility for the tragedy one hundred years earlier.[7]

Satisfaction with the joint meeting of 1928 seemed general, but there was no stated intention of repeating the experiment. For the following five years the Affiliated Service Committee did administer an annual John Bowne Lecture, which featured a prominent speaker to give the same talk at sessions of each yearly meeting and allowed members of the two branches a common experience. Later, a number of other lectures and dinners were arranged in the New York City area, usually in cooperation with the American Friends Service Committee.

The 1939 World's Fair in New York provided another occasion when unity rather than division among Friends was called for. The Affiliated Service Committee provided the vehicle for this cooperation, and an exhibit at the Bowne House in Flushing was developed and staffed with Quaker volunteers.

As important a role for the committee as arranging joint meetings and enterprises was keeping Friends informed of moves toward understanding and unity at the local or monthly meeting level, movement that the Affiliated Service Committee often encouraged.

Reunion at the Grass Roots

Because of the prominent role that the new American Friends Service Committee played in relief and reconstruction during and after the world war and in promoting the cause of peace as well, there was attraction to the Society of Friends that had not existed for more than one century. The Depression and the appearance of the Service Committee as a leader in Christian social reform attracted still more people of liberal, or even radical, political bent to seek out Quaker meetings or to join together to investigate whether Quakerism might have the answers they were seeking. A few of these new "seekers" had remote connections to the Society, most were of a religious inclination, but few were drawn to the fine distinctions of theology and practice that divided Friends into Gurneyites, Hicksites, and Wilburites, and confused them when they reached out to find a congenial fellowship. The formation of these new and united meetings is covered in chapter 13.

Young Friends and Peace Concerns Ignore Division

A strong indicator that reunion of the two yearly meetings would eventually take place was the joining in 1938 of the two groups of young Friends, the Young Friends Movement, with General Conference connection, and the Young Friends Board, with Five Years Meeting connection to form the Young Friends Fellowship. Actually, in the New York City area, they had been joined for three or more years. Moreover, the two groups had been holding joint conferences at Minnewaska, at the Holden farm in Dutchess County, and at other places around New York State. In its detailed report to the Hicksite Yearly Meeting in 1935 the Young Friends Movement reported appointment of a committee to consider a program for complete unification of Young Friends in New York and New Jersey and of another committee to study the Jenkins Plan "for the unification of all Friends." So by 1938, plans for a united group were worked out by the Young Friends, following a plan outlined in a letter of George Badgley, which stated: "We have not lived long enough to have theologies which cannot be mutually reconciled. We have no property nor financial affairs which tend to serve as difficult legal barriers. On the other hand, we do have numerous friendly experiences upon which to look. We have a genuine desire that the Society of Friends recapture some of its lost vitality."[8] The proposal was approved by the Hicksite Yearly Meeting in April and by the Orthodox in July with apparent enthusiasm in both cases.

The Young Friends Fellowship received some financial support from both yearly meetings but appointed its own officers, who were listed in the directories included with the published minutes of each body along with an annual report of the Fellowship. Busy with military and social concerns, the new Fellowship reported no further consideration of organic union of the yearly meetings.

During and after World War II the organized Young Friends apparently became less able to carry on a program throughout the year. They did usually meet during the annual business sessions of the yearly meetings and issue an epistle "to Young Friends everywhere" through 1968. The last appearance of the Young Friends Fellowship in the budget of the yearly meeting, by then unified, was 1971.

Nearly as anxious as the Young Friends to break down walls between the two yearly meetings were the two committees concerned with peace and social issues. The threat of a new world war and the close relations both committees had with the American Friends Service Committee made cooperation a near necessity and organizational unity an obvious advantage. From 1938 on the reports of the Hicksite Peace and Social Order Committee and the Orthodox Friendly Relations Committee show an increase of common efforts led by the Joint Peace and Service Committee of the two New York Monthly Meetings and the Young Friends of United Montclair Meeting. The subcommittees lending support to Civilian Public Service became joint in 1944, and the main groups, each renamed Peace and Service Committee, became one under the two New York Yearly Meetings on March 31, 1945, with Howard L. Carey of the Lafayette Avenue Meeting, Brooklyn, as chair.

The Theological Wall Crumbles

Probably the one thing that created the most hesitancy among Hicksite Friends leaning toward the reunion of the two New York Yearly Meetings was retention of the 1901 *Uniform Discipline* by the Orthodox group. In some respects this document was barely acceptable even to many Orthodox members. Its use of many evangelistic terms and its inclusion of the declaration issued by the Richmond Conference of 1887, even though placed in the appendix, made it unthinkable for the Hicksites. The Five Years Meeting of 1940 authorized development of a new *Book of Faith and Practice* whose several draft versions were more to the liking of the liberal yearly meetings. None of the tentative drafts proved acceptable to all the Five Years Meeting groups, but in 1945 New York Yearly Meeting approved use of the new book by local meetings on an experimental basis. In spite of a warning open letter signed by fifteen ministers from eight other yearly meetings[9] several monthly meetings in New York did adopt it. The united meetings had already chosen to use some Discipline other than that of 1901, so the new *Faith and Practice* only further reduced its use. In 1950 the statistician reported, "6 Meetings use the old *Uniform Discipline,* 11 use *Faith and Practice,* 3 use the 15th Street Discipline, 7 say they use several different ones, and 10 did not answer." With this degree of confusion and dissatisfaction within the Orthodox ranks, the 1901 Discipline had ceased to be a formidable barrier to the coming together of the two groups.

For their part, the Hicksite group had been in the process of revising or replacing its own Discipline. A Committee for Revision of the Discipline, appointed in 1946, brought together a new "Queries and Advices" but decided to substitute what it called the "Uniform General Conference Discipline" for New York's 1930 book. Essentially, this discipline was the *Practice and Procedure* adopted by Philadelphia Yearly Meeting in 1927. New York Yearly Meeting accepted the committee's recommendation in 1950. It would appear that, with reunion of New York Friends almost certain, the Committee for Revision was unwilling to undertake a project that would soon become irrelevant. Working out a book of practice and procedure for future use would have to follow actual organic union.

Background to Reunion

Between the world wars, American Friends of all branches were rethinking their relationship to the wider world and to the Bible and their own tradition as well. This pattern was found throughout Protestantism as it no longer unthinkingly dominated American culture. Threatened by the doubling in membership of Nazarenes, Assemblies of God, and other fundamentalist groups from 1926 to 1936, the "main-line" churches found sectarian differences less crucial. National church leaders and local clergy in America and Europe increasingly turned to each other in crises as they shared a renewal of the Social Gospel as "neo-orthodox" or Barthian theology probed deeper into social and personal sources of evil.

Southern and northern Methodists reunited in 1939 after one century, although still without their black and fundamentalist fellow churchgoers. Three decades later, the several branches of Presbyterians did the same. The Congregationalists united with one Christian connection in 1931 and, in 1951, with four already merged Evangelical and Reformed branches of German Reformed churches to form the United Church of Christ.

Interchurch councils for missions, religious education, and social service opened the way for expanding the 1908 Federal Council of Churches into the wider National Council of Churches; Five Years Meeting and Philadelphia (Orthodox) Friends, part of the process from the beginning, were exempted from the otherwise required creedal limits. World church conferences in 1925 on Faith and Order and on the Churches' Life and Work were continued in 1927; these led to meetings at Utrecht and Amsterdam in 1938, which continued in 1948 and created the World Council of Churches. In debates on sacraments and ministry Friends helped these bodies transcend conflicts over details. On peace and service they were welcomed as leaders. In local interchurch councils, however, Friends' own disunity was embarrassing.

Most of the leading American Quaker pastors between the wars had attended interdenominational seminaries, and most weighty Friends in the unprogrammed tradition were by then graduates of nonsectarian colleges and universities. These two groups led Friends toward reunion.

In New England, where many conferences and the AFSC had brought Friends together, the merged Boston and Cambridge Meetings and new meetings in academic communities such as Hartford and New Haven protested the continuing division of New England Friends into Gurneyite and Wilburite Yearly Meetings and refused to join either. This stand helped to reunite the two New England Yearly Meetings in 1945.[10]

Philadelphia Yearly Meeting had divided one year earlier than the New York meeting, but both the resulting meetings had kept to unprogrammed worship and had met together since the 1920s in a united Young Friends Movement, in the AFSC and in many other joint committees, and in common support of Quaker work in Japan.[11] After careful negotiations these yearly meetings reunited in 1955. In the same year their journals, *The Friend* and *Friends Intelligencer,* merged into *The Friends Journal.* Although many New York Friends traveled constantly to Boston and Philadelphia, the interaction of these reunions with developments in New York Yearly Meeting has not been studied. New York's Quarterly Meetings moved ahead with reunion more than had Philadelphia's, but, unlike New York Yearly Meeting, Philadelphia was able to produce a common *Book of Discipline* before the merger.

The Reunion Process Begins

When the Joint Committee on Affiliated Service made its report to both yearly meetings in 1944 and suggested that it should be laid down because its assigned task was essentially completed, it doubtless was referring to action taken in the 1943 sessions. The Orthodox Yearly Meeting, in minute no. 10 of that year, recorded: "As a result of the report of the State of Society, a concern was expressed that the 250th session of New York Yearly Meeting, two years hence, might be a united session with the New York Yearly Meeting of General Conference affiliation." A

18. New York Yearly Meeting. Clerks' table at the first joint Business Session
of the Orthodox and Hicksite Branches at Silver Bay in 1948.
Left to right: Ruth Craig, C. Frank Ortloft, George Badgley,
Howard E. Kershner, Blanche E. Brown, and Stephen LeRoy Angell.
Courtesy Haviland Records Room, New York Yearly Meeting.

committee was appointed not only to consider united sessions in 1945
but also to consider joint sessions in 1944. Restrictions on travel and
other problems incidental to conditions during and immediately after
World War II resulted in delay in achieving these goals.

Concrete steps that steadily led to joint sessions of the two yearly
meetings began in 1945 with appointment of a committee to explore
and arrange for a joint conference with members from each yearly
meeting. This conference was held in Lisle, New York, during September 1946. It forwarded two recommendations to each yearly meeting:
(1) that quarterly meetings of both yearly meetings consider any opportunity to cooperate or unite; (2) that concurrent yearly meetings be
held in 1947 at some place new to both yearly meetings. The Representative Committee of the Hicksite group accepted the Lisle conference
recommendation but suggested that separate business sessions by the
two yearly meetings be held and be adjourned to a joint session for
consideration of committee reports and concerns common to both.
Thus, after separate meetings, joint business sessions were held at the
Quaker-connected resort at Minnewaska, New York, June 25–30, 1947.
Full-time joint sessions were held at the YMCA Conference Center at
Silver Bay on Lake George, New York, in 1948. Joint sessions continued
at Silver Bay each following year through 1955, except for 1950 when
only a joint conference was held there. United sessions had to wait until the Fourth Day evening at the conclusion of joint sessions in 1955.

The sense of the inevitability and the desirability of reunion, which was present in the leadership of the two yearly meetings in 1943, was not shared by all members of many of the local meetings in either of the yearly meetings. One and one-quarter centuries of separate growth and life were not to be erased quickly. During the next dozen years many adjustments in organization and ways of thinking were made. In fact, it was still another nine years before the reunion could really be considered completed. One adjustment that was difficult for the Long Island and New York City Hicksite Friends was giving up the yearly meetings at 15th Street for sessions upstate. Within a few years, however, the advantages of having a site where a large and lively program for children and young people could take place won them over to favoring the Lake George facilities.

Annual sessions in 1953 approved Ministry and Counsel's proposal that a committee be appointed to investigate obstacles to be overcome if organic union was to come about. This committee of thirteen, listed in the minutes as "Joint Committee to Consider Problems for Organic Union of New York Yearly Meetings," selected attorney Herman J. Compter as its chair. In its first report to the Permanent Board of the Orthodox group in December 1953, and to the Representative Committee, the equivalent body of the Hicksite Yearly Meeting, in January 1954, the committee stated specific problems that needed to be addressed. The report stated that the committee was united in favoring organic union in principle, concluding: "Although many knotty problems confront us the Committee feels none of them present a serious obstacle, if there is a will to unite."

The Representative Meeting had already been testing the "will to unite" in the Hicksite branch in response to a September 1952 minute from Shrewsbury and Plainfield Half-Yearly Meeting, which requested the "Representative Committee of New York Yearly Meeting to take immediate action looking to the organic union of the two New York Yearly Meetings." Of the twenty-two replies to its March 1953 request for responses by monthly and quarterly meetings to the Shrewsbury minute only one voiced objection to reunion, and thirteen approved with no conditions. The Orthodox group did not poll its monthly meetings until a letter from its clerk, Alfred J. Henderson, dated March 9, 1954. A report to the Permanent Board in May found that within the thirteen meetings responding by that time "there was general approval." Of course, more than half of these were united meetings, which, naturally, were highly favorable to reunion.

The stated unity of the committee appointed to explore the problems of organic union needed some qualification. One member, J. Kennedy Sinclaire, in a letter to Compter in July 1954, wrote: "I am sorry to have to be one of the minority that while not opposed to organic union as a marriage of convenience don't recognize just how it will strengthen the Religious Society of Friends. After all, we are a religious society, and it seems to me that a joining such as is contemplated is not a religious joining at all, but simply a face-saving idea to offset the complaint some make that guests and new members wonder why the Society cannot get together."[12] Similar sentiments were voiced by Albert Schreiner, appointed to fill a vacancy in the committee in May 1955. In a letter to Compter he remarked, "If the condition of being united in organization were good in itself I should see no reason for not joining with *any* existing religious group whatever its beliefs."[13] Levinus K. Painter, another committee member and pastor of a small meeting at Collins, near Buffalo, at first had his enthusiasm for reunion tempered by the reluctance of the Hicksites to accept the pastoral system and support for foreign missions as legitimate concerns for a united yearly meeting. By June 1955 he had come to feel that union should take place at the approaching sessions, particularly because reunion was already taking place between the two Philadelphia Yearly Meetings.[14]

Although the climate before joint sessions of the two yearly meetings in July and August 1954 was encouraging, it still remained to be seen whether approval for reunion in principle would support adjustments necessary to make one functioning body. Ever since its appointment, the Committee on Organic Union had been hammering out "A Basis for Consolidation of the Two New York Yearly Meetings." This plan, largely the work of Herman Compter, was presented to the yearly meetings in joint session on August 2, 1954, and approved for distribution to all subordinate meetings for their consideration and suggestions. Final action was to wait another year during which the committee was directed to continue study and make reports.

In brief, the sixteen points of the plan proposed to:

—Combine the organizational structure of the yearly meetings at the yearly meeting level only, including officers, committees, budgets, property, and legal identity.

—Retain connections to Friends General Conference and the Five Years Meeting of Friends but to reconsider that to the New York State Council of Churches.

—Adopt a uniform practice and procedure but to make no attempt to adopt a uniform statement of faith and beliefs.

—Continue recognition of gifts in the ministry.

—Leave local meetings free to determine their own forms of worship and qualifications for membership.

Reactions to the Basis for Consolidation were directed to the committee. Because many meetings had responded positively to the queries from the Representative Committee and the Permanent Board and had few reservations about going ahead with unification, they needed urging to reply again. To elicit responses from those meetings who had made them when the sixteen points were presented at Silver Bay in August 1954 the Organic Union Committee sent a letter on May 5, 1955, in which it requested replies to the question of whether consolidation should be approved at the yearly meeting session in July and August. Of all the letters received during the year between annual sessions only two opposed reunion in 1955.[15] One was a Hicksite meeting that, despite assurances in the "Basis," voiced fear that it would have to adopt the pastoral system. One united meeting recommended more study before proceeding. Brooklyn Hicksite minuted: "a necessary prerequisite to formal union of the two New York Yearly Meetings is the preparation of a common book of Discipline acceptable to members of both Yearly Meetings." Suggestions for modification of the sixteen points dealt with committee structure, recognition of ministers, and the budget. Yet several of the united meetings were chafed that the reunion process was taking so long. Typical was a minute of All Friends Quarterly Meeting of May 14, 1955: "Each passing day, week and month makes us more eager for the accomplishment of organic union." It is notable that theological issues were essentially unmentioned by any meeting as an obstruction.

At its final meeting before 1955 yearly meeting sessions, at the home of committee member David F. Lane in Poughkeepsie, the Committee on Organic Union concluded that "in light of the great preponderance of expression favoring proceeding promptly" that its report would recommend that the two yearly meetings unite at those sessions on the unmodified basis of the sixteen points presented in 1954.

Immediately preceding presentation of the report to the yearly meeting session on Monday evening, August 1, the meeting received a minute from the high school group expressing the hope that organic union would be effected. Although this sequence of events was not staged, a more favorable climate for prompt acceptance of the committee's recommendation could scarcely be imagined. When the presiding clerk, Horace Stubbs, heard no objections to the recommendation of the Organic Union Committee, he cautioned, "Wait a minute, Friends, do you know what you are approving?"[16] His remarks failed to suppress the overwhelming joy of most Friends that the long hoped-for union was finally taking place. The minute recorded, "With a complete sense of unity the Meeting approved the recommendations of the committee set forth in its report." Before thanking and discharging the Organic Union Committee, the meeting sent a message to Martha and L. Hollingsworth Wood. Hollingsworth's appointment to the Joint Committee on Affiliated Service in 1916 had begun a lifetime devotion to the reunion just realized.

The business meeting then promptly adopted minutes to effectuate the sixteen-point plan. Among these was establishment of a Committee on Yearly Meeting Practice and Procedure. Appointed to this new committee of eight were four of the members of the Organic Union Committee, including Herman E. Compter, who became its chair, and David Lane and Paul Schwantes, who had already been preparing a first draft of a united discipline on business procedures.

Tying Up the Loose Ends

In 1947 the New York Yearly Meeting with General Conference affiliation and the New York Yearly Meeting with Five Years Meeting affiliation were only two of four yearly meetings with local meetings in the area that had been covered by New York Yearly Meeting in 1828. In 1834 Hicksite Friends in western New York State had been set off to Genesee Yearly Meeting, which also included Friends in Canada. By 1947 only one of its regional meetings, Farmington Half-Yearly Meeting, with one local meeting, East Hamburg Executive Meeting, survived in the United States. A few weeks after the reunion at Silver Bay in 1955 Canadian Friends brought together their three branches, Orthodox, Hicksite (Genesee), and Conservative, into Canadian Yearly Meeting. This left East Hamburg's forty-two members and its meeting houses at Orchard Park and Collins in the Canadian meeting. This inconvenient situation was corrected in 1958 when East Hamburg Friends were transferred to Farmington Quarterly Meeting as Orchard Park Monthly Meeting.

The Wilburite or Conservative Friends that remained in New York in 1947 were organized as Scipio Four-Months Meeting, which had become a part of Canada Yearly Meeting, Conservative. Very few in number, these Friends laid down the Four-Months Meeting in 1954 and, as individuals, joined monthly meetings of the United Scipio Quarterly

Meeting. Thus, in spite of all the separations, by the end of 1958 all the meetings in the area that had been in New York Yearly Meeting in 1828 were members of the one New York Yearly Meeting, if in the United States, or of the one Canadian Yearly Meeting, if in Canada.

To an extent the organic union of 1955 was an anticlimax, after eight years of holding all or part of the business of the two yearly meetings in joint sessions. A noticeable change was joining the interim bodies for conducting business, the Representative Committee of the Hicksite group and the Permanent Board of the Orthodox body, into the Representative Meeting. The Representative Meeting was described as an "interim Yearly Meeting" with representatives named from subordinate meetings to ensure broad participation, but open to all. It had its own clerk and agenda committee; the clerk reported significant business to the yearly meeting, treating it as a separate body. Not until 1986 did the yearly meeting approve a change in *Faith and Practice*, providing for the same clerk for the two bodies.

As previously noted, each of the yearly meetings that had just joined had been in a state of flux as far as its "discipline," or "book of faith and practice," was concerned. Such a defining document has always been the mark of a yearly meeting in the Society of Friends, a yearly meeting answering to no higher human authority. Arriving at a suitable organizational plan of practices and procedures was simplified by the practical experience of working together over the years since the Records Committee had become joint in 1904 and particularly during the years of joint yearly meeting sessions. The continuation of the members of the Committee to Consider the Problems of Organic Union on to the Committee on Practice and Procedure under the continued chairmanship of Herman Compter showed the confidence Friends had in the group and doubtless made adoption of the Practice section (Part II) of a new discipline much smoother than it might have been. Progress might have seemed glacial to non-Friends, who saw that only after eight years was a document produced for "trial" use. Approval, however, required nearly unanimous acceptance from a diverse group, acceptance that was made possible by constant reference back to the scattered monthly and quarterly meetings. In accordance with the "Basis" there was as little disturbance with monthly meeting autonomy as was possible. Matters that impinged on religious views, such as membership and granting of "Letters of Travel" to Friends who have a message to deliver to distant Friends and others, proved more troublesome, and were among the last sections to be approved.

Much more difficult than arriving at agreement on practices and procedures was crafting a statement of faith and belief that would describe and satisfy a yearly meeting with numbers of members ranging from those who could be characterized as agnostics to those who could be labeled Biblical literalists. Many of the newer members, particularly those in the newly formed meetings, had been attracted to Friends by the absence of any creed or requirement of a declaration of faith before being accepted as members. The 1950 *Book of Discipline* of the yearly meeting with Friends General Conference connection made a minimal Christian statement: "This manifestation of God in man was most fully exemplified in Jesus of Nazareth. The Divine Spirit became so wholly Jesus' own that his teaching, example, and sacrificial life are the complete revelation in humanity of the will of God."[17] Even this was faulted by one meeting in the All Friends Quarterly Meeting, which felt it excluded "other persons who may not be Christian but who seek God through the Light within."[18]

The yearly meeting was fortunate to gather a committee with rather constant membership from its first appointment in 1955 to its discharge upon completion of a draft of a "Faith" section (Part I) of a proposed discipline approved for three-year trial use in 1964. Through all these years it had had the sensitive and skillful leadership of its chair, A. Keith Smiley, who now continued to serve on a standby committee for a trial period. In his reports to the yearly meeting he emphasized that the writing did not attempt to present a complete theology and that the intent was not to take any specific position in the wide spectrum of current religious opinion. The section entitled "Life of the Spirit," defining some beliefs that were distinctively Quaker, reached a final form only after the circulation of preliminary drafts to the local meetings for discussion and suggestions. The section was then rewritten by the committee and recirculated.

Illustrating the theological differences within New York Yearly Meeting was the controversy that continued from 1956 through 1967 about whether the yearly meeting should approve an application for membership in the National Council of Churches by Friends General Conference. The National Council had adopted a constitution that included a statement of rather minimal Christian doctrine to which its members were expected to subscribe. Friends who particularly valued Friends' traditional avoidance of any creedal statement, and especially those of a more unitarian faith, felt that Friends could not in good conscience be part of the council. A proposal to allow Friends to interpret the doctrinal statement in their own ways as a condition of membership did not completely satisfy. Discussions took place in many monthly and quarterly meetings and at Silver Bay and a special seminar at the Powell House conference center. Still, no unity was found, and there was no further consideration after 1967.

Actually, New York Yearly Meeting, in its refusal to sanction Friends General Conference application, was put in the anomalous position of already being a member of the National Council through its membership in the Five Years Meeting of Friends (later Friends United Meeting), which was a member of the council. Nevertheless, after ten years of consideration, the yearly meeting could not unite in granting approval for the General Conference also to join. In an exhibit of equity a proposal for Friends General Conference to join the International Association for Liberal Christianity and Religious Freedom was never approved either.

Final reports of the Practice and Procedure and the Faith and Beliefs committees were received by the yearly meeting at the sessions in 1967. The "Faith" section, Part I, remained essentially the same as that submitted in 1964. The "Practice and Procedure" section, Part II, was mostly unchanged, except for a revision of the provisions on membership. The committees were both laid down, but a new committee consisting of their members was formed with two further appointments to do the final editing of the finished book, *Faith and Practice*. The reunion process might be considered to have been completed when the yearly meeting approved the report presented by Keith Smiley on July 26, 1968.

Adjusting to New Realities

Among the practical considerations requiring immediate attention by the united body that had not invited confrontation during the years of joint sessions was a unified budget to meet organizational expenses, such as salaries of staff, committee expenses, and support of larger bodies with which the yearly meeting was associated. Adjustments were made easier because the former two yearly meetings had memberships and staffs of comparable size and many of the committees had already become joint and were being supported by the two meetings. At the time of reunion the amount to be raised per member in each was nearly the same. This had not been true ten years earlier when the Hicksite group's cost per member was somewhat larger than that for the Orthodox. The latter had seen its costs rise some 60 percent as a result of more adequate salary for its field secretary and greater demands from the Five Years Meeting. So, immediately after reunion, assessments on local meetings did not change dramatically, and resentment about raises in "quotas" could not be automatically blamed on reunion. About the only complaints were from former Hicksite meetings that resented the sending of some of their dollars to support foreign missions.

At the time of joining the only real property owned by either yearly meeting was the New York Yearly Meeting Friends Home, which the Hicksite Yearly Meeting had acquired by gift from non-Friends in 1950. The McCutchen, as the boarding home came to be called in honor of the donors, became the property of the united meeting. A nursing home was added in 1965 and six apartments in 1975 to bring total capacity of the facility to nearly sixty residents. An attempt to establish a larger, or life-care, retirement community by New York Friends in later years was unsuccessful.

Trends in total membership in the yearly meeting might be considered a measure of the satisfaction from bringing the long-separated society back together. The period from 1955 through 1965 probably was one of the most stable in the history of New York Friends. The annual State of Society reports to the yearly meeting by Ministry and Counsel in the years through 1960 showed many local meetings experiencing growth of attendance and building or improving their meeting houses. The 1964 report noted the laying down of several meetings. Additionally, seven surviving small rural meetings, mostly pastoral and formerly Orthodox, that for 1955 reported 250 members reported only 83 ten years later. Because all the growth that counterbalanced these losses was in newly established unprogrammed meetings or in a few of the older unprogrammed meetings, the complexion of the yearly meeting was changing but certainly more for demographic reasons than as a result of reunion.

Assessing the results of the 1955 action of the joint session at Silver Bay ten years later, it seems that reunion was an almost unqualified success. There was little reason to change the Ministry and Counsel's 1957 summary of the State of Society that showed "'resurgence of love and unity from waiting on God together,' 'solemn joy,' and, because of the organic union of two Quarterly Meetings, 'a revitalized period in the life of our Meetings'." For a time the century and one-quarter of steady membership decline of Friends in the New York area was arrested.[19]

16

Peace and Social Concerns: The Last Forty Years, 1955–1995

NANCY C. SOREL
and
LLOYD AND MARGARET BAILEY, HUGH BARBOUR,
THOMAS BASSETT, EMMA FLECK, DANIEL A. SEEGER,
MARY SEXTON, JANE B. SIMKIN, MARY ELLEN SINGSEN,
KATHERINE SOREL, ALSON D. VAN WAGNER,
GEORGE H. WATSON, HENRY A. WHEELER

The Cold War and Nuclear Disarmament

From the middle of the 1950s, if not before, many members of New York Yearly Meeting were deeply concerned about the threat of atomic-nuclear war and the proliferation of nuclear testing. That war could now escalate to where all civilization would be destroyed was an undeniable fact, and it changed the perspective of Friends and non-Friends alike. Even people who did not call themselves pacifists became ardent antinuclear activists.

The Hiroshima Maidens Project

One effect of this awareness within the yearly meeting was the co-operation of many Friends with Norman Cousins of the *Saturday Review*

A major and invaluable source throughout this chapter has been Lawrence Apsey's *Following the Light for Peace* (Katonah, N.Y.: Kim Pathways, 1991). Also widely consulted were oral histories of present and past members of New York Yearly Meeting. References to Yearly Meeting actions may be found in yearbooks of New York Yearly Meeting for the years cited. Transcripts of oral histories and the yearbooks are available at the Haviland Records Room at 15 Rutherford Place, New York City.

on the Hiroshima Maidens Project. In 1955 twenty-five young women, severely burned as children when the United States dropped atomic bombs over Japan, were brought to New York for treatment and plastic surgery at Mount Sinai Hospital. During the year they lived with families, Quaker and non-Quaker, some attending meeting for worship on Sunday morning. Where this happened, Friends became more aware of the nuclear issue and were left with enduring impressions.

One of the most active New York Yearly Meeting Friends to play a role in the antinuclear issue was Albert (Bert) Bigelow. Serving as a navy lieutenant-commander during World War II, he had been profoundly affected by the news of Hiroshima as he stood on the bridge of his ship on August 6, 1945. He and his wife, Sylvia, an early member of the Stamford-Greenwich Meeting, provided a home for two of the "Hiroshima Maidens," an experience that provided him the impetus for becoming a Quaker himself.[1]

Demonstrations at the New Mexico and Nevada Testing Sites

Albert Bigelow, along with Dorothy Day, David Dellinger, A. J. Muste, Bayard Rustin, and Lawrence Scott, formed the Non-Violent Action Against Nuclear Weapons (NVAANW) and later, under Muste's leadership, the Committee on Non-Violent Action (CNVA). Another central figure was William (Bill) Huntington, who had been a conscientious objector and a founder of the Episcopal Pacifist Fellowship during World War II. His contact with Quakers in CPS camps influenced his decision to become a Friend himself. After the war he worked with Stephen Cary as co-commissioner of postwar refugee relief in Europe for AFSC. On his return to the United States he joined Westbury Meeting and in 1955 went with other members of CNVA to New Mexico to a vigil at Los Alamos. Some of the demonstrators, Bigelow among them, entered the restricted area and were arrested. When the nuclear device was detonated some thirty-five miles away, the vigilers stood with their backs to the blast in symbolic protest. Demonstrations at the New Mexico and Nevada testing sites continued intermittently. More than three decades later New York Yearly Meeting Friends were still making the trip, compelled to continue the witness against nuclear warfare. One of these, Nancy First of Purchase Meeting, for four years in the early 1980s wrote daily to the president about nuclear warfare and was among the thousands of vigilers in Nevada who were arrested for their vigil—a fruitful inheritance of the little CNVA group of 1955.[2]

The Voyage of the Golden Rule

Another CNVA project was the voyage of the *Golden Rule,* conceived to alert the world to the dangers of nuclear testing and to protest the U.S. decision to prohibit navigation in an area around the uninhabited Eniwetok atoll in the central Pacific. A crew of four planned to sail the *Golden Rule,* a thirty-foot ketch, into the testing area, accepting the risks of contamination and possible death as representatives of humanity. Albert Bigelow was captain, William Huntington, first mate; George Willoughby and Orion Sherwood and, later, James Peck made up the crew. The first three were Quakers, Sherwood was a teacher on leave from Oakwood School, and Peck had been imprisoned for three years as a conscientious objector during World War II. Many members of New York Yearly Meeting supported the crew's decision to act by the light of their conviction.

Testing had already begun when in late April 1958, with the *Golden Rule* scheduled to sail from Honolulu, the Atomic Energy Commission —in a ruling clearly directed at the project—issued a "regulation" making it a crime for U.S. citizens to enter the Eniwetok-Bikini testing area. The day before the sailing a federal court in Hawaii issued a restraining order and scheduled a hearing for an injunction. To sail in the face of a court injunction meant contempt of court—civil disobedience of a high order. After hours of thinking and praying, the crew decided they would risk it. The injunction was granted, and the *Golden Rule* sailed, only to be stopped, boarded by the Coast Guard, and towed back to port where the crew was promptly arrested and jailed. They were released on appeal, but appeal was denied, and they set out again. This time only Bigelow was arrested. Huntington took the helm and carried the *Golden Rule* well past the three-mile limit into international waters before it was once more overtaken by the Coast Guard and forced to return. By the time the crew was freed from jail two months later, testing in the Eniwetok area was completed.

But conviction of belief can be contagious. Another yacht, the *Phoenix,* arrived and tied up beside the *Golden Rule.* Its crew consisted of Earle Reynolds, a scientist who had studied the radiation effects of the atom bombings on the children of Hiroshima and Nagasaki, his wife, Barbara, their children, and a young Japanese yachtsman. They were to sail back to Hiroshima. As the two crews became friends, the Reynolds family found themselves of one mind with the crew of the *Golden Rule* and decided to take on their cause. Bigelow, Huntington, and the others were still in jail when they learned that the *Phoenix* had broken through and sailed successfully into the Eniwetok atoll.[3]

The Fort Detrick, Pentagon, and Times Square Vigils

Many New York Yearly Meeting Friends participated in the vigil at Fort Detrick between July 1959 and March 1961. The Department of Defense was actively, if quietly, engaged in chemical and germ warfare experiments at Fort Detrick in Frederick, Maryland, and the protest, organized by Lawrence Scott, was designed to make this fact more widely known to the American people. From 1959 to 1961 Friends came from all over to stand in silent vigil—twenty-four hours a day, seven days a week—at the entrance to the fort near a single large sign that read: "Vigil at Fort Detrick—An Appeal Against Germ Warfare." Most people, like Prudence Wayland-Smith of Mohawk Valley Meeting, went down once or several times for a few days, staying in the house Scott had rented or with sympathetic families in the area; others, such as Lawrence and Virginia Apsey of Scarsdale Meeting, remained for weeks at a time. There was some local hostility, but the vigil received wide national publicity and played a part in the eventual discontinuation of the germ warfare program.

In the Quaker Peace Witness of November 1960 more than one thousand Friends came together from all over the country to stand vigil at the Pentagon. They walked in silence across the bridge from Washington and ringed the Pentagon, holding signs that spoke their abhorrence of war and desire for peace. As Jeremy Mott, a teenager and one of a large contingent from Ridgewood Meeting, said later, "It was a vigil to witness to the terrible waste and folly and evil of military spending and preparations for war." On the second day small groups of Friends visited and spoke with persons in all branches of the government.

New York City Friends began their Easter peace vigil in 1961. From the evening of Good Friday until Easter Sunday morning, Friends stood vigil around the traffic island in Times Square, handing out leaflets explaining their mission to passersby. At sunrise on Easter morning a meeting for worship was held in front of the recruiting station. This vigil continued through much of the Vietnam period.

Loyalty Oaths

Friends had anguished over and resolved individually the question of loyalty oaths for more than two decades, but in 1963 the entire yearly meeting was confronted with one Friend's battle against a New York State requirement that all teachers under its employ sign a certificate—in effect, a "loyalty oath"—or be dismissed from their jobs. A 1940 state civil service law "made ineligible of appointment or continu-

ance in public employ in the State of New York any person who will-
fully and deliberately advocates the overthrow of the government by
force and violence or who organizes or becomes a member of any society or group which teaches or advocates the overthrow of government
by such means." The law, aimed at Communists, was made applicable
to public schools, including state colleges and universities, by a later
provision known as the Feinberg Law.

Newton Garver, lecturer in philosophy at the (previously private)
State University of New York at Buffalo, objected. Garver acknowledged
that he understood that the "Regents Rules on Subversive Activities"
were part of the terms of his employment. Still, he crossed out the final
sentence, "I further certify that I am not now a member of the Communist Party and that if I have ever been a member of the Communist
Party I have communicated that fact to the President of the State University of New York." He informed the university administration that to
sign would run counter to his religious tradition and its custom of
speaking plainly and directly, of avoiding judicial oaths and hollow for-
malities. "Quite a number of [my colleagues] feel that the Feinberg
provisions are a formality to placate the super-patriots, rather than
something to be taken seriously," he wrote. "A practice which promotes
such cynicism, and which urges people (as it has me) away from whole-
some principles, is surely evil."[4]

With the university administration still unsympathetic to his position, Garver decided to lay the matter before Friends to determine
whether his interpretation of the Quaker commitment to plain speech
was sound. The Committee on Ministry and Counsel of Buffalo Meeting pondered his action, determined that it was consistent with Quaker
testimony, but felt that the spiritual guidance of the wider body of
Friends was desirable. They asked the 1964 Yearly Meeting to consider
the issue, and the approved minute reads, in part, as follows:

> It is affirmed, first, that Newton Garver is a member in good standing
> of our Religious Society and is known as a Friend of integrity and
> sensitivity of conscience. It is affirmed, second, that Friends have,
> from their beginnings, maintained a testimony for freedom of con-
> science and against the imposition of test oaths and other 'vain
> protestations.' The interpretation of this tradition is a matter of indi-
> vidual decision guided by the Inner Light. We are confident that New-
> ton Garver's refusal to subscribe to the required certificate is the
> result of careful searching and that it is fully in harmony with Friends'
> testimonies and practices.[5]

With such affirmation, Garver informed SUNY officials that he was more confirmed than ever in his conviction that the principles and traditions of Friends were not consistent with his signing any disclaimer certificate or loyalty affidavit. He understood that this meant they would probably seek his dismissal, but "since my choice is, as I see it, between God and Mammon, I am hardly in a very good position to compromise further."[6] He noted that he and four others on the Buffalo faculty and staff had joined in a class action suit in federal court to have the Feinberg Law declared unconstitutional. In the end neither Garver nor any other faculty member at SUNY Buffalo was dismissed. The suit to declare the Feinberg Law unconstitutional moved through the judicial system until, on January 23, 1967, New York State's antisubversive laws, the Feinberg Law among them, were declared unconstitutional by the Supreme Court.[7]

Quakers at the United Nations

The story of Quaker House and the Quaker U.N. Office (QUNO) began in 1947 when a property was made available to AFSC so that United Nations diplomats might join Friends in discussing matters of international concern. Later a small group of donors enabled the purchase of a house in the historic Turtle Bay area, a few blocks from U.N. Plaza. The house is a quiet island in the turbulent currents of Manhattan and the United Nations.

Neither Quaker House nor QUNO, at 77 United Nations Plaza, is formally connected with New York Yearly Meeting, but over the years staff members there have regularly attended meetings for worship and spoken before New York City and other meetings. Many members of the yearly meeting have served on the QUNO governing committee and participated in the programs. Until this point the directors have always been a married couple, with the husband serving as director of QUNO and the wife, of Quaker House. The first three directors were members of New York Yearly Meeting. Elmore and Elisabeth Jackson served from 1948 to 1961 and provided an inspired direction for the program. George and Eleanor Loft followed, coming from a three-year stint as Quaker representatives in British Central Africa. They were succeeded in 1963 by William and Leonie Huntington, who had just completed two years service with AFSC in North Africa. The QUNO / New York program staff is composed of Friends from the United States and abroad with experience in U.N. issues of concern to Friends.

Although QUNO and Quaker House may play a part in major

conflicts, their influence is more often felt in the quieter building of relationships. For example, during the Lofts' tenure, a key Western European ambassador who had never before talked with African representatives met with black nationalist leaders and a white former official from British Central Africa at Quaker House. Two separate nationalist factions from Angola were also able to meet and talk privately there. During the Huntingtons' directorship (1963–69), the ambassador from Malta requested that they bring together a number of U.N. representatives at Quaker House so that he could present before them his concerns on the need for a "Law of the Sea." On another occasion African ambassadors met with American civil rights workers, enabling both sides to gain a better understanding of each other's racial problems.

A further function of Quaker House is to provide a place for delegates from various countries to meet socially on "safe ground." Both Eleanor Loft and Lee Huntington regretted never having managed to get the Arabs and the Israelis into the same room, although Lee did accomplish it with the Indians and Pakistanis and with other groups that were antagonistic. There is a sense of privacy at Quaker House; people can discuss important matters informally over breakfast, lunch, tea, or dinner. There has long been a Wednesday luncheon worship for Friends from the U.N. community and the city.

New York Yearly Meeting Friends have served at QUNO, facilitating such matters as assistance received from various Friends' funding agencies. Another informal but vital connection has been Friends' participation in the Lake Mohonk conferences that QUNO has sponsored for diplomats on such subjects as Africa, disarmament, the restructuring of the Economic and Social Council, and the Earth Summit. Powell House, too, has regularly provided space for QUNO / Quaker House staff and committee retreats.

Right Sharing of the World's Resources

A more equable sharing of the world's resources has long been a concern of New York Yearly Meeting Friends. Many have lived in countries where people's income can scarcely provide for their basic necessities, an ever-present reminder of what needs to be done in this regard.

Even before the 1967 World Conference of Friends at Guilford College, a specific concern was emerging. In 1965 New Paltz Meeting, at the instigation of Keith Smiley and others at Lake Mohonk, approved a minute on care for the "Good Earth," which was carried to the Guilford Conference. A program called "Right Sharing of World

Resources" emerged from these sessions. The Friends World Committee for Consultation adopted the project and suggested a goal of giving "One Percent More" of income after taxes toward international development. The program, endorsed by New York Yearly Meeting in its 1968 sessions, was established as a yearly meeting committee in 1972. In 1973 Friends expressed continued uneasiness and regret that they had not "found clearness as to what right sharing means in terms of money or lifestyle. . . . We sense a growing need to reorder our lives so as to consume less, and in so doing to help provide for the liberation of those oppressed by poverty, disease, and ignorance, in our country as well as the rest of the world."

The committee, which receives its main source of revenue from the Sharing Fund, has aided various institutions over the years with special emphasis on Friends College in Kenya in its work of assistance to developing nations. Alfred H. Cope of Syracuse Meeting established scholarships for Friends to study right sharing at Pendle Hill and Friends World College.[8] Projects included work camps, such as one in Honduras in 1991, which combined labor for construction work with firsthand experience of the conditions of life in Central America. Not many Friends, however, have set aside that original goal of "One Percent More," and each year the committee must turn down many applications for funds from indigenous cooperatives in the Third World.

New York Yearly Meeting and the
American Friends Service Committee

During the late 1950s New York Yearly Meeting Friends active in AFSC projects in the New York City area began to wish for a more local administrative committee to work with rather than the Middle Atlantic Regional Office in Philadelphia (later, Baltimore). In time a group of Friends concluded arrangements with the national AFSC office for a regional office to be established in the New York metropolitan area, its territory roughly incorporating counties within a one-hundred mile radius of Columbus Circle. Although Robert Gilmore, who had worked tirelessly to build local New York programming, left the AFSC at this time, other Friends—in particular, George and Margery Rubin, Doris Shamleffer, Edward Doty, Daniel Seeger, and Jack Patterson—carried on his work.

One of the earliest and most successful programs of the new regional office was the Southern Student Project, which brought academically gifted African-American high school students from the South to live and study in the larger New York area. Conciliation and peace-building work among youth gangs in East Harlem was another important endeavor.

New York Yearly Meeting members Nicholas Paster, Robert Vogel, and Faye Honey Knopp served as early, but short-term, executive secretaries of the new office. Eventually, Daniel Seeger took on the post, which he held for more than twenty years. Many other yearly meeting Friends joined the staff or served on committees. Work of the regional office in peace and social justice was characterized by an attempt at responsible radicalism rooted in the faith and practice of the Religious Society of Friends. Both the civil rights and anti-Vietnam War movements attracted elements of angry, near-violent militants not above demagogic appeal. While trying not to stand aloof, the New York AFSC sought to uphold a standard of love and compassion, intellectual clarity, and spiritual authenticity in the face of much that went awry in the social and political establishment during those difficult times.

Relations between New York Yearly Meeting and the New York AFSC remained strong and vital. The regional office sought relevant programming that did not submerge Quaker values in the intellectual and political fashions of the moment. The great strength of the office was the wide range of local Friends who were actively involved in the spiritual, programmatic, and deliberative life of the office. A substantial staff delegation attended yearly meeting sessions, became acquainted with New York Yearly Meeting Friends, and deepened their grasp of Friends' values and of the movement of the spirit among them. Dan Seeger was committed to the idea that the AFSC only made sense if rooted in the experience and practice of Friends; as a New York Yearly Meeting Friend, he cared about, and focused on, the life of the Religious Society in its own right.

In 1991 Seeger resigned his post to become executive director of Pendle Hill. He was succeeded by Elizabeth Enloe, who had previously served as regional executive secretary in Atlanta, had grown up a member of Scarsdale Meeting, and has brought her own wide experience and spiritual foresight to the New York regional office.

Friends World College: A Dream of a New Education

Friends World College, sponsored by New York Yearly Meeting, was unique in its program of world education through experiential learning. It began with the dream of a peace college on Long Island, con-

ceived in the early 1960s by a group of Friends in Westbury Meeting led
by George Nicklin. Approved by the yearly meeting after much deliber-
ation and with the proviso of requiring no yearly meeting financial
support, it was put under the care of a yearly meeting committee,
which obtained the necessary charter from the State of New York.

The radically innovative four-year program was introduced in the
fall of 1965 by the first president, Morris Mitchell, a Friend and retired
faculty member of Columbia University Teachers College. It was his
concept to divide the world into seven major cultural regions with a
study center in each. A class of students would enter each center for a
semester of study, at the close of which they would move on to the next
center, traveling eastward around the world. The eighth and final semester, at the home center, would complete the program for a bachelor's degree.

In 1965 the first class arrived at war surplus military barracks in
Westbury to begin a semester of intense study of North American culture, involving substantial travel. A center was opened in Mexico for
the second semester and one in Denmark for the third. In a short time
there were centers in Austria, Israel, Kenya, India, and Japan. Although
many students had exceptionally rich learning experiences, it became
clear early that one semester was too short to learn a new language, a
new culture, and new academic subject matter. Graduates who attended in those years call themselves "the survivors." There were few
models to follow in this new approach to higher education, and inevita-
bly mistakes were made. Morris Mitchell retired in 1968, after which
there was a two-year interval with Sidney Harman as president, followed
by two more years under a three-person "troika," including an educator, a head of finance, and a student executive. Decisions were
reached, with extensive faculty and student participation, by the sense
of the meeting, and in the regional centers by community meeting.
The curriculum was modified to allow students to spend more time in
individual field-study projects and to spend an entire year in a single
cultural region. The "two culture requirement" for graduation, much
debated over the years, called for a student to spend two study periods
of at least one full year each in two foreign cultural areas. In 1972 the
college moved to the 93-acre Livingston Campus in Lloyd Harbor, a
beautiful old abandoned estate. During the same year George Watson,
a political scientist and a Quaker, took over as "moderator" of the presi-
dential troika. An important figure during this time was Mary-Cushing
Niles of Baltimore Yearly Meeting, clerk of the Board of Trustees, who

set up the center in Bangalore, India, and directed it for a time. She was convinced that Friends World College was the will of God and was determined that it prevail.

During the 1970s the program was subject to continual reshaping in the light of experience gained. As it finally evolved, the student began with a year in his or her home region learning the techniques of independent field study and planning and carrying out a field-study project. The learning plan for the project included the design of the work to be done and the intellectual expectations, both academic and practical. During each year, students kept journals in which they reported on the environment in which they were living, the work accomplished, the learning achieved, variations from the original plan, and personal growth. The final weeks of each academic year were spent back home at the center completing the journal and evaluation and preparing for the next year in another world region with a new language to learn. The fourth and final year, which could be spent either in another region or at one's home center, included a senior thesis or project requiring intensive work in the student's field of concentration. When the faculty approved a student for graduation, the thesis was read and the student examined by an external examiner, a specialist in the student's field, who then recommended whether the bachelor's degree should be conferred. Graduates have had almost no difficulty entering graduate and professional schools; the quality of their journals, theses, and recommendations easily overcame the lack of conventional grade point averages. A disappointment for the college was that it seemed impossible to create a true world college with proportional numbers of students from other regions. Substantial financial aid was provided for U.S. students by both national and state governments, but this aid was not available to other nationalities. Students in most parts of the world, however, can attend local universities tuition-free and do not have the resources for private institutions like Friends World College. The college's own limited aid funds were used for these students, but only a few could be covered at any given time.

During the 1970s American society turned away from innovation and internationalism, and enrollment dropped. The college had never managed to obtain regional accreditation, first because of its unorthodox program and later because of financial weakness. In 1980 George Watson retired, and Lawrence Weiss, a brilliant young China specialist from Columbia University's International Studies program, came in as president. Weiss gained permission to open a program in China and improved the college's finances by selling part of the campus and using the funds to pay off bonds, build new dormitories, and substantially enlarge the budget. Weiss sought additional income-producing programs; one such program was found by New York State to violate its funding regulations. Friends World College was ordered to repay more than six million dollars received in student financial aid; the result was expensive litigation and a final settlement of two million dollars.

Virginia Lester, a Friend, took the helm in 1990. Shortly thereafter, the State Education Department issued an ultimatum: the college must either merge with another institution or close its doors. Lester and the board favored a merger with Long Island University (LIU), which agreed to take on the college as an autonomous program, with its faculty, student body, and curriculum. Although this proposal met with strong opposition from a number of yearly meeting members, the transfer took place during the 1991–92 academic year. Friends World College became known as the Friends World Program at LIU in expectation of financial stability and full accreditation. The board of the college (mostly Friends) became the Council of Overseers of the program, and two of the overseers were named to the board of LIU. The transfer is still disputed at this writing, and doubts surround the future of the program and of the college's assets.

It must be conceded that Friends World College has not met all the expectations with which it was conceived, but in no sense did it fail. Students have learned to make essential educational decisions at an early age, to manage their own lives, and to participate in the governance of an institution. They have been influenced by a faculty and administration believing in human equality and in achieving justice through nonviolent social change. They have experienced the enrichment received from cultural diversity. There have been many problems, as in any institution drawing from the people and customs of many countries. Opportunities for grievances and misunderstandings have been multiplied by cultural differences of all kinds. But students have continued to thrive on the challenges and to learn prodigiously. They have truly become world citizens.

Nonviolence in New York and Mississippi:
The Peace Testimony Restated and Relived

The Peace Testimony of Friends has always met with some resistance within New York Yearly Meeting. Not all Friends afford it unqualified acceptance, and it has sometimes proved a stumbling block to attenders who are unsure of their commitment to it and, therefore, whether they should apply for membership. Most meetings have welcomed attenders who express a sincere desire for peace and a willingness to work toward it.

The Wilton Minute

In 1959 Virginia Repenning of Wilton (Connecticut) Meeting resolved that her meeting and the yearly meeting should look squarely at the issue. At her urging the members of Wilton Meeting minuted "an urgent need for a worldwide reaffirmation of faith in the principles of love and reconciliation" and called upon "Friends throughout the world to re-examine our testimony against war." The minute expressed the hope that "during the year 1960, which commemorates the 300th anniversary of the Quaker Statement Against War, there might again be a great upsurge of conviction . . . in support of the Peace Testimony."[9] Scarsdale Meeting added its own recommendation that monthly meetings study "specific methods by which love and reconciliation can be applied to overcoming force and tyranny" and the contemporary viability of those "nonviolent methods applied by Friends and others throughout the years."

The Wilton minute and Scarsdale recommendation came before the 1959 yearly meeting, which approved sending them to the Friends World Committee for Consultation to forward to other yearly meetings. Although there was widespread interest, the hoped for "great upsurge of conviction" did not occur. The major impact remained within New York Yearly Meeting. Monthly meetings were asked to reexamine the Peace Testimony and report back to a special yearly meeting committee formed for that purpose. This committee then brought to the 1960 yearly meeting a modern restatement of the historic Peace Testimony, which the yearly meeting adopted as follows:

> The hydrogen bomb has thrown its sinister shadow on the earth. That shadow stands for fear, retaliation, for the infliction of suffering, for hatred, for death. Again, as in the declaration of Friends to Charles II in 1660, "We utterly deny all outward wars and strife, and fighting with outward weapons for any end or under any pretence whatsoever and this is our testimony to the whole world. . . ." We believe that love and compassion consciously applied with steadfast refusal to cooperate with evil, and with joyous acceptance of the suffering involved, will reconcile the differences between the men and nations of our own day. We proclaim our faith that by this means the shadow of fear, hatred, and tyranny can be lifted from the earth.

The Peace Institute

In 1960 the yearly meeting also approved that the Peace and Service Committee undertake development of a peace program to strengthen and expand the work of our existing agencies and to develop new ideas, methods and means of outreach in our search for peace. The subcommittee named for that purpose settled on the need for a Friends Institute "to formulate and recommend an action program for peace." The 1961 yearly meeting approved, and a steering committee was named that brought together at Lake Mohonk in March 1962 some seventy representatives appointed by local meetings for the first Peace Institute.

It was hoped that with the advice of experts in international affairs, the institute could formulate a peace action program for New York Yearly Meeting and other Friends. The group at that first meeting proposed a number of desired actions but did not set priorities. As a result, it fell to the Steering Committee to select the programs for action. The course of the New York Yearly Meeting Peace Action Program (and, subsequently, the Peace and Social Action Program [PSAP]) was, thus, largely determined by the Steering Committee rather than, as had originally been intended, by the institute. In action taken at the 1966 yearly meeting the old Peace and Service Committee was abolished, and Agnes Morley, its clerk, took on the post of executive secretary of the Steering Committee. The Peace Institute was defined as a body with representatives appointed by the monthly and preparative meetings, with only the Steering Committee appointed by the yearly meeting. Subcommittees were generally named by it, rather than by the institute or the yearly meeting.

In the years after 1962 the annual institutes served as a gathering point for peace activists of the yearly meeting and a source of ideas for the Steering Committee. The monthly meetings, however, tended to appoint as representatives members who wished to become better acquainted with Friends' Peace Testimony, rather than those most knowledgeable and capable of developing and executing an effective plan. Programs generally included speakers prominent in the field of peace and social concerns, such as Daniel Berrigan, Samuel Levering, and Canby Jones. Participants reported spiritual strengthening from worship sharing and role-playing exercises included in the programs.

Interest continued high for a number of years, attendance rising to 308 from forty-three meetings in 1971. After six years at Lake Mohonk, the institute spent four years at neighboring Minnewaska and another four at Painted Post in west-central New York State. In 1976 the institute moved most of its annual gatherings to the yearly meeting's conference center, Powell House. The last year that attendance exceeded 150 was 1975. After the termination of PSAP and its Steering Committee in 1980, sponsorship fell to the Witness Coordinating Committee. Beginning in 1984 the institute changed from a conference of named representatives to an informational and inspirational gathering for Friends desiring to uphold their Peace Testimony. The 1992 Peace Institute Planning Committee reported "a fine program, well received, with an attendance of only sixty-five participants." Nevertheless, the institute has proved an unusual program to have survived for more than thirty years.

Peace and Social Action Program (PSAP)

What is difficult to realize in 1995 is that before 1960 the yearly meeting had seldom dealt with peace as a practical goal toward which it might work as a corporate body. Peace concerns had generally been left to other existing organizations such as the AFSC. But Friends were beginning to realize that there was more to be done—not only internationally, where the AFSC was superb, but in the cities and towns and villages within New York Yearly Meeting and that this might best be done by Friends already living there. The Peace Action Program was formed in 1961 to further peace work within the monthly meetings themselves and to provide Friends with means to study and work toward international peace and methods to help bring about solutions to a variety of local problems. Besides reaffirming the promotion of goodwill and understanding between citizens of East and West, it recommended concrete activities such as the vigil—public witness for peace in the spirit of Friends—on a local and a national level as well.

Arts for World Unity was one of the successes of the Peace Action program. It was initiated by two Friends—noted artist Fritz Eichenberg, whose wood engravings adorned the American editions of many Russian classics, and Vally Weigl of Morningside Meeting, widow of the well-known composer Karl Weigl and a composer and musician herself. During some fifteen years Arts for World Unity helped sponsor and organize concerts, dance programs, and poetry readings on the theme of peace. The group backed a project for teaching art in one of New York City's Houses of Detention and was the force behind a three-days-a-week arts program at the Brooklyn Museum of Art. A moving exhibit of Vietnamese art depicting the agony of the war and the efforts of the people to overcome it was brought to one of the Peace Institutes by Arts for World Unity.

By 1966 the Peace Action Program had become the Peace and Social Action Program, or PSAP. It was the umbrella for many of the special projects that came out of that period: Training in Nonviolence workshops, the Mississippi Church-Building Project, the Quaker Project on Community Conflict, Police Relations and Training workshops, the Homeless People Project, the Peace Squad, the Children's Creative Response to Conflict program, the Imagining a World Without Weapons Project, the Friendly Outreach Peacemaking Project, and the Alternatives to Violence Project.

Albert Bigelow, skipper of the *Golden Rule,* and Lawrence Apsey devised the first Training in Nonviolence workshops under PSAP. Larry Apsey was a lawyer who worked as counsel for a large corporation by day and for Quaker causes at night. A convinced Friend committed to Gandhian principles, he had already led workshops in nonviolence in Scarsdale Meeting. Now, with the willing support of his wife, Virginia, he began to train volunteers in their New York City apartment and to mold a traveling team prepared to go out across New York Yearly Meeting to hold workshops in nonviolence.

The heart of the workshop was role playing, the enactment of a typical conflict—family, workplace, racial, political—to which the players responded in varying ways. Each dramatic situation was followed by a critique of the players' reactions and a discussion of other nonviolent responses that might have been more effective. David Hartsough enlivened sessions with stories of lunch counter sit-ins in the South as did Bigelow with an account of his days as a Freedom Rider attempting to desegregate the whites-only waiting rooms of southern bus stations. James Farmer of the Congress of Racial Equality (CORE) had described how "Bert . . . stepped right between the [white] hoodlums and [black] John Lewis. . . . They clubbed Bigelow and finally knocked him down, and that took some knocking because he was a pretty strapping fellow, and he didn't hit back at all."[10] Some Friends who were not as big and strapping as he was were less sure of their capacity to absorb shock. Others were not convinced of the value of learning from "set-up" situations, but participants left the workshops with some idea of what a violent confrontation was like and more confidence in their ability to deal with it.[11]

The Mississippi Church-Building Project

During the summer of 1964 thousands of young people poured into Mississippi to help with voter registration and to set up "Freedom Schools" for African-American students. Most white Mississippians were

19. Rebuilding Cedar Grove Baptist Church,
Canton, Mississippi, October 1964.
Courtesy Peace Collection, Swarthmore College.

deeply hostile to what they saw as an invasion from the North. In an attempt to intimidate African-Americans and keep them from joining the movement, forty-four of their churches were burned to the ground. Friends at yearly meeting sessions that summer felt called upon to respond. They collected more than one thousand dollars and sent Thomas Purdy, headmaster of Oakwood School, and Ross Flanagan, a convinced Friend who had previously worked as a peace educator with the AFSC in California, to Mississippi to explore what role the yearly meeting might play in the project to rebuild the churches.

Once there Purdy and Flanagan joined in the creation of the interracial, interfaith Committee of Concern in Mississippi to raise money for the project. Most of the money came from white Baptist Mississippians who felt an obligation to help but were not ready to invite their black neighbor Baptists to share their own churches. Ross remembered "some very scary moments driving along the back roads of Mississippi near sundown looking for churches that had been burned down," thinking of three young men—James Chaney, Andrew Goodman, and Michael Schwerner—who only a few weeks before had been murdered for doing exactly what they themselves were doing, driving on back roads investigating burned churches.

Pine churches were rebuilt in brick. Money raised by the Mississippi Committee of Concern paid for the materials, with labor supplied by volunteers, many of them college students, including more than fifty white Mississippians. Lawrence Scott of Philadelphia and Robert Swann, a professional builder and a leader of the New England Committee on Non-Violent Action, were in charge. White volunteers worked side by side with black members of the congregation. During the 1964 Christmas season Richard Hathaway of New Paltz Meeting worked with them and made plans to return to Jackson after Scott and Swann left. Part of the work Hathaway and his wife, Shirley, would do the next year was regular Saturday teaching in a black community center near Canton built with financial assistance from New York Friends. Richard also took part in the Selma to Birmingham march and was invited by Andrew Young to be the Quaker representative on days when participation was restricted.

In October 1964 Lawrence Apsey went down to Jackson to volunteer his services to the Lawyers' Constitutional Defense Committee for the handling of civil rights cases. Only four members of the Mississippi bar—three black, one white—consented to handle cases involving the rights of African-Americans. After so turbulent a summer an enormous backload of cases had piled up. Other lawyers, too, had opted to spend their vacation in Mississippi that year, representing civil rights workers, black and white, who had been arrested under a statute that made it a felony to advocate "unlawful acts" to effect political or social change. Passing out leaflets urging African-Americans to register to vote was a felony.

Apsey came back with harrowing tales of obstructions placed by local law enforcement officers on civil rights workers, particularly black ones. But there were heartwarming stories, too, such as the rally he attended in a black church to support "the boys in jail." There was preaching and hymn singing, and the civil rights workers talked about why they had come to Mississippi and the difficulties they had experienced. One northern African-American said that if someone struck him, he intended to strike back. Larry spoke of nonviolence and its power to change people's thinking, and he was glad when the preachers who followed him pledged themselves to nonviolence, and the congregation offered resounding support.

Women went to Mississippi, too. Virginia Apsey and Faye Honey Knopp—New York Yearly Meeting women of great strength of character and commitment—traveled about the state in their own quiet campaign to build support for civil rights among Mississippi women. With the help of Ann Hewitt, a Mississippi Friend living in New York, they set up teas and invited white women advocates of civil rights to meet with sympathetic local women in an atmosphere where discussion could take place without anyone feeling threatened. Apsey and Knopp also visited black women working to better the conditions of their people, who sometimes took their new white associates with them to prayer meetings—often the first time these women had ever attended a black church.

The Hathaways, back in Jackson in the fall of 1965, were present for two landmark desegregation events. Richard was teaching at Millsaps College, which became that fall the first white college in Mississippi to integrate without force or incident. Besides gathering a Friends worship group in their home, they attended Galloway Memorial Methodist Church where they worked from within for integration. An earlier attempt, to no one's surprise, had failed. Now the Hathaways served as a bridge between liberal members of the church and a group of students and faculty, mostly black, from Tougaloo College. One Sunday morning this group again approached the church but were blocked by the ushers standing with their backs against the doors. Shirley Hathaway, invited to enter, chose not to, and Richard, at first excluded but then asked in, also remained outside. The group at the foot of the church steps invited the Hathaways to join them, but Richard replied, "If we come down there, we can't be a bridge between you and the church any more; if you come up here, we can all stand together." They came, included the hostile ushers in their new circle, and remained in silent communion through the hour of worship. Within one month the doors were open.

Quaker Project on Community Conflict

The Quaker Project on Community Conflict came out of the 1965 Peace Institute. Lawrence Apsey and Ross Flanagan were its guiding lights and devoted fund-raisers, and by midsummer it also had office space and a sizable budget. Flanagan presented the project to the yearly meeting as a challenge to Friends to leave the comfort of their meeting houses for the discomfort of the streets and do what they could to combat violence in their communities. Virginia Apsey spoke in strong support and offered herself as a full-time volunteer. The yearly meeting approved enthusiastically. Support was indeed far-reaching across the yearly meeting. By fall seventy-eight Friends had volunteered. At its first planning session a variety of potential problems were addressed from domestic violence to the function of the police, extremism, and the role of Friends in crisis situations.

Buffalo Police Relations Program

Buffalo Friends Meeting saw the deteriorating relations between their police and their African-American community as perhaps their greatest civic problem. They attempted to address it in 1964 after Victor Paschkis, a German refugee professor of physics at Columbia and a founder of Morningside Meeting, stood up at yearly meeting to express his great concern about the increasing racial divisions in the United States. Paschkis offered to give one month of his time to any meeting that wished to work intensively with him on the problem of racial interrelations.

Buffalo Meeting accepted the challenge. Early in October Paschkis came to live at the meeting house, which was in a changing neighborhood, and by the end of the month the Citizens Council on Human Relations (CCHR) was born. CCHR—interracial, largely professional, and with younger members than preexisting organizations—had a very real impact on housing, employment, and education. Work on police-community relations had begun.

CCHR plowed the ground for the next stage of police-community relations work, which began when Buffalo Meeting asked if the Quaker Project on Community Conflict (QPCC) might come to help mitigate hostility between black citizens and the police. QPCC agreed to try, and Ross Flanagan, along with six members of Buffalo Meeting, met with representatives of the Police Department, who themselves were increasingly unhappy with the situation. Together they worked out a project proposal that included a series of interviews with community leaders, black residents, and patrol officers, a citizen's conference to air grievances, and the establishment of an experimental police-community relations program implemented by a special staff in the Police Department. Flanagan also met with leaders of the African-American community and with the Ira Aldrich Players, a black dramatics group who proved central to the project.

As chair of public meetings held in June and July of 1966, Newton Garver, a member of CCHR, joined local pastors in setting a tone of sincere and open inquiry into the causes of the recognized tension. Flanagan moderated the panel and tried to turn heated comments from the audience into constructive channels. Impromptu skits illustrating common problems were performed, first with the police and African-Americans playing themselves, then with the roles reversed. Later QPCC proposed that the police commissioner incorporate such workshops into the general police training program on an experimental basis in the belief that role playing of critical incidents was a more effective educational tool than lecturing. A six-month project of this nature, incorporating the Ira Aldrich Players and six white police "actors" and funded by the Ford Foundation, was begun in 1968.

The program was, at best, partially successful. Role-playing techniques helped patrol officers understand how their actions and reactions were perceived by the "other side." Police learned that their behavior could raise or lower the level of hostility and that brutalization of any part of the community only enhanced the difficulties. To the disappointment of many, the Police Department chose not to incorporate role-playing techniques for nonviolence into their regular training program. And Ross Flanagan began classes at the New York City College of Police Science. "NYYM did me a great favor by helping me de-romanticize my commitment to nonviolence," he said. "The criminal justice system was one place we could begin."

The Homeless People Project

One Sunday morning in the fall of 1966 Friends approaching the 15th Street Meeting House had to pass a shabbily dressed young man lying face-downward on the sidewalk. Nearer the entrance another young man passed out leaflets suggesting that perhaps there was something wrong when Quakers could step around someone lying in their path, unaware that he was one of their own attenders acting the part of a local derelict. Many Friends agreed. At the next meeting for business money was allocated and members and attenders volunteered to help organize a pilot rescue project among the homeless.

There were an estimated nine thousand persons living on the streets of New York at that time, many of them on the Bowery (and, thus, not far from the meeting house), most of them alcoholics, and all of them subject to freezing to death that winter. Margery Haring of Brooklyn Meeting was asked to coordinate rescue patrols. Every night teams of two or three persons, equipped with blankets, coffee, a flash-light, and a first aid kit, patrolled the area on foot with extensive instructions on what to do or not to do for homeless persons encountered. One result of that winter's work was a booklet called *Out of Community*, which discussed ways in which the needs of homeless people might be met.

Joni Ross of 15th Street Meeting served as leader of the Rehabilitation Subcommittee, which with its limited resources of time and money attempted to help Bellevue patients who were also alcoholics. In the summer of 1967 she inherited the supervision of the Homeless People Project, which then was transferred from QPCC to 15th Street Meeting and renamed "Toward Community." Ross Flanagan and Ned Towle, a young conscientious objector, organized the patrols and counseled the alcoholics. Friends in the New York area kept the project going in the face of enormous difficulties. Even after the patrols were later dropped, the work continued, with 15th Street Meeting providing a supervised space where a small number of homeless people could spend each night.

Community Peace Squad and Other Work of QPCC

Under Larry Apsey's guidance QPCC grew and evolved in a variety of different programs. The Community Peace Squad was formed; its activities included (1) entering into dialogue with members of the John Birch Society; (2) aiding parade marshals in protecting participants during a mass draft card burning in Central Park; (3) helping with peacekeeping at an Armed Services Day parade; (4) opening exchanges with several black nationalist groups, including the Black People's Party and the Organization of Afro-American Unity; (5) bringing Arabs and Jews together for discussion immediately after the Six Day War; (6) helping prevent violence during peaceful activities of the Direct Action Project; (7) advising Friends in other areas of the yearly meeting on peacekeeping methods to avert riot during racial disturbances; and (8) joining in citywide plans to counter expected riots during the summer of 1968 (which did not occur). In addition, the Community Peace Squad assisted in the Poor People's Campaign for Jobs and Income by preparing a leaflet on nonviolent power for ghetto youth—who had known little but violence in their short lives—to take with them to Washington. They also helped to keep order on Solidarity Day when the nonpoor came to the capital to show their support.

Meanwhile, the QPCC parent body helped to organize and train more than four hundred volunteers to serve as marshals at the Moratorium March of November 1969 in Washington, the nation's largest peace march. Many New York Yearly Meeting Friends who attended that overnight event were unaware that the young people who so effectively kept the march orderly and nonviolent had been trained under Quaker direction.

The Children's Creative Response to Conflict Program

In 1968 Larry Apsey resigned from the Quaker Project on Community Conflict. The Peace and Social Action Program of New York Yearly Meeting, which included QPCC, had grown to the point where a full-time administrator was needed, and Lee Stern accepted that position, which he held for the next thirteen years. Stern was a midwesterner who had gone to prison as a conscientious objector during World War II and afterward joined Cleveland (Ohio) Meeting where he met his wife, Ruth. In 1956 he took a job with the Fellowship of Reconciliation in Nyack, New York, and he and Ruth became active in Rockland Meeting.

Four important projects came out of PSAP while Lee Stern headed it. The Alternatives to Violence Project is described later. Of the others —the Imagining a World Without Weapons Project, the Friendly Outreach Peacemaking Project, and the Children's Creative Response to Conflict Program (CCRC)—the last was the most significant. It emerged from QPCC's training for peacekeeping projects. As Stern said, "the seeds of conflict, the hostility, and the counter-productive ways of dealing with conflict were endemic in our society, and had started when we were children."[12] It was important to work with children before the negative aspects of society became ingrained in their thinking.

The project really got off the ground when Priscilla Prutzman, Leonard Burger, Gretchen Bodenhamer, and Edward Hayes put together a program for the schools. The curriculum was based on the four themes of cooperation, communication, conflict resolution, and affirmation, or positive self-concept, because as Lee said, "until children feel good about themselves, they really can't feel good about others."[13] Funding came from Brooklyn Meeting and several foundations, and workshops were introduced into five public, one parochial, and the two Quaker private schools in New York City. From the start it was a success. Workshops blossomed across the country, then around the world, and its "Friendly Handbook for a Small Planet" has been widely translated. After CCRC became national and then international the yearly meeting felt it could no longer oversee it properly. It was turned over to FOR, and became an affiliate of their program.

Intercultural Education and Race Relations:
Rachel Davis DuBois

"It is the not-me in thee that makes thee precious to me" ran the old Quaker proverb that Rachel Davis DuBois often wore on a pendant around her neck. It expressed the belief that led her toward a lifelong career in intercultural education and race relations. Born Rachel Miriam Davis in 1892, she grew up on the farm her Quaker family had owned since the seventeenth century. Although she was born and died a member of Woodstown Friends Meeting, she was an active member of 15th Street Meeting and New York Yearly Meeting for much of her life. She graduated from Bucknell University, began a teaching career, and married Nathan DuBois (they were later divorced). World War I awakened her concern for pacifism. In 1920 she attended the First International Conference of Friends in London and traveled to Germany to observe the feeding stations set up by English and American Friends for German children. She became involved with the Women's International League for Peace and Freedom; in 1922 she traveled to The Hague for a conference of women on the economic consequences of the Versailles treaty.

About this time DuBois came upon an article by W. E. B. DuBois, "Race and War," which maintained that worldwide racial injustices are the underlying causes of war and that to overcome war one must first overcome racial injustice. His words marked a turning point in her life. "Now I felt I had reached my Concern," she wrote. "Now I knew what I must dedicate the rest of my life to."[14]

DuBois returned to teaching in 1924. She opposed the postwar emphasis on the melting pot theory in schools because she believed in a sharing of ethnic richness; she established an intercultural assembly program, using student dramatizations to highlight the contributions of various ethnic groups. A Ph.D. candidate at Columbia Teacher's College, she also taught a course in intercultural education for teachers at New York University.

Anxious to counteract growing prejudice against ethnic groups in the 1930s, DuBois began experimenting with friends and students on how to bring diverse groups of people together. A spontaneous sharing of early memories of harvest festivals indicated how the communication of childhood memories could highlight the similarities underlying ethnic and religious differences and create a feeling of community. The result was "group conversation." In 1941 DuBois and a few friends formed the Workshop for Cultural Democracy, and she devoted the next two decades to demonstrating group conversation and training community leaders across the United States and Europe. She published three books on these experiences.

In the late 1950s, DuBois became interested in adapting group conversation to Friends' needs at the local level. She developed a "Quaker Dialogue" to help them talk over meeting concerns and their role as Friends at a time of world tension, visiting more than four hundred meetings in the United States, Canada, and Mexico and traveling to eight European countries for that purpose.

DuBois was a strong follower of Martin Luther King, Jr. At the 1963 Civil Rights March on Washington, she rededicated herself to the issue of race relations, specifically to facilitating honest, ongoing communication between people of all ethnic groups so they could work more effectively together. Under the auspices of FGC, she held group conversation training sessions in southern meetings. Later, she and her colleague, Mew-soong Li, were asked by King to join the Southern Christian Leadership Conference staff. For six months they ran "Operation Dialogue" to facilitate mutual understanding, acceptance, and reconciliation between blacks and whites. In the 1970s when an influx of African-American students on previously white campuses brought new tensions, DuBois began leading group conversations between students, faculty, and townspeople of all races in college communities.

In 1976 DuBois moved back to Woodstown, New Jersey, but not to retire. Recognizing how art could reach across differences, she developed the "Living Room Gatherings," combining group conversation with artistic expression. Funded by the New Jersey Committee for the Humanities, these gatherings were successful in bringing people of diverse cultures together.

Rachel Davis DuBois was more than 90 when she finished her autobiography, *All This and Something More: Pioneering Intercultural Education*. She died on March 30, 1993, at the age of 101.[15]

Civil Rights, Human Rights: Bayard Rustin

Few New York Yearly Meeting Friends have done more to shape the wider world than Bayard Rustin. Born in 1912 in West Chester, Pennsylvania, he was brought up by his grandfather, son of a Maryland slave, and his Quaker grandmother, Julia Davis Rustin, a Delaware Indian who instilled in him her pacifist outlook. Quakerism was the backdrop against which he acted out many dramatic roles of his life. Just before his thirtieth birthday, he joined New York Monthly Meeting and remained a member until his death forty-five years later. His Quakerism was a source of his strength, and its tenets of nonviolence and social justice became the themes of his life.

No black child in this country escaped unscarred, but Bayard's natural talents gave him a confidence that allowed him to follow his leadings. He was an honor student in high school and graduated as valedictorian. He trained his tenor voice at the local African Methodist Episcopal church. Much of his tuition for Wilberforce College in Ohio and Cheyney State near home came from singing with folksingers Leadbelly and Josh White.

In the 1930s Rustin transferred to City College in New York where his dismay at the Scottsboro case prompted him to organize black students for the Young Communist League. (He was never a party member, however, and broke with the Communists in 1941 when, after Hitler invaded Russia, they abandoned issues of race and peace to campaign for America's entry into the war.) On his return from a period of study at the London School of Economics, A. J. Muste hired him as race relations secretary for the Fellowship of Reconciliation. He remained with FOR for twelve years.

Rustin was always a rebel. After Pearl Harbor he went to the west coast with the AFSC, working in an internment camp with Japanese-Americans to help them find ways to protect their property. On speaking engagements at colleges, Quaker work-camps, and Civilian Public Service camps across the country, he asked why African-Americans should fight for a segregated America. He himself defied Jim Crow laws that kept blacks, including servicemen, from seats on crowded buses and trains. One of his mentors was A. Philip Randolph, who had built the Brotherhood of Sleeping Car Porters on a national and interracial basis, earning respect among all races for his vigorous but nonviolent tactics. Now Rustin joined Randolph in planning a mass march on Washington aimed at opening war industry to black labor. With only five days to spare, President Roosevelt signed Executive Order 8802 on fair employment, declaring an end to discrimination in defense industry jobs. The march was called off.

As a Quaker, Rustin was granted conscientious objector status and designated for hospital work, but when a similarly scrupulous Methodist was turned down, Bayard's integrity would not allow him to accept alternative service. During the next twenty-eight months spent in federal penitentiaries at Ashland, Kentucky, and Lewisburg, Pennsylvania, he transferred his fight to one against racism in federal prisons. After his release, he took on the direction of Randolph's Committee Against Discrimination in the Armed Forces, which contributed to President Truman's executive order that prohibited segregation in the armed forces.

The war had changed the position of African-Americans in the United States, but had not much improved the attitude of their white neighbors. When the U.S. Supreme Court ruled against segregation on interstate bus travel, FOR joined with the Congress of Racial Equality (CORE)—which A. J. Muste, James Farmer, George Houser, and Rustin had helped form in 1942—to organize what they termed a journey of reconciliation. The plan was to test the Supreme Court ruling by sending eight blacks and eight whites on a bus trip through four states of the upper South. Rustin was among those arrested under various Jim Crow laws, and after losing on appeal he served more than three weeks on a chain gang in North Carolina. His 1949 *New York Post* article, describing his steps to become reconciled with guard captain Jones, was instrumental in ending the Carolina chain gangs.

The bus trip generated a new kind of resistance. Now executive secretary of the War Resisters League, Rustin took a leave of absence to help shape the Civil Rights movement in America. The 1955 bus boycott in Montgomery, Alabama, building on a decade of freedom rides and restaurant sit-ins, rallied wide support among southern blacks and northern liberals. Martin Luther King, Jr., turned for assistance to Rustin, whose extensive background in the theory and tactics of nonviolent action (including a 1948 visit to India) made him invaluable. Rustin helped prepare the charter for uniting churches and activists in the Southern Christian Leadership Conference (SCLC). He also served as chief organizer of the 1963 March on Washington for Jobs and Freedom, bringing together 250,000 workers, labor leaders, and liberals. King's dream was his dream, too.

Through the A. Philip Randolph Institute, which he helped found in 1964, Rustin worked tirelessly for improved relations between the labor movement and the black community. But daily work was regularly disrupted by calls for help after the Mississippi church bombings or the ghetto riots or court cases in connection with the massive voter registration drive in the South. In 1964 Rustin organized a school boycott for integration in New York City, considered at the time the largest civil rights demonstration of its kind. He was often photographed in those years at King's side, tall and slender, in Selma or Birmingham or, finally, in the 1968 sanitation workers strike in Memphis, Tennessee. He managed to collect one hundred thousand dollars for the strikers. When King died there in Memphis, Rustin put aside his grief to organize, with Walter Reuther of the United Auto Workers (UAW), the massive march of mourning.

Some people blamed Rustin for not actively opposing the war in Vietnam, but he contended that that was not his fight, and surely his fight was large enough to excuse him from others. The "black power" effort of the 1970s was not his either, and he felt increasingly lonely, writing in *Commentary* or *Harper's* or the *Amsterdam News* for peace and nonviolence and union with workers of all races and against black rage, separatism, and anti-Semitism in the African-American community. He saw the need for basic social change in the ghettos, for education rather than black political power, and deplored the condoning of violence by black leaders. He went into Harlem during one riot to try to persuade people to stop, only to find himself mocked by other civil rights leaders. He was also shunned by some because he was gay and did not hide it; it is difficult to assess how much this affected his work.

These were, perhaps, the years Rustin took consolation in the wonderful art he had been collecting over a long period. Mother and child images stood out, from medieval Catholic sculpture and Orthodox icons to African and Asian images. Some of these last he had acquired on his journey to India and on later trips to work with Kwame Nkrumah in Ghana and Nnamdi Azikewe in Nigeria. Over time he also assembled a fine collection of beautifully carved walking sticks and another of antique stringed instruments, including a Stradivarius guitar. Art and music—he loved to sing gospel songs and spirituals—remained to him expressions of universal human experience and a great joy in his daily life.

Late in his career and concerned about apartheid, Rustin started Project South Africa, an attempt to link the proponents of nonviolence in that country with those in his own. He traveled about Latin America and to Thailand to observe the condition of the Cambodian refugees. It seemed never to occur to him to retire.

An eloquent speaker, Bayard Rustin addressed many Quaker gatherings over the years. On his death in 1987 Friends spoke of him as "a penetrating political philosopher and analyst" but also as someone who "practiced good humoredness and conciliation on a personal level toward those who opposed him."[16] They noted that he often spoke of his Quaker grandmother's convictions—egalitarianism, tolerance of dissent, simplicity, truthfulness, nonviolence—as central to his life.[17]

Peacemaking During the Vietnam War

Quaker witness against the war in Vietnam was widely and variously experienced within New York Yearly Meeting. Many monthly meetings found their Sunday morning worship revolving around messages of heartfelt concern and dismay with the government's actions in continuing and escalating the Vietnam conflict. During the early phases of the war, before the antiwar effort reached sizable proportions, Quaker meetings were one of the few places where protesters of both sexes and all ages could expect support. For young men of draft age considering conscientious objector status, counseling was available. Often meetings on or near college campuses doubled their size during this period. Not all Quakers were strong in their pacifism, however, and some members never approved of antiwar activity in their meetings.

New York Yearly Meeting Friends Pledge to Bind the Wounds

Friends' group witness against the war dated from the beginning of U.S. bombing in Vietnam. Early in 1965 New York Yearly Meeting Friends stood vigil outside the U.S. Mission to the United Nations, bearing blankets and other relief supplies to be sent to the victims of the bombings. This and subsequent acts of protest were organized by Ross Flanagan as part of the Peace and Social Action program. Flanagan spoke out on a dilemma that bothered many Friends—our apparent passive complicity in war. "When nations start fighting," he asked, "what is the appropriate role for the person of Quaker nonviolent conviction?"

New York Yearly Meeting Friends concluded that the historic role was to bind the wounds on both sides. The difficulty lay in U.S. Treasury Department regulations, which ruled that sending anything to North Vietnam without a special license violated the Trading with the Enemy Act. Violators were subject to fines and imprisonment. Many Friends felt that accepting this proscription implied a complicity irreconcilable with Quaker beliefs. A plan to send medical supplies impartially to the Red Cross societies serving North and South Vietnam and the National Liberation Front through the Canadian Red Cross or other Canadian agencies was brought to the 1965 yearly meeting by the Peace and Service Committee and Subcommittee on Vietnam. Such action, it was made clear, would place the yearly meeting as a corporate body in the position of performing acts of civil disobedience and could

20. Members of Quaker Action and Relief sending parcels to
Vietnam, March 1965.
Photograph by Ross Flanagan. Courtesy Peace Collection,
Swarthmore College.

only be construed as an intentional violation of the Treasury Department's interpretation of the Trading with the Enemy Act.

With this firmly in mind the gathered meeting at Silver Bay felt
moved by the Spirit to take a stand against the inhumanity of war. General approval of the proposed action was voiced. Later, some Friends at
home who had not experienced the force of the meeting made known
their discomfort with the proposed action. Coming so early in the war,
while antiwar sentiment was still minimal, the project was difficult for
some Friends to explain, particularly those in rural communities who
lived closely among neighbors with sons already fighting in Vietnam.
Friends active in the effort visited with Friends who had deep objections, trying to understand their distress. A dialogue with Canadians
was also considered important; Walter Ludwig of Scarsdale Meeting

and Newton Garver of Buffalo Meeting, who delivered the funds to the Canadian Friends Service Committee on behalf of New York Yearly Meeting, went on prime time Canadian television to explain the action. Many Canadians did not appreciate the intimidation of the U.S. government and were pleased with the New York Yearly Meeting plan. The 1965 New York Yearly Meeting minute inspired similar action in Baltimore, Philadelphia, Ohio, Illinois, and Pacific Yearly Meetings.

The Easter Sunday Peace Bridge Pilgrimage

The 1967 Easter Sunday pilgrimage across the Peace Bridge from Buffalo was one implementation of the New York Yearly Meeting minute. Several hundred Friends from across the yearly meeting came together to carry money and boxes of medical supplies labeled for both North and South Vietnam into Canada. On Saturday evening Friends met in the darkened nave of a Unitarian church to review the course of action and possible consequences of civil disobedience. For those with young children the question of what would happen to the children if their parents were arrested was a disquieting one, but the worship fostered a renewed commitment and trust. The pilgrimage had been publicized to increase public awareness of the suffering in Vietnam, and all that night Friends stood vigil in two-hour shifts by the bridge, harassed by antagonistic local citizens.

Easter Sunday dawned clear and cold, but it turned into the first warm day of spring. Friends gathered for what Lee Stern of PSAP remembered as a powerful meeting for worship "with a sense of unity and a purposefulness, but more than anything the leading of God's hand in what we were doing." At the bridge the group was confronted by a representative of the U.S. Bureau of Foreign Assets Control, who warned all who stepped onto the bridge that they might be arrested, charged with trading with the enemy, and given ten years in prison and $10,000 fines. Many were aware they had never before stood so strongly and clearly for what they believed. Friends walked without incident as far as the Canadian Entry of Customs where a customs official informed them that Canada was not authorized at that time to receive any parcels bound for Vietnam. Feeling that they had no recourse but to wait and see where they might be led, the group settled into a silent meeting for worship. They had not been there long when they heard a phone ring in another room followed by excited discussion. The customs official reappeared to inform them that the Canadian government had changed its policy. The considerable pressure in Canada against caving in to the U.S. government had had its effect. For those present, however, success had a more personal flavor, and the return walk was accomplished in the glow of Friends' confirmed testimony.

Conscientious Objection Before Vietnam

The Central Committee for Conscientious Objectors (CCCO) was formed in 1948—the year the draft law came back into effect—to handle cases in which the National Service Board for Religious Objectors was not especially interested, such as nonregistrants who would not cooperate at all with the draft and nonreligious conscientious objectors. John Mott of Ridgewood Meeting, who had been a conscientious objector during World War II, was one of the original members of the CCCO board. Between then and the outbreak of the Korean War there were few actual inductions into the armed services from the draft; the law's main effect was to require men to register. Almost everyone who openly refused to register was prosecuted and sent to prison; probably half of these were Quakers. Newton Garver, a student at Swarthmore but not yet a Quaker, was sentenced to serve one year and one day, primarily at the Danbury, Connecticut, federal penitentiary. Some men served more than one prison term; it was possible to be released from prison only to be redrafted and to have to go through the whole process again. During the Korean conflict large numbers of men were drafted and inducted, and afterward the draft and inductions continued right through to the end of the Vietnam war.

United States versus Seeger

In 1962 Daniel Seeger, an attender at Morningside Meeting who had been brought up a Catholic, was indicted for failing to submit to induction into the armed forces. His story had begun five years earlier when, in preparation for being reclassified 1A after the lapse of his student deferment, he claimed on draft board documents that because of his religious beliefs, he was a conscientious objector exempt from combatant and noncombatant training. In reply to the question "Do you believe in a Supreme Being?" he checked neither "yes" nor "no" but attached a written statement of his beliefs. He claimed not to be an atheist, but an agnostic, noted that he believed in a "devotion to goodness and virtue for their own sakes," and admitted that "the cosmic order does, perhaps, suggest a creative intelligence." On the subject of war he wrote that it was futile and self-defeating and unethical as well.[18]

Man pays a great spiritual price for his willingness to destroy human life, he said.

The question for the draft board was whether Seeger's position could be reconciled with a 1948 addition to the Selective Service Act, Section 6(j), which honored the refusal of a person "conscientiously opposed to participation in war in any form" but defined religious training and belief as "an individual's belief in a relation to a Supreme Being involving duties superior to those arising from any human relation." After the local draft board decided against Seeger, the FBI and Justice Department conducted investigations. The hearing officers of the FBI found him sincere and recommended that he receive conscientious objector status, but the Justice Department insisted that his religious beliefs were not in accordance with Section 6(j) of the Selective Service Act, and, thus, he was not entitled to exemption.[19]

In May 1964 Seeger was sentenced to one year and one day in prison. He appealed, arguing that the Selective Service law gave priority to one type of religion—belief in a Judeo-Christian Supreme Being—and punished others who might be religious but did not have a religion defined in that manner. He claimed that Section 6(j) violated the First Amendment, which states, "Congress shall make no law respecting an establishment of religion" and the due process clause of the Fifth Amendment as well and questioned whether belief in a standard definition of "Supreme Being" should be required for exemption or conscientious objector status. On January 29, 1964, the Second Circuit of the U.S. Court of Appeals unanimously reversed the conviction. The court declared itself convinced of Seeger's sincerity, based as it was on "religious training and belief," noting that he had been brought up in a Catholic home, had gone to parochial school, was an attender of Quaker meeting and well-read in Quaker thought, and agreed with Friends' opposition to war in any form. The court felt that Seeger's refusal to admit belief in a Supreme Being was not a reason to deny him exemption. The judge observed that many religions (e.g., Taoist or Buddhist) do not teach a belief in a Supreme Being, but the conscientious decisions made by their adherents could not be held in lesser regard than those of believers in a traditional God. Thus, the Court ruled Section 6(j) of the Selective Service Act unconstitutional as violating the due-process clause of the Fifth Amendment.[20]

The government's reaction, as usual with a decision that strikes down federal law, was to appeal to the Supreme Court immediately. In *United States v. Seeger* (1965) Justice Tom Clark, speaking for the court, stated that "the test of belief 'in a relation to a Supreme Being' is whether a given belief that is sincere and meaningful occupies a place in the life of its possessor parallel to that filled by the orthodox belief in God of one who clearly qualifies for exemption." A unanimous court found that "beliefs which prompted his objection occupy the same place in his life as the belief in a traditional deity holds in the lives of his friends, the Quakers"[21] and gave him the decision, but not on the grounds he had proposed. Seeger had hoped the Supreme Court would declare Section 6 (j) of the Selective Service and Training Act unconstitutional, forcing Congress to write a new law. The court chose instead to change the meaning of the words used, expanding the statute so as to include Seeger's belief, thus ignoring the constitutional issue.

Within two years the question, "Do you believe in a Supreme Being?" was eliminated from the Conscientious Objector status application form, and the "parallel to God" test guided future decisions of draft boards in the United States. Eventually, after the case was settled, Dan Seeger, and his wife, Betty Jean, joined Morningside Meeting. Seeger went on to serve many years as head of the New York office of the AFSC.

Draft Resistance During Vietnam

In the mid-1960s when the Vietnam conflict began to heat up, a number of draft-eligible young Friends began to examine what was the best thing for them to do. In those days deferments were readily granted for college, graduate school, teaching, joining the Peace Corps, or becoming a father. But some Friends were uncomfortable with deferments that were not always available to their less-well-heeled contemporaries. Some preferred to take a stand—to file as a conscientious objector and, if approved, to complete the required two-year alternative service.

One of these was John Mott's son, Jeremy, who dropped out of Harvard after his second year, in the spring of 1965, and signed on with the Church of the Brethren Volunteer Service. After training in Maryland (where he also served a stint as an experimental subject at the National Institutes of Health), he was sent, like others in his position, to work at the Bethany Brethren Hospital on Chicago's West Side. But as the war escalated and public reaction against it mounted, Jeremy Mott concluded that what mattered was ending, or at least hindering, the war. The next step was active resistance to the draft. As part of the April 15, 1967, antiwar protest in New York—in company with some

150 others and guarded by the Community Peace Squad of PSAP— Mott burned his draft card in Central Park. Then he went back to Chicago, resigned from his alternative service job, and went to work full time—ten hours a day, six days a week—as a draft counselor.

Although the government chose not to prosecute the Central Park draft-card burners, it did try many of the young men active in the Chicago antiwar movement for draft resistance. Mott's trial, in which he defended himself, took place in December 1967, and he was, as expected, convicted. He began his prison sentence the following month at the federal prison in Marion, Illinois, which he found a tense and violent institution. It was not long, however, before the prison administration apparently began to fear the effect of the incarcerations of conscientious objectors so near to Southern Illinois University with its considerable Vietnamese student population and antiwar sentiment. In July, in the middle of a prison visit from his family, Mott was whisked off, eventually to arrive at "the farm" at Lewisburg, Pennsylvania, among some twenty other draft resisters. His last stop was the prison at Ashland, Kentucky. There for the first time he encountered other draft-resisting Quakers, enough in fact to hold regular meetings for worship; it was also the first time he saw forced sex and other brutal activities among the inmates themselves. Banding together, the Friends found they had just enough power to effect a change of status for a few very young men unable to fend for themselves. Quakers and others imprisoned as war objectors were regularly visited by Faye Honey Knopp of Wilton Meeting, who represented the Central Committee for Conscientious Objectors. Knopp had been visiting internees in state, county, and federal prisons since 1955. In 1968 she and the Reverend Robert Horton, a Methodist minister, founded Prisoner Visitation and Support (PVS). By 1972 they were allowed to visit any internee in the prison system. Knopp visited hundreds of war objectors during the Vietnam years; since that time local volunteers have visited persons in more than fifty federal and military prisons across the country.

Jeremy Mott, whom Honey Knopp visited, was released after sixteen and one-half months. Ironically, the parole board allowed him to return to draft counseling (he would otherwise have stayed in jail, he said), and from then until the end of the war he wrote, edited, typed, and mailed a monthly newsletter to draft counselors across the United States. He attended the 1969 yearly meeting as a resource person on draft resistance and counseling.

Almost every meeting provided draft counseling to a large number of eligible young men from diverse backgrounds. The object was not to encourage them to evade the draft or in any other way to violate the law but to help them think through their own individual convictions in full knowledge of their options. Robert Blanc of Manhasset Meeting, a conscientious objector from World War II, then chairman of PSAP's Committee on Militarism and the Draft, visited meetings throughout the state, explaining the problems facing young men trying to become COs and advising them how to prepare statements and obtain supporting material.

Meetings on or near college campuses were especially involved. Cornell was a hotbed of protest against the war, and Ithaca Meeting was very active in draft counseling and providing support to draft resisters and their families. Rochester, Syracuse, Buffalo, and many other meetings were similarly involved. Albany Meeting even went so far as to harbor a group of idealistic, if anarchistic, antiwar protesters. The presence of these sometimes disruptive young people in the meeting house caused much searching within Albany Meeting; some Friends felt they were not in the tradition of Quakerism and should leave, whereas others were more receptive but felt a few rules were necessary. The matter was largely resolved when the group moved to other quarters, and those who had attended meeting for worship continued to do so. Richard Accetta-Evans, one of the young rebels, remembered Albany Friends as having been "very open and willing to listen and talk."[22] They invited the Capital Area Peace Center to establish an office in the meeting house and were very supportive of draft resisters during their court trials. To Accetta-Evans they came to represent an alternative set of values. "They offered me a place where there was some balance and perspective, a place not in the mainstream of society, but grounded in something other than my own momentary ideas of what was right and what was wrong."[23] At the time he turned in his draft card and became an active draft resister he also joined Albany Meeting.

Seven Years of Testimony at Yearly Meeting

From 1965 through 1971 the spectre of Vietnam hovered over the yearly meeting sessions at Silver Bay. In 1965 Clarence Yarrow of the AFSC recalled a prophetic AFSC statement from eleven years before, suggesting the possibility of the United States "backing into an unwanted war." He spoke of the great seriousness of the situation and the need to make another effort at finding ways to cut through national pride and prestige to help the Vietnamese people. The yearly meeting approved a lengthy minute on Vietnam, which described "a growing national acquiescence in terror" as "bombings, torture, and reprisals mount in ferocity." It reaffirmed the primacy of people, the well-being of the Vietnamese people, "not merely the requirements of American security or national honor," and suggested that a neutral fact-finding team go to both North and South Vietnam. During the 1966 sessions the PSAP Vietnam subcommittee presented "A Message to Friends on Vietnam from New York Yearly Meeting"—one of the strongest statements ever to come out of yearly meeting sessions. "Our Nation, using the greatest military power the world has known, is devastating a small and relatively defenseless country and destroying the people we claim to be protecting." The message called upon Friends, among other things, to stand unequivocally for the Peace Testimony, to examine their consciences on the question of more fully dissociating themselves from the war machine by tax refusal, and "to urge that young men consider whether they can submit to a military system that commands them to kill and destroy." It was the approval of this message that had caused concern and dismay in the more conservative areas of the yearly meeting.

An adviser to the East Asian and Pacific Affairs Division of the State Department attended the 1967 yearly meeting and explained the mechanics and difficulties of supervision in regard to sending supplies to North Vietnam. Friends' lack of sympathy with State Department views was evidenced by approval of a statement in support of the crew of the *Phoenix*, Earle Reynolds's boat that nine years before had sailed to the Eniwetok atoll to protest nuclear testing and now had twice transported medical supplies through the U.S. fleet to Haiphong and the Red Cross of North Vietnam. The crew's passports had been rescinded, and the Treasury Department had recommended that they be prosecuted. New York Yearly Meeting Friends expressed a unity of spirit with providing medical relief to any who suffer.

In 1968 Friends heard from Marjorie Nelson, an Indiana Friend who had been working as a doctor in the Friends clinic in Quang Ngai, Vietnam. She described the agony of the war casualties and her experience under siege during the Tet offensive in Hue and as a prisoner of the Viet Cong, who evacuated her into the mountains for safety. A Letter on Conscription was approved to be sent to Friends at home with a supporting minute from the high school group that read in part: "As many of the Young Friends will be facing this decision [draft resistance] in the near future, we feel that it is imperative that they feel support of their position by the Meeting. As this is an illegal stand, we also feel these young people should not have to stand alone." This was not the first time, nor would it be the last, that the high school group, having been informed of issues relating to the war under consideration by the yearly meeting, drew up their own minute and sent it in to the larger meeting.

Conscription was a major concern of the 1969 sessions as well, and the yearly meeting approved a "Letter to Friends Troubled by Conscription" for distribution to the monthly meetings. They also agreed that the yearly meeting should refuse to honor liens on the wages of its employees made for collecting taxes that were not being paid for reasons of conscience. In the 1971 sessions Friends were urged to protest against taxation for war by refusing to pay the federal telephone tax, and the yearly meeting agreed to publicize its own refusal to pay this tax "imposed for the specific purpose of procuring funds for the support of the military action in Vietnam."

The last American forces withdrew from Vietnam in the spring of 1973. Friends felt relief that the goal toward which they had worked for so long had at last come to pass, but the degree of suffering and loss of life had been too great to find any satisfaction in the outcome. And although small compared to that undergone by the soldiers and Vietnamese people, the pain and distress undergone by the war protestors also took its toll in damaged lives.

New Swarthmoor: Nursery for Quaker Leaders, 1969–1974

One good thing to come out of the Vietnam struggle was an experiment in Quaker living known as New Swarthmoor. A group of young Friends, a few to more than one dozen, on conference weekends perhaps up to one hundred, occupied Hazel and Walter Haines's old farmhouse between Marshall and Clinton, New York. At the peak of the antiwar sentiment, Young Friends of North America (YFNA) sought to awaken Friends to the whole range of Quaker concerns. The testimonies of equality for women and other undervalued groups, simplicity, community, and concern for the environment all worked into a broadbased set of drives. It was the hope of some to keep the branches of Friends in touch by visitation.

Stimulated by the International Young Friends Summer after their gathering at the World Conference at Guilford-Greensboro in 1967, young Friends felt the need of a place to rest and talk things over after presenting their radical testimony to whatever Friends they could reach. They knew that Swarthmoor Hall had filled that function for early Friends. Deborah Haines, on the YFNA executive committee, consulted her parents, who were about to leave for one year in Kenya, and got their permission to use the farm. Several young Friends picked apples at Friends' orchards near Barnesville, Ohio, and earned fifteen hundred dollars for winter supplies.

Their deficit home economy relied on supplements from friends and neighbors. A jug marked "Well, water" could be filled from the farm's uncertified well for body- and dishwashing; neighbors' wells supplied drinking water. Grocery carton material tacked onto inside walls improved the insulation. Two wood stoves warmed the downstairs area and the space directly overhead; the other bedrooms, called "Inner" and "Outer Siberia," were for the rugged. Vegetarian meals included experiments with native herbage, whole grain staples, and apples, strawberries, and vegetables in season sharepicked or donated.

These intensely searching youths believed that worship must be central and that leadings should be checked by much verbal threshing and study. Grace at meals might blossom into a half-hour's "thankfulness for being alive and together and hungry" as Pamela Haines wrote. They also believed in playing and enjoying the beauties of the countryside. They sang a lot, skinny-dipped in the pond in summer, explored sex, and let love be without dissimulation. They banned tobacco, alcohol, and other addictive drugs. They were joyfully honest not only with each other but also with outsiders, including police. Pastors and professors, such as Levinus Painter, Canby Jones, and William Taber, visited, and casual wanderers as well. A few residents may bear scars. Nobody died. Mohawk Valley Monthly Meeting had the care of one marriage, and another couple celebrated their commitment without institutional sanction. Questions about going back to college, turning in one's draft card, or the myriad matters of close living might also lead to gatherings for worship sharing or into clearness committees when the spirit moved in order to discover what God wanted in the situation. They conducted both business and worship in the manner of Friends although they appointed no clerks except for the moment, recorded few minutes, and had neither formal membership nor discipline.

Outside New Swarthmoor, Mohawk Valley Meeting gave tangibly and received an intangible vitality. They welcomed the young people, fed them, provided baths, supported their trials, appointed them representatives, and attended to their messages, even when their ministry might include song and dancing in the spirit. New Swarthmoorites made their presence known far and wide as marshals at demonstrations, at the hearings, arraignments, and trials of members, or as they hitchhiked thousands of miles. Eli Hostetler's and Geoffrey Kaiser's broad-brims, Marian Baker's Quaker bonnet, and Anne Wilson's plain dress attracted attention, usually favorable. Other members, including Elizabeth Cazden, Peter Blood-Patterson, Lee Garner, and Deborah Haines, among others, have continued to travel in the ministry and provide leadership within several yearly meetings. New Swarthmoor, a household of faith that tried to keep God at the center of its personal and collective struggles, was formally laid down in 1974.

New York Yearly Meeting Friends and the Nuclear Freeze

Many New York Yearly Meeting Friends were dedicated members of local and regional committees of the campaign for a nuclear weapons freeze that swept the country in the early 1980s. There were strong organizations in Albany, Rochester, Ithaca, Purchase, Scarsdale, and Long Island meetings, among others. AFSC's New York office was the center of action and education for Friends and others in the area convinced that a rough parity of nuclear forces existed between the United States and the Soviet Union, allowing both sides freedom to "freeze" their nuclear activities. Training sessions in the AFSC office gave confidence to neophyte peaceworkers who feared that the escalating numbers of nuclear weapons might somehow be used and could wipe out human life on the planet. Grass-roots groups like the one that originated in the Peace and Social Action committee of Scarsdale Meeting persuaded their local mayors and trustees to pass resolutions asking the president for a multilateral, verifiable nuclear weapons freeze.

In 1982 the United Nations Special Session on Disarmament was the impetus for the June 12 march from the United Nations to Central Park in which New York Yearly Meeting Friends joined several hundred thousand other nuclear freeze supporters in a demonstration for peace. Locally, Friends set up regional freeze offices in their meeting houses. One of the most active was at Scarsdale where a county-funded coordinator fielded questions from all over Westchester and dispensed tapes, literature, promotional materials, and press releases, published a newsletter, and organized the annual walkathon.

Changing Times for Native Americans and New York Yearly Meeting

Over the past forty years native Americans have increasingly focused on family roots, preserving tribal culture, and finding ways to overcome poverty, unemployment, and disease. They have faced major problems in gaining recognition of treaty obligations and rights to tribal lands and in protecting and improving the environment on existing reservations.

In a decade of struggle beginning in the late 1950s the New York Yearly Meeting Indian Affairs Committee (IAC) and other involved Friends witnessed to their concerns by standing alongside native Americans to prevent the flooding of the tribal lands of the Seneca Nation for the federal Kinzua Dam. They were unsuccessful. IAC also worked with the Friends Committee on National Legislation to foster legislation to preserve and restore native lands taken in violation of treaty agreements. In 1971 Syracuse Friends stood in witness with the Onondagas and other members of the Six Nations to prevent the confiscation of tribal lands for the widening of Interstate 81; the courts later upheld the Onondagas' claim to their land.

New York State's plan to industrialize the north country resulted in the confiscation of the tribal lands of the Mohawks to build locks and to widen and deepen the St. Lawrence River. Industries were sited near the seaway, the ecology of the river was changed, and tribal lands were contaminated by industrial wastes. Beginning in 1986, IAC worked with AFSC and the Akwesasne Task Force on the Environment of the Mohawk Nation to implement remedial action plans for pollution cleanup. The task force also planned economic development projects such as fish farming, planting black ash trees for future basket-making, and a seed project for family vegetable gardens.

E. Russell Carter, Levinus K. Painter, and Glad Schwantes were early and devoted members of IAC. Carter led committee members to understand that many of the problems native Americans confront come from being forced into a mold not of their making. Painter became an adopted member of the Six Nations Agricultural Society in 1969; he and Schwantes encouraged native Americans to learn about their roots. He was opposed to any attempt to make Indians over into the image of the dominant culture, preferring to help them seek what God gave uniquely to them. He encouraged the Senecas on the Cattaraugus Reservation to start language classes in their native tongue for their children. Friends remember storytelling by Levinus and David Owl, a Cherokee minister who worked with Levinus in preserving Indian folk tales. Glad Schwantes and Red Wing, a Winnebago who was associated with IAC for a number of years, helped Friends appreciate the beauty and art of native American crafts.

New York Yearly Meeting is actively represented on and contributes financial support through IAC to the Associated Committee of Friends on Indian Affairs. IAC has granted small scholarships to students enrolled in the American Indian Program at Cornell University, supported native American colleges and schools, and maintained an active interest in the four ACFIA-affiliated Friends Centers in Oklahoma, the Mowa Choctaw Friends Center and school in Alabama, and the Mesquakie Friends Center in Iowa.

The New York Yearly Meeting IAC has been troubled by growing conflicts among native Americans. A federal law enacted in 1988 allowed a tribe to operate on its reservation any form of gambling establishment that is allowed in the state where the reservation is located. The profits of such enterprises have often not been shared communally, and there have not always been consensual decisions about the acceptability of these enterprises. In 1990 Friends from Canada, New York, and Philadelphia Yearly Meetings responded to a call from traditional Mohawk chiefs to stand with them in peaceful witness against the violence threatened by the operators of high-stakes bingo and casino gambling. The people of the reservation were divided into factions with the Warrior Society opposing the traditional chiefs. After the ensuing violence Friends withdrew their presence but not their concern.

Latin American Concerns and Sanctuary for Refugees

During the 1982 New York Yearly Meeting sessions a small group of Friends formed who felt some sense of connection to Central America. At the December Representative Meeting they drafted a proposal for the Latin American Concerns (LAC) task group. Although crises in certain Central American countries were claiming the most attention, they intended to include all of the Americas south of the U.S. border and all people who came to the United States from there.

The first cut-and-paste newsletter, using material gathered from trusted alternative publications, was mailed that fall. Yearly meeting interest groups and participation in Peace Institutes were other ways LAC tried to offer a more complete picture of the situation in Central America than appeared in the mass media. Even Quakers showed symptoms of denial: there was reluctance to believe published accounts of the violence and doubt that our own government could be offering substantial assistance to armed forces that regularly participated in atrocities. As awareness grew, some reacted with "There's a war going on and we've got to stop it!" whereas others, shocked at the treatment of refugees here, stressed help and protection, even for a few.

At early meetings Elizabeth Millet shared her experiences in Nicaragua before 1979. Later, other New York Yearly Meeting Friends visited Central America and returned to share their impressions. Carol Tobkes brought valuable insights from her long-term experience in El Salvador, which was partially sponsored by New York Yearly Meeting.

Albany Meeting was the first in New York Yearly Meeting to declare sanctuary. At least eight more monthly meetings became involved in sanctuary or other activities with refugees in their localities. Some emphasized practical assistance or a forum for refugees to speak about the conditions from which they had fled.

In 1986 the task group became a committee. One of its objectives —"to seek ways in which we can help Latin Americans solve the problems to which they give priority, such as hunger, genocide, intervention by the United States, and violent repression"—was articulated by a refugee and emphasized the committee's focus on learning from Latin Americans. This same learning was available to the entire yearly meeting in 1988 when eight Central Americans, mostly leaders of self-help organizations, came to Silver Bay, camped with members of the committee, and joined Friends at meals and other events.

LAC has facilitated opportunities for Central Americans to share a piece of their lives. In response Friends have sought ways to join with and support Central Americans who fled to the United States, those who stayed at great risk in their own countries, and those who witness by openly returning from exile. Even when open warfare ends, as it has in some countries, and the spotlight of attention moves away from the region, justice issues remain unresolved. The need to better understand the problems is ongoing.

Alternatives to Violence Project

The germ of the Alternatives to Violence Project lies in an encounter Larry Apsey had in 1974 with inmates at Green Haven prison in Dutchess County, New York. One of them, Roger Whitfield, had organized a group called the Think Tank Concept and had arranged for delinquency-prone teenagers from New York City to come up for sessions on what it was like to spend time in prison and how to avoid it. Whitfield had heard of Apsey's work in nonviolence training and contacted him about leading a workshop for the Think Tank. The first workshop occurred in March 1975 under the auspices of the New York Yearly Meeting Peace and Social Action Program; Bernard LaFayette, Jr., and Paul Tillquist of Gustavus Adolphus College in Minnesota, and Steven Stalonas, Peter Matusewitch, and Apsey of the Quaker Project on Community Conflict were the facilitators. The program included inmate discussion, role-playing of conflict situations within the prison, instruction in the basic techniques of nonviolent direct action, and reminiscences by LaFayette of his experiences with Martin Luther King, Jr., and in the 1968 Poor People's Campaign.

The workshop was a great success, and there were immediate requests for more from other New York prisons. Auburn prison near Syracuse was the site of the second workshop with Janet Lugo, Ellen Lindop (Flanders), Charles Wilson, and Gary Eikenberry of the AFSC Syracuse office assisting Apsey and LaFayette. Nonviolence is not passiveness, Apsey told the men, but a way to change tyranny and oppression. LaFayette described how the civil rights marchers had "overcome" in the South, walking right past the troopers' guns and tanks into Montgomery, Alabama. The Auburn workshop was also successful.

From the start Lee Stern was involved, bringing to the program the four themes—affirmation, community building, communication, and cooperation—of the Children's Creative Response to Conflict project. Steven Levinsky, a young behavioral scientist knowledgeable in conflict resolution, added to the curriculum with exercises in human relations, trust, and dealing constructively with negative stereotyping. The Movement for a New Society in Philadelphia sent trainers to introduce the so-called Light and Livelies—games, usually physical, interspersed with more serious matter to keep the men from getting restless and to provide opportunity for laughter, creativity, and a sense of community. Flanders and Lugo formalized an advanced course, published more sophisticated manuals, and introduced a variety of innovations. Soon there were three levels of courses: the basic for newcomers, the advanced for graduates of the basic, and the training course for facilitators.

With demand so great the prison project outgrew its subsidiary position within PSAP and in 1979 became the Alternatives to Violence Project, Inc. (AVP), a not-for-profit corporation under New York State laws with Larry Floyd as its first clerk. Although still partly under the control and direction of the yearly meeting (which as of 1993 appointed six of the nine members on its board of directors), it has a broader constituency, drawing loyal supporters from Christian, Jewish, Islamic, and Buddhist groups alike.

Prisons remained the major concern, but in time AVP began to provide community workshops as well. These attracted new people who could be trained as facilitators, aides constantly in need of replenishment as the demand for workshops continued to exceed the supply. Besides some thirty prisons in New York State, AVP has become active in institutions in other states and countries. From the beginning inmates were welcomed as co-facilitators, their insights adding significant dimension to the program. Actively involved non-Quakers have also included a number of former prisoners.

A major feature of AVP workshops has been the introduction of the concept of "transforming power," the power to change violence into peaceful resolution of conflict. Larry Apsey described "transforming power" as rising out of one's attitude and behavior toward self and others. Anyone high on drugs or alcohol or carrying a weapon is unlikely to be open to "transforming power," which depends on one's ability to listen, to try to understand, and to reach for that something in the other person that at its center is good. It depends on being truthful, risking one's ego, and trusting one's inner sense of what is needed in the situation. Although "transforming power" is not presented as a religious concept and promotes no religious doctrine, it relies in practice and theory on spiritual growth. Deborah Wood has spoken of going into a prison with another outside facilitator, two or three inside facilitators, and a group of, perhaps, twenty men "who society has decided are of no value" and creating in three days a community of trust, "which in the best workshops has changed lives."

When Stephen Angell first participated in an AVP workshop, he found it so energizing that he soon became an active facilitator and the coordinator of the program at Fishkill. After the death of his wife, Barbara, he took on AVP as a kind of ministry. With a travel minute from Bulls Head–Oswego Meeting, endorsed by the yearly meeting, he crisscrossed the United States and Canada telling people about AVP, and later expanded his mission overseas. He was perhaps most successful in the United Kingdom, Australia, and New Zealand. On one of his trips he arranged for Robert Martin to come to New Zealand; Martin had been an inmate and inside coordinator at Fishkill who, after he was released, came and spoke very persuasively at the yearly meeting session. As a savvy African-American, Martin was very effective with the weirdly tattooed Maoris. Prison authorities were amazed to find Maoris from rival gangs in friendly conversation before the workshop was over.

Not surprisingly, AVP has helped those persons who have gone into the prisons as well as those already there. Perhaps the experience of Nettie West of Bulls Head–Oswego Meeting is in some way typical: "I went into AVP when my life was at a standstill, and I needed to reach out. Little did I know how much I would grow and become. I was given more than I gave. Green Haven prison became a familiar place, and those workshops, for all their difficulties, invariably brought a sense of joy and discovery of shared humanity and inner peace to us all."[24]

Unity and Diversity since Reunion

Hugh Barbour
and
Robin Alpern, John E. Brush, Miriam K. Brush,
Mary Foster Cadbury, Victoria Baker Cooley,
Anne-Marie Eriksson, Cheshire Frager,
Edward Myers Hayes, Lewis W. Hoskins,
Eloise C. Kayton, Janet L. Lugo, John Maynard,
Patricia Hayes Myers, Elizabeth H. Moger,
Noel Palmer, Daniel A. Seeger, Henry A. Wheeler

Changes in Structure and Constituency since 1955

Among the sixteen points that were the basis for consolidation of the two New York Yearly Meetings (discussed in chapter 15) was the stipulation that "the autonomy of the Quarterly and Monthly Meetings be preserved, and that no pressure be brought to have meetings in the same locality unite." There were already united monthly meetings, however, and after Reunion others merged. Some monthly meetings were laid down; new meetings and worship groups were formed.

All Friends was already a united quarter; in 1955–56 the two Purchase Quarters joined. Soon thereafter New York and Westbury Quarters became New York–Westbury Quarter. In 1959 meetings in the Hudson valley realigned to form Nine Partners Quarter. By 1986, after further mergers in both western and northeastern New York State, there were nine regional meetings in contrast to the original fourteen,

In this chapter and in chapter 16 we have asked for input from the Friends most directly involved. We have checked facts but have not attempted to present the variety of beliefs and attitudes held on each issue by New York Friends. Any value judgments implied are not necessarily shared by the whole yearly meeting.

each made up of all the monthly meetings in a particular geographical area.

With Reunion most of the committees of the two New York Yearly Meetings were continued; some were combined, a few were laid down, Yearly Meeting Executive and Administrative Committees were formed, and later committees arose, reflecting such new concerns as disabilities and women's rights. Efforts toward strengthening and expanding the work for peace began with creating a Fund for Peace in 1960 and evolved into the formation of the Peace and Social Action Program. As shown in chapter 16, PSAP initiated and implemented diverse projects and was a semiautonomous body for several years. In 1971 the yearly meeting could provide office space for PSAP, thus allowing for greater communication and some coordination of office functions.

In 1972 the Executive Committee reported some "uneasiness" in the yearly meeting with regard to staff activities and oversight and the functioning of committees, especially those on social concerns. At the same time the clerk of the yearly meeting and the Administrative Committee were aware of the absence of coordination among yearly meeting committees and their limited accountability to the yearly meeting. An ad hoc committee, after two years of study, recommended a plan for grouping all yearly meeting committees and representatives to associated bodies into four large Sections, each based on a common focus: Ministry and Counsel; Nurture; Witness; and General Services. Section coordinating committees provided oversight, guidance, and coordination. This plan was approved by the yearly meeting in 1976 and, with some modifications dictated by practicality and changed circumstances, is in place today.

Other ad hoc committees have been employed over the years to tackle problems or concerns beyond the scope of a single committee. The work of the Ad Hoc Committtee on Resource Development (AHCORD) led to the establishment of the Sharing Fund, a combined appeal for the voluntary support of the programs of the yearly meeting peace and social justice committees and of Powell House until 1992. At about the same time the yearly meeting set up the Ad Hoc Committee on Renewal to respond to the cry for spiritual revitalization in the Society. The yearly meeting newsletter *SPARK* and the worship-sharing and interest groups during the yearly meeting sessions are tangible outcomes of that committee's work. Concerns about the adequacy of financial support for yearly meeting activities, however, and for the state of spiritual vitality of yearly meetings are never completely and finally resolved, and in 1992 another Ad Hoc Committee on Renewal was set

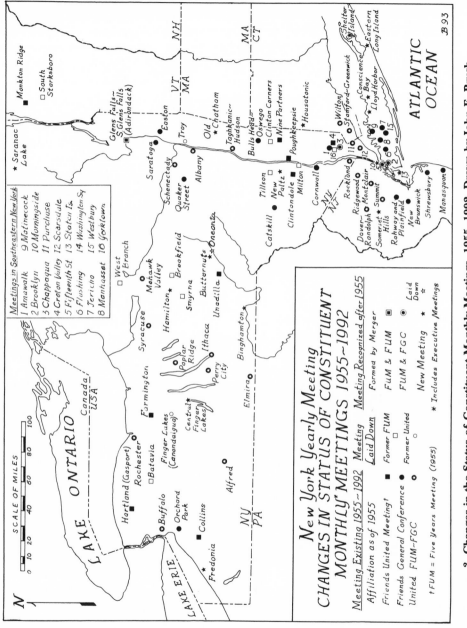

3. **Changes in the Status of Constituent Monthly Meetings, 1955–1992. Drawn by John E. Brush.**

up and charged with the task of pursuing ways to deal with financial issues, declining membership, and, seen by some as the core issue, the need for spiritual reinvigoration in the local meetings. While the committee struggles to define its task and develop recommendations to present to the yearly meeting in 1994, many local meetings have engaged in new study programs, and regional meetings have cooperated in religious education and outreach work.

In the forty years from 1952 to 1992, the total membership of the yearly meeting(s) shrank from 5,940 to 4,270. The sharpest decline was in the number and membership of the pastoral meetings, whereas the unprogrammed meetings, by averaging steadier overall, have increasingly become the dominant voice in the reunited yearly meeting. There are in 1994 now only three New York Friends churches with Quaker pastors; some pastors are part-time. The seeming loss of children and youth is partly the result of ways of reckoning numbers: 440 junior or associate members (11 percent of the total) were listed, crucial for growth.[1] More Friends were entering meetings as adults than by birth or upbringing. In 1952 the joint Religious Education Committee of the two yearly meetings had visited both the FGC and FUM national offices, held three conferences for young people, and reported 1,782 children, average attendance 1,104, in thirty-five First-Day schools under 227 teachers. Margaret Garone acted as traveling staff. In 1991 the Religious Education Committee reported "few Friends willing to contribute time and energy" and in 1992 "overwhelming inertia," despite various meetings and training institutes.

"Every community that wants to last beyond a single generation must concern itself with education," says Walter Brueggemann.[2] Friends are committed to the possibility of continuing revelation and do not want to copy "religious education" from churches where it is creedal indoctrination. Nor should teachers simply convey a prescribed body of facts. Friends recognize that even small children "know" God and can teach adults who are now reticent about sharing their religious lives for fear of "imposing." Thus, New York Friends have few regular and frequent programs for teens and adults. Many monthly meetings limit themselves to First-Day Schools for children or are mired in choosing an appropriate curriculum. A few meetings offer a full spectrum of religious education for all ages. At the yearly meeting level there are excellent programs for youth at Powell House and Silver Bay, and some teacher training workshops. James Toothaker served as religious education secretary from 1968 to 1977 but was not replaced. Religious education is sharing and discovering religious lives. All growth and health depends on this.

21. New York Yearly Meeting at Silver Bay, 1991.
Photograph by Hugh Barbour.

Joseph Vlaskamp came as General Secretary to New York Yearly Meeting in 1976 after serving as youth or religious education minister for three midwestern churches and as Assistant Secretary for Religious Education of Friends General Conference with an eight-year interim as a fundraiser for Farmers and World Affairs. Like many pastors, he was a graduate of Earlham College and Hartford Seminary. He edits the yearly meeting newspaper, *SPARK,* and lends support to the administrative functions of all the yearly meeting committees. He has served on many national Quaker committees and boards of FGC, FUM, and FWCC. Other staff at the 15th Street central yearly meeting office, many of whom have given the best years of their lives and been much loved by Friends, have included Floy Cullinan, Barbara Houser, Viola Purvis, Marge Rubin, Marge Schlitt, and Helen Toppins.

Witnessing to Quaker unity, New York, Canadian, New England, and Baltimore Yearly Meetings have played an important role in broadening the Five Years Meeting, rechristened Friends United Meeting (FUM) after it began meeting triennially in 1960, and in preventing its "realignment" along theological lines in 1991. Becoming members of FUM had been one cause of hesitancy for some Hicksites in the 1955

reunion, but evangelical Friends from the West and Midwest have regularly been invited to Silver Bay to give messages or lead Bible study. The
yearly meeting's financial support has been divided between FUM and
FGC, but a full quota of active New York delegates have taken part in
FUM Board and national committee meetings, which support schools,
hospitals, and missions overseas. FUM's 1993 Triennial was held at
Clinton, New York.

When the biennial gatherings of Friends General Conference
(FGC) were moved away from Cape May, New Jersey, near Philadelphia, in 1970, they were next held at Ocean Grove and at Ithaca,
within New York Yearly Meeting. Having no missions, schools, or hospitals overseas, FGC has not needed to carry on much business at its
gatherings, now annual, which bring together up to two thousand
Friends each year for worship, spiritual sharing, and study and create a
nationwide network of friendships. Thus, FGC's network of representative committees and its office in Philadelphia undertake FGC's decisions and services to monthly meetings.

The Haviland Records Room and the Keepers of the Records

The longest-serving employee, although unpaid, of New York
Friends was John Cox, Jr., who continued as Keeper of the Records of
the two yearly meetings from 1904 until 1948 when he was succeeded
by Percy E. Clapp. In this period Cox had supervised the moving of the
precious minutes and registers from the huge safes in the 15th Street
Meetinghouse to a special room in the adjacent Friends Seminary in
1924, to storage in Central Valley, Rockland County, during World War
II, and back to the Records Room at Friends Seminary. During Clapp's
term the two yearly meetings permitted the Church of Jesus Christ of
Latter Day Saints to microfilm those records begun before 1850 that
contained vital statistics. Thus, most of the early minutes and registers
of the monthly meetings, some one hundred thousand pages, were
made available in convenient form for historians and genealogists at
the Records Room at Haverford and at Swarthmore. Clapp was succeeded in 1958 by Agnes H. Campbell. During her term and while
Gerald McDonald was clerk of the Society of Friends Records Committee of the newly reunited yearly meeting, the committee's "heart's desire" of securing more archivally adequate space for the records was
made possible in the new building of the Friends Seminary through the
gift of Elizabeth Haviland. In December 1965 the Records Committee
was able to meet for the first time in the Haviland Records Room.

22. John Cox, Jr. (1860–1951).
Courtesy Haviland Records Room, New York Yearly Meeting.

During the following year, 1966, Mary G. Cook became the Keeper, to be followed, through the date of this writing, by Elizabeth H. Moger.

Organization of the Haviland Records Room holdings are based on the *Catalogue of the Records in Possession of, or Relating to, the Two New York Yearly Meetings of the Religious Society of Friends and Their Subordinate Meetings,* the culmination of forty years work by John Cox, Jr., published in 1940 by the Historical Records Survey of the Works Projects Administration as part of the Inventory of the Church Archives in New York City. From this catalog Agnes Campbell prepared the basic card file of the records, which in a modernized form serves as the finding aid to the collection.[3]

The collections in the Haviland Records Room have been used by scholars and genealogists and by Friends of New York and other yearly meetings as well, but its use has been restricted by limited time available, limited space, and lack of professional archival expertise. New York is unique among yearly meetings maintaining archival collections in not being able to share facilities or staff with any other historical or academic institution. In 1986 at the Keeper of the Records' urging, the yearly meeting approved the establishment of the John Cox, Jr., Memorial Endowment Fund, still open for contributions, whose income is to be expended for professional archival services to enhance the preservation, care, and use of New York Yearly Meeting records.

Powell House and Pearl and Francis Hall

In May 1960 Elsie Knapp Powell offered a large frame house with associated buildings and land in the Town of Chatham, Columbia County, New York, as a gift to the yearly meeting. The property, beginning in 1902 with a small tenant farmhouse, was part of the farm of her family, acquired by her husband, Isaac Hopper's great-grandson, Wilson M. Powell, a New York attorney who was counsel and president for New York Hospital. By extensive additions and remodeling, the Powells had made it into their summer residence, which they called "Pitt Hall," with fourteen bedrooms, seven baths, and comfortable common rooms. After Wilson Powell's death in 1935 the farm had been used as a summer camp for teen-age girls learning to ride horses while the Powell House in Manhattan was given to the AFSC, which used it to house wartime refugees.

Projected uses of the Columbia County house were either as a residential community for retired couples and creative persons (as suggested by Elsie) or as a rural meeting center that could be used for worship retreats, committee workshops, Young Friends activities, and for conferences on Quaker concerns or social outreach matters as envisioned by New York Friend Rachel Davis DuBois. The committee appointed to investigate reported to the yearly meeting sessions in July 1960 that basic alterations would be required at a cost of seventeen thousand dollars to convert the house for winter use and estimated that fifteen thousand dollars would be necessary for operation in the first year.

In 1960 the yearly meeting accepted the house with 57 acres and proceeded with steps necessary for incorporation of the Elsie K. Powell House. A standing committee of the yearly meeting was created with responsibilities for finances, operation, and appointment of staff. The yearly meeting's goals of converting the property to accommodate conferences, retreats, and committee meetings and developing a center for youth programs were soon fulfilled with the leadership of Francis and Pearl Hall, who came as directors in 1961, and with Robert and Elizabeth Bacon, who came the following year as youth directors. Bob Bacon also became business manager. Their energy and imaginative pioneering during its first thirteen years established the role that Powell House has had in renewing the yearly meeting.

Friends had known the Halls, originally from Colorado, as members of the Bruderhof Community, and earlier of another "intentional community" in Georgia. In 1940 their Newark Ashram, a residential settlement house in a black ghetto, had been an inspiration for the leaders of the Student Christian Movement out of all the colleges and universities of New England and the Middle Atlantic States. With David Dellinger and other Union Theological Seminary students, Fran Hall refused a divinity deferment under the draft and spent the war years in Danbury Penitentiary. When they stopped on a trip to Connecticut, the Halls found interesting the brief experience of Adelyn Holden and her husband, Henry Wheeler, William and Dorothy Bruff, and Dan and Rosalie Wilson, with a small intentional community, Bentley Farm, later the nucleus of Bulls Head Meeting, and said that "if the way would open" they would join Friends and accept the role at Powell House. A Friend at home in Christ-centered theology, Fran gained the respect of Friends across the yearly meeting by visiting widely among them and was asked by Keith Smiley to present at the yearly meeting session the draft of the new New York Yearly Meeting Discipline. For FWCC he edited two unbiased books on the branches of Friends in the Americas. Yet both he and Pearl were best loved as devotional leaders, as writers on spiritual growth and aging, and as personal counselors. They went on to head the Quaker Hill Conference Center in Indiana.

Subsequent Powell House directors and staff, such as Matt Drake and Evelyn Dane, provided valued leadership in the evolving religious experience of both adult and youth participants in the formative years. George Badgley and Rachel Davis DuBois were among the most active planners; a Youth Committee was also formed.[4] Pete Seeger and Fritz Eichenberg were among those who brought music and art to Powell House. By 1993 the annual operating budget had grown to exceed three hundred thousand dollars and the staff has increased to nine, including office workers, cooks, and buildings and groundskeepers. Contributions of Friends through three major fund drives supported the construction of The Knoll House for the directors' residence plus additional housing for the youth directors. The central Pitt Hall has rooms for some thirty-five adults, serves up to fifty in the enlarged din-ing room, provides three staff offices, and seats up to one hundred in the meeting rooms. One dozen camping sites, a two-acre swimming pond, a playing field, a children's playground, and a garden allow varied outdoor activities. In 1992 the number of registrations in adult programs exceeded 1,509, in the youth programs, 750. Under stress of financial crisis, an Ad Hoc Committee on the Future of Powell House studied carefully the programs there. Their exhaustive report and 1988 fund appeal were approved by the yearly meeting: Powell House would be phased out of the Sharing Fund over a three-year period, and direct support from the Yearly Meeting budget would continue for Powell House as a yearly meeting resource.

The Powell House Youth Program began in 1962. Bob and Betty Bacon had run the high school group at yearly meeting sessions in Silver Bay's Paine Hall. In 1967 the old carriage house became the Anna Curtis Youth Center, named for a 15th Street Friend who had enriched the lives of children at yearly meeting for many years with her stories of Quaker lore. Bob and Betty retired in 1970 and were succeeded by Bob and Anne Rommel, Joan and Austin Wattles, Tom and Barbara Rindge in 1975, and Patsy and Ed Myers-Hayes from 1979 to 1990.

Throughout the years the youth program provided for the yearly meeting's young people a place where they were accepted and nurtured as they coped with growing up. Each year, up to two dozen conferences, varying in length and in focus, were held. The capacity of the center grew from mid-twenties to mid-forties. Occasional large celebrations of more than one hundred provided an intensity of community for young people who were often the only Quakers or pacifists or vegetarians in their schools and communities. While conference topics varied, an experiential learning focus was constant through the years, as were training in group process and in leadership. The youth directors all shared a preference not to proselytize but encouraged young people to find their own path and their own answers. Conferences examined Quakerism and spirituality and also sexuality, peace concerns, racism, drug and alcohol use, friendship, and personal ethics. As many conference attenders brought friends from school, the youth program became a significant outreach to non-Friends.

Conferences balance an unconditional acceptance of each attender with a challenge to grow and be the best person each can be. The youth program has felt the brunt of changing social values and behaviors as it maintained a program trusted by the parents and meetings. From these struggles the young people took responsibility for the tone and behavior of conferences, and thrived.

Theological Standpoints: Lewis Benson, Dean Freiday, and Universalist Quakers

The revision of the Yearly Meeting Book of Discipline, begun in 1968, brought out again the differences of belief among New York Friends. Some Friends held to traditional liberal or orthodox lines. The moral trauma of the two world wars evoked in most American Protestant circles the "neo-orthodox" movement led by Manhattan's Reinhold Niebuhr, who described human ambiguity in *The Nature and Destiny of Man.*[5] Among Friends there was no corresponding reexamination of the nature of God and humans. Meetings and members of New York Yearly Meeting are primarily liberal in theology and unprogrammed in worship, affirming human goodness and finding it easier to talk about Jesus than about Christ, appealing to truth rather than to the Bible. Along with the age-long Quaker witness against dogma and intellectualism, New York Friends have learned from ex-Catholics and ex-evangelical members to reject authoritarianism. The changes of twentieth-century urban mores, which drove some rural Friends back into conservatism, brought most also to resent any discussion of guilt and depravity. The most outspoken forms of both evangelical and humanist religion have been so far apart that they have been led by anxiety and pride into mutual intolerance. Though Friends shared Niebuhr's awareness of the demonic self-righteousness of those who are proud to be white, American, middle-class, or male, his rejection of pacifism kept Friends from learning his humility about all religious ideals. Partly for this reason, two outspoken Quaker theological minds within New York Yearly Meeting have been prophets without honor there although influential among groups of Friends elsewhere.

Lewis Benson (1906–1986) was a birthright Friend of Manasquan Meeting. He worked as a messenger boy on the Hoboken docks and was an avid but in time disillusioned student of Gurdjieff. He then became an intense, diligent, self-taught student of George Fox's writings, studying at Woodbrooke, Pendle Hill, and briefly at the University of Chicago while supporting himself as a printer and meeting secretary. With the help of his wife, Sarah, he traveled widely to speak among Friends and wrote and published (at first by himself) two influential studies of Fox's teachings: *Prophetic Quakerism* (1943) and *Catholic Quakerism* (1966), and a dozen articles as well in *Quaker Religious Thought* (two issues of which in 1970 and 1987 were devoted entirely to his thought), in the *Friends Journal,* the British *Friends Quarterly* and *The Friend,* and in two series of publications centering on his ideas, *The Call* (1954–1959) and *New Foundations Publications* (1976–). He called

Friends to total obedience to the inward voice of God, to Christ as prophet:

> Fox's first public act was to proclaim . . . that "Christ has come to teach his people himself." Christ, the teacher of righteousness, is the new way that God has chosen to bring all men to himself. Fox's message is . . . not about the nature of man. He encounters God the Creator as lawgiver. . . . "That of God in every man" is not a human means of knowing, . . . but the voice and wisdom of the Creator. . . . The call is to repentance, . . . a voice that is personal and transcendent. . . . That of God in man is not answered without a person to person relationship to Christ who must be obeyed in all things.[6]

Benson wrote also about Christ as sacrificial Priest and as King, but like Fox was impatient with any stress on mere forgiveness and atonement. He rejected all Christianity that accepted moral compromise; hence, his "Catholic" Quakerism was meant to be a totally new faith, the only true way for everyone. He consistently carried this ethic into life by trying to form committed communities, the Woolman Settlement in New Jersey in the 1940s, Philadelphia's "Brudercoop" with Mennonites in the 1950s, "The Call" in the 1960s. Nobody continued obedient to the vision as he saw it. An injury in youth had wrecked Benson's hearing and made dialogue difficult for him. When asked what Christ's commands are, which must be inwardly heard and obeyed, Benson usually declined to specify, but he felt them to be laws, not guidances for specific occasions. The New Foundation Fellowship of scattered individuals and study groups in the 1970s and 1980s grew by the influence of Benson's speaking tours in England and America and of broader-spirited disciples such as Joseph Pickvance, leading its members to a new dedication to Quakerism. He and Manasquan Meeting, whose language was more conservative than the New Foundations', were never easy members of the New York Yearly Meeting. Manasquan accepted the new *Faith and Practice,* but Benson had protested by a letter he sent throughout the yearly meeting that it did not describe Christ rightly. (In fact, Christ's name was used as often in the new *Discipline* as in the old.)

A second pillar of the Manasquan Meeting has been Dean Freiday. Theologically trained, he, too, has written and spoken as an individual although he has represented FGC at the 4th and 5th World Conferences on Faith and Order of the World Council of Churches in 1963 and 1993 and was clerk of FGC's Christian and Interfaith Relations Committee in 1966–72. He has a wide grasp of the history of theology and has been strongly influenced by Donald Nesti, a charismatic priest of the Holy Ghost Fathers. With Nesti and Calvin Keene, a gifted Quaker theologian formerly at St. Lawrence University, Freiday has co-written or coedited a series, *Catholic and Quaker Studies,* including a work on seventeenth-century Quaker and Catholic pioneers in Bible study. Freiday's best known publication was the 1967 modern English edition of Barclay's *Apology.* His own thought is best shown in his articles in *Quaker Religious Thought*[7] for which he also served as editor from 1979 to 1989. That quarterly was sponsored by the Quaker Theological Discussion Group, founded by Wilmer Cooper on a national basis, but usually meeting in the Midwest. It publishes a wide theological range of papers read at its sessions. The group and journal have included Dan Seeger, Benson, and Freiday and many from New Foundations groups.

By their warmth of insight into the religious experiences of others, the Christ-centered Francis Hall and Universalist Daniel Seeger acted as reconcilers. Seeger, from a Catholic background, called himself an agnostic and became a Friend after seeking draft counseling at the AFSC. The concurring opinion of Justice William O. Douglas in the Seeger case, likening Seeger's views to those of Buddhists, sparked his interest in world religions. As New York regional executive secretary of AFSC, he became convinced that its faith was becoming less clear and saw his universalist interest in common human destiny as a way to project spiritual themes within such a diverse group. He sought to acknowledge the Christian roots of Quakerism while encouraging Friends' appreciation of the way other faiths revealed the activity of God. He never regarded an intolerance of Christianity coupled with esteem for other spiritual traditions as a legitimate form of universalism. He participated in the Quaker Theological Discussion Group and took pains to reach out to Evangelical Friends, seeking to make unprogrammed Friends aware of the value of their religious experience and their outreach to groups in society that unprogrammed Friends were unable to draw in. He shared the platform with Lewis Benson at an evening plenary session of the yearly meeting to defuse a polarization of universalist and New Foundation Friends and spoke before the Anglo-American Quaker Universalist Fellowship,[8] asking how Friends can express Jesus' uniqueness and humanity without dogma. He wrote a thoughtful, reconciling statement, *The Boundaries of our Faith,* in 1990 in response to divisions in New York Yearly Meeting between a group of Friends who were exploring pre-Christian religions, women's rituals, and goddess spirituality, and critics, notably in Clintondale Meeting, who in 1989 had minuted their objection to paganism. In response,

New York Yearly Meeting's Ministry and Counsel Coordinating Committee brought to the 1991 sessions a statement urging mutual listening and sharing and circulating a series, *Statements of Belief.*

Ethical Issues and Disagreements:
Sex Education and Abortion Rights

New York City was the home of Margaret Sanger, Dr. R. L. Dickinson, Clarence Gamble, and other pioneers of birth control and founders of Planned Parenthood. New York Quakers could not escape concern as these issues reached young Friends, immigrants, and long-term citizens and blacks and Hispanics in the ghettos. The Friend who became a national pioneer in sex education, Dr. Mary Calderone, was the daughter of the famous photographer Edward Steichen. Schooled in France, she did premedical studies at Vassar, switching to acting before returning to medicine. She married a fellow physician in public health and through her daughters' First-Day School found her way into Quakerism. In 1953 she became medical director of the Planned Parenthood Federation and called and published the results of a national conference on *Abortion in the United States* (1958) that dramatized the need for new birth control methods such as "the pill." Demands for her manuals and talks extended her concern to other human dimensions of sexuality, and she founded the Sex Information and Education Council of the United States for which, as executive director from 1964 to 1982, she responded to ever-increasing calls for information by articles and one hundred speeches a year.[9]

In 1971–72 the yearly meeting united in a minute that affirmed women's responsibility and prerogative in making choices about bearing children:

> Friends recognize that restrictive abortion laws discriminate against poor and middle class women, because well-to-do women can afford to pay the high cost of a competent practitioner or travel to a place where abortion is legal. Friends affirm a commitment to life. We believe that contraception is preferable to abortion as a way of avoiding unwanted pregnancies. We further feel that laws restricting the distribution of contraception information and contraceptive devices should be repealed. The right of women to decide with their partners to have only those children they want should be protected. When they consider it necessary, legal and safe abortion should be readily available.

The yearly meeting session two years later united in an action designed to work for the protection of civil space within which women could exercise this responsibility: "The Meeting approved the joint proposal from the Human Relationships and Sexuality Committee and the Women's Rights Committee, . . . that the New York Yearly Meeting appoint a representative to the Religious Coalition for Abortion Rights . . . sponsored by the New York State Council of Churches."[10]

Over the years grave reservations about the moral character of abortion emerged within the yearly meeting, felt by some Friends as a source of profound religious struggle and perceived by others as a clear moral prohibition. After several years in which bitter disagreements were expressed the yearly meeting's minute in 1986, prepared by a Task Group on Abortion, explicitly noted that it did not supersede the 1972 minute:

> Among Friends in New York Yearly Meeting there is much diversity of feeling and opinion on . . . abortion. The abortion issue is an emotional one, and the debate as to its rightness or wrongness has very often caused deep division and pain. This struggle will continue but . . . even those of us with profound differences of opinion have much that we can agree upon: . . . the preciousness of life and the right of everyone to follow his or her own path through life as guided by the Inward Light. We know that we must be loving, supportive, and nonjudgmental and that our continuing search for truth on the abortion issue must take place on this common ground. We must "listen to God and listen to one another for what comes from God."[11]

Yearly meeting representatives continued to participate in the Religious Coalition for Abortion Rights because no one had raised the issue. But a comment in the 1988 Advance Reports, stating that the coalition was no longer under the State Council's direct sponsorship, drew the attention of those opposing abortion, and the issue of yearly meeting participation was brought to the floor of the yearly meeting session. The yearly meeting had minuted its intention to participate in this coalition in 1974 without any contingency that the Council of Churches sponsor it, so no new decision seemed needed. The raising of the issue by those strongly opposed to abortion was one of several signs of a change in the state of the yearly meeting. The yearly meeting session was unable to unite on rescinding the appointment, which was for 1988–1990. The Nurture Coordinating Committee was asked to examine that question. In December 1989 the yearly meeting, on the Nurture Coordinating Committee's recommendation, let the appointment remain and charged Ministry and Counsel to consider "ways and resources by which the Yearly Meeting might consider . . . the broad issues of conscience, rights and abortion."[12] In December 1990 the 1988 appointment expired. The yearly meeting heard that the Nurture Coordinating Committee could not reach unity on a recommendation. The final minute on this matter reflects the diverse views within the yearly meeting: "Friends did not have unity in filling the New York YM position on the New York Religious Coalition for Abortion Rights at this time."[13] In spite of the 1986 minute's allusion to "our continuing search" no further action had been taken nor even proposed by 1993. The task group on Abortion Concerns was laid down by Ministry and Counsel in July 1991. The lack of unity loomed so large that common ground was difficult to find.

The various conflicts the yearly meeting has experienced since the 1980s have led to much talk and consideration of "Quaker process," "Gospel Order," and other ways of handling conflicts. "We seem to act from crisis to crisis," as Vicki Cooley said. "We get bogged down in issuing general statements or debating membership in organizations instead of seeking truth through hard questions. . . . It seems that we expect almost miraculous results if we just use the process correctly [but] the process does not create or establish the truth. It is designed to help us recognize, test, and act, but the truth remains whether we engage in the process or not."[14] As Herbert Lape put it, "The only thing that . . . will help us is a recovery of the gospel, not just gospel order."[15]

Ethical Disagreements: Gay and Lesbian Friends

A group of gay and lesbian Friends, some other Quakers, and Morningside Preparative Meeting in New York City persuaded the 1971 yearly meeting session to set up a committee to study "the implications of homosexuality" and consider a call to apply civil rights to gay men and lesbians. In 1972 this committee asked the yearly meeting to advocate "the repeal of all legislation imposing penalties upon homosexual persons as homosexuals." The high school group of Young Friends also urged approval. The yearly meeting at once agreed that "Homosexuals suffer serious discrimination; . . . that civil rights laws should protect homosexuals," asking "revision of all legislation imposing disabilities." After long laboring a minute urging meetings to "continue to examine these questions" in light of "the great diversity in relationships that people develop with one another" received applause.[16]

Part of the impulse for this proposal was London Yearly Meeting's

1963 publication, *Towards a Quaker View of Sex,* which chronicled British Friends' unease with the plight of young gay Friends who had no one to talk to about their own feelings of love in circumstances in which to act on that love was illegal. It was the subject of many discussions among Friends in New York Yearly Meeting. In addition, many Friends applied the principle that God continually inspires and concluded that Friends are free to differ with the sanctions against homosexuality in Leviticus and in Paul's Epistles. One Friend wrote, "We are called to live in the new covenant, not the old one." Beginning in the 1960s, gay, lesbian, and bisexual Friends and associates met for weekend conferences, meals, worship-sharing, and socializing in various towns within the yearly meeting. They often discussed political issues, civil rights, and same-gender marriage. Many had been involved in gay civil-rights activities that had new drive and publicity after 1969. In the 1960s and 1970s gay and lesbian Friends' groups went on invitation to Bulls Head, Croton Valley, Brooklyn, 15th Street, and Westbury Meetings to share in discussions with Friends on their experiences of being gay. In 1990–91 one gay member of New Paltz Meeting was invited to travel to talk about his meeting's process in approving the taking of same-sex marriage under its care. Some talked with the teenagers at the yearly meeting sessions at Silver Bay to help them understand thoughts and struggles gay Friends had had so that young gay Quakers would know others to talk to and so that young Friends might appreciate the variety of Quakers they would come to meet. For many years Friends held "gay-straight" dialogues on the inn porch.

In the 1990s several gay Friends felt that the heated discussions about same-sex marriage put their lives under more and longer scrutiny than was comfortable. They sought the Society's support of long-term same-sex relationships and wished Friends to see them as wholly human. By 1993 Morningside, Rochester, and Cornwall Meetings had taken one or more same-sex marriages under their care, and several more had supported such events. But in 15th Street Meeting some members protested the holding of a same-sex ceremony in the meeting house although not under the monthly meeting's official care. During eleven years of ensuing discussion that meeting found it difficult to agree on how to interpret and when to undertake any specific marriages under its care. In Albany, after five years, such discussions ended as a result of the deep emotions associated with the issue.

During this period the yearly meeting charged a committee to revise the Book of Discipline, *Faith and Practice.* The committee presented an emphasis on spiritual search and relationships with which many

Friends agreed. Others vehemently objected, saying that the rewritten and retitled section on marriage and family relations left too much to individuals and presented lawful marriage and chastity as only two alternatives among many relationships equally sanctioned when the others are neither biblical nor within Friends tradition. Deliberations about these proposed revisions indicated to some Friends in this and other yearly meetings that New York Friends had gone far beyond biblical and Quaker standards. This perception, along with several matters of Christian faith, helped spark the "movement" of 1989–92 within FUM because of which Southwest Yearly Meeting proposed to withdraw with others of like mind from Friends United Meeting or to reorganize it so as no longer to include united yearly meetings affiliated with both FUM and FGC. In 1993 Southwest Friends did withdraw.

As of 1993 most gay and lesbian New York Friends kept their business and relationships independent of their meetings. Some felt driven from their meetings, but others became better in coping with arguments and able to present themselves forthrightly and with love to all, believing that to be the way the Spirit had directed them. Many meetings declined to unite around any condemnatory minutes. Gay and lesbian Friends had become acquainted across the yearly meeting, working on all Friends' concerns. The name of the yearly meeting committee begun in 1971 was changed to the Human Relations and Sexuality Committee and deliberately included some gay, lesbian, and bisexual members to bring cares and concerns. Many meetings and the yearly meeting had gay and lesbian officers and teachers. Gay couples attended in dozens of meetings, and gay parents' and couples' children shared in local religious education classes.

Developments among Women

At the end of the 1960s a new feminist movement emerged in the United States. It dealt, as had the first wave in the nineteenth and early twentieth centuries, with equity issues but also reflected the context of the time when movements focused on liberation and self-identification. Many women became conscious of "woman" not just as a neutral fact of genetics or biology but as an identity: political, spiritual, social, sexual, cultural, historical. In the light of their self-definition as women many analyzed institutions, societies, and experiences and challenged what they found by organizing, by writing, and by developing new tools and models of expression and self-development. These trends directly affected all social institutions from marriage and the workplace to the church.

To trace these trends within New York Yearly Meeting, perhaps the clearest index is the twenty-year history of its Women's Rights Committee. It began in 1972 with a shared concern on the Inn Porch at Silver Bay among a group of like-minded women who set themselves "the task of challenging sexist attitudes and structures in New York Yearly Meeting." Approved in 1973, the committee's charter was to

> serve as a source of information to men and women, to encourage Friends to reassert . . . our historic testimony on the equality of men and women, to increase awareness of the issues that are being identified in the contemporary women's movement, to provide a network of support to women who are troubled or suffering because of women-related conflicts, and to strive to promote a spirit of love, caring and understanding when dealing with the tensions that feminism is bringing to the surface.

In the first few years there was repeated discussion about whether the committee should be principally a support group or should emphasize outward witness on women's needs and rights. It was settled in part by leaving the choice to the local meeting-based or regional women's groups in the yearly meeting. Another question regarded eligibility for membership; the standard chosen was support for the committee's goals, not gender.

In its "outward witness" role, the committee early recommended the review of *Faith and Practice* to see whether it reinforced stereotyped gender roles or used sexist language. It first asked for and then organized child care during yearly meeting sessions. It recommended a change in the Eleventh Query to improve its language and update its vision. It issued a set of queries on sexism in monthly meetings, initiated a Mother's Peace Day campaign to reclaim the holiday's original vision, reaffirmed the yearly meeting's 1971 minute supporting a woman's right to abortion, endorsed the Seneca Women's Encampment, helped fund a film on women's images of women and Claire Simon's video *Crones* on elder Quaker women, and promoted it among Friends. In 1976–77 the committee coordinated publication of the newsletter *Friendly Woman* (the task rotates among yearly meetings every two years).

The committee early began sponsoring programs at Powell House. These became the women's weekends, a spring event of intense "sharing, fun and energizing relaxation," as well as exploration of themes and issues, and a fiercely treasured time of community. Traditions developed, such as sharing artistic or craft creations, and attendance eventually reached more than sixty, undercutting intimacy. A second weekend, in winter, was initiated. The themes of these weekends ranged from sociopolitical issues, such as "Racism, Sexism and Quakerism" or abortion, to spirituality in "The Feminine Element of Godhead," and self-development: "Making Decisions," "Women, Anger and Forgiveness." Many weekends focused on building self-understanding, others on sheer joy: "How Can I Keep from Singing?" Through the 1980s the committee also held nonthematic autumn women's retreats, usually at a home or a farm.

When the committee first moved to sponsor Women's Worship Sharing at yearly meeting sessions, there was opposition stemming from a sense that such separatism was out of keeping with Friends' principles. But so many women found this experience becoming essential to them that it needed to break into multiple groups. At Silver Bay the committee has always sponsored interest groups (usually two) that reflect the same broad concerns as the weekends. The first focused on traditional images of godhead.

Many women have found female imagery, particularly traditional "goddess" figures, important in helping them discover and assert their own spiritual power and strength. They derive great empowerment from a sense of continuity with a spiritual tradition going back to earliest prehistory in which the female is identified with the holy, and the divine is immanent. These themes—the holiness and goodness of the physical world and a deep sense of holy connectedness with it—are also intimately connected for many women with the environmental movement. Although some women see these as additive to their Quakerism, many see in them other expressions of Friends' traditional teachings of immanence and direct experience of the divine. Many feel deep connection between the feminist views of "power with" and Quaker experience of power as nonhierarchical, inward, and nonviolent.

Many question whether exclusively male images of the divine justify male dominance of human institutions, including the Church. Feminism brings many to new definitions and understandings of power: what it is, how it is used, how it is institutionalized and operative in structures of societies. They define as patriarchy a twenty-five-hundred-year-old pattern of dominators and dominated in all relations, from the family to nation-states. Relationships become hierarchies not only in social structures but also in thought, leading to exploitation and dehumanization of the dominated, an understanding of power that is the reverse of both the feminist and the pacifist definition. Defining divine power in traditionally female terms leads to women broadening, deepening, enriching, and renewing their experience of Quaker faith, to reclaim the history of women and the strong role of women in the story of Quakerism past and present.

Incest and Crisis Survivors

Meetings in New York and other yearly meetings have founded or fostered various groups for crisis survivors, "Twelve-Step" programs, such as Substance Abuse, Alcoholics Anonymous, Alanon, marriage enrichment groups, and others for individuals recently separated or divorced. In many such groups, within or independent of meetings, individuals have found, just as in the gay and lesbian Friends groups, both reassurance and strength for rebuilding and experiences of rebirth or rediscovery of their identity and a divine "greater power" on which to rely.

Anne-Marie (Eriksson), an attender at 15th Street Meeting, was responsible for the formation of the yearly meeting's Task Force on Family Trauma. Gradually, she had come to realize that the problems she was having in her marriage were directly related to the trauma she had experienced as a victim of incest in childhood. With the help of Elders Larry Floyd and Arthur Waring and of Eloise Kayton a peer group for survivors of incest was formed in 1983 at 15th Street, an early effort to bring male and female survivors together to address the issue and liberate themselves from their previously hidden shame and anger. Erik Eriksson attended the first meeting. After he and Anne-Marie were married a second group was begun at Westbury, and in 1984 the yearly meeting Task Group on Incest Prevention was accepted under the care of the Nurture Coordinating Committee, later called the Task Group on Family Trauma. Its goal has been to provide information and insight to help Friends deal with problems of sexual abuse of the children in their meetings. Similar programs are now active in many other yearly and monthly meetings across America.

Blacks in New York Yearly Meeting

Quakers were among the leaders in the abolition of slavery and remain strong advocates of equal rights and good race relations, but in spite of Friends' record of goodwill, the number of African-American Friends is minuscule. In New York Yearly Meeting they comprise less than 1 percent, and many of these were members, before migrating to the United States, of meetings with pastors and planned orders of ser-

23. Barrington Dunbar (1901–1978), at New York Yearly Meeting, 1976.
Courtesy Haviland Records Room, New York Yearly Meeting.

vice. The basic tenet that worship is the experience of the individual
being in fellowship with God makes it possible for Friends of varying
orientations to worship and work together.

   Among the black Quakers active in New York Yearly Meeting was
Barrington Dunbar, whose biography[17] tells how from childhood he
learned the meaning of "experimental religion" and had a deep concern for the dignity of people long before he became a Quaker. Dunbar served the United Nations Relief and Rehabilitation Agency as a
welfare officer to displaced Poles and Estonians in Germany. He also
served Church World Service in France and was appointed in 1950 by
UNICEF as a representative to the government of Haiti. He later served
as director of the Newberry Avenue Center, a Chicago settlement house
for blacks of all ages. While in Chicago Barrington became a Quaker,

joining 57th Street Meeting. Later he was a trustee of Friends Seminary and a resident at Pendle Hill and Friends World College.

He followed keenly the developments in the civil rights movement in the 1960s. He was by then a member of 15th Street Meeting in New York. Stimulated by a May 1969 speech by James Forman, former leader of the Student Nonviolent Coordinating Committee, Dunbar during the yearly meeting session at Silver Bay that year challenged Friends to set up their own Black Development Fund to help meet the needs of disadvantaged black people. He recommended that Friends commit 1 percent of their annual income to this fund and estimated that fifty thousand dollars a year could be raised to advance this cause. Although the amount estimated was never raised, as a result of his urging, the yearly meeting's Black Development Fund Committee was established under the Sharing Fund by which allocations are made and a budget is administered. Many scholarships have been given to students at different educational levels and seed money provided for small business and innovative projects.

Barrington Dunbar's influence has remained strong in the yearly meeting. He is fondly remembered by many young people he led at Powell House. After his death in 1978 the Black Development Fund Committee incorporated his name as the Barrington Dunbar Fund for Black Development. Over the years many black Quakers have served on this committee.

Another African-American Friend of cherished memory was Hessye Castlen of Albany Meeting. She served on the yearly meeting Nominating Committee and became clerk of the Race Relations Committee after its name was changed in 1980 to Friends Committee for Black Concerns.[18] Hessye Castlen was active in the monthly meeting and the Albany community as well. She was the cofounder of the Thacher Home Day Care Center where disadvantaged parents found a place to leave their children while they went to work. She came to Friends when well up in years and of frail but stately frame. She would rise early to take the bus from Albany to New York City or any place where she attended a meeting. She was an eloquent spokesperson and gave her life unstintingly. When she died in 1988 her memorial service filled the large St. John's Church of God in downtown Albany.

Winifred Jacobs Rashford was a Quaker from Jamaica, West Indies, where her father was for many years pastor of the Port Antonio Meeting. On coming to New York Winifred became a member of 15th Street Meeting and was active both on the monthly meeting and yearly meeting levels. She had a special concern for New York area Friends accustomed to pastoral meetings. In 1976, 15th Street Meeting approved her request for a programmed service on first Sundays each month at 9:30 a.m. Rashford relocated to Charleston, South Carolina, and started Charleston Meeting of which her son became clerk. She died in 1992.

James Fletcher was a member of Poughkeepsie and then of Chappaqua Meeting. He had a particular interest in South African apartheid. He returned from a visit with zeal for raising funds for the building of the meeting house in Soweto and collecting books for its library. His interest in African-American history led him to research the life of Paul Cuffee, the New England black Quaker sea captain and wealthy merchant.[19] Fletcher worked for IBM, and later accepted a position as vice-president for fiscal affairs of Howard University.

The Fellowship of Friends of African Descent was born of the need of black Friends to get together. It was the feeling that there are not many black Quakers in the United States, so the idea was circulated that it would be good for them to meet and know each other. The first gathering was at Pendle Hill in August 1990. A second gathering was held at Howard University in August 1992. The fellowship is incorporated and has a Continuing Committee that manages its affairs. The clerk in 1993 was Stephen Braunginn, and the Recording Clerk Philip M. Lord. New York Yearly Meeting members and liaisons on the Continuing Committee are Noel Palmer, Helen Toppins, and Daisy Westra. The black Quakers in New York Yearly Meeting, although few in number, are active and effective in their undertakings. They are generally professionals in given fields and have come to Quakerism by convincement or have been nurtured in that quality of life that reflects "that of God."

Prison Worship Groups

Auburn Prison Friends Meeting was the first Quaker meeting held in a New York State prison. Begun as a worship group in 1974, it soon became the only known prison Preparative Meeting. As its members were transferred to other New York prisons, they have organized new Quaker worship groups in Attica, Green Haven, Wallkill, Taconic, Eastern, and Sing Sing.

In the aftermath of the Attica uprising of 1971 the brutal role of the state in suppressing it aroused a widespread citizens' movement to reform the prison system morally and politically, backed by church and community organizations, working with and informed by inmates' organizations. The New York Yearly Meeting Prisons Committee was a member of a grass-roots lobbying coalition for legislative prison reform. High-ranking state prison officials, fearing further disturbances, themselves asked the coalition to lobby for a Temporary Release Bill by which prisoners nearing parole could share in work, education, community services, and religious events. The bill passed in May 1974, and Friends General Conference, meeting in Ithaca in June, applied under it for two eligible inmates to attend. The prison bureaucracy, who had not yet written regulations to restrict the law for their own purposes, refused. Under pressure, they classified FGC as a religious organization and said any appropriate Quakers in the prison system could attend. There were none; but the Wider Quaker Fellowship, a membership organization for people in sympathy with Quakerism but unable to join because of isolation or other religious ties, "as in the case of prisoners," provided a hurdle over the obstacle. The president of the Auburn inmates' Jaycee chapter passed on the news. Another inmate asked Janet Lugo and Syracuse Friends to start a Quaker worship group. Friends were not accused of proselytizing because inmates kept their former church memberships. The Auburn Prison Friends Meeting met that fall in the prison's Osborne School, named for a non-Quaker warden, a son-in-law of Lucretia Mott. Both had visited the prison, he incognito.

Two of the early prison worship groups, those at Auburn and Green Haven, continue with support from Friends and meetings on the outside. Groups also continue at Sing Sing and Eastern, and Avenel in New Jersey. In 1993 a group began at the Sullivan Correctional Facility.

For those inside prison the worship group is an oasis of quiet, of relaxation of tension, of friendship and community, and of connection with the world outside prison walls. It is also a place where many learn to relate to people more positively, more trustingly, with more self-esteem. Some find opportunity to develop leadership skills in themselves. Friends who come in from outside find the experience enriching. To be with people who are trying to change their lives for the better challenges the visitors to be better. To be asked about Quakerism and about one's own beliefs and experience of God forces one to try to put into words one's deepest self. To share spiritual experience and to build fellowship among people of diverse cultural and racial backgrounds offers great opportunities for learning and growth for everyone involved.

Prison worship groups act as much like monthly meetings as they can, choosing clerks and committees as needed. They hold day-long seminars, usually annually, with worship, fellowship, speakers, and discussion. They have developed programs for the wider prison population: family relationship classes, victim-offender mediation, even job training. The sense of connection with Friends outside is sustaining and affirming to many inmates. Few have kept close to Friends upon release, however, and Friends have offered very little to help people being released.

New York Yearly Meeting: A Concluding Reflection

Since 1948 the idea of the yearly meeting has centered for many Friends on what is visible at Silver Bay: miles of clear water, steep mountains thick with trees and wildlife, familiar friends and new ones on the inn porch, committee meetings, worship-sharing groups, and worship and business in the auditorium. Others remember Representative Meetings at 15th Street and Brooklyn, on Long Island, in New Jersey, up the Hudson, and in central and western New York. These are the pictures in the memories of Friends active in the affairs of the yearly meeting. The common undertaking of both the "Yearly Meeting Friends" and of the two-thirds of Friends who have never been to Silver Bay is attention to God in solitude and in knots of connection or communities. Friends create places for seeking and finding together in many locations: at Silver Bay, in Quaker Studies classes, on committees, at Powell House weekends, but most fundamentally in monthly meetings.

It is difficult to characterize what is happening in seventy monthly meetings or where they are going. Themes recur: change as growth; and struggle leading to strength. Demographic changes are reported by many local meetings. Some which had no children for a period now have growing First-day Schools. All meetings are affected by the aging of the United States population, and many have lost active older members who have moved to retirement communities in other states. Children's programs matter to Friends. They often go through cycles, reported as either richly rewarding or as a matter of concern about lack of children, lack of adult willingness to participate, or challenges about content. A number of meetings have recently reported new success with First-day Schools. Youth programs at Powell House and Junior Yearly Meeting at Silver Bay continue stable and inspiring.

Changes in numbers that seem threatening are difficult to interpret. Overall membership continues to decline slowly, but attendance at Silver Bay remains constant or increases. In some meetings attendance at business meeting and occasions for corporate worship have substantially increased; some others have shrunk to a handful of elderly worshippers. Several prison groups have become stable worshipping communities since 1974.

In the 1990s change challenges Friends not so much through numbers as through questions about belonging and community commitment at both the monthly and yearly meeting levels. In the 1950s and 1960s Quaker history records actions mingled with practices of reflection and mutual exchange in PSAP, Powell House, and Quaker Dialogues. In the 1970s and 1980s action continued, nourishing to individuals but less visible in monthly meetings or on the floor of the yearly meeting sessions. Friends seem to have turned attention to questions of self-definition. Members challenge each other with demands about identity: Do all Friends not believe the same things? Are Friends not willing to trust each other? Can Friends not be faithful to their Quaker heritage? Why are Friends not all present and engaged for witness activities and for religious education? Are Friends not open to continuing revelation of truth? Are Friends not committed to the truth they have recognized and honored for generations?

In response to the question, "Is the Society of Friends a community of belief or practice or action?" one wise Friend answered "Yes." New York Yearly Meeting Friends may be functionally divided between those determined to *settle* the question of identity in favor of belief or practice or action, and those devoted to religious community as mutual ministry.[20] In yearly meeting Friends find communities in which they are sustained and challenged in paying attention to God. The spiritual strength of their knots of connection can be seen as these hold the spaces around and between them open and available. They are linked by belief, action, practice, perhaps by history, and ultimately also by difference.

Experiences of difference teach Friends, but they are not docile or even willing learners. Nevertheless, when one finds meetings for worship deepening, when one sees vital new Friends drawn into Quaker communities, when those whom one perceives as different work together fruitfully, one comes to know experimentally that faithful struggle with differences may strengthen the religious community. For Friends now God is troubling the water.

Appendix
Notes
Glossary
Selected Quaker Sources
Bibliography
Index

Appendix
Yearly Meeting Clerks

New York Yearly Meeting

Men's Meeting

Edward Burling	1763–1774	George Bowne	1793–1797
George Bowne	1775	Richard Mott	1798
Oliver Hull	1776	John Murray, Jr.	1799–1800
William Rickman	1777	Richard Mott	1801–1803
Oliver Hull	1778–1779	John Murray, Jr.	1804–1806
Silas Downing	1780–1783	Richard Mott	1807
Edmund Prior	1784–1786	John Barrow	1808
George Bowne	1787–1789	Richard Mott	1809–1816
James Mott	1790–1792	Samuel Parsons	1817–1828

Women's Meeting

Margaret Dobson	1775	Anne Mott	1803
Eleanor Moode	1776	Anna Merritt	1804
Anne Willis	1777	Anne Mott	1805–1807
Hannah Haydock	1778–1788	Anna Merritt	1808
Anne Willis	1789–1792	Anne Mott	1809–1813
Hannah Pearsall	1793–1795	Anna Merritt Thorne	1814
Amy Bowne	1796	Anne Mott	1815–1817
Hannah Cornell	1797	Abigail Evernghim	1818–1821
Phebe Downing	1798–1799	Abigail E. Thurston	1822–1823
Elizabeth Bowne	1800	Anna M. Willis	1824
Phebe Downing	1801–1802	Abigail E. Thurston	1825–1828

New York Yearly Meeting (Orthodox)

Men's Meeting

Samuel Parsons	1828–1841	William Wood	1869–1870
Richard Mott	1842–1850	Robert L. Murray	1871–1874
Richard Carpenter	1851–1856	Augustus Taber	1875–1881
William Wood	1857–1867	James Wood	1882
Stephen Wood	1868	Augustus Taber	1883–1884

Women's Meeting

Anne Mott	1828–1831	Maria Willets	1861–1873
Anna W. Willis	1832	Ruth C. Flagler	1874–1880
Sarah Waring	1833–1838	Caroline E. Ladd	1881–1885
Elizabeth U. Willis	1839–1860		

Joint Meeting

Augustus Taber	1885–1890	David F. Lane	1932–1936
Charles H. Jones	1891	George H. Wood	1937–1942
James Wood	1892	Ruth E. Craig	1943–1947
Charles H. Jones	1893	George A. Badgley	1948–1950
James Wood	1894–1895	Alfred J. Henderson	1951
Charles H. Jones	1896	C. Frank Ortloff	1952
James Wood	1897–1925	Alfred J. Henderson	1953–1955
L. Hollingsworth Wood	1926–1931		

Secretaries

J. Lindley Spicer	1903–1910	Emmet Gulley	1925–1928
Richard R. Newby	1910–1912	Elizabeth L. Hazard	1928–1950
Albert G. Shepherd	1916–1922	George A. Badgley	1950–1955
Mary E. Pennington	1924–1925		

New York Yearly Meeting (Hicksite)

Men's Meeting

Stephen Mott	1828–1830	Nathaniel S. Merritt	1864–1871
Stephen Underhill	1831–1839	Charles A. Macy	1872–1874
Thomas Wright	1840–1846	Nathaniel S. Merritt	1875–1879
Samuel Willets	1847–1852	Robert S. Haviland	1880–1888
George T. Trimble	1853–1863	William H. Willets	1889–1903

Women's Meeting

Mary Bristol	1828–1829	Hannah M. Frost	1852–1856
Ann M. Comstock	1830–1842	Rachel Hicks	1857–1866
Abigail M. Thurston	1843–1844	Mary Jane Field	1867–1882
Mary U. Hicks	1845	Amanda K. Miller	1883–1888
Abigail M. Thurston	1846–1849	Jane W. Carpenter	1889–1893
Deborah M. Field	1850–1851	Emily P. Yeo	1894–1903

Joint Meeting

William H. Willets	1904–1908	George B. Corwin	1943–1944
James S. Haviland	1909–1914		(Acting)
Ellwood Burdsall	1915–1929	George B. Corwin	1945
Josephine Tilton	1927 (Acting)	Howard E. Kershner	1946–1949
		Horace R. Stubbs	1950
Edward Cornell	1930–1937	Howard E. Kershner	1951
J. Franklin Brown	1938–1939	Henry A. Wheeler	1952
Stephen Holden	1940	Horace R. Stubbs	1953–1955
J. Hibbard Taylor	1941–1944		

Secretaries

J. Elliott Janney	1928–1931	Gladys S. Seaman	1944–1955
Elizabeth M. Lantz	1931–1943		

New York Yearly Meeting (United)

Clerks

Horace R. Stubbs	1956	Miriam K. Brush	1970–1974
Paul C. Schwantes	1957–1961	Katherine A. Nicklin	1975–1977
George B. Corwin	1962–1965	Henry A. Wheeler	1978–1981
Delbert E. Replogle	1966	Willard Gaeddert	1982–1984
Francis B. Compter	1967–1968	Mary Foster Cadbury	1985–1990
Paul H. Myers	1969	George Rubin	1991–1993

General Secretaries

Gladys S. Seaman	1955–1960	Viola E. Purvis	1968–1976
Rachel K. Wood	1961–1967	Joseph A. Vlaskamp	1977–

Field Secretaries

George A. Badgley	1955–1969	Daniel P. Whitley	1978–1982
James Toothaker	1970–1977	Janice M. Greene	1982–

Genesee Yearly Meeting

Men's Meeting

Joseph Jones	1834–1835	Jonathan D. Noxon	1892–1893
Thomas J. Alsop	1836–1838	Samuel P. Zavitz	1894
Thomas M'Clintock	1839–1843	Jonathan D. Noxon	1895–1898
Sunderland P. Gardner	1844–1846	Samuel P. Zavitz	1899–1904
Caleb Carmalt	1847–1859	Jonathan D. Noxon	1905–1906
John Searing	1860	Samuel P. Zavitz	1907–1910
John J. Cornell	1861–1874	Jonathan D. Noxon	1911
Jonathan D. Noxon	1875–1883	Samuel P. Zavitz	1912
John J. Cornell	1884	Charles A. Zavitz	1913–1921
Jonathan D. Noxon	1885–1890	C. Harold Zavitz	1922–1928
John J. Cornell	1891		

Women's Meeting

Mary B. Durfee	1834–1836	Jane R. Searing	1872–1874
Margaret Brown	1837	Phebe Jane Noxon	1875–1882
Anna R. Brown	1838	Mary T. Freeman	1883–1887
Rhoda DeGarmo	1839–1843	Rebecca Wilson	1888–1889
Mary A. White	1844–1845	Rebecca Zavitz	1890–1893
Hannah Loines	1846	Serena Minard	1894
Mary A. White	1847–1848	Phebe Jane Noxon	1895
Sarah Carmalt	1849–1859	Agnes Haight	1899
Catharine E. Bosworth	1860	Rebecca Zavitz	1900
Anna R. Brown	1861	Ida Haight Zavitz	1901
Jane R. Searing	1862–1867	Charlotte C. Talcott	1902–1910
Phebe W. Cornell	1868–1871	Rebecca Zavitz	1911

Notes

1. Quaker Beginnings in England and New York

1. George Fox, *The Journal of George Fox*, ed. John L. Nickalls (Philadelphia: Religious Society of Friends, 1985), 1–14, 18, 27.

2. The name Friends, based on Jesus' words to his disciples in John 15:15, was already used in some Separatist groups in Nottinghamshire (cf. Fox, *Journal*, 709).

3. Perry Miller, *Errand into the Wilderness* (Cambridge, Mass.: Harvard Univ. Press, 1956), chap. 1.

4. Margaret Fell was one of the early converts to Quakerism. She later married George Fox.

5. Robert Barclay, *An Apology for the True Christian Divinity* (London: s.n., 1678), 254–57.

6. Richard Bauman, *Let Your Words Be Few: The Symbolism of Speaking and Silence among Seventeenth-Century Quakers* (New York: Cambridge Univ. Press, 1983). Howard Brinton describes leadings to speak in meetings for worship and calls to wider ministries as distinct stages in a typical Quaker's maturing, in his study of one hundred Quaker journals. See Howard Brinton, *Children of Light* (New York: Macmillan, 1938), 383–406.

7. Frederick B. Tolles, *Meeting House and Counting House* (Chapel Hill: Univ. of North Carolina Press, 1948), chap. 3, describes the Quaker business ethic as a combination of the Anabaptist ethical position with the Calvinist attitude toward the material world.

8. For initial Quaker activities in New Netherland see George L. Smith, *Religion and Trade in New Netherland: Dutch Origins and American Development* (Ithaca, N.Y.: Cornell Univ. Press, 1973), in which he discusses the Company's efforts to turn a profit and to tolerate dissenters for business reasons. For the balance of Quaker inroads see Arthur J. Worrall, *Quakers in the Colonial Northeast* (Hanover, N.H.: Univ. Press of New England, 1980), 20–24.

9. E. B. O'Callaghan, ed., *Documents Relative to the Colonial History of New York* (Albany, N.Y.: Weed, Parsons, 1853–87), 1:554.

10. Jessica Kross, *The Evolution of an American Town: Newtown, New York 1642–1775* (Philadelphia: Temple Univ. Press, 1983), 114–15; Worrall, *Colonial Northeast*, 64–67.

11. As viewed by late seventeenth- and early eighteenth-century New York Friends, ranters were one-time Friends who, like the Cases, refused to come under the control of Quaker business meetings and frequently behaved in a manner scandalous to the local community. Worrall, *Colonial Northeast*, 66.

12. Christopher Densmore, "The Samuel Bownas Case: Religious Toleration and the Independence of Juries in Colonial New York," *Long Island Historical Journal* 2 (1990): 177–88; Worrall, *Colonial Northeast*, 55–56.

13. Worrall, *Colonial Northeast*, 57.

2. Building Traditions and Testimonies

1. See Frederick B. Tolles, *Quakers and the Atlantic Culture* (New York: Macmillan, 1960). For variation in the English reaction, however, see Worrall, *Colonial Northeast,* chaps. 4, 5.

2. Europeans still usually ask permission before using these forms to friends. But American Quakers who said "thee is right" or "is thee going" were preserving a north-of-England regional dialect learned from the Danes and Vikings who taught all England to say "he goes" instead of "he goeth." See Hugh Barbour, *Quakers in Puritan England* (New Haven, Conn.: Yale Univ. Press, 164–65).

3. George Fox, *The Line of Righteousness and Justice stretched fourth* (London: Robert Wilson, 1661), 3, 4.

4. For differing views see Barry Reay, *Quakers and the English Revolution* (New York: St. Martins Press, 1985), chap. 6, and Peter Brock, *Quaker Peace Testimony, 1660 to 1914* (York, England: Sessions Book Trust, 1990), chap. 3. Brock and Reay overlook the dynamic thrust of early Quaker nonviolence.

5. J. William Frost, *The Quaker Family in Colonial America* (New York: St. Martins Press, 1973); Barry Levy, *Quakers and the American Family* (New York: Oxford Univ. Press, 1988); J. William Frost, ed., *Quaker Origins of Anti-Slavery* (Norwood, Pa: Norwood Editions, 1980).

6. William Penn, *No Cross, No Crown* (London: s.n., 1669), 61.

7. Amelia Mott Gummere, *The Quaker, A Study in Costume* (Philadelphia: Ferris and Leach, 1901), chap. 1.

8. William Penn, *A Defense of the Duke of Buckingham, Against the answer to his Book* (London: Printed for W.C., 1685), 4.

9. Gummere, *Costume,* chaps. 4, 5.

10. Worrall, *Colonial Northeast,* chap. 7.

11. Ibid., chap. 8.

12. For this section see ibid., chaps. 4, 5.

13. New England Yearly Meeting, 1695 (Rhode Island Historical Society).

14. Samuel Fothergill to Israel Pemberton, Flushing, 26/V/1755 in George Crosfield, ed., *Memoirs of the Life and Gospel Labours of Samuel Fothergill. . . .* (Liverpool: D. Marples, 1843), 187.

3. New York Quaker Settlements and Immigrants

1. Rufus M. Jones, ed., *Journal of George Fox* (New York: Capricorn Books, 1963), 511–12; Purchase Monthly Meeting, Apr. 9, 1725; Flushing Quarterly Meeting, Mar. 20, 1684; Flushing Monthly Meeting, Apr. 28, 1684.

2. Worrall, *Colonial Northeast,* 109.

3. Purchase Quarterly Meeting, June 3, 1745. Reflecting the continued growth of numbers was the setting up of preparative meetings at Oswego (1758), Poughquaig (1771), the Creek (1776), New Milford, Connecticut (1777), Branch (1783), Valley (1785), Crum Elbow (1797), and on the west side of the Hudson at Cornwall (1777), Marlborough (before 1782), and Newburgh Valley (1799).

4. Rufus Hall, *Journal of . . . Rufus Hall* (Byberry, Pa.: John and Isaac Comly, 1840), 16–17.

5. Hiram Rawson Whitney in Abby Maria Hemenway, ed., *Vermont Historical Gazetteer* (Burlington, Vt.: Hemenway, 1867–92), 2:370.

6. Although family limitation may have already started among urban Friends, rural Friends do not appear to have joined the practice.

7. "Timothy Rogers His Journal" (manuscript at Pickering College, Newmarket, Ontario), 1–9, 13–14. Rogers's dates are from memory. He recalled the Vergennes Falls deal as in 1787, but a history of Vergennes, apparently based on land records, describes Bowne buying and Rogers transferring to Jacob Fitch as of 1789. H. P. Smith, ed., *History of Addison County* (Syracuse, N.Y.: D. Mason, 1886), 653.

8. William Savery, "Journal," *Friends Library* 1 (1837): 350, 354; Alexander Stewart, "The Sesquicentennial of Farmington, New York, 1789–1939," *Bulletin of the Friends Historical Association* 23 (1940): 37–43; John Cox, Jr., *New York Church Archives: Religious Society of Friends* (New York: WPA, 1940), 156, 179–81. Monthly meetings established in this area were Farmington (1803), Scipio (1808), DeRuyter (1809), East Hamburg (1814), Junius (1815), Collins (1820), Hector (1820), Hartland (1821), and Rochester (1825). New quarterly meetings were Farmington (1810) and Scipio (1825).

9. Norwegian sailors had established two Quaker meetings between 1814 and 1816. They became convinced Friends after contact with English Friends imprisoned during the Napoleonic Wars. Suffering persecution from the established church, they decided to move to North America in 1824 and had help from New York City Friends in settling in Kendall. Rasmus B. Anderson, *The First Chapter of Norwegian Emigration* (Madison, Wis.: R. B. Anderson, 1906), 45–131; John Cox, Jr., "Quakers in Rochester and Monroe County," *Rochester Historical Society Publication Fund Series*, no. 14 (1936): 100–103; "A Brief Account of the Rise of Friends in Norway," *Friends Miscellany* 8(1836): 11–18.

10. Monthly meetings in central New York were Duanesburg (1806) and Laurens (1810); new meetings to the north and west were LeRay (1815) and Lowville (1819).

11. Elias Hicks, *The Journal of the Life and Religious Labours of Elias Hicks*, 5th ed. (New York: Isaac T. Hopper, 1832), 120.

12. Data are derived from Loren Fay, "Arrivals of Friends in Scipio Monthly Meeting," *Yesteryears* 22 (1978): 28–33.

13. Hicks, *Journal*, 129.

14. Arthur G. Dorland, *The Quakers in Canada: A History* (Toronto: Ryerson Press, 1968), chaps. 3–11 provided source material for this chapter. For a brief discussion on Friends in Lower Canada see the section on the Upper Hudson and Champlain valleys.

15. The schism of the Children of Light in 1812 led to the departure of some members. For discussion of this episode see the next section of this chapter.

16. For a basic account of the rise of Shakers see Edward Denning Andrews, *People Called Shakers* (New York: Oxford Univ. Press, 1953); 3–39.

17. Joshua Evans, "Joshua Evans's Journal," *Friends Miscellany* 10 (1837): 94–97.

18. Herbert A. Wisby, Jr., *Pioneer Prophetess* (Ithaca, N.Y.: Cornell Univ. Press, 1963).

19. The quotation is from David Hudson, *History of Jemima Wilkinson* (Geneva, N.Y.: S. P. Hull, 1821), 103; see also Charles Lowell Marlin, "Jemima Wilkinson: Errant Quaker Divine," *Quaker History* 52 (1963): 90–94; and Edwin B. Bronner, "Quakers Labor with Jemima Wilkinson—1794," *Quaker History* 58 (1969): 41–47.

20. Dorland, *Quakers in Canada*.

21. Ibid., 104–11; Albert Schrauwers, *Awaiting the Millennium: The Children of Peace and the Village of Hope, 1812–1889* (Toronto: Univ. of Toronto Press, 1993); and Albert Schrauwers, "The Separation of the Children of Peace," *Quaker History* 79 (1990): 1–19.

22. George Fox, *George Fox: An Autobiography* (Philadelphia: Ferris and Leach, 1904), 22, 76, 93.

23. For a description of meeting house architecture, with several examples drawn from New York, see David M. Butler, "Quaker Meeting House Architecture in America and England: Impressions and Comparisons," *Quaker History* 79 (1990): 93–104. The Historic American Buildings Survey drawings reproduced in *Historic American Buildings, New York* (New York: Oxford Univ. Press, 1979), 6: 332–38, 364–68, 382–91; 7: 220–30, document New York Quaker meeting houses.

4. Wars, Revolutions, and the Peace Testimony

1. Fox, *Journal*, 400.

2. See Alan Cole, "The Quakers and the English Revolution," *Past and Present* 10 (1956): 39–54; Christopher Hill, "George Fox and the English Revolution" (Paper for the George Fox Commemorative Conference, Univ. of Lancaster, March 25, 1991, based on Hill's earlier works, such as *The World Turned Upside Down* [1975]); also Reay, *Quakers and the English Revolution*, and Brock, *Quaker Peace Testimony*.

3. Fox, *Journal*, 402; from 2 Cor. 1:4.

4. For James Naylor's "Lamb's War" and his "dying words" see Hugh Barbour and Arthur O. Roberts, *Early Quaker Writings, 1650–1700* (Grand Rapids, Mich.: William B. Eerdmans, 1973), 102–115. Where Friends defended their Testimonies by legal strictness in obeying the Bible text, as with oaths and titles, they were basically concerned with continuing an ethical stand that had seemed self-evident to the Baptists and other radical Puritans. On violence they reached a new Testimony by a more inward and inclusive logic.

5. Robert Barclay even allows arms to Christians who have not reached the full "measure" of Light given to Quakers (*Apology*, Prop. 15, sec. 13–15).

6. Worrall, *Colonial Northeast*, chap. 8; Brock, *Quaker Peace Testimony*, chaps. 4, 5.

7. See Randall Balmer, *A Perfect Babel of Confusion: Dutch Religion and English Culture in the Middle Colonies* (New York: Oxford Univ. Press, 1989), 31–37.

8. Material for this section is from Worrall, *Colonial Northeast*, 134–35, and from Brock, *Quaker Peace Testimony*, chap. 3.

9. A wider presentation of this material is Arthur J. Mekeel, *The Relation of the Quakers to the American Revolution* (Washington, D.C.: Univ. Press of America, 1979).

10. Ibid., 149.

11. Ibid., 245.

12. Ibid., 247.

13. Ibid., 246.

14. Ibid., 149.

15. Ibid., 249.

16. Ibid., 249–50.

17. Ibid., 251.

18. Ibid., 250.

19. Hall, *Journal*, 16–17.

20. Mekeel, *Relation of the Quakers to the American Revolution*, 248.

21. Ibid., 318.

22. Few New York Friends had done so. An exception was William Morris, a Friend on the New York Council in 1686. See Worrall, *Colonial Northeast*, 134.

23. Mekeel, *Relation of the Quakers to the American Revolution*, 315.

24. Ibid., 316.

25. Ibid., 316.

26. Alson Van Wagner, "Dutchess County Quakers Maintain Their Testimony Against Military Participation," in *Dutchess County Historical Society Yearbook* 70 (Poughkeepsie: Dutchess County Historical Society, 1985), 50–52.

27. William C. Kashatus, *Conflict of Conviction: A Reappraisal of Quaker Involvement in the American Revolution* (Lanham, Md.: Univ. Press of America, 1990), chap. 1.

28. See Mark Philp, *Paine* (New York: Oxford Univ. Press, 1989); Thomas Paine, *Political Writings,* ed. Bruce Kuklick (New York: Cambridge Univ. Press, 1989).

29. This also explains the unwillingness of Thetford to put up a memorial to Paine offered by Americans in our own time.

30. See Rufus Jones, *Later Periods of Quakerism* (New York: Macmillan, 1921), 1:161–64.

31. Page Smith, *The Shaping of America* (New York: Penguin, 1989), 3: chap. 31.

32. See Samuel Knapp, *Life of Thomas Eddy* (New York: Conner and Cooke, 1834), 155, and works on the Erie Canal. Brock, in *Quaker Peace Testimony,* 156–58, shows that after one failed effort in 1789 by James Madison to insert into the Constitution a clause exempting conscientious objectors, issues of military training and taxes were left to the individual states.

33. See *Friends Library* 4 (1840), 303. As a boy, Hull three times had to escape northward through Westchester County as the British army pressed forward against Washington's army in 1776.

34. Talcutt Patching, *A Religious Convincement and Plea for the Baptism and Communion of the Spirit* (Buffalo, N.Y.: H. A. Salisbury, 1822); I. D. Steward, *History of the Freewill Baptists* (Dover, [N.H.]: Freewill Baptist Print, 1862).

35. Hoag, 201–202.

36. John Mott, *Lawfulness of War for Christians Examined* (New York: Samuel Wood, 1814), 21.

37. Adna Heaton, *War and Christianity Contrasted* (New York: Samuel Wood and Sons, 1816), 21, 57. See also John I. Wells, *An Essay on War* (Hartford, Conn.: Hudson and Goodwin, 1808; New York: Samuel Wood, 1812). The expanded 1812 edition of Wells was approved by the Meeting for Sufferings of New York Yearly Meeting.

38. Brock, *Quaker Peace Testimony,* 157–58.

39. See Peter Brock, *Freedom from War: Nonsectarian Pacifism, 1814–1914* (Toronto: Univ. of Toronto Press, 1991), 37, 66–72, 80–85, 341 (n. 22); idem, "The Peace Testimony in A Garden Enclosed," *Quaker History* 54 (1965): 67–80.

40. Dorland, *Quakers in Canada,* 319–23; Brock, *Quaker Peace Testimony,* chap. 17.

5. Slavery and Abolition to 1830

1. Elias Hicks, *A Series of Extemporaneous Discourses* (Philadelphia: Parker, 1825), 61.

2. Mary S. Wood, *Social Hours with Friends* (New York: William Wood, 1867), 271–75.

3. Manumission records, Nine Partners Monthly Meeting and Westbury Monthly Meeting, in the Haviland Records Room, New York Yearly Meeting.

4. John Cox, Jr., *Quakerism in the City of New York, 1657–1930* (New York: Privately printed, 1930), 61–64.

5. John B. Shiel, "175 Years in One Book," *Long Island Forum* 33 (Mar. 1970): 45–50.

6. Lynda Day, "Friends in the Spirit: Blacks and Quakers on Long Island, 1789–1865" (Paper for the Conference on New York State History, Colgate Univ., June 1987).

7. Edythe Ann Quinn, "The Hills in the Mid-Nineteenth Century: The History of a Rural Afro-American Community in Westchester County, New York," *Afro-Americans in New York History and Life* 14 (July 1990): 35–50.

8. Edgar J. McManus, *History of Negro Slavery in New York* (Syracuse, N.Y.: Syracuse Univ. Press, 1966), 150–78.

9. Microfilm of the Records of the New York Manumission Society (NYMS) from the New York Historical Society; Thomas Robert Moseley, "History of the New York Manumission Society, 1785–1849" (Ph.D. diss., New York University, 1963).

10. NYMS Minute Book, 1806, New York Historical Society.

11. NYMS Membership, HRR, New York Yearly Meeting; Raymond A. Mohl, *Poverty in New York, 1783–1825* (New York: Oxford Univ. Press, 1971), 176.

12. Knapp, *Life of Thomas Eddy*, 20–21.

13. Ibid., 20.

14. Timothy Rogers Journal, Canada Yearly Meeting Archives, Pickering College, Newmarket, Ontario. Thomas E. Drake, *Quakers and Slavery in America* (New Haven, Conn.: Yale Univ. Press, 1950), 119, and Dorland, *Quakers in Canada*, 294, interpret the story differently.

15. Hildegard F. Graf, "Abolition and Anti-Slavery in Erie County" (Master's thesis, Univ. of Buffalo, 1939), 76, 80.

16. Letter from Jonathan Pierce to Wilmer Kearns, 1938, in the Haviland Records Room.

17. Lydia Maria Child, *Isaac T. Hopper: A True Life* (Boston: Jewett, 1853), 457.

18. "Letter from C. E. Putnam," *Liberator* (Jan. 16, 1857).

19. Jean R. Soderlund, *Quakers and Slavery: A Divided Spirit* (Princeton, N.J.: Princeton Univ. Press, 1985), developing an idea by J. William Frost.

20. H. Larry Ingle, *Quakers in Conflict: The Hicksite Reformation* (Knoxville: Univ. of Tennessee Press, 1986), 6; Thomas E. Drake, *Quakers and Slavery in America* (New Haven, Conn.: Yale Univ. Press, 1940), 117; Hugh Barbour, ed., *Slavery and Theology: Writings of Seven Quaker Reformers, 1800–1870* (Dublin, Ind.: Prinit Press, 1985).

21. Drake, *Quakers and Slavery*, 89, 95–99, 102–12. Elias Hicks was among those drafting the 1786 petition. Yet Drake thought (89) that "conservatism marked the New York Friends, as it did New Yorkers in general."

22. Barbour, *Slavery and Theology*, 10–16.

23. Elias Hicks, *A Series of Extemporaneous Discourses* (Philadelphia: Parker, 1825), 79, 81.

24. Drake, *Quakers and Slavery*, 118.

25. *New York State Assembly Journal* (1824): 741.

6. City Philanthropists and Social Concerns, 1787–1857

1. Cox, *Quakerism*, 120.

2. Ibid., 73–74, based on *Documentary History of the State of New York* (Albany, N.Y.: Weed, Parsons, 1849–51) 3:623. On the Murrays, see especially Stephen Allott, *Lindley Murray, 1745–1826: Quaker Grammarian of New York and Old York* (York, England: Sessions, 1991), 35.

3. Figures from Edward Countryman, *A People in Revolution: The American Revolution and Political Society in New York, 1760–1790* (Baltimore, Md.: Johns Hopkins Univ. Press, 1981), 24, 109. Mohl, *Poverty in New York*, 6; Richard F. Hixson, *Isaac Collins: A Quaker Printer in 18th Century America* (New Brunswick, N.J.: Rutgers Univ. Press, 1968), 161;

Stephen Longstreet, *City on Two Rivers: Profiles of New York* (New York: Hawthorn Books, 1973); William L. Stone, *History of New York City from the Discovery to the Present Day* (New York: Virtur and Yorston, 1872). Annually reported deaths in a table published by City Inspector Thomas K. Downing grew from 2,125 in 1804 to 2,507 in 1814 to 3,542 in 1822 (yellow fever) and 4,341 in 1824 (a smallpox epidemic) to 10,359 and 9,082 in 1832 and 1834 (cholera years), and to 8,875 in 1844 and 22,702 in 1854.

4. The *Encyclopedia of New York Biography and Genealogy,* published as volume 3 of Daniel Van Pelt, *Leslie's History of Greater New York* (New York: Arkell Publishing, 1898), only remembered one Quaker, Valentine Mott, in its list of one thousand names. James Grant Wilson's *The Memorial History of the City of New York* (New York: New York History, 1895) in its biographical section named none.

5. It seems impossible to verify the legend that British General Lord Howe was distracted by a dinner party at the Murrays and did not notice the escape of Washington's forces.

6. Cox, *Quakerism,* 5. Thomas Eddy, *Memoir of the Late John Murray, Jun., Read Before the Governors of the New York Hospital* (New York: E. Conrad, 1819).

7. The others were Thomas Eddy, John Griscom, and Valentine Mott, succeeded by Thomas Cock, and later by Isaac Collins, Jr. See data in the archives of the American Bible Society. Unlike the largely financial board of the American Bible Society (ABS), its officers and staff were mostly clergy and included no Friends until 1911. The independent Philadelphia-based Bible Society of Friends in America probably diverted Quaker concerns although the ABS sent seventy-five Bibles each year to the New York Free School and used Quaker Isaac Collins's Bible editions. Credit for founding the bank was given to John Pintard, the pioneer staff member of the American Bible Society, by Mohl, *Poverty in New York.*

8. Robert A. Davison, *Isaac Hicks: New York Merchant and Quaker, 1767–1820* (Cambridge, Mass.: Harvard Univ. Press, 1964).

9. Bliss Forbush, *Elias Hicks, Quaker Liberal* (New York: Columbia Univ. Press, 1956), 130, called Isaac Hicks "the largest shipowner in the city. His *Solon* was the first vessel to carry the newly adopted American flag into the Black Sea; his *Sally Hicks* was known . . . as 'Queen of the Whaling Fleet,' " but the *Sally* was a trading schooner, and the whaler *Sarah* was only leased to Hicks.

10. Knapp, *Life of Thomas Eddy,* 43, 44, 45, 343.

11. Ibid., 52, 53, 54, 55.

12. Harry Elmer Barnes, *The Story of Punishment* (Boston: Stratford, 1930), 133.

13. Knapp, *Life of Thomas Eddy,* 59.

14. Ibid., 161.

15. Knapp, *Life of Thomas Eddy,* 117–23. *Report of the Commissioners Appointed by . . . the State of New York, . . . 1810, to Explore the Route of an Inland Navigation from Hudson's River to Lake Ontario and Lake Erie* (New York: Prior and Dunning, 1811); see also Nathan Miller, *The Enterprise of a Free People: Aspects of Economic Development in New York State During the Canal Period, 1792–1838* (Ithaca, N.Y.: Cornell Univ. Press, 1962), 23–43, 88–89; George E. Condon, *Stars in the Water: The Story of the Erie Canal* (Garden City, N.Y.: Doubleday, 1974), 14–28; Eddy drove as hard a bargain as the commissioners could with the land speculators.

16. Cadwallader Colden, quoted in Knapp, *Life of Thomas Eddy.* This material and much more can be found in Peter J. Wosh, "Bibles, Benevolence and Emerging Bureaucracy: The Persistence of the American Bible Society, 1816–1890" (Ph.D. diss., New York Univ., 1988), 63–78; see also *Dictionary of American Biography,* 3:15.

17. On the coherence of New York's elite during this period see M. J. Heale, "From City Fathers to Social Critics: Humanitarianism and Government in New York, 1790–1860," *Journal of American History* 63 (June 1976): 21–41; Thomas Bender, *New York Intellect: A History of Intellectual Life in New York City from 1750 To Beginnings of Our Own Time* (New York: Alfred A. Knopf, 1987), 46–88; and Mohl, *Poverty in New York*, 241–58.

18. Knapp, *Life of Thomas Eddy*, 29–30, 42–43, 57–58, 137–243. The *Daily Advertiser* obituary was reprinted on p. 260 of Knapp's biography. Concerning Eddy's efforts to introduce Lancasterian pedagogical techniques into the public schools see Carl Kaestle, *The Evolution of an Urban School System: New York City, 1750–1850* (Cambridge, Mass.: Harvard Univ. Press, 1973), 80–84. On solitary confinement see David J. Rothman, *The Discovery of the Asylum: Social Order and Disorder in the New Republic* (Boston: Little, Brown, 1971), 92–93, 96–101.

19. Knapp, *Life of Thomas Eddy*, 34–35; Edward Pessen, *Riches, Class and Power Before the Civil War* (Lexington, Ky.: D. C. Heath, 1973), 146, on family ties of antebellum urban elites.

20. Knapp, *Life of Thomas Eddy*, 8, 14–15, 40.

21. Miller, *Enterprise of a Free People*, especially xi–xii, 11–19; Sean Wilentz, *Chants Democratic: New York City and the Rise of the American Working Class, 1788–1850* (New York: Oxford Univ. Press, 1984), 87–97, uses the 1825 celebration of the canal's completion as a symbol of cultural unity.

22. Manuscript book of members / contributors at Haviland Records Room, New York Yearly Meeting.

23. Knapp, *Life of Thomas Eddy*, 59–75; 18–19, 78–92.

24. Mohl, *Poverty in New York*, chap. 8.

25. Knapp, *Life of Thomas Eddy*, 21.

26. Bloomingdale Hospital moved to White Plains about 1900. Knapp, *Life of Thomas Eddy*, 250; 12–13, 28–29. D. Hack Tuke, *The Insane in the United States and Canada* (London, 1885; reprint, New York: Arno Press, 1973), 143. The hospital at Utica, opened in 1843, was more inclusive. Daniel Rothman, *Discovery of the Asylum*, sees the early builders as obsessed with architecture. Compare communes like New Lanark and the Phalansteries. The best statement of the ideal was by Thomas Kirkbride of Philadelphia, *Remarks on the Construction, Organization and General Arrangements of Hospitals for the Insane* (Philadelphia: R. K. and P. G. Collins, 1847).

27. Robert S. Pickett, *House of Refuge: Origins of Juvenile Reform in New York State, 1815–1857* (Syracuse, N.Y.: Syracuse Univ. Press, 1969), 25. Tuke, *Insane*, 2. Of the five oldest asylums in the United States, McLean's in Boston and the Hartford Retreat also used Tuke principles.

28. Mohl, *Poverty in New York*, 114; cf. Rothman, *Discovery of the Asylum*, chap. 7; Pickett, *House of Refuge*, chap. 1.

29. Knapp, *Life of Thomas Eddy*, 178–81, 214–15, 230.

30. The Quaker printer Mahlon Day published both 1824 editions of this document, issued over the signature of Cadwallader Colden. He used the same arguments as in Thomas Eddy's 1823 presentation to the Pauperism Society plus case histories from New York police and from England and France, probably supplied by Eddy and Griscom, who (with Isaac Collins) were on the drafting committee. It was funded by a tax on immigrants and "sin-taxes" on theaters and taverns as sources of the children's corruption.

31. Pickett, *House of Refuge*, xvi.

32. Data summarized from Pickett, *House of Refuge*, chaps. 4–9, especially 6, 13, 110, 190.

33. Bayard Tuckerman, ed., *Diary of Philip Hone, 1821–1851* (New York: Dodd, Mead and Co., 1910), 64, quoted in Pickett, *House of Refuge*, 2.

34. See, for instance, Knapp, *Life of Thomas Eddy*, 163–70.

35. By 1850 there were only 2,000 Friends in a population of 630,000. Pickett, *House of Refuge*, 2, 112.

36. Edgar F. Smith, *John Griscom, 1774–1852, Chemist* (Philadelphia: s.n., 1925), 5. John H. Griscom [his doctor son] *Memoir of John Griscom, Ll.D.* (New York: Robert Carter, 1859) includes Griscom's journal.

37. David Hosack (1768–1835), not a Friend, studied at Princeton, taught medicine at Columbia, was elected to the Royal Society, and wrote the life of his friend DeWitt Clinton. He prompted Colonel Samuel Knapp to write the *Life of Thomas Eddy*.

38. Haverford's Quaker Collection includes letters from Griscom to Silliman and one from Eddy to Griscom in care of Allen, reporting on the pauperism society and the House of Refuge.

39. John Griscom, *A Year in Europe . . . in 1818 and 1819* (New York: Collins, 1823). Following Lavoisier, Friend John Dalton of Manchester worked with gases, J. J. Berzelius with oxides of metals to understand molecules. Barons George L. C. F. D. Cuvier and F. H. A. von Humboldt established the species and genera of many living animals.

40. Lecture at the New York Lyceum, Dec. 1, 1841, abridged in Griscom, *Memoir*, 269–79. He left his collection of three thousand rock specimens to his school.

41. Valentine Mott, *Travels in Europe and the East* (New York: Harper and Brother, 1942); see also *DAB*; Alfred C. Post, *Eulogy of the late Valentine Mott, M.D., Ll.D.* (New York: Bailliere, 1866), and S. D. Gross, M.D., *Memoir of Valentine Mott, M.D.* (New York: D. Appleton, 1868).

42. In 1830 Griscom was given a bottle of chloroform by Samuel Guthrie, who called it "a lively cordial" (Smith, *Griscom*, 13). Valentine Mott, *Pain and Anaesthetics* (Washington, D.C.: McGill and Witherow, 1863).

43. Cox, *Quakerism*, 152–53; notes by the American Bible Society.

44. See Christopher Densmore, "Quaker Publishing in New York State, 1784–1860," *Quaker History* 72 (1985): 39–57; and Harry R. Weiss, "Mahlon Day, Early New York Printer, Bookseller and Publisher of Children's Books," *Bulletin of the New York Public Library* 45 (1941): 1007–21.

45. Richard F. Hixson, *Isaac Collins*. This book contains lists of all the published imprints in each of these firms in the years Collins worked with them.

46. Pickett, *House of Refuge*, 42, 63–64, 99, must refer to Isaac, Jr.

47. Pickett, *House of Refuge*, 178–79.

48. See Christopher Densmore, "New York Quakers among the Brotherton, Stockbridge, Oneida, and Onondaga, 1795–1834," *Man in the Northeast* 44 (1992): 83–93; Rayner W. Kelsey, *Friends and the Indians, 1655–1917* (Philadelphia: Associated Executive Committee on Indian Affairs, 1917), 114–31. On overall policies see Robert F. Berkhofer, *Salvation and the Savage* (Lexington, Ky.: Univ. of Kentucky Press, 1965).

49. New York Yearly Meeting, Meeting for Sufferings Minutes, Mar. 12, 1793; on the Treaty of Canandaigua see the *Journal of William Savery*, e.g., in *Friends Library* 1: 349–68. New York Yearly Meeting, Meeting for Sufferings, Minutes, Dec. 8, 1795; *Friends Review* 5–6 (1852): 778ff.

50. See Society of Friends, Philadelphia Yearly Meeting, *Brief Account of the Proceedings of the Committee, Appointed in the Year 1795 . . . for the Improvement and Gradual Civilization of the Indian Natives* (Philadelphia: Kimber, Conrad, 1805); also the Records of the Indian Committee of Philadelphia Yearly Meeting at the Friends Historical Library, spe-

cifically the Minutes of Jan. 15, 1796 and Feb. 2, 1796, and Letters of May 27, 1796 and Nov. 4, 1797; also Samuel Kirkland, *Journals of Samuel Kirkland,* ed. Walter Pilkington (Clinton, N.Y.: Hamilton College, 1980), 332.

51. William Love, *Samson Occom and the Christian Indians of New England* (Boston: Pilgrim Press, 1899); Daniel E. Wager, *Our County and Its People—A Descriptive Work on Oneida County, New York* (Boston: Boston History Co., 1896); New York Yearly Meeting, Minutes, 1804, and New York Yearly Meeting, Indian Committee, Minutes, 1810–17, both in the Haviland Records Room; letters from Samuel Kirkland, Nov. 19, 1801 and Nov. 21, 1802 in the Philadelphia Yearly Meeting, Indian Committee Records (Friends Historical Library).

52. New York Yearly Meeting (Hicksite), Minutes, 1834, includes Corey's summary of his work.

53. The papers of the Joint Committee on the Indian Concern in the Haviland Records Room of New York Yearly Meeting have been arranged by A. Day Bradley.

7. The Orthodox-Hicksite Separation

1. Gerald R. Cragg, *The Church and the Age of Reason, 1648–1789* (Harmondsworth, England: Penguin, 1960).

2. William Penn, *William Penn on Religion and Ethics,* ed. Hugh Barbour (Lewiston, N.Y.: E. Mellen, 1991). In contrast, Robert Barclay's *Apology* (1678) described his own experience in Quaker worship.

3. See Jack D. Marietta, *The Reformation of American Quakerism* (Philadelphia: Univ. of Pennsylvania Press, 1984). Michael Birkel is writing on Woolman's library and its impact on his thought.

4. William Hodgson, *Select Historical Memoirs of the Religious Society of Friends* (Philadelphia: s.n., 1844), chap. 43. The book praised Shillitoe and condemned Barnard for the United Irish "rebellion."

5. Sydney E. Ahlstrom, *A Religious History of the American People* (New Haven, Conn.: Yale Univ. Press, 1972), chap. 24; Earl Morse Wilbur, *A History of Unitarianism* (Cambridge, Mass.: Harvard Univ. Press, 1945–52), 1:395–96.

6. Elizabeth Fry, *A Memoir of the Life of Elizabeth Fry* (Philadelphia: H. Longstreth, 1847), for 8th Month 1st, 1799. On the London elders and "chanting" women ministers see James Jenkins, *Records and Recollections of James Jenkins,* ed. J. William Frost (Lewiston, N.Y.: E. Mellen Press, 1984).

7. John Bevans, *Some Tracts Relating to the Controversy Between Hannah Barnard and the Society of Friends* (London: Denton and Harvey, 1802). Was this the first clash over a letter to the Governor of Barbados written by Fox's Quaker shipmates in 1671 to prove Friends' orthodoxy?

8. "A Summary of Hannah Barnard's Faith," included in Bevans, *Some Tracts,* 5–6.

9. Thomas Foster, *A Narrative of the Proceedings in America in the Case of Hannah Barnard* (London: C. Stower, 1804), 38. A manuscript copy is in the New York State Library in Albany. Foster said that the "original faith of the Society of Friends was Unitarian" (vi).

10. On a list of seventy-six early Unitarian divines all were New Englanders (Conrad Wright, *Beginnings of Unitarianism in America* [Boston: Beacon, 1955]). Richard Earle Mooers, "Origin and Dispersion of Unitarianism in America" (Master's thesis, Syracuse Univ., 1971) shows that their home missionaries skipped upstate New York to follow New Englanders to Michigan.

11. Frederick B. Tolles, "The New Light Quakers of Lynn and New Bedford," *New England Quarterly* 22 (1959): 291–319.

12. Ultra-Universalists, who believed in no punishment after death, separated on this issue after 1830 from Restitutionists under Adin Ballou (Elmo Arnold Robinson, *American Universalism* [New York: Exposition Press, 1970] 140–44). See Richard Eddy, *Universalism in America: A History* (Boston: Universalist Publishing House, 1886); also Abel C. Thomas, *A Century of Universalism in Philadelphia and New York* (Philadelphia: s.n. 1872), which describes the Reverend Abner Kneeland's friendship with Frances Wright and Robert Owen (278).

13. Robinson, *American Universalism*, 48, 174. Philadelphia was a partial exception. The merger of Unitarians and Universalists came only in 1961.

14. In 1830 Maine had 60 "societies" and 30 clergy; New Hampshire, about 35 and 8; Vermont, 50 and 16; upstate New York, 148 and 40; as against only 2 churches and 6 pastors in New York City and only 70 and 38 in all of Massachusetts and less than 12 in Connecticut (Thomas Whittemore, *Modern History of Universalism* [Boston: The author, 1830], chaps. 10–11).

15. First printed by Robert Porter in his local *Christian Repository*, reprinted in Philadelphia by Joseph Rakestraw, 1823. See also H. Larry Ingle, *Quakers in Conflict: The Hicksite Reformation* (Knoxville: Univ. of Tennessee Press, 1986), 98–102.

16. See Penn, *Religion and Ethics*, pt. 2. Penn and Ferris said the words *Trinity* and *Person* are not biblical. Ferris added Mosheim's history to Penn's Eusebius on the relativity of creeds.

17. *Friends Weekly Intelligencer* 5 (1848): 306, 313–14, 321–23.

18. Randsome Family Papers, New York Historical Society, Cooperstown.

19. Jones, *Later Periods*, 1: chap. 7; see also Elbert Russell, *History of Quakerism* (New York: Macmillan, 1942), 234–35; Ingle, *Quakers in Conflict*, chap. 2; Forbush, *Elias Hicks*, chaps. 12, 14.

20. Within New York Yearly Meeting the organization dates of the most-visited northern Quaker communities—Easton-Saratoga, Adams, and East Hoosack—dated from the 1770s, but West Hartford, Coeymans, Duanesburg, Plains-Esopus-Otsego, Ferrisburgh and Monkton, and Galway, and, in Canada, Adolphustown were preparative meetings in the 1790s and monthly meetings within about one decade after, Queensbury-Glens Falls, Granville and Danby, Hudson, and Keeseville-Grand Isle, further north, were monthly meetings before 1800; See map 2.

21. Marietta, *Reformation*.

22. *Journal of the Life, Travels, and Gospel Labours of . . . Job Scott* (New York: Isaac Collins, 1797); Hicks, *Journal;* Isaac Martin, *Journal of . . . Isaac Martin* (Philadelphia: William P. Gibbons, 1834), William Savery, *Journal of . . . William Savery,* comp. Jonathan Evans, *Friends Library* 1 (1837): 327–459, as was Henry Hull, *Memoir of . . . Henry Hull, Friend's Library*, 236–325; Hall, *Journal;* David Sands, *Journal of . . . David Sands* (London: Collins and Brother, 1848); Joseph Hoag, *Journal of the Life of Joseph Hoag* (Auburn, N.Y.: Knapp and Peck, 1861). The publishers and editors are worth noting: for example, the *Memoir of . . . Martha Routh* (1822) was reprinted by the Orthodox in *Friends Library* 12 (1848): 413–77. The Diary of *Deborah Darby of Coalbrookdale* kept in manuscript in her own family was condensed with notes for publication by Rachel Lady Labouchere (York, England: Sessions, 1993).

23. See the memoir of Routh, 426; and the journals of Savery, 370–73, and Hall, 18.

24. Hall, *Journal,* 5; Hull, *Memoirs,* 38.

25. Fry, *Memoir,* entry for July 10, 1797.

26. Martin, *Journal*, 153.

27. Woolman's use of this image is discussed by Michael Birkel, in "John Woolman on the Cross" in Michael L. Birkel and John Newman, eds., *The Lamb's War: Essays to Honor Hugh Barbour* (Richmond, Ind.: Earlham College Press, 1992).

28. Hall, *Journal* 63, 65. On the danger of speaking without a leading, from "a slavish fear lest some should go away without being benefitted," see Martin, *Journal*, 77.

29. Hicks, *Journal*, 238, 323.

30. Sands, *Journal*, 5, 44, 27, 54–70; cf. Hull, *Memoir*, 42. On Sands see also Rufus Jones, *Quakers in the American Colonies* (London: Macmillan, 1911), 133–35, 254–55; idem, *Later Periods*, 281–84.

31. Joseph Hoag felt a leading to warn New York in 1789, as Sands had done in Philadelphia: Hoag, *Journal*, 57. Besides this memoir see John C. Smith, "Joseph Hoag, Vermont Quaker" (Master's thesis, Earlham School of Religion, 1971).

32. Labouchere, *Deborah Darby*, 194–98. Stephen Grellet, *Memoirs of the Life and Gospel Labors of Stephen Grellet*, ed. Benjamin Seebohm (Philadelphia: H. Longstreth, 1860), 18–21. He showed courage in his 1816 travel throughout French-speaking Haiti, which was since Toussaint L'Ouverture's slave revolt a leading candidate for repatriating American ex-slaves. His trips through Europe, including Finland and Constantinople, totaled fourteen years.

33. Hicks's *Journal* is a summary of his ministry up to 1813, noting as Woolman did the events, miles, and days of each journey; after 1813 it becomes a daily diary of all aspects of his life. There are four hundred manuscript letters by Elias Hicks in the Swarthmore College Friends Historical Library, others in Baltimore and the Haviland Records Room in New York. On Hicks's letters see Forbush, *Elias Hicks*, 294.

34. Hicks, *Journal*, 188. A hereditary illness may have run in Jemima Seaman's family; all their four sons died in their teens of a progressive, weakening disease; none walked past age ten.

35. Hicks, *Journal*, 11, 15. Hicks told the same experience at Little Creek, Delaware, on Dec. 30, 1826.

36. *The Quaker* 4 (1828): 41.

37. Hicks, *Journal*, 16; on Long Island, see Countryman, *People in Revolution*, 148–49. Hicks noted that all wars were claimed as defensive, but Jesus gave up his own life rather than kill (*The Quaker* 4 [1828]: 57).

38. Data are summarized in Forbush, *Elias Hicks*, 290–93; details in Hicks's *Journal*. Here we combine twenty-two thousand miles from Hicks's own estimates with four thousand added by Forbush and add for twenty-two journeys reckoned by neither. On horses, see Forbush, *Elias Hicks*, 107, 109, 126. Methodists Francis Asbury, Peter Cartwright, and other "circuit rider" clergy were credited with one hundred thousand miles apiece in the same years.

39. *The Quaker* 4 (1828): 36; letter of Dec. 7, 1828, quoted in Forbush, *Elias Hicks*, 59.

40. Hicks, *Journal*, 355, 326, 104, 338, 343; *The Quaker* 4 (1828): 24; Hicks, *Journal*, 275, 336; *The Quaker* 4 (1828): 113. He rejected his Universalist friends' belief that a loving God condemns no one in final judgment (see Forbush, *Elias Hicks*, 84). On evil thoughts, see *The Quaker* 4 (1828): 326–37; on predestination, 4 (1828): 46. Hicks's *Journal* told more fully than most Public Friends the content of his messages. It was published posthumously. Marcus Gould printed some transcripts from Hicks's ministry in 1826 in the Philadelphia area (described in only one short paragraph in Hicks's *Journal*, 276) in vols. 1 and 4 of *The Quaker*. A few of Hicks's doctrinal letters were printed many

times over, along with the "orthodox" replies of Friends like Anna Braithwaite. Otherwise the only writing by Hicks published in his lifetime was his fiery *Observations on the Slavery of Africans and their Descendants*, first published in 1811. For a Hicks sermon against war, see *The Quaker* 1 (1827): 48.

41. *The Quaker* 1 (1827): 6; 4 (1828): 9, 22.

42. *The Quaker* 4 (1828): 25, 38; 1 (1827): 17, 121; 4 (1828): 29, where as often he identified the two "slain witnesses" of Rev. 11, whom men would not heed, with the Spirit within and rational understanding; on his dualism, see *The Quaker* 2 (1827): 264.

43. *The Quaker* 1 (1827): 136, 131; 4 (1828): 281, 271; on Deism see also Forbush, *Elias Hicks*, 107, 116; *The Quaker* 1 (1827): 106; Hicks, *Journal*, 103; *The Quaker* 4 (1828): 92, 273; 1 (1827): 219, 47, 132; 3 (1828): 99; 4 (1828): 82, 273, 63.

44. *The Quaker* 4 (1828): 16; Hicks, *Journal*, 29, 273, 94, 289, 314.

45. Hicks, *Journal*, 153, 103 (cf. 190, 353), 116, 104; *The Quaker* 4 (1828): 103.

46. *The Quaker* 1 (1827): 16; cf. 3 (1828): 99.

47. Ibid., 4 (1828): 82, 272. He was doctrinally a Sabellian. Jesus' miracles he saw as part of his outward ministry to the Jews (see *The Quaker* 1 [1827]: 17, 105ff. and Hicks's credal statement to Phebe Willis printed in *The Quaker* 4 [1828]: 283–87). On Jesus as showing people (the inward) Christ, the way, truth, and life, see also *The Quaker* 3 (1828): 105, 108.

48. *The Quaker* 1 (1827): 5; he preached this at the Ohio Yearly Meeting sessions in 1828, intensifying their division; 3 (1828): 215, 255; 4 (1828): 288; cf. 1 (1827): 5, 41. This was the teaching of Fox and Samuel Fisher in the 1650s.

49. Hicks, *Journal*, 383; *The Quaker* 4 (1828): 273, cf. 1 (1827): 19, 37; 3 (1828): 256. The Scriptures, although they can do nothing themselves, "can point us to that which is able to do everything." See also Forbush, *Elias Hicks*, 84.

50. Transcript of Butler's letters in the Haviland Records Room, New York Yearly Meeting; Society of Friends, Jericho Monthly Meeting, *Testimony from the Monthly Meeting of Jericho Concerning Elias Hicks, Deceased* (New York: Isaac T. Hopper, 1830), signed by Clerks Willett Robbins and Abigail Hicks.

51. Ingle, *Quakers in Conflict*, 76, 132. Compare his chaps. 6–9 with Forbush, *Elias Hicks*, chaps. 16–21, and Jones, *Later Periods*, chap. 12, and the more obviously partisan histories by Samuel Janney, *An Examination of the Causes which Led to the Separation of the Religious Society of Friends in America* (Philadelphia: T. E. Zell, 1868), and *History of the Religious Society of Friends* (Philadelphia: T. E. Zell, 1859–1867). See also Barbour, *Slavery and Theology*, chap. 1.

52. Robert Waln, *Seven Letters to Elias Hicks* (Philadelphia: s.n., 1825), 4.

53. Hicks, *Journal*, 174; on the debate see *A Review of Elias Hicks' Letter to Thomas Willis on the Miraculous Conception of Our Lord and Saviour Jesus Christ* (Philadelphia: Printed for the Reader, 1824), which publicized his reply to Atlee, "we cannot believe what we do not understand." Another was Anna Braithwaite, *A Letter from Anna Braithwaite to Elias Hicks on the Nature of His Doctrines* (Philadelphia: Printed for the Reader, 1825).

54. For example, *A Letter from a Friend in the Country to a Friend in the City* (Philadelphia: s.n., 1825), 4. Forbush and Ingle credit Ferris's ideas in *Letters of Paul and Amicus* (Philadelphia: Joseph Rakestraw, 1823) to Hicks's many letters to William Poole, but Ferris proudly noted that he found them in the writings of William Penn.

55. Elias Hicks, *The Substance of Two Discourses, Delivered in New York, Dec. 17, 1824* (New York: J. V. Seaman, 1825), 6; *Sermons delivered by Elias Hicks and Edward Hicks in Friends Meetings, New-York, in 5th Month, 1825* (New York: Seaman, 1825), 23, 130. Four

better-known volumes of *The Quaker* came out only in 1827 and 1828 after the split was inevitable.

56. *The Cabinet, or Works of Darkness Brought to Light* (Philadelphia: s.n., 1824).

57. See Jeremiah J. Foster, *An Authentic Report of the Testimony . . . in the Court of Chancery . . . Between Thomas Shotwell, Complainant, and Joseph Hendrickson and Stacy Decow, Defendants* (Philadelphia: J. Harding, 1831). Robert W. Doherty, *The Hicksite Separation: A Sociological Analysis of Religious Schism in Early Nineteenth Century America* (New Brunswick, N.J.: Rutgers Univ. Press, 1967), a statistical study of some Philadelphia and rural meetings, concludes that on average the Orthodox were wealthier and more urban, the Hicksites proportionately more rural and less worldly, but that there was division within every group and community.

58. *Friends Library* 6: 309–10; *Memoir of Griscom,* 258.

59. James Mott to Elias Hicks, Aug. 5, 1805, Elias Hicks Papers, Friends Historical Library, Swarthmore College. See also John Murray to Hicks, Feb. 3, 1808, Elias Hicks Papers; Aaron Legget to [unknown], Dec. 1827, George H. Burr Papers; Evan Lewis to Benjamin Ferris, Feb. 19, 1828, Benjamin Ferris Papers, all in Friends Historical Library.

60. Jacob Willets to Hicks, Aug. 18, 1828, Elias Hicks Papers.

61. Evan Lewis, *A Review of the Testimony Issued by the Orthodox Seceders from the Monthly Meetings of Westbury and Jericho Against Elias Hicks* (New York: A. Ming, Jr., 1829); Thomas Willis, *The Answers by Elias Hicks to the Six Queries Addressed to him . . . Contrasted with . . . the Doctrines of the Society of Friends* (New York: Mahlon Day, 1831).

62. Society of Friends, New York Monthly Meeting (Hicksite), *Correspondence between the Committee Appointed by the Monthly Meeting of Friends in the City of New York and a Committee of Those Called Orthodox . . . in Relation to the Property Belonging to the Monthly Meeting . . .* (New York: Isaac T. Hopper, 1838), a series of ever more self-righteous and doctrinal statements by both sides.

63. New York State, Supreme Court, *Opinion of the Supreme Court of the State of New York, James Field, Plaintiff, versus Charles Field, Defendant* (Philadelphia: William Brown, 1833), an Orthodox document.

64. Data from Thomas C. Hill, "Monthly Meetings in North America: An Index," (Cincinnati, Ohio: T. C. Hill, 1992), Feb. 21, 1992.

65. Dorland, *Quakers in Canada,* chap. 9.

8. After the Separation

1. Orthodox figures from John Cox, Jr., "List of the Members of NYYM at the Time of the Separation" (Haviland Records Room), Typescript; Hicksite figures are from Foster, *Report of the Testimony,* 2:463–64.

2. *Friends' Review* 25 (1872): 380–81.

3. Richard Pointer, *Protestant Pluralism and the New York Experience* (Bloomington: Indiana Univ. Press, 1988), 4; New York State, *New York Census for 1845,* vol. 2, *Recapitulation* (New York: Carroll and Cook, 1846), nos. 6–8.

4. See John Cox, Jr., "The Quakers in Michigan," *Michigan History* 59 (1945): 512–21; Carlisle G. Davidson, "A Profile of Hicksite Quakerism in Michigan, 1830–1860," *Quaker History* 59 (1970): 106–12; and Edith Haviland, "Reflections on some Quaker Activities," *Michigan History* 46 (1962): 147–52.

5. Jacob Barker, *Incidents of My Life and Life Work of 84 Years* (Richmond, Ind.: Nicholson, 1911), 15.

6. The early history of Quaker settlement is described in John E. Pomfret, *The Province of East New Jersey, 1609–1702* (Princeton, N.J.: Princeton Univ. Press, 1962), 381–96.

7. Dorland, *Quakers in Canada*, 157–79.

8. Sunderland P. Gardner, *Address to the Children and Youth of the Religious Society of Friends* (Rochester, N.Y.: Daily Advertiser, 1846), 9.

9. A. Day Bradley, "Progressive Friends in Michigan and New York," *Quaker History* 52 (1963): 95–103.

10. Ann Braude, *Radical Spirits: Spiritualism and Women's Rights in Nineteenth-Century America* (Boston: Beacon Press, 1990), 12–15.

11. Isaac Post, *Voices from the Spirit World* (Rochester: Charles H. McDonnell, 1852), 22–27, 28–30, 79–82, 91–95.

12. Anthony to E. C. Stanton, Sep. 29, 1857, in Ellen DuBois, ed., *Elizabeth Cady Stanton / Susan B. Anthony: Correspondence, Writings, Speeches* (New York: Schocken Books, 1981), 64–67.

13. "Progress of Disunionism in the West" *National Anti-Slavery Standard*, Oct. 31, 1857. See also Lucy Colman, *Reminiscences* (Buffalo, N.Y.: H. L. Green, 1891), 23–27.

14. Loren V. Fay, *Quaker Census of 1828* (Rhinebeck, N.Y.: Kinship, 1989).

15. Rachel Hicks, *Memoir of Rachel Hicks* (New York: G. P. Putnam's Sons, 1880), 119–20.

16. Sunderland P. Gardner, *Memoirs of the Life and Religious Labors of Sunderland P. Gardner* (Philadelphia: Friends Book Association, 1895), 69.

17. Ibid., 20.

18. Ibid., 636.

19. John J. Cornell, *Autobiography of John J. Cornell* (Baltimore, Md.: Lord Baltimore Press, 1906).

20. Cornell, *Autobiography*, 405.

21. See especially, Whitney Cross, *The Burned-Over District: The Social and Intellectual History of Enthusiastic Religion in Western New York, 1800–1850* (Ithaca, N.Y.: Cornell Univ. Press, 1950), and Paul E. Johnson, *A Shopkeeper's Millennium: Society and Revivals in Rochester, New York, 1815–1837* (New York: Hill and Wang, 1978).

22. Some radical Hicksites, including George Prior and John Orvis, were briefly involved with the Skaneateles Commune. See Thomas D. Hamm, "The Limits of the Peace Testimony: Hicksite Friends and the Nonresistant Movement" (1993), typescript (copy in Haviland Records Room).

23. For John Wilbur's theological position, see his *Letters to a Friend on Some of the Primitive Doctrines of Christianity* (London: Harvey and Denton, 1832).

24. New York Hicksites also followed the Beacon controversy. Isaac T. Hopper reprinted Isaac Crewdson, *A Beacon to the Society of Friends* (New York: Isaac T. Hopper, 1835); and Joseph John Gurney, *Brief Remarks on Impartiality in the Interpretation of Scripture* (New York: Isaac T. Hopper, 1840); and published Thomas M'Clintock, *Observations on the Articles Published in the Episcopal Recorder* (New York: Isaac T. Hopper, 1837).

25. Joseph Hoag, *Journal of Joseph Hoag* (Auburn, N.Y.: Knapp and Peck, 1861), 366–57.

26. John Wilbur, *A Narrative and Exposition of the Late Proceedings of New England Yearly Meeting* (New York: Piercy and Reid, 1845).

27. A. Day Bradley, "New York Yearly Meeting at Poplar Ridge and the Primitive Friends," 68 (1979): 75–82; Christopher Densmore, "New Information on the Wilburites of New York: Discovery of the Wilburite Friends' Meeting for Sufferings Minute Book (1853–68)," *Quaker History* 72 (1983): 130–33; Alson D. Van Wagner, "Minutes of Meet-

ings of New York and Ohio Yearly Meetings, Conservative, Retrieved," *Quaker History* 77 (1988): 122-23.

9. Quaker Education

1. Society of Friends, London Yearly Meeting, *Collection of Epistles from the Yearly Meeting of Friends in London* (Baltimore: Cole and Hewes, 1806), 38.

2. Frost, *Quaker Family in Colonial America* (New York: St. Martin's Press, 1973), 159-60.

3. Tolles, *Meeting House*, 205.

4. William Penn, *Works* (London: William Phillips, 1825), 3: 354; see also Howard Brinton, *Quaker Education in Theory and Practice*, 3d rev. ed. (Wallingford, Pa.: Pendle Hill, 1967), 78.

5. Tolles, *Meeting House*, 210-13.

6. Ibid., 159, quoting English Quaker schoolmaster Christopher Taylor.

7. Brinton, *Quaker Education*, 66, 49-50, 54.

8. Cox, *Quakerism*, 164.

9. Ibid., 166-68.

10. Ibid., 200; Nancy Reid Gibbs, *Children of Light: Friends Seminary, 1786-1986* (New York: Friends Seminary, ca. 1986), 32.

11. Cox, *Quakerism*, 171.

12. Gibbs, *Children of Light*, 55, 51.

13. Ibid., 61, 80.

14. Ibid., 87, 92, 103.

15. Ibid., 103, 123, 141, 201.

16. Stephen Allott, *Lindley Murray, 1745-1826: Quaker Grammarian* (York, England: Sessions, 1991), 48.

17. Frost, *Quaker Family in Colonial America*, 103.

18. Joseph Tallcot, *Memoirs* (Auburn, N.Y.: Miller, Orton and Mulligan, 1855), 16-17.

19. Tallcot, *Memoirs*, 79-81.

20. William J. Reagan, *A Venture in Quaker Education at Oakwood School* (Poughkeepsie, N.Y.: Oakwood School, 1968).

21. Edgerton Grant North, *Seventy-five Years of Brooklyn Friends School* (New York: Brooklyn Friends School, 1942), p. 7.

22. Ibid., 11.

23. Ibid., 23.

24. Ibid., 28.

25. Tallcot, *Memoirs*, 74-75.

26. Ibid., 79.

27. Ibid., 277.

28. Ibid., 280, 264.

29. Ibid., 111, 141.

30. New York Yearly Meeting (Orthodox), Minutes, 1846.

31. Ibid., 1838.

32. Ibid., 1837.

33. Ida Husted Harper, *Life and Work of Susan B. Anthony*, 3 vols. (New York: Arno, 1969), 23, 39.

34. Judith Colucci Breault, *The World of Emily Howland: Odyssey of a Humanitarian* (Milbrae, Calif.: Les Femmes, 1975), 9–11.

35. William M. Masland, "The Story of Friends Academy," *Nassau County Historical Society Journal* 38 (1983): 18–35.

36. John Griscom, *Considerations Relative to an Establishment for Perfecting the Education of Young Men Within the Society of Friends* (New York: Samuel Wood, 1815).

37. Rufus Jones, *Haverford College: A History and an Interpretation* (New York: Macmillan, 1933), 2–20.

38. Katharine E. Cook and A. Day Bradley, "The Young Ladies Collegiate Institute—Howland School," *Yesteryears* 20 (Spring 1977): 96–102.

39. *Friends Review* 3 (1850): 551–52; 7 (1854): 355–57; 17 (1863): 82–83; 21 (1868): 705–6; *Friends Intelligencer* 17 (1860–61): 615–16, 711–12.

40. Cox, *Quakerism*, 62–63.

41. Ibid., 176–77.

42. Ibid., 180.

43. Carl F. Kaestle, *Joseph Lancaster and the Monitorial School Movement* (New York: Teachers College Press, 1973), 124, 3.

44. Ibid., 41, 3–4.

45. Ibid., 98.

46. Ibid., 77.

47. Ibid., 17.

48. Brinton, *Quaker Education*, 62.

49. Ibid., 62, 63.

50. Ibid., 65.

51. Kaestle, *Joseph Lancaster*, 18.

52. William O. Bourne, *History of the Public School Society of the City of New York* (New York: William Wood, 1870), 328, 348.

53. Kaestle, *Joseph Lancaster*, viii.

54. Ellwood P. Cubberley, *Public Education in the United States* (Cambridge, Mass.: Riverside Press, 1962), 134.

55. Griscom, *Year in Europe*, 1: 416–27.

56. Ibid., 2: 336, 375–93.

57. Griscom, *Memoir*, 356–57.

58. Bourne, *Public School Society*, 660.

59. Griscom, *Memoir*, 201–8.

60. Ibid., 209–12.

61. For Lindley Murray's life, see Allott, *Lindley Murray*.

62. Ibid., viii.

63. Ibid., 68.

64. Ibid., 30.

65. Ibid., 56.

66. See the "Introductory Essay" by Richard L. Venezky in *American Primers: Guide to the Microfiche Collection* (Bethesda, Md.; Univ. Publications of America, 1990), xv–xvi.

67. Christopher Densmore, "Quaker Publishing in New York State, 1784–1860," *Quaker History* 74 (Fall 1985): 47–48.

68. Tallcot, *Memoirs*, 193.

69. Ibid., 187–88.

70. James Mott, "Observations on the Education of Children," *Friends Miscellany* 11(1838): 2, 10, 22; "Memoirs of James Mott," *Friends Miscellany* 9 (1837): 341–42.

10. Women's Rights and Roles

1. New York Yearly Meeting, Minutes, 1804.

2. *Friends Intelligencer* 1 (1838): 98.

3. *Friends Intelligencer* 1 (1838): 65–66.

4. *Friends Review* 30 (1874): 681.

5. "Basis of Religious Association," reprinted in Elisabeth Potts Brown and Susan Mosher Stuard, eds., *Witnesses for Change: Quaker Women over Three Centuries* (New Brunswick, N.J.: Rutgers Univ. Press, 1989), 116, 119.

6. Margaret Hope Bacon, "A Widening Path: Women in Philadelphia Yearly Meeting Move Toward Equality," in *Friends in the Delaware Valley*, ed. John M. Moore (Haverford, Pa.: Friends Historical Association, 1981), 188 passim.

7. New York Yearly Meeting (Orthodox) *Discipline* (1890), 30; New York Yearly Meeting (Hicksite), *Discipline* (1893), 11.

8. On the role of women in the early history of the Society of Friends, see Phyllis Mack, "Gender and Spirituality in Early English Quakerism, 1650–1665," in Brown and Stuard, *Witnesses for Change*, 31–63.

9. Rufus M. Jones, *Later Periods*, (1921; reprint, Westport, Conn.: Greenwood Press, 1970), 129, 32–33. See also Margaret Hope Bacon, *Mothers of Feminism: The Story of Quaker Women in America* (San Francisco: Harper and Row, 1986), chaps. 1–3.

10. The discussion that follows on the effects of the schisms on Quaker women's role and rights is adopted from Nancy A. Hewitt, "The Fragmentation of Friends: The Consequences for Quaker Women in Antebellum America," in Brown and Stuard, *Witnesses for Change*, 93–108.

11. Quote from Jones, *Later Periods*, 1: 293, 283. See also Bacon, *Mothers of Feminism*, 40–41, 78–79. Barnard was accompanied on this ministry by Elizabeth Coggeshall, who made a second visit to England from 1813–15.

12. Ingle, *Quakers in Conflict*, 126, 127–29.

13. Mary Kirby Willis to Amy Kirby, 182?, Isaac and Amy Post Family Papers (IAPFP), University of Rochester. This is only one of dozens of letters in this one set of family papers that focuses on the schism of the 1820s.

14. Much of the information on individual Quaker women from New York Yearly Meeting has been compiled by Sabron Newton from the records of those meetings.

15. Hannah Kirby Post to Amy Kirby, January 29, 1826, IAPFP.

16. John Ketcham to Isaac and Amy Post, January 20, 1829, IAPFP.

17. Mary Robbins Post to Amy Post, October 183?, IAPFP. See also Bacon, *Mothers of Feminism*, 93.

18. Sarah [Thayer] to Amy Post, March 9, 1853, IAPFP.

19. Biographical information on Chandler is taken from Benjamin Lundy's memoir of her, published as an introduction to Chandler, *The Poetical Works of Elizabeth Margaret Chandler* (Philadelphia: Lemuel Howell, 1836), 7–44; see also Merton R. Dillon, "Elizabeth Chandler and the Spread of Antislavery Sentiment to Michigan," *Michigan History* (1955): 481–94. The portrait is included in Chandler, *Essays, Philanthropic and Moral* (Philadelphia: Lemuel Howell, 1836). The poems appear on the title pages of the two works.

20. Laura Smith Haviland, *A Woman's Life Work* (Cincinnati: Walden and Stowe, 1882), 32–34.

21. Caroline Hare, *The Life and Letters of Elizabeth Comstock* (London: Headley Brothers, 1895), 150–51, 272–73, and 468–70; and Thomas D. Hamm, "Elizabeth Leslie Rouse Wright Comstock," *American National Biography* (New York: Oxford Univ. Press, forthcoming).

22. Sojourner Truth, *Narrative of Sojourner Truth* (Battle Creek, Mich.: Published for the author, 1878), 133–35, 187; Bernice Lowe, "Michigan Days of Sojourner Truth," *New York Folklore Quarterly* 12 (1956): 127–35; Nell Irvin Painter, "Sojourner Truth in Life and Memory: Writing the Biography of an American Exotic," *Gender and History* 2 (1990): 3–16; and Carleton Mabee, *Sojourner Truth—Slave, Prophet, Legend* (New York: New York Univ. Press, 1993).

23. Material on upstate New York women Friends is taken primarily from Nancy A. Hewitt, *Women's Activism and Social Change: Rochester, New York, 1822–1872* (Ithaca, N.Y.: Cornell Univ. Press, 1984).

24. Phebe Post Willis to Isaac and Amy Post, April 5, 1837, IAPFP.

25. Genesee Yearly Meeting of Women Friends, Minutes, 1837, Haviland Records Room, New York City.

26. See Genesee Yearly Meeting of Women Friends, Minutes, 1838, 1839, and 1840.

27. John Ketcham to Isaac and Amy Post, March 11, 1841, IAPFP.

28. Colman, *Reminiscences,* 84.

29. Amy Post to Abby Kelley, December 4, 1843, Abby Kelley Foster Papers, American Antiquarian Society, Worcester, Massachusetts.

30. See, for an early example, the call for an antislavery fair published in the *National Anti-Slavery Standard,* February 2, 1843.

31. Material on the June 1848 schism is taken from Nancy A. Hewitt, "Feminist Friends: Agrarian Quakers and the Emergence of Woman's Rights in America," *Feminist Studies* 12 (Spring 1986): 27–49; Judith Wellman, "The Seneca Falls Woman's Rights Convention: A Study of Social Networks," *Journal of Women's History* 3 (1991): 9–37; and Christopher Densmore, personal correspondence in author's possession.

32. Quoted in Wellman, "Woman's Rights Convention," 25.

33. "Basis of Religious Association," Brown and Stuard, *Witnesses for Change,* 114, 116.

34. See Wellman, "Woman's Rights Convention," for a detailed discussion of the three groups whose efforts intersected at Seneca Falls, New York.

35. Wellman, "Woman's Rights Convention," 27.

36. Woman's Rights Convention, *Report of the First Woman's Rights Convention, Held at Seneca Falls, New York, July 19th and 20th, 1848* (Rochester, N.Y.: John Dick, 1848), and Rochester Woman's Rights Convention Minutes, August 2, 1848, in the Phebe Post Willis Papers, University of Rochester. At the Seneca Falls Convention, James Mott, husband of convention co-organizer Lucretia Mott, presided. For a detailed discussion of the Rochester convention see Hewitt, "Feminist Friends."

37. Rochester Woman's Rights Convention, Minutes, August 2, 1848.

38. Information on Quaker women's participation in the temperance cause is abstracted from Sabron Newton, "New York Friends and the Concern about Alcohol," 1–7, a typescript essay in the author's possession (with a copy in Haviland Records Room).

39. Ibid., 3.

40. Daniel Anthony to Susan B. Anthony, July 16, 1848, Anthony Papers, Schlesinger Library, Radcliffe College, Cambridge, Mass., quoted in Wellman, "Woman's Rights Convention," 25–26.

41. The major sources for this portrait of Susan B. Anthony are Katherine Sorel,

"Susan B. Anthony," typescript manuscript in the author's possession; Kathleen Barry, *Susan B. Anthony: A Biography of a Singular Feminist* (New York: Ballantine Books, 1988); and Ida Husted Harper, *The Life and Works of Susan B. Anthony* (1898–1908; reprint, New York: Arno, 1969).

42. Barry, 8–9. Daniel Anthony espoused a liberal version of Quakerism and nurtured his daughter's autonomy.

43. Barry, *Susan B. Anthony*, 18, 30.

44. Harper, *Susan B. Anthony*, 1:65.

45. Newton, "Concern about Alcohol," 4–5.

46. Information on Emily Howland was compiled by Katherine Sorel. The major source on Howland's life remains Breault.

47. Breault, *Emily Howland*, 10.

48. William P. McDermott, "The Rev. Amanda Halstead Deyo (1838–1917): A Chrononarrative of a Preacher of Peace," *Hudson Valley Regional Review* 8 (1991): 1–23.

49. Quoted in Barry, *Susan B. Anthony*, 90.

11. Quakers, Slavery, and the Civil War

1. Society of Friends, New York Yearly Meeting, *Discipline* (New York: Collins and Perkins, 1810), 48.

2. Dillon, "Elizabeth Chandler," 487.

3. *Friends Intelligencer* 1 (1838–39): 115–16, 145–47, 273–77, 309–12.

4. Aaron M. Powell, *Personal Reminiscences of the Anti-Slavery and Other Reforms and Reformers* (New York: Caulon Press, 1899), 156–57.

5. *National Anti-Slavery Standard (NASS)*, Mar. 25, 1841, 167; Apr. 8, 1841, 174. The *NASS* carried articles on the controversy throughout the next year. Many of the articles and documents were later included in Isaac T. Hopper, *Narrative of the Proceedings of the Monthly Meeting of New-York* (New York: Hopper, 1843). Lydia Maria Child, a resident of the Hopper household in New York and one-time editor of the *NASS*, wrote about the affair in *Isaac T. Hopper*, 386–99, 465.

6. *NASS*, June 2, 1852, 202.

7. *NASS*, Sep. 14, 1842, 59; June 8, 1843, 2.

8. Cornell, *Autobiography*, 22–23.

9. The records of the New York Association are at the Friends Historical Library, Swarthmore College; reports and documents of the association were printed in the *NASS*, July 8, 15, 29, 1841; July 21, 1842; and June 15, 1843.

10. "Letter from Miss C. F. Putnam," *Liberator* (Jan. 16, 1857).

11. Christopher Densmore, "The Dilemma of Quaker Anti-Slavery: The Case of Farmington Quarterly Meeting, 1836–1860," *Quaker History* 82 (1993): 84–85; see also the *Non-Slaveholder*, a free-produce journal from Philadelphia, 1846–1850, 1853–1854, for reports from New York and contributions from New York Yearly Meeting Friends David Irish, Henry Miles, and Thomas Willis.

12. *Friends Review* 11 (1858): 558, 12 (1859): 315–316.

13. Albert J. Edmunds, *The Vision, in 1803, of Joseph Hoag* (Philadelphia: Innes and Sons, 1915); a letter from David Thomas to William H. Seward, May 20, 1861, in the Seward Papers at the University of Rochester, claims that he had seen manuscript copies of the vision "nearly 25 or 30 years ago."

14. Various undated broadside printings and manuscript copies of the "Vision" exist. The quotation here is from a copy at the Friends Historical Library, Swarthmore College.

15. Priscilla Hunt Cadwallader, *Memoirs* (Philadelphia: Book Association of Friends, 1864), 109.

16. New York Yearly Meeting, Minutes, 1863: 16.

17. Pringle's journal was reprinted with an introduction by Rufus Jones in 1918, edited by Henry J. Cadbury as a Pendle Hill pamphlet, and even given a fourth edition in a Mennonite periodical.

18. *Friends Intelligencer* 21 (1864): 518–19.

19. *Friend* 37 (1864): 171–72.

20. New York Yearly Meeting, Minutes, 1865.

21. "Address to the Members of the Religious Society of Friends," *Friends Review* 14 (1861): 582–83.

22. C. Rous Hare, *Life and Letters of Elizabeth Comstock* (London: Headley, 1895), 109.

23. Jacquelyn S. Nelson, *Indiana Quakers Confront the Civil War* (Indianapolis: Indiana Historical Society, 1991), 20–21, 101–5.

24. Gardner, *Memoirs*, 98–100, 106–7, 123–24, 127–29, 400–431.

25. A. J. H. Duganne, *The Fighting Quakers, A True Story of the War for Our Union*, 2d. ed. (New York: J. P. Robens, 1866), 112–13.

26. *Friends' Review* 17 (1863–64): 168, 330–32; *NASS*, July 28, 1863.

27. See the annual reports [1]–9 (1862–70) of the "Committee of the Representatives of New York Yearly Meeting of Friends upon the Condition and Wants of the Colored Refugees" in the Minute book of the Representative Committee of New York Yearly Meeting (Orthodox), Haviland Records Room.

28. *Friends Intelligencer* 19 (1862–63): 603–4, 679–80; 20 (1863–64): 743, 794–96; 21(1864–65): 757–60; 22(1865–66): 734–35.

12. Evangelicals and Hicksites, 1870–1917

1. New York Yearly Meeting Minutes, 1870, passim; William H. S. Wood, *Friends of the City of New York in the Nineteenth Century* (New York: s.n., 1904).

2. Thomas D. Hamm, *The Transformation of American Quakerism Orthodox Friends, 1800–1907* (Bloomington: Indiana Univ. Press, 1988), 36–73; New York Yearly Meeting (Orthodox), *Discipline of the Society of Friends of New York Yearly Meeting* (New York: Samuel S. and William Wood, 1859), 65–66.

3. Hamm, *Tranformation*, 2–5, 21–22, 77–95.

4. David B. Updegraff, *Open Letters for Interested Readers* (Philadelphia: s.n., 1880), 22.

5. "New York Yearly Meeting," *Friends Review*, June 17, 1871, 681; J. E. R., "Some Lessons of a Christian Life," ibid., June 19, 1890, 742; "Aggressive Christianity," *Christian Worker*, Sep. 15, 1871, 159; Ann Burton and Conrad Burton, *Michigan Quakers: Abstracts of Fifteen Monthly Meetings of the Society of Friends, 1831–1960* (Decatur, Mich.: Glendwr, 1989), 195–417; Thomas W. Ladd obituary, *Gospel Expositor*, Jan. 12, 1883, 3; Ellen C. L. Conklin, *Autobiography and Extracts from the Diaries of Caroline E. Ladd* (n.p., n.d.), 8–9, 17–18.

6. "New York Yearly Meeting," *Christian Worker*, June 15, 1871, 91–92.

7. Ibid., New York Yearly Meeting, Minutes, 1871, 10.

8. "General Meeting at Farmington, New York," *Christian Worker*, Sep. 15, 1871, 151–152, Nathan T. Frame and Esther G. Frame, *Reminiscences of Nathan T. Frame and Esther G. Frame* (Cleveland, Ohio: Britton, 1907), 129.

9. Editorial, *Friend*, Jan. 6, 1872, 157–59; "Brooklyn General Meeting," *Friends Review*, Dec. 16, 1871, 257–58; ibid., Dec. 23, 1871, 274–77; "General Meeting at Glens Falls," *Christian Worker*, Mar. 15, 1872, 53.

10. New York Yearly Meeting, Minutes, 1872, 15, "The Church at Work," *Christian Worker,* Feb. 1, 1873, 43, ibid., Apr. 1, 1873, 107, Luke Woodard, *Sketches of a Life of 75* (Richmond, Ind.: Nicholson Printing, 1907), 58.

11. "Correspondence," *Friends' Review,* Oct. 31, 1889, 221; New York Yearly Meeting, Minutes, 1877, 35.

12. Woodard, *Sketches,* 38–101; Thomas W. Ladd obituary, Elizabeth Mallison obituary, *Christian Worker,* Aug. 11, 1883, 383. Henry Stanley Newman, *Memories of Stanley Pumphrey* (New York: Friends Book and Tract Committee, 1883), 258–59.

13. New York Yearly Meeting, Minutes, 1891, 81–83; "The Late Thomas Kimber, Minister in the Society of Friends," *Friends Review,* Apr. 23, 1891, 612–13; "Editorial Notes," *Friends Expositor,* 4 (Oct. 1890), 457; Thomas Kimber, Jr., "Early Quakerism, Scriptural Christianity," *Christian Worker,* June 1, 1874, 161–64; ibid., June 15, 1874, 177–80; ibid., July 1, 1874, 193–96.

14. New York Yearly Meeting, Minutes, 1891, 82–83; William Wade Hinshaw, ed., *Encyclopedia of American Quaker Genealogy,* 6 vols. (Ann Arbor: Edwards Brothers, 1936–50), 3:192.

15. Arthur J. Mekeel, *Quakerism and a Creed* (Philadelphia: Friends Book Store, 1936), 84–86; New York Yearly Meeting (Gurneyite), Representative Meeting Minute, Mar. 6, 1873 (Haviland Records Room, New York), New York Yearly Meeting (Gurneyite) of Ministers and Elders, Minutes, May 25, 1875 (Haviland Records Room, New York); "Conference of ministers and elders in New York," *Friends Review,* June 26, 1875, 713. New York Yearly Meeting, Minutes, 1875, 36; Society of Friends, New York Yearly Meeting (Orthodox), *Discipline* (1876), 41–43, "New York Yearly Meeting," *Christian Worker,* June 15, 1875, 186.

16. "Is It a Creed?" *Friends' Review,* July 10, 1875, 744–45, "Doctrinal Queries," ibid., May 27, 1876, 648; Mekeel, *Quakerism and a Creed,* 86–87, John J. Thomas to Henry Hartshorne, July 31, 1876, box 12, Hartshorne Family Papers (Quaker Collection, Haverford College), David B. Updegraff, "The Few Queries," *Christian Worker,* June 1, 1876, 64–65.

17. Society of Friends, New York Yearly Meeting, *Discipline,* 43; Mekeel, *Quakerism and a Creed,* 85–87, New York State Yearly Meeting, 1880, 62; John W. Graham, "American Papers—V," *British Friend,* Feb. 1897, 32; "Brooklyn General Meeting," *Friends Review,* Dec. 23, 1871, 277; New York Yearly Meeting, Minutes, 1876, 36.

18. New York Yearly Meeting, Minutes, 1871, 23–24; ibid., 1875, 7, 20, 27; Woodard, *Sketches,* 53–54; "Leray Monthly Meeting, New York," *Friends Review,* Feb. 26, 1876, 442; Butternuts Quarterly Meeting (Gurneyite), Men's Minutes, Nov. 12, 1874, Feb. 18, 1875 (Haviland Records Room), Scipio Quarterly Meeting (Gurneyite), Men's Minutes, Apr. 29, 1876 (HRR); Representative Meeting, Minutes, Dec. 1, 1885, Dec. 5, 1899, Abm S. Underhill, "Historical Account of Le Ray Friends Meeting, at LeRaysville, Jefferson County, N.Y.," 1938. Typescript, Haviland Records Room.

19. New York Yearly Meeting, Minutes, 1878, 63; Butternuts Quarterly Meeting, Men's Minutes, May 16, 1878.

20. Editorial, *Christian Worker,* Aug. 7, 1879, 380, "Recall of Helen Balkwill," ibid. Sept. 25, 1879, 461, "Helen Balkwill," *British Friend,* Sep. 1, 1879, 926–27. Hamm, *Transformation,* 133–36.

21. "Recall of Helen Balkwill," *Christian Worker,* Sept. 25, 1879, 461; "The Conference at Glens Falls," *Christian Worker,* Oct. 30, 1879, 520–21.

22. Timothy Nicholson to Joel and Hannah E. Bean, May 2, 1881, box 4, Joel Bean Papers (Friends Historical Library, Swarthmore College, Swarthmore, Pa.); Luke Wood-

ard letter, *Christian Worker*, Dec. 25, 1879, 619–20; Representative Meeting, Minutes, Apr. 28, 1881; J. J. Thomas to C. W. Allis, Apr. 22, 1881, Caleb W. Allis Papers (Haviland Records Room); Luke Woodard to Allis, Apr. 19, [1881], ibid.; Call for Representative Meeting, Apr. 11, 1881, ibid.; "New York Yearly Meeting," *Friends Review*, June 20, 1885, 732; ibid., Jun. 13, 1889, 730; "Editorial Notes," *Friends Expositor*, 3 (April 1889): 263–64. Vocal opponents of the ordinances in New York Yearly Meeting were Thomas Kimber, William H. Ladd, and Alexander M. Purdy. See Thomas Kimber, "Water Baptism and the Outward Supper, No Institutions of Christ," *Friends' Review*, Jan. 24, 1880, 371–73; Alexander M. Purdy letter, ibid., Sep. 23, 1886, 126, W. H. Ladd; "The Ordinances Again," *Christian Worker*, Oct. 30, 1879, 519.

23. New York Yearly Meeting, Minutes, 1887, 32; ibid., 1910, 13–14; Alexander H. Hay, "The Rise of the Pastoral System in the Society of Friends, 1850–1900" (Master's thesis, Haverford College, 1938), 65 New York Yearly Meeting, Minutes, 1882, 30.

24. Hay, "Pastoral System," 64; Isaac Hazard to Allen Jay, Mar. 24, 1887, G–L box, Allen Jay Papers (Archives, Lilly Library, Earlham College, Richmond, Ind.); Thomas Kimber, "Pastorates in the Society of Friends," *Friends' Review*, Sep. 23, 1886, 113–16; James Wood, "The Pastoral Question," ibid., May 10, 1894, 451–53.

25. Hay, "Pastoral System," 79; "Meetings in New York," *British Friend*, July 1, 1886, 175; Representative Meeting, Minutes, Oct. 7, 1886; Editorial, *Friends Review*, Sep. 16, 1886, 105–6; "Society Intelligence," ibid., Mar. 7, 1889, 507.

26. Graham, "American Papers," 32–33; Alexander M. Purdy, "Are We on the Right Track?" *Christian Worker*, Apr. 13, 1893, 226; "The Pastoral System," *Friends Review*, Mar. 8, 1894, 227.

27. For Friends and missions generally see Christina Jones, *American Friends in World Missions* (Richmond, Ind.: American Friends Board of Missions, 1946). For the Protestant missionary impulse in this period see William R. Hutchison, *Errand to the World: American Protestant Thought and Foreign Missions* (Chicago: Univ. of Chicago Press, 1987).

28. James Purdie Knowles, *Samuel A. Purdie: His Life and Letters* (Plainfield, Ind.: Publishing Association of Friends, 1908).

29. Walter Rollin Williams, *These Fifty Years with Ohio Friends in China* (Damascus, Ohio: Friends Foreign Missionary Society of Ohio Yearly Meeting, 1940), 52–53, 57, 127–31. New York Yearly Meetings, Minutes, 1902, 9; 1904, 47; 1908, 46.

30. New York Yearly Meeting, Minutes, 1904, 47, Mary H. Thomas, "A Paper Read at the Public Meeting of Women Friends Missionary Association at Poughkeepsie, Fifth Mo. 27, 1891." *Friends Review*, June 11, 1891, 724; Errol T. Elliott, *Quakers on the American Frontier* (Richmond, Ind., Friends United Press, 1969), 317–18.

31. Wood, *City of New York*, 54–56; Francis Charles Anscombe, "The Contribution of the Quakers to the Reconstruction of the Southern States" (Ph.D. diss., Univ. of North Carolina, 1926), 62; Representative Meeting, Minutes, Dec. 1, 1870.

32. "New York Yearly Meeting," *Christian Worker*, May 15, 1873, 155; New York Yearly Meeting, Minutes, 1878, 47; 1881, 32; 1897, 42.

33. Seth B. Hinshaw, *The Carolina Quaker Experience, 1665–1985: An Interpretation* (Greensboro: North Carolina Friends Historical Society, 1985), 171–72, New York Yearly Meeting, Minutes, 1908, 43–44.

34. Rufus M. Jones, *The Trail of Life in the Middle Years* (New York: Macmillan, 1934), 27–28.

35. Elizabeth Gray Vining, *Friend of Life: The Biography of Rufus Jones* (Philadelphia: Lippincott, 1958), 65; Rufus M. Jones, "James Wood," *American Friend*, Dec. 31, 1925, 896–97.

36. Letter, James Wood to James T. Shinn, Mar. 27, 1891, from Damascus. Material on James Wood is from family archives of Wood family at Braewold, plus data courtesy of Peter Wosh, archivist of the American Bible Society, and from Thomas Hamm, and from Cox, *Quakerism.*

37. Society of Friends, Richmond Conference (1887), *Proceedings including Declaration of Christian Doctrine of the General Conference of Friends held in Richmond, Ind., U.S.A., 1887*, especially 301.

38. Society of Friends, Five Years Meeting, *Proceedings of the Conference of Friends in America held in Indianapolis, 1897* (Philadelphia, 1898); Society of Friends, Five Years Meeting, *Minutes and Proceedings of the Five Years Meeting . . . 1902* (Philadelphia, 1903).

39. Hamm, *Transformation,* chap. 7.

40. "Field News and Notes," *Evangelical Friend,* July 26, 1907, 477; "Scipio Quarterly Meeting," ibid., Jan. 17, 1907, 44; Note, ibid., Jan. 24, 1907, 58; New York Yearly Meeting, Minutes, 1914, 22–23; "New York Yearly Meeting," *American Friend,* June 14, 1917, 464; Edward Mott, *Sixty Years of Gospel Ministry* (Portland, Oreg.: n.p., n.d.), Samuel H. Hodges to Elbert Russell, Sep. 2, 1906, box 3, Elbert Russell Papers, Earlham College, Richmond, Ind.

41. Hamm, *Transformation,* 167; James Wood, "The Relation of Quaker Doctrine to Modern Thought, Read at the Educational Conference, Richmond, Ind., Seventh Mo. 31, 1905," *American Friend,* Dec. 28, 1905, 868–70; "New York Yearly Meeting," ibid., June 15, 1916, 458; Homer J. Coppock, "Theological Education for Friends Ministers," ibid., Aug. 27, 1914, 552–53; "The Church at Work," ibid., Apr. 27, 1916, 320; Leonard S. Kenworthy, *Living in a Larger World: The Life of Murray S. Kenworthy* (Richmond, Ind.: Friends United Press, 1986), 43–48; Elliott, *Quakers on the American Frontier,* 396.

42. Elbert Russell, *The Separation after a Century* (Philadelphia: Friends Intelligencer, 1928), 64–67; New York Yearly Meeting, Minutes, 1907, 68; 1908, 83–84, 87–88; 1909, 52–54; 1914, 35–36; E. Thomas, "The Message of Quakerism," *American Friend,* Sep. 24, 1914, 616; L. Hollingsworth Wood, "The Friend in Need," ibid., July 2, 1914, 422–23; "Peace Department," ibid., Apr. 6, 1916, 256; "News Items," ibid. July 30, 1914, 492–93; Society of Friends, New York Yearly Meeting, *Constitution and Discipline for the American Yearly Meetings* (New York: Friends Book and Tract Committee [1901]).

43. Condensed from Sabron Reynolds Newton, "New York Friends and the Concern about Alcohol" (unpublished article, 1992) based on New York Yearly Meeting, Five Years Meeting and Women's Christian Temperance Union minutes and sources. Copy in Haviland Records Room.

44. Olive Floyd, *Phebe Anna Thorne, Quakeress, 1828–1909* (Rye, N.Y., privately printed, 1958).

45. Powell, *Personal Reminiscences;* Powell, *The National Purity Congress* (New York: American Purity Alliance, 1895); David J. Pivar, *Purity Crusade: Sexual Morality and Social Crusade, 1868–1900* (New York: Greenwood, 1973).

46. Material from Sabron Reynolds Newton, by personal correspondence.

47. Society of Friends, Friends Union for Philanthropic Labor, *Proceedings of Friends Union for Philanthropic Labor at Its Fifth Conference Held in New York . . . 1888* (New York: Collies, Macy, 1888), 4, source also for the following data.

48. Society of Friends, Friends General Conference, *Proceedings of the Friends General Conference* (Philadelphia: The Conference, 1902); Russell, *History of Quakerism,* 495–96. Rufus Jones, being Orthodox, does not mention FGC in his *Later Periods* (1921). The Committee on Philanthropic Labor was chaired by John William Hutchinson of New York, the Committee on Advancement of Friends Principles by New Yorker Henry W. Wilbur; the conference was chaired by Baltimore's Edward Janney.

49. At this time New York Yearly Meeting Hicksites reported eighteen First Day Schools with 553 scholars, Genesee four with 209, Philadelphia seventy-six with 5,045 pupils, Baltimore twenty-six with 1,046, Ohio, Indiana, and Illinois between them only twenty-two with 583 attenders.

13. Liberal Pastors and New Intellectual Meetings, 1900–1945

1. The movements discussed in this chapter are more fully covered in Ahlstrom, *Religious History,* chaps. 24, 36, 37, 46, 47; William R. Hutchison, *The Modernist Impulse in American Protestantism* (Durham, N.C.: Duke Univ. Press, 1992), and idem, ed., *American Protestant Thought: The Liberal Era* (New York: Harper, 1968).

2. Adolf von Harnack's *Das Wesen des Christentums* (literally "The Essence of Christianity," but translated as *What is Christianity?* [New York: G.P. Putnam's Sons, 1901]) and William James's *The Varieties of Religious Experience* (London: Longmans, 1902) were key books for American liberal Christianity.

3. Robert T. Handy, ed., *The Social Gospel in America, 1870–1920* (New York: Oxford Univ. Press, 1966); Charles H. Hopkins, *The Rise of the Social Gospel in American Protestantism, 1865–1915* (New Haven, Conn.: Yale Univ. Press, 1940).

4. Braude, *Radical Spirits,* chaps. 2, 4.

5. Rufus M. Jones, *The Inner Life* (New York: Macmillan, 1916), 101. See also Jones, *Social Law in the Spiritual World* (Philadelphia: Winston, 1904), 227–45. In the late twentieth century, aware of the limits to the human mind that are shown by psychology, sociology, quantum mechanics, and quarks, many Quakers see the Oversoul as oversold.

6. Elizabeth Isichei notes that Boehme and Tauler were popular among Victorian Quakers in *Victorian Quakers* (London: Oxford Univ. Press, 1970), 39.

7. Caroline Stephen, *Quaker Strongholds* (London: K. Paul, Trench, Trubner, 1890), 30–33.

8. His favorite mystics were Eckhart and Tauler, and he studied them with Karl Schmidt and philosophy with Kuhno Fischer in Germany. In America, although he studied later at Harvard under George Herbert Palmer, Josiah Royce, and Hugo Muensterberg, his ideas owed more to Emerson and the poets Dante and Lowell.

9. Rufus Jones, *Social Law,* 152, 155, 156.

10. Rufus Jones, *Studies in Mystical Religion* (London: Macmillan, 1909), xviii; idem, *Spiritual Energies in Daily Life* (New York: Macmillan, 1922), 137.

11. Rufus Jones, *The Trail of Life in College* (New York: Macmillan, 1929), quoted in Vining, *Friend of Life,* 51.

12. Rufus Jones, *The Luminous Trail* (New York: Macmillan, 1947), 163–64.

13. Vining, *Friend of Life,* 65, 60–61.

14. Woodard, *Sketches,* 6, 9, 77, 89.

15. Transcript of oral history interview with Gus Benedict by Mary Ellen Singsen, July 29, 1981, p. 7, in Oral History Collection, Haviland Records Room.

16. Transcript of oral history interview of George Badgley by Alson Van Wagner, May 2, 1992, in Oral History Collection, Haviland Records Room.

17. Data on Glens Fall from Joshua Brown, "Keeping Up to Date" (Paper in Haviland Records Room), 1990; information on Hannah Pratt supplied by Sabron Reynolds Newton; on Jesse Wilmore from Francis E. Willard, *American Women* (New York: Mast, Crowell and Kirkpatrick, 1897); on Brooklyn from Henry Isham Hazelton, *The Buroughs of Brooklyn and Queens* . . . (New York: Lewis Historical Publishing, 1925), vol. 3; on Will Reagan, see his *Venture in Quaker Education.*

18. Transcript of an oral history interview with Rachel Osborn, n.d., in Oral History Collection, Haviland Records Room.

19. Memorial minute for Jeannette Hadley; see Levinus Painter and George Badgley, *Elizabeth Lawton Hazard, 1880–1968* (New York: New York Yearly Meeting, 1970).

20. Between 1905 and 1940 Penn College sent ten students to Hartford, three to Auburn, one to Colgate Rochester, and twenty-eight to other liberal seminaries; in the 1950s, after its turn to conservative evangelicalism, they sent no one to any of these (except to Drew and Garrett) but sent five to the Holiness Wesleyans' Asbury and six to other Bible schools and Evangelical seminaries. Few Bible school students had college degrees.

21. Levinus King Painter, *Hill of Vision: The Story of the Quaker Movement in East Africa, 1902–1965* (Kaimosi, Kenya: East Africa Yearly Meeting of Friends, 1966). Quaker students at Hartford, but not in New York churches: Joseph Peele, Thomas E. Jones, Hershel Folger.

22. Newton, "Leroy Willard Reynolds," (Manuscript).

23. Transcripts of oral history tapes of interviews with George Badgley, Jan. 22, 1982, by Mary Ellen Singsen, of discussion between Badgley and Alson Van Wagner May 2, 1992, and Van Wagner with Lewis Hoskins, May 9, 1992.

24. Unidentified material in this section is from the Tercentenary, Society of Friends, New York Yearly Meeting, *Directory 1993,* (New York: New York Yearly Meeting, 1993).

25. Christopher Densmore, *Society of Friends in Buffalo and Western New York* (Buffalo, N.Y.: Buffalo Friends Meeting, 1990), in his centenary history in 1990.

26. Society of Friends, Montclair Monthly Meeting, *Founding and Early History of Montclair Monthly Meeting* (S.l.:s.n., 1960).

27. Sources on Albany Meeting are from Margallen Fichter and Warder Cadbury and the meeting's pamphlet *Albany Friends Meeting, A Short History, 1942–72* (s.l.: s.n., 1973).

28. Syracuse material from Alfred H. Cope and Adelaide Webster, Marjorie Banks, and Roger Riffer, "History of Syracuse Friends Meeting" (1982, Typescript.)

29. Stamford data from Thomas P. Johnson, "Quaker Activists in the Peace and Civil Rights Movements, 1955–1975: A Study of Stamford-Greenwich Friends Meeting" (Richmond, Ind.: Earlham College, 1990); Scarsdale from Mary Ellen Singsen, *The Quaker Way in Old Westchester* (Scarsdale, N.Y.: Scarsdale Historical Society, 1982). The Conscience Bay story from Daisy Newman, *A Procession of Friends* (Richmond, Ind.: Friends United Press, 1980), 359–60.

30. Edwin A. Burtt, *In Search of Philosophic Understanding* (New York: New American Library, 1965), 249. Data for this section come from memorials to Burtt in *Proceedings and Addresses of the American Philosphical Society,* 64, no. 5: 62–64, and Ithaca Monthly Meeting Minutes of Oct. 14, 1989.

31. Edwin A. Burtt, *Types of Religious Philosophy* (New York: Harper, 1939), gave Jesus only four pages and Plato a dozen, bracketing all Protestants as Fundamentalists and capitalists. Burtt surveys his contemporaries, such as Russell and Whitehead, and positivists and idealists.

32. Edwin A. Burtt, *Man Seeks the Divine: A Study in the History and Comparison of Religions* (New York: Harper, 1957) 9, 13.

33. Edwin A. Burtt, *The Metaphysical Foundations of Modern Physical Science: A Historical and Critical Essay* (New York: Harcourt, Brace, 1925), 330.

34. Kenneth Morgan, *Reaching for the Moon on Asian Religious Paths* (Chambersburg Pa.: Anima Press, 1990), 3.

35. His own meditation discipline is Buddhist. He views prayer as "an expression of aspiration, of hope, of longing . . . for the ability to act in closer harmony with . . . the Sacred Reality." Morgan, *Reaching for the Moon,* 170.

36. Morgan, *Reaching for the Moon,* 154; transcript of his oral history interview by Hugh Barbour for New York Yearly Meeting, Nov. 15, 1991, 10.

37. Morgan, *Reaching for the Moon,* 184–85, 183.

38. Transcript, of Morgan's oral history interview for New York Yearly Meeting, Nov. 15, 1991, 10.

39. Kenneth Morgan, *The Religion of the Hindus* (New York: Ronald Press, 1953); idem, *The Path of the Buddha* (New York: Ronald Press, 1956); and idem, *Islam: The Straight Path* (New York: Ronald Press, 1958).

40. Morgan, *Reaching for the Moon,* 179.

41. Guidebook for the exhibition, John Brzostoski, *Art of Tibet* (Greenville N.C.: (Gray Art Gallery, East Carolina Univ., 1989), 3. The art collection was transferred to the Rose Gallery at Brandeis University, and Brzostoski moved to teaching at the Cooper Union.

42. Henry J. Cadbury, "Hebraica and the Jews in Early Quaker Interest," in *Children of Light,* ed. Howard Brinton (New York: Macmillan, 1938), 135–63. Margaret Fell wrote two tracts for Rabbi Israel ben-Manasseh of Amsterdam.

43. Transcript of New York Yearly Meeting oral history tape, 2.

14. Quaker Service and Peacemaking, 1900–1948

1. Christina Jones, *World Missions,* 254. She lists Micajah Binford, Elizabeth Hazard, William Taber, and Carolena Wood among only 11 New Yorkers in the 250 who served on the Foreign Mission Board from 1859 to 1944 and only 4 from New York Yearly Meeting of the 350 who served in home or foreign missions.

2. David Thomas, *Travels Through the Western Country in the Summer of 1816* (Auburn, N.Y.: David Rumsey, 1819), 80.

3. Larry E. Burgess, (archivist, A. K. Smiley Public Library, Redlands, CA), *Mohonk: Its People and Spirit* (Mohonk, N.Y.: Mohonk Mountain House, 1980); Frederick Partington, *The Story of Mohonk* (Fulton, N.Y.: Morrill Press, 1911). Lyman Abbott, *Silhouettes of my Contemporaries* (Garden City, N.Y.: Doubleday, Page, 1921), 28–43; *DAB.*

4. Clyde A. Milner II, *Churchmen and the Western Indians* (Norman, Univ. of Oklahoma Press, 1985), chap. 5; Francis Paul Prucha, *American Indian Policy in Crisis* (Norman, Univ. of Oklahoma Press, 1976); Larry E. Burgess, *The Lake Mohonk Conference of Friends of the Indian: A Guide to the Annual Reports* (New York: Clearwater Publishing, 1975), based on his Ph.D. diss., Claremont Univ., 1972.

5. Lake Mohonk Conference of Friends of the Indian, *Proceedings of the Seventh Annual Meeting of the Lake Mohonk Conference of Friends of the Indian* (Lake Mohonk, N.Y.: Lake Mohonk Conference, 1889), 44.

6. Laurence M. Hauptman, ed. *The Lake Mohonk Conference on the Negro Question: A Guide to the Annual Reports* (New York: Clearwater Publishing, 1975).

7. Lake Mohonk Conference on International Arbitration, *First Lake Mohonk Conference on International Arbitration* (Mohonk Lake, N.Y.: Lake Mohonk Conference, 1895), 5. On this whole conference series see Michael A. Lutzker, "Patrician Peace Advocates: The Lake Mohonk Conferences on International Arbitration, 1895–1916," 2, based on his paper at the New York State Historical Association, May 1975, from a copy at the Swarthmore College Peace Collection, which also holds the whole archive of these con-

ferences. See C. Roland Marchand, *The American Peace Movement and Social Reform, 1898–1918* (Princeton, N.J.: Princeton Univ. Press, 1972); and David S. Patterson, *Toward a Warless World: The Travail of the American Peace Movement, 1887–1914* (Bloomington: Indiana Univ. Press, 1976).

8. See Brock, *Peace Testimony,* 296.

9. Willis H. Hall, *Quaker International Work in Europe since 1914* (Chambery: Reunies de Chambery, 1938), examined the options chosen by British Quaker conscientious objectors and their impact on the founding of postwar Quaker Centers in continental Europe. Martin Ceadel, *Pacifism in Britain, 1914–1945* (Oxford: Oxford Univ. Press, 1980), summarized and expanded in America by Thomas C. Kennedy, *Hound of Conscience* (Fayetteville: Univ. of Arkansas Press, 1981), and his articles, "Fighting about Peace," *Quaker History* 69, no. 1 (1980): 3–22, and "They in the Lord Who Firmly Trust," *Quaker History* 78, no. 2 (1989): 87–102; citing also Leigh Tucker, "English Quakers and World War I" (Ph.D. diss. Univ. of North Carolina, 1972). E. W. Orr, *Quakers in Peace and War, 1920 to 1967* (Eastbourne: W. J. Offord and Sons, 1974), 15, cites John W. Graham, *Conscription and Conscience: A History 1916–1919* (Allen and Unwin, 1922), reckoning 6,261 British conscientious objectors arrested of whom 1,543 refused any form of conscription and at least 1,400 spent two or more years in prison. Ass also Charles Chatfield, *For Peace and Justice: Pacifism in America* (Knoxville: Univ. of Tennessee Press, 1971), chaps. 1–3.

10. George H. Nash, *The Life of Herbert Hoover,* vol. 2 (New York: W. W. Norton, 1988).

11. Chatfield, *Peace and Justice,* 20.

12. Gertrude Bussey and Margaret Tims, *Pioneers for Peace: Women's International League for Peace and Freedom, 1915–1964* (London: WILPF, 1980).

13. Margaret Hope Bacon, "The Friends and Academic Freedom: Some Experiences and Thoughts of Henry J. Cadbury" in *Seeking the Light,* J. William Frost and John M. Moore, ed. (Wallingford, Pa.: Pendle Hill, 1986). Anna L. Curtis, *Mary S. McDowell, Peace Crusader* (New York: New York Monthly Meeting, 1960); material from Elizabeth Moger.

14. J. William Frost, "Our Deeds Carry Our Message," *Quaker History* 81, no. 1 (1992): 3–51; see also Rufus M. Jones, *A Service of Love in Wartime* (New York: Macmillan, 1920); Mary Hoxie Jones, *Swords into Ploughshares* (New York: Macmillan, 1937); John Forbes, *The Quaker Star under Seven Flags, 1917–1927* (Philadelphia: Univ. of Pennsylvania Press, 1962). The British Friends Service Committee, later merged into the War Victims Committee, had begun in 1915.

15. Combining the manuscript diary of Leroy Willard Reynolds (from Sabron Newton), and AFSC's oral history interview no. 26, France, World War I (copyright 1989), used by permission.

16. Marvin Weisbord, *Some Form of Peace* (New York: Viking, 1968), chap. 1.

17. Frost, "Our Deeds," 15, 31. More than two-thirds had attended college as compared with 17 percent in the same ages in the U.S. population; but two-thirds had farm experience.

18. Russell, *History of Quakerism,* 515; Lawrence S. Wittner, *Rebels Against War: The American Peace Movement, 1933–1983* (Philadelphia: Temple Univ. Press, 1984), 41n. On camps, see Chatfield, *Peace and Justice,* chap. 2, 69, 75; half were Mennonites, less than one-quarter Friends. For prison camp treatment see Harold Studley Gray, *Character "Bad": The Story of a Conscientious Objector . . . Harold Studley Gray* (New York: Harper, 1934). In 1936, American Friends numbered 93,697, Mennonites 114,337, Brethren 188,290 (Wittner, *Rebels Against War,* 13).

19. Frost, "Our Deeds," 38. Daily distribution was by German teachers and social workers.

20. Letter from Alfred Scattergood to Edward Brinton, May 24, 1921, Wood Family Archives. She had already volunteered to go to Germany in October 1918; see Jones, *Service of Love,* and Vining, *Friend of Life,* 170. They were the first U.S. civilians admitted to postwar Germany (Frost, "Our Deeds," 35).

21. Howard Brinton, "Friends for Seventy-Five Years," *Bulletin of the Friends Historical Association* 49 (1960): 16; Mary Hoxie Jones, *Swords into Ploughshares,* 75– 77, both courtesy of Sabron Reynolds Newton; letter from Carolena to James Wood, May 4, [1921?], Wood family archives at Braewold.

22. Hall, *Quaker International Work,* 188, 191. His data lists (71) 251 relief workers from Five Years Meeting, 600 in noncombatant service and 2,313 in the armed forces. His corresponding figures for FGC are 67, 29, and 298; for Philadelphia Yearly Meeting (Ortho), 76, 24, and 82. AFSC's European relief totaled more than twenty-five million dollars in supplies. In France alone there were 1,070 English and 780 American workers (Chatfield, *Peace and Justice,* 380, citing Anna Ruth Fry, *A Quaker Adventure: The Story of Nine Years' Relief and Reconstruction* (New York: Frank Maurice, 1927). On Russia, see Weisbord, *Some Form of Peace,* chap. 3.

23. Letter from Carolena Wood to Hollingsworth Wood, from San José, Costa Rica, Nov. 1927, in Wood Family Archives.

24. Letter, May 15, 1909, from the Working Girls Vacation Society. The Board of Advice and Information of the charity organizations said only four places admitted a few, healthy colored children. The five boxes of files of the Colored Mission at Haverford seem all to be Wood's own. Their twenty-odd sacks of Wood's papers are still not inventoried.

25. Albert N. Keim, *The Politics of Conscience: The Historic Peace Churches and America at War, 1917–1955,* (Scottsdale, Pa.: Herald Press, 1988); Chatfield, *Peace and Justice,* 30, 40, and, generally, chaps. 4–8; cf. Abraham John Muste, *Not By Might* (New York: Harper, 1947); Nat Hentoff, *Peace Agitator: The Story of A. J. Muste* (New York: Macmillan, 1963); Jo Ann Robinson, *Abraham Went Out: A Biography of A. J. Muste* (Philadelphia: Temple Univ. Press, 1981), based on her doctoral dissertation and idem, *A. J. Muste, Pacifist and Prophet* (Wallingford, Pa.: Pendle Hill, 1981), stressing his Quakerism.

26. Lester Jones, *Quakers in Action: Recent Humanitarian and Reform Activities of American Quakers* (New York: Macmillan, 1929), chaps. 15–16.

27. Weisbord, *Some Form of Peace,* chaps. 4 and 5.

28. Cynthia Eller, *Conscientious Objectors and the Second World War: Moral and Religious Arguments in Support of Pacifism* (New York: Praeger, 1991) 15, 12.

29. Chatfield, *Peace and Justice,* 267, shows AFSC's and Ray Newton's central role in the National Peace Conference of 1936 and the Emergency Peace Campaign.

30. Of their men near draft age 42 percent of Mennonites, 10 percent of Friends, and 8 percent of Brethren claimed conscientious objector status (Eller, *Conscientious Objectors,* 50).

31. Letter from Elizabeth Hazard to Yearly Meeting Friends, Nov. 11, 1941, in Haviland Records Room.

32. Wittner, *Rebels Against War,* (41n) reckons 11,887 were given 4-E status, 25,000 were classified 1-A-O for noncombatant service in uniform, and 6,086 went to prison of the 10,022,367 drafted. The National Service Board of Religious Objectors, *Directory of Civilian Public Service* (Washington, D.C.: National Service Board of Religious Objectors, n.d.), lists 11,966 of whom 951 were Friends.

33. Hobart Mitchell, *We Would Not Kill* (Richmond Ind.: Friends United Press, 1983), vii.

34. American Friends Service Committee, *The Experience of the AFSC in Civilian Public Service under the Selective Training & Service Act of 1940, 1941–45* (Philadelphia: American Friends Service Committee, 1945), 22–25. The 1,733 Civilian Public Service men under AFSC were from a national total of 10,723. The others were in camps under Brethren, Mennonite, Catholic, Methodist, or secular leadership.

35. *The Compass* (Campton camp journal, Nov. 1942), 24. Liceum data, 22–23.

36. Mary Ellen Singsen, "Looking Back at the CPS Experience," and other articles in *Friends Journal* 38, no. 1 (1992): 22–24; cf. also personal narratives in *The Southern Friend, Journal of the North Carolina Friends Historical Society* 14, nos. 1, 2, 1992.

37. Memorial letter by Jean Young to Syracuse Meeting, Dec. 17, 1967, from Norman Whitney's papers in the Swarthmore College Library Peace Collection. See also *Friends Journal* (April 1992) 2; Lloyd Harbor's meeting house was named for him and Mildred Whitney.

38. See Robert L. Hale, Jr., "Report of a Housing Project Undertaken by the Monthly Meeting of . . . Friends in Syracuse, N.Y., September 1954 to March 1955," copy in Haviland Records Room.

39. See Painter, *Hill of Vision;* Wilma Wilcox, *Quaker Volunteer: An Experience in Palestine* (Richmond, Ind.: Friends United Press, 1977).

15. Reunion

1. Society of Friends, New York Yearly meeting (Hicksite), "Alfred Moore," *Memorials Concerning Deceased Friends* (New York: J. J. Caulon, 1889), 97–98.

2. Nine Partners Quarterly Meeting, Minutes, May 8, 1855.

3. New York Yearly Meeting (Orthodox), Minutes, 1899, 75.

4. New York Yearly Meeting (Orthodox), Minutes, 1904, 52–55.

5. New York Yearly Meeting (Orthodox), Minutes, 1908, 63–84.

6. New York Yearly Meeting (Orthodox), Minutes, 1944, 26–27.

7. New York Yearly Meetings, 1928, 4.

8. New York Yearly Meeting (Orthodox), Minutes, 1938, 74.

9. Myron L. Tripp and A. Ashley Stuart, "Open letter to urge Orthodox Friends of the Five Years Meeting to retain the old Discipline and to reject the proposed Faith and Practice," June 1946, Clinton Corners file, vertical files, Haviland Records Room.

10. George Selleck, *Quakers in Boston* (Boston: Friends Meeting at Cambridge, 1976), 212–18.

11. John M. Moore, ed., *Friends in the Delaware Valley* (Haverford, Pa.: Friends Historical Association, 1981), chap. 4 by Herbert Hadley.

12. J. Kennedy Sinclaire, letter to Herman Compter, July 23, 1954, correspondence file, Herman Compter Collection, Haviland Records Room.

13. Albert Schreiner, letter to Herman Compter, June 29, 1955, Organic Union Committee correspondence file, Herman Compter Collection, Haviland Records Room.

14. Levinus K. Painter, letters to Herman Compter, May 14, 1954, and June 27, 1955, Organic Union Committee correspondence file, Compter Collection, Haviland Records Room.

15. See "Monthly Meeting Letters 3/54–7/55," Herman Compter Collection, Haviland Records Room.

16. Transcript of "John and Miriam Brush, 7/24/1991" and "George Badgley, 1/22/1982" taped interviews, Oral History Collection, Haviland Records Room.

17. Society of Friends, New York Yearly Meeting (Hicksite), "Introductory Statement," *Book of Discipline of the Religious Society of Friends* (New York: New York Yearly Meeting, 1950), 7.

18. Society of Friends, New York Yearly Meeting, "State of Society Summary," Minutes, July 25–August 1, 1956, 105.

19. The author of this chapter was heavily dependent on the advice and corrections of Elizabeth H. Moger. The recollections of George A. Badgley, Lewis W. Hoskins and Elizabeth A. Hoskins, and Irene H. Van Wagner were further resources.

16. Peace and Social Concerns: The Last Forty Years, 1955–1995

1. Johnson, "Quaker Activists," 11–13.

2. Ibid., 13–16.

3. Ibid., 16–18; Albert Bigelow, *The Voyage of the Golden Rule: An Experiment with Truth* (Garden City, N.Y.: Doubleday, 1959).

4. Newton Garver to J. Lawrence Murray, June 8, 1964, in the Richard Lipsitz Papers, University Archives, State University of New York at Buffalo. The Lipsitz Papers concern the challenge to the Feinberg Law of 1949 made by Newton Garver and other members of the State University of New York at Buffalo faculty in the 1960s.

5. New York Yearly Meeting, Minute #54, July 1964.

6. Newton Garver to David S. Price, Vice President of SUNY, Aug. 11, 1964. Lipsitz Papers.

7. *New York Times,* Jan. 24, 1967.

8. For an example of what was produced, see Vince Buscemi, "A Study of the Right Sharing of World Resources" (Dec. 1986), on file at the Haviland Records Room.

9. Minutes of Wilton (Connecticut) Monthly Meeting, Spring 1959, as noted in Lawrence S. Apsey, *Following the Light for Peace* (Katonah, N.Y.: Kim Pathways, 1991).

10. Johnson, "Quaker Activists," 20–21.

11. Ibid.

12. Transcript of Interview with Lee Stern, July 28, 1989, p. 6, in the Oral History Collection, Haviland Records Room.

13. Ibid.

14. Rachel Davis DuBois, *All This and Something More: Pioneering in Intercultural Education* (Bryn Mawr, Pa.: Dorrance, 1984), 38.

15. DuBois, *All This;* also New York Yearly Meeting Memorial Minute, 1993.

16. New York Yearly Meeting Memorial Minute, 1987.

17. Sources include material on Rustin from Charles Bloomstein and Fr. Michael Kerper (manuscript biography in author's possession); Bayard Rustin, *Down the Line: The Collected Writings of Bayard Rustin* (Chicago: Quadrangle Books, 1971); Kenneth Ives and Leonard Kenworthy, "Bayard Rustin" in Kenneth Ives, ed., *Black Quakers: Brief Biographies* (Chicago: Progresiv Publishr, 1991); Aldon D. Morris, *The Origins of the Civil Rights Movement: Black Communities Organizing for Change* (New York: Free Press, 1994); Thomas M. Shaw, *Bayard Rustin as Art Collector* (Newark, N.J.: Kean College of New Jersey, 1989); Robert Penn Warren, *Who Speaks for the Negro?* (New York: Random House, 1965).

18. Lillian Schlissel, *Conscience in America: A Documentary History of Conscientious Objection in America, 1757–1967* (New York: Dutton, 1968), 260; Margery W. Rubin, "The Chal-

lenge of U.S. vs. Seeger to the United States Supreme Court" (Master's Thesis, C.W. Post College, New York, 1982); Edward Banzal, "Part of the Draft Act Is Upset by Court," *New York Times,* Jan. 21, 1964.

19. Schissel, *Conscience in America,* 261.

20. Ibid., 267; "Excerpts from Ruling on Conscientious Objection," *New York Times,* Jan. 21, 1964; United States vs. Seeger, 380 U.S. (1965).

21. Paul Freund, *Constitutional Law: Cases and Problems,* 3d ed. (Boston: Little, Brown, 1967), 1198; Schissel, *Conscience in America,* 267.

22. Transcript of Interview with Richard Accetta-Evans, Nov. 15, 1992, p. 2, in Oral History Collection, Haviland Records Room.

23. Ibid, 3.

24. Nettie West, personal letter to the author.

17. Unity and Diversity since Reunion

1. See Joshua Brown, mimeographed manuscripts, "You Can't Get There from Here" (1986), "Looking for the Promised Land" (1988), and "Keeping Up to Date" (1990), mainly aimed at reorienting staff work from social action toward ministry. Copies in HRR.

2. Walter Brueggemann, *The Creative Word: Canon as a Model for Biblical Education* (Philadelphia: Fortress Press, 1982), 1.

3. Beginning in 1979, the proceeds of the Sheldon and Mary Budd Rymph Fund, shared with Powell House, made possible the securing of archival supplies and of archival services that supplemented those provided from yearly meeting funds. This money permitted them to acquire a computer, overhaul the air conditioning, undo the results of an indoor flood, briefly hire an archival consultant, and pay the expenses of a volunteer so that Agnes Campbell's card file was computerized, updated, and extended to more of the collection.

4. Many anecdotes of the Powells and of early days at Powell House are preserved by Dorothy K. Garner, comp., *Reminiscences of Powell House Beginnings for Its 25th Anniversary* (n.p., 1985?).

5. Reinhold Niebuhr's Gifford Lectures, published as *Nature and Destiny of Man* (New York: Scribner, 1941–43).

6. Lewis Benson, "That of God in Every Man—What Did George Fox Mean by It?" *Quaker Religious Thought* 12, no. 2 (1970): 2–24. Francis Hall responded.

7. See Dean Freiday, "The Early Quakers and the Doctrine of Authority," *Quaker Religious Thought* 15, no. 1 (1973): 4–38, and idem, "Atonement in Historical Perspective," *Quaker Religious Thought* 21 (1987): 13–32.

8. Daniel A. Seeger, *Quaker Universalists, Their Ministry Among Friends and in the World* (Media, Pa.: Quaker Universalist Fellowship, 1988). His paper, "Is Coexistence Possible? Christianity and Universalism in the Religious Society of Friends," was published in the first *Universalist Reader* of the Quaker Universalist Fellowship.

9. Natalie A. Naylor, "Mary Calderone, Crusader for Sex Education," paper read for the Conference on New York State History, Seneca Falls, New York, June 5, 1993.

10. New York Yearly Meeting Minutes, 1972, #68; 1974, #88.

11. Ibid., 1988, #183.

12. New York Yearly Meeting Representative Meeting Minutes, 1988, #27.

13. Ibid., 1990, #22.

14. Victoria Cooley to Nurture Coordinating Committee, Sept. 1988.

15. Herbert Lape, private letter to Mary Foster Cadbury.

16. New York Yearly Meeting Minutes, 1972.

17. Carleton Mabee and James Fletcher, *A Quaker Speaks from the Black Experience: The Life and Selected Writings of Barrington Dunbar* (New York: New York Yearly Meeting, 1979).

18. Other members included Iceline Curtis, Janet Fletcher, Henry and Margaret Mulindi, Cecil Seale, Helen Toppins, Jane Kerina, Marvea Thompson, Philip LaViscount, and Roosevelt Weaver.

19. Lamont D. Thomas, *Rise to be a People* (Urbana, Ill.: Univ. of Illinois Press, 1986); idem, *Paul Cuffee, Black Entrepreneur and Pan-Africanist* (Urbana, Ill.: Univ. of Illinois Press, 1988).

20. Similarly, Michael Sheeran, S.J., in *Beyond Majority Rule: Voteless Decisions in the Religious Society of Friends* (Philadelphia: Philadelphia Yearly Meeting, 1983), identified the key line of distinction among Philadelphia Friends as their focus, or lack of it, upon the "gathered meeting."

Glossary

Acknowledgment: Formal apology given by an offender for an infraction of Quaker rules. The formal apology accepted by the business meeting.

Advices: Rules or recommended practices stated in the Quaker discipline.

Affirmation: A statement of a fact by a Quaker to a public official or body. By most English and American law now accepted in lieu of a judicial oath by Quakers and others.

Allowed / Indulged Meeting: A meeting for worship at a place and at times appointed by a monthly meeting. If attendance and conduct is acceptable, the group may become a preparative or monthly meeting.

Birthright Member: A person recorded as a member when both parents are members.

Clearness: The state of readiness to take action free of violations of the discipline as determined by a meeting for business.

Clerk: The person selected to conduct a meeting for business. The duties may also include giving and receiving communications on behalf of the meeting.

Complaint: A charge of violation of the discipline against an individual brought to a monthly meeting for business.

Concern: An urge to take an action on the basis of a testimony or conscientious scruple.

Convincement: Quaker convincement means conversion. Acceptance of Quaker faith and practice as stated in the discipline.

Dealing: Process by which a business meeting brings a violator of Quaker rules to account.

Discipline: Rules established by yearly meetings for members in their jurisdictions.

Disownment: The expulsion from membership of a Quaker for violation of rules. See **Restoration.**

Distraint: The seizure of property by public authorities for nonpayment of taxes, fines, or nonperformance of services.

Facing Benches: The seats at the front of the meeting room sometimes reserved for ministers and elders. The seats faced the main seating and were generally elevated one or more steps.

Inward Light: The light or seed of God that Quakers believe lies within all people. Light Within or Inner Light.

389

Leading: A personal conviction, believed to be divinely guided, requiring new individual or group action. The individual may bring it before a Quaker meeting for testing.

Meeting for Sufferings: The executive committee of a yearly meeting. Later, Representative Meeting or Permanent Board.

Minister: A person recognized by his or her monthly meeting as having a special gift in the ministry. In modern programmed meetings a pastor may also be a minister.

Minute: The resolve of a business meeting determined and recorded by the clerk as being the will of the meeting without voting. (verb) To record such a determination.

Monthly Meeting: The basic Quaker organization that oversees membership, owns property, enforces Quaker rules, and conducts business. The meeting for business of this unit.

Plain Dress: Clothing of simple cut devoid of ornament. Historically, simple clothing of an earlier style.

Plain Speech: Use of singular form of speech in referring to one person. Avoidance of names of months and days of the week honoring non-Christian deities.

Preparative Meeting: The local congregation that refers matters to the monthly meeting. The meeting for business of this unit. Today, monthly meetings generally have only one congregation.

Programmed Meeting: A meeting for worship at an appointed time with a pastor or other person in charge and an order of service.

Quarterly Meeting: The organization of a region of a yearly meeting that meets four times a year and to which monthly meetings report. The meeting for business of this unit.

Restoration: The formal restoration to membership of disowned members upon acceptance of their acknowledgments by the monthly meeting for business.

Sufferings: The financial losses, imprisonments, physical or mental abuse endured because of conscientious observance of Quaker practices and beliefs.

Testimonies: Quaker behavioral requirements that at relevant times could include plain dress or speech, refusal to take oaths, refusal of military service, and others.

Unprogrammed Meeting: A meeting for worship at an appointed time without a prearranged order. There may be spoken messages or only silence.

Witness: Action taken to conform with a testimony or conscientious belief. (verb) To take such an action.

Yearly Meeting: The organization for a geographic area that makes rules and oversees constituent quarterly and monthly meetings. The meeting for business of this unit.

Selected Quaker Sources

The best place to begin any study of New York Quaker history is in the Haviland Records Room in New York City, which contains the archives and related papers of New York Yearly Meeting from 1663 to the present. Extant records of business meetings are found there. For the most part these holdings are complete from the late eighteenth century although some key meeting records for the early period have been lost. This collection also contains many secondary works pertaining to New York and Quaker history at large. Many, although not all, of the meeting records were microfilmed in the 1950s and are available on microfilm throughout the country at the genealogical libraries of the Church of Jesus Christ of Latter Day Saints. Of interest also for New York Quaker history are records of Canadian meetings at Pickering College in Newmarket, Ontario, and Orthodox Michigan Friends at Malone College in Canton, Ohio.

The substantial holdings of the Friends Historical Library at Swarthmore College, the Swarthmore College Peace Collection, and the Quaker Collection at Haverford College usefully supplement official collections and also contain microfilm of many official records. Among the larger collections of personal papers at other institutions are the Emily Howland Papers at Cornell University; the Tallcot-Howland Family Papers at the University of Rochester (there are also Howland and Tallcot family papers at Swarthmore and Haverford); the Post Family Papers at the University of Rochester; the Rachel Davis DuBois Papers at the Immigration History Research Center at the University of Minnesota; records of the New York Manumission Society at the New-York Historical Society; the Henry Miles Papers at the Houghton Library, Harvard University; the Mary Stone McDowell Papers at the Schlesinger Library, Radcliffe College; the Bowne Family Papers at the Bowne House, Flushing, New York; the Robinson Family Papers at the Rokeby Museum, Ferrisburg, Vermont; and the Parsons Family papers at the Winterthur Library and at the Queensborough Public Library.

Despite the wealth of primary sources, relatively little has been written specifically about New York Friends in any period. The two chapters on New York in *Quakers in the American Colonies* by Rufus Jones, Isaac Sharpless, and Amelia Gummere, remained the standard account for many years. Reflecting the many studies of Quaker history since 1950 is Arthur J. Worrall, *Quakers in the Colonial Northeast,* which is thematic in approach and also covers New England. Henry

391

Onderdonk, *The Annals of Hempstead,* gives a detailed account of Friends there through 1828, while John Cox, Jr., *Quakerism in the City of New York, 1657–1930,* provides a useful introduction to Friends in the city. A. Day Bradley, "Progressive Friends in Michigan and New York," and Bradley, "New York Yearly Meeting at Poplar Ridge and the Primitive Friends," detail two religious controversies of the nineteenth century. Bliss Forbush, *Elias Hicks: Quaker Liberal,* is a useful biography about a key figure in the separation that bears his name, while Robert Davison, *Isaac Hicks: New York Merchant and Quaker,* is a model business study of a less well-known relative of the famous Quaker minister.

Arthur G. Dorland's study of Canadian Friends first appeared in 1927; its revised and updated version is *The Quakers in Canada: A History.* It covers the meetings in Ontario that were part of the New York Yearly Meeting (Orthodox) until 1867 and of the Genesee Yearly Meeting until 1955. Other studies on related areas are Charles W. Hughes and A. Day Bradley, "The Early Quaker Meetings of Vermont"; Carlisle G. Davidson, "A Profile of Hicksite Quakerism in Michigan, 1830–1860"; John Cox, Jr., "The Quakers in Michigan"; and Nelson R. Burr, "The Quakers in Connecticut."

The journals of a number of New York Friends have been published, most notably the *Journal of the Life and Religious Labors of Elias Hicks,* the *Journal of . . . Rufus Hall,* the *Memoirs of the Life and Religious Labors . . . Henry Hull,* the *Memoirs of the Life and Gospel Labors of Stephen Grellet,* the *Journal of the Life of Joseph Hoag, Memoir of Rachel Hicks, Memoirs of the Life and Religious Labors of Sunderland P. Gardner,* and the *Autobiography of John J. Cornell.* Samuel L. Knapp, *Life of Thomas Eddy, Memoir of John Griscom,* and Lydia Maria Child, *Isaac T. Hopper: A True Life,* contain much primary material.

Bibliography

Archives/Manuscript Collections

American Antiquarian Society, Worcester, Mass.
  Abby Kelley Foster Papers
Earlham College, Richmond, Ind.
  Allen Jay Papers
  Elbert Russell Papers
Haverford College—Quaker Collection, Haverford, Pa.
  Hartshorne Family Papers
  Philadelphia Yearly Meeting. Indian Committee.
    Records
  Wood Family Papers
Haviland Records Room, New York Yearly Meeting, New York City
  Caleb W. Allis Papers
  Genesee Yearly Meeting Records
  Herman Compter Collection
  Joint Committee on the Indian Concern Records
  List of Members of New York Yearly Meeting at the Time of the Separation
    (typescript by John Cox, Jr.)
  New York Manumission Society Membership List
  New York Yearly Meeting Records
  Oral History Collection
  Jonathan Pierce to Wilmer Kearns, Letter, 1938
  Purchase Quarterly Meeting Records
New York Historical Association, Cooperstown, N.Y.
  Randsome Family Papers
New-York Historical Society, New York City
  New York Manumission Society Records
Pickering College, Newmarket, Ontario
  Timothy Rogers Journal
Rhode Island Historical Society, Providence, R.I.
  New England Yearly Meeting Archives
State University of New York at Buffalo
  Richard Lipsitz Papers

Swarthmore College—Friends Historical Library, Swarthmore, Pa.
    Joel Bean Papers
    George H. Burr Papers
    Benjamin Ferris Papers
    Elias Hicks Papers
    New York Association for the Relief of those Held in Slavery . . . Papers,
        1839–1844
Swarthmore College—Peace Collection, Swarthmore, Pa.
    Norman J. Whitney Papers
University of Rochester, Rochester, N.Y.
    Amy and Isaac Kirby Post Papers
    William Seward Papers
    Phebe Post Willis Papers
Wood Family Archives, Braewald, Mt. Kisco, N.Y.
    Wood Family Papers

Periodicals

American Friend (Philadelphia), 1894–1960
British Friend (Glasgow), 1843–1913
Bulletin of the Friends Historical Association (Philadelphia), 1906–61
Christian Worker (Chicago), 1871–94
The Compass (Campton CPS Camp), 1942
Evangelical Friend (Cleveland), 1906–14
Friend (Philadelphia), 1827–1955
Friend, or Advocate of Truth (Philadelphia and New York), 1828–33
Friends Expositor (Mt. Pleasant, Ohio), 1887–92
Friends Intelligencer (New York), 1838–39
Friends Intelligencer (Philadelphia), 1844–1955
Friends Journal (Philadelphia), 1955–
Friends Library (Philadelphia), 1837–50
Friends Miscellany (Philadelphia), 1831–39
Friends' Review (Philadelphia), 1847–94
Gospel Expositor (Columbus, Ohio), 1883–84
Liberator (Boston, Mass.), 1831–65
National Anti-Slavery Standard (New York), 1840–70
New York State Assembly Journal (Albany, N.Y.), 1824
New York Times, 1964
Non-Slaveholder (Philadelphia), 1846–50, 1853–54
Quaker (Philadelphia), 1827–28
Quaker History (Philadelphia), 1962–
Quaker Religious Thought, 1959–
Southern Friend (Greensboro, N.C.), 1992

Books, Booklets, and Pamphlets

Abbott, Lyman. *Silhouettes of My Comtemporaries*. Garden City, N.Y.: Doubleday, Page, 1921.

Ahlstrom, Sydney E. *A Religious History of the American People*. New Haven, Conn.: Yale Univ. Press, 1972.

Allott, Stephen. *Lindley Murray, 1745–1826: Quaker Grammarian of New York and Old York*. York, England: Sessions, 1991.

American Friends Service Committee. *Experience of the American Friends Service Committee in Civilian Public Service under the Selective Training and Service Act of 1940*. Philadelphia: American Friends Service Committee, 1945.

American Primers: A Guide to the Microfiche Collection. Introduction by Richard L. Venezky. Bethesda, Md.: Univ. Publications of America, 1990.

Anderson, Rasmus B. *The First Chapter of Norwegian Emigration*. Madison, Wis.: R. B. Anderson, 1906.

Andrews, Edward Deming. *People Called Shakers*. New York: Oxford Univ. Press, 1953.

Apsey, Lawrence S. *Following the Light for Peace*. Katonah, N.Y.: Kim Pathways, 1991.

Bacon, Margaret Hope. *Mothers of Feminism: The Story of Quaker Women in America*. San Francisco, Calif.: Harper and Row, 1986.

Balmer, Randall. *A Perfect Babel of Confusion: Dutch Religion and Culture in the Middle Colonies*. New York: Oxford Univ. Press, 1989.

Barbour, Hugh. *Quakers in Puritan England*. New Haven, Conn.: Yale Univ. Press, 1964.

———. *Slavery and Theology: Writings of Seven Quaker Reformers, 1800–1870*. Dublin, Ind.: Prinit Press, 1985.

Barbour, Hugh, and Arthur O. Roberts, eds. *Early Quaker Writings 1650–1700*. Grand Rapids, Mich.: William B. Eerdmans, 1973.

Barclay, Robert. *An Apology for True Christian Divinity*. London: s.n., 1678.

Barker, Jacob. *Incidents of My Life and Life Work of 84 Years*. Richmond, Ind.: Nicholson, 1911.

Barnes, Harry Elmer. *The Story of Punishment*. Boston: Stratford, 1930.

Barry, Kathleen. *Susan B. Anthony: A Biography of a Singular Feminist*. New York: Ballantine Books, 1988.

Bauman, Richard. *Let Your Words Be Few: The Symbolism of Speaking and Silence Among Seventeenth-Century Quakers*. New York: Cambridge Univ. Press, 1983.

Bender, Thomas. *New York Intellect: A History of Intellectual Life in New York City from 1750 to Beginnings of Our Own Time*. New York: Alfred A. Knopf, 1987.

Berkhofer, Robert F. *Salvation and the Savage*. Lexington: Univ. of Kentucky Press, 1965.

Bevans, John. *Some Tracts Relating to the Controversy Between Hannah Barnard and the Society of Friends*. London: Denton and Harvey, 1802.

Bigelow, Albert. *The Voyage of the Golden Rule: An Experiment with Truth*. Garden City, N.Y.: Doubleday, 1959.

Birkel, Michael L., and John Newman, eds. *The Lamb's War: Essays to Honor Hugh Barbour.* Richmond, Ind.: Earlham College Press, 1992.

Bjorklund, Victoria Baum. *A Century of Friends, 1877–1977.* Locust Valley, N.Y.: Friends Academy, 1977.

Bourne, William O. *History of the Public School Society of the City of New York.* New York: William Wood, 1870.

Braithwaite, Anna. *A Letter from Anna Braithwaite to Elias Hicks, on the Nature of his Doctrines.* Philadelphia: Printed for the Reader, 1825.

Braude, Ann. *Radical Spirits: Spiritualism and Women's Rights in Nineteenth-Century America.* Boston: Beacon Press, 1989.

Breault, Judith Colucci. *The World of Emily Howland: Odyssey of a Humanitarian.* Milbrae, Calif.: Les Femmes, 1976.

Brinton, Howard, ed. *Children of Light.* New York: Macmillian, 1938.

———. *Quaker Education in Theory and Practice.* 3d rev. ed. Wallingford, Pa.: Pendle Hill, 1967.

Brock, Peter. *Freedom from War: Nonsectarian Pacifism, 1814–1914.* Toronto: Univ. of Toronto Press, 1991.

———. *Quaker Peace Testimony.* York, England: Sessions, 1990.

Brown, Elisabeth Potts, and Susan Mosher Stuard, eds. *Witnesses for Change: Quaker Women over Three Centuries.* New Brunswick, N.J.: Rutgers Univ. Press, 1989.

Brueggemann, Walter. *The Creative Word: Canon as a Model for Biblical Education.* Philadelphia: Fortress Press, 1982.

Brzostoski, John. *Art of Tibet.* Greenville, N.C.: Gray Art Gallery, East Carolina Univ., 1989.

Burgess, Larry E. *The Lake Mohonk Conference of Friends of the Indian: A Guide to the Annual Reports.* New York: Clearwater Publishing, 1975.

———. *Mohonk: Its People and Spirit.* New Paltz, N.Y.: Mohonk Mountain House, 1980.

Burton, Ann, and Conrad Burton. *Michigan Quakers: Abstracts of Fifteen Monthly Meetings of the Society of Friends.* Decatur, Mich.: Glendor, 1989.

Burtt, Edwin A. *In Search of Philosophic Understanding.* New York: New American Library, 1965.

———. *Man Seeks the Divine: A Study in the History and Comparison of Religions.* New York: Harper, 1957.

———. *The Metaphysical Foundations of Modern Physical Science: A Historical and Critical Essay.* New York: Harcourt, Brace, 1925.

———. *Types of Religious Philosophy.* New York: Harper, 1939.

Bussey, Gertrude, and Margaret Tims. *Pioneers for Peace: Women's International League for Peace and Freedom, 1915–1965.* London: WILPF, 1980.

The Cabinet, or Works of Darkness Brought to Light. Philadelphia: Printed for the Compiler, 1824.

Cadwallader, Priscilla Hunt. *Memoirs.* 2nd ed. Philadelphia: Book Assocation of Friends, 1864.

Ceadal, Martin. *Pacifism in Britain, 1914–1945.* New York: Oxford Univ. Press, 1980.

Centennial Temperance Conference (1885: Philadelphia). *One Hundred Years of Temperance*. New York: National Temperance Society and Publication House, 1885.

Chandler, Elizabeth Margaret. *Essays, Philanthropic and Moral*. Philadelphia: Lemuel Howell, 1836.

——. *The Poetical Works of Elizabeth Margaret Chandler*. Philadelphia: Lemuel Howell, 1836.

Chatfield, Charles. *For Peace and Justice: Pacifism in America, 1914–1941*. Knoxville: University of Tennessee Press, 1971.

Child, Lydia Maria. *Isaac T. Hopper: A True Life*. Boston: Jewett, 1853.

Colman, Lucy N. *Reminiscences*. Buffalo, N.Y.: H. L. Green, 1891.

Condon, George E. *Stars in the Water: The Story of the Erie Canal*. Garden City, N.Y.: Doubleday, 1974.

Conklin, Ellen C. L. *Autobiography and Extracts from the Diaries of Caroline E. Ladd*. N.p, n.d.

Corder, Susanna. *Life of Elizabeth Fry*. Philadelphia: H. Longstreth, 1855.

Cornell, John J. *Autobiography of John J. Cornell*. Baltimore, Md.: Lord Baltimore Press, 1906.

Countryman, Edward. *A People in Revolution: The American Revolution and Political Society in New York, 1760–1790*. Baltimore: Johns Hopkins Univ. Press, 1981.

Cox, John, Jr. *New York Church Archives: Religious Society of Friends*. New York: WPA, 1940.

——. *Quakerism in the City of New York, 1657–1930*. New York: Privately printed, 1930.

Cragg, Gerald R. *The Church and the Age of Reason, 1648–1789*. Harmondsworth, England: Penguin Books, 1960.

Crewdson, Isaac. *A Beacon to the Society of Friends*. New York: I. T. Hopper, 1835.

Crosfield, George, ed. *Memoirs of the Life . . . of Samuel Fothergill*. Liverpool, England: D. Marples, 1843.

Cross, Whitney R. *The Burned-Over District: The Social and Intellectual History of Enthusiastic Religion in Western New York, 1800–1850*. Ithaca, N.Y.: Cornell Univ. Press, 1950.

Cubberley, Ellwood P. *Public Education in the United States*. Cambridge, Mass.: Riverside Press, 1962.

Curtis, Anna L. *Mary S. McDowell, Peace Crusader*. New York: New York Monthly Meeting of Friends, 1960.

Davison, Robert A. *Isaac Hicks: New York Merchant and Quaker, 1767–1820*. Cambridge, Mass.: Harvard Univ. Press, 1964.

Densmore, Christopher. *Society of Friends in Buffalo and Western New York*. Buffalo, N.Y.: Buffalo Friends Meeting, 1990.

Documentary History of the State of New York. 4 vols. Albany, N.Y.: Weed, Parsons, 1849–51.

Doherty, Robert W. *The Hicksite Separation: A Sociological Analysis of Religious Schism in Early Nineteenth Century America*. New Brunswick, N.J.: Rutgers Univ. Press, 1967.

Dorland, Arthur G. *A History of Friends (Quakers) in Canada.* Toronto: Macmillan, 1927.

———. *The Quakers in Canada: A History.* Toronto: Ryerson Press, 1968.

Drake, Thomas Edward. *Quakers and Slavery in America.* New Haven, Conn.: Yale Univ. Press, 1950.

DuBois, Ellen, ed. *Elizabeth Cady Stanton / Susan B. Anthony: Correspondence, Writings, Speeches.* New York: Schocken Books, 1981.

DuBois, Rachel Davis, *All This and Something More: Pioneering in Intercultural Education.* Bryn Mawr, Pa.: Dorrance, 1984.

———. *Neighbors in Action: A Manual for Local Leaders in Intergroup Relations.* New York: Harper, 1950.

DuBois, Rachel Davis, and Mew-Soong Li. *The Art of Group Conversation: A New Breakthrough in Social Communication.* New York: Association Press, 1963.

Duganne, A. J. H. *The Fighting Quakers: A True Story of the War for Our Union.* 2d ed. New York: J. P. Robens, 1866.

Eddy, Richard. *Universalism in America: A History.* 2 vols. Boston: Universalist Publishing House, 1886.

Eddy, Thomas. *Memoir of the Late John Murray, Jun., Read before the Governors of the New York Hospital.* New York: E. Conrad, 1819.

Edmunds, Albert J. *The Vision, in 1803, of Joseph Hoag.* Philadelphia: Innes and Sons, 1915.

Eller, Cynthia. *Conscientous Objectors and the Second World War: Moral and Religious Arguments in Support of Pacifism.* New York: Praeger, 1991.

Elliott, Errol T. *Quakers on the American Frontier.* Richmond, Ind.: Friends United Press, 1969.

Fay, Loren V. *Quaker Census of 1828.* Rhinebeck, N.Y.: Kinship, 1989.

Fletcher, James, and Carleton Mabee. *A Quaker Speaks from the Black Experience: The Life and Selected Writings of Barrington Dunbar.* New York: New York Yearly Meeting, 1979.

Floyd, Olive B. *Phebe Anna Thorne, Quakeress, 1828–1909.* Rye, N.Y.: Privately printed, 1958.

Forbes, John. *The Quaker Star under Seven Flags, 1917–1927.* Philadelphia: Univ. of Pennsylvania Press, 1962.

Forbush, Bliss. *Elias Hicks: Quaker Liberal.* New York: Columbia Univ. Press, 1956.

Foster, Jeremiah J. *An Authentic Report of the Testimony . . . in the Court of Chancery . . . between Thomas Shotwell, Complainant, and Joseph Hendrickson and Stacy Decow, Defendants.* 2 vols. Philadelphia: J. Harding, 1831.

Foster, Thomas. *A Narrative of the Proceedings in America in the Case of Hannah Barnard.* London: C. Stower, 1804.

Fothergill, Samuel. *Memoirs of the Life and Gospel Labours of Samuel Fothergill.* Liverpool, England: D. Marples, 1843.

Fox, George. *George Fox: An Autobiography.* Edited by Rufus M. Jones. Philadelphia: Ferris and Leach, 1904.

———. *Journal of George Fox.* Edited by Rufus M. Jones. New York: Capricorn Books, 1963.

————. *Journal of George Fox.* Edited by John L. Nickalls. Philadelphia: Religious Society of Friends, 1985.

————. *A Line of Righteousness and Justice Stretched Forth.* London: Printed for Robert Wilson, 1661.

Frame, Nathan T., and Esther G. Frame. *Reminiscences of Nathan T. and Esther G. Frame.* Cleveland, Ohio: Britton, 1907.

Freund, Paul. *Constitutional Law: Cases and Problems.* 3d. ed. Boston: Little, Brown, 1967.

Frost, J. William. *The Quaker Family in Colonial America.* New York: St. Martin's, 1973.

————, ed. *Quaker Origins of Anti-Slavery.* Norwood, Pa.: Norwood Editions, 1980.

Frost, J. William, and John M. Moore, eds. *Seeking the Light.* Wallingford, Pa.: Pendle Hill, 1986.

Fry, Anna Ruth. *A Quaker Adventure: The Story of Nine Years' Relief and Reconstruction.* New York: Frank Maurice, 1927.

Fry, Elizabeth. *Memoir of the Life of Elizabeth Fry.* Philadelphia: H. Longstreth, 1847.

Gardner, Sunderland P. *Address to the Children and Youth of the Religious Society of Friends.* Rochester, N.Y.: Daily Advertiser, 1846.

————. *Memoirs of the Life and Religious Labors of Sunderland P. Gardner.* Philadelphia: Friends Book Association, 1895.

Garner, Dorothy K., comp. *Reminiscences of Powell House Beginnings for Its 25th Anniversary.* N.p., 1985.

Gibbs, Nancy Reid. *Children of Light: Friends Seminary 1786–1986.* New York: Friends Seminary, 1986.

Graham, John W. *Conscription and Conscience: A History, 1916–1919.* London: Allen and Unwin, 1922.

Gray, Harold Studley. *Character "Bad": The Story of a Conscientious Objector.* Edited by Kennith I. Brown. New York: Harper, 1934.

Grellet, Stephen. *Memoirs of the Life and Gospel Labors of Stephen Grellett.* Edited by Benjamin Seebohm. 2 vols. Philadelphia: H. Longstreth, 1860.

Griscom, John. *Considerations Relative to an Establishment for Perfecting the Education of Young Men Within the Society of Friends.* New York: Samuel Wood, 1815.

————. *A Year in Europe . . . in 1818 and 1819.* 2 vols. New York: Collins, 1823.

Griscom, John H. *Memoir of John Griscom, LL.D.* New York: Robert Carter, 1859.

Gross, Samuel D. *Memoir of Valentine Mott, M.D.* New York: D. Appleton, 1868.

Gummere, Amelia Mott. *The Quaker, A Study in Costume.* Philadelphia: Ferris and Leach, 1901.

Gurney, Joseph John. *Brief Remarks on Impartiality in Interpretation of Scripture.* New York: Isaac T. Hopper, 1840.

Hall, Rufus. *Journal of . . . Rufus Hall.* Byberry, Pa.: John and Isaac Comly, 1840.

Hall, Willis H. *Quaker International Work in Europe since 1914.* Chambery: Reunies de Chambery, 1938.

Hamm, Thomas D. *The Transformation of American Quakerism: Orthodox Friends, 1800–1907.* Bloomington: Indiana Univ. Press, 1988.

Handy, Robert T., ed. *The Social Gospel in America, 1870–1920.* New York: Oxford Univ. Press, 1966.

Hare, C. Rous. *The Life and Letters of Elizabeth Comstock.* London: Headley Brothers, 1895.

Harnack, Adolf von. *What is Christianity? [Das Wesen des Christentums].* New York: G. P. Putnam's Sons, 1901.

Harper, Ida Husted. *Life and Work of Susan B. Anthony.* 3 vols. 1898–1908. Reprint. New York: Arno, 1969.

Hauptman, Laurence M. *The Lake Mohonk Conference on the Negro Question: A Guide to the Annual Reports.* New York: Clearwater Publishing Company, 1975.

Haviland, Laura Smith. *A Woman's Life Work.* Cincinnati: Walden and Stowe, 1882.

Hazelton, Henry Isham. *The Boroughs of Brooklyn and Queens, Counties of Nassau and Suffolk, Long Island, New York, 1609–1924.* 5 vols. New York: Lewis Historical Publishing, 1925.

Heaton, Adna. *War and Christianity Contrasted.* New York: Samuel Wood and Sons, 1816.

Hemenway, Abby Maria, ed. *Vermont Historical Gazetteer.* 5 vols. Burlington, Vt.: Hemenway, 1867–1892.

Hentoff, Nat. *Peace Agitator: The Story of A. J. Muste.* New York: Macmillan, 1963.

Hewitt, Nancy A. *Women's Activism and Social Change: Rochester, New York, 1822–1872.* Ithaca, N.Y.: Cornell Univ. Press, 1984.

Hicks, Elias. *Journal of the Life and Religious Labors of Elias Hicks.* 5th ed. New York: Isaac T. Hopper, 1832.

———. *Observations on the Slavery of Africans and their Descendants.* New York: Samuel Wood, 1811.

———. *A Series of Extemporaneous Discourses.* Philadelphia: Parker, 1825.

———. *Sermons Delivered by Elias Hicks and Edward Hicks in Friends' Meetings, New-York, in 5th Month, 1825.* New York: J. V. Seaman, 1825.

———. *Substances of Two Discourses Delivered in New-York, Dec. 17, 1824.* New York: J. V. Seaman, 1825.

Hicks, Rachel. *Memoir of Rachel Hicks.* New York: G. P. Putnam's Sons, 1880.

Hill, Christopher. *The World Turned Upside Down.* New York: Viking, 1975.

Hill, Thomas C. *Monthly Meetings in North America: An Index.* Cincinnati, Ohio: T. C. Hill, 1992.

Hinshaw, Seth B. *The Carolina Quaker Experience, 1665–1985.* Greensboro, N.C.: North Carolina Yearly Meeting, 1985.

Hinshaw, William Wade. *Encyclopedia of American Quaker Genealogy.* 6 vols. Ann Arbor, Mich.: Edwards Brothers, 1936–50.

Historic American Buildings Survey. *Historic American Buildings, New York.* 8 vols. New York: Oxford Univ. Press, 1979.

Hixson, Richard F. *Isaac Collins: A Quaker Printer in 18th Century America.* New Brunswick, N.J.: Rutgers Univ. Press, 1968.

Hoag, Joseph. *Journal of Joseph Hoag.* Auburn, N.Y.: Knapp and Peck, 1861.

Hodgson, William. *Select Historical Memoirs of the Religious Society of Friends*. Philadelphia: s.n., 1844.

Hone, Philip. *Diary of Philip Hone, 1821–1851*. Edited by Bayard Tuckerman. New York: Dodd, Mead, 1910.

Hopkins, Charles H. *The Rise of the Social Gospel in American Protestantism, 1865–1915*. New Haven, Conn.: Yale Univ. Press, 1940.

Hopper, Isaac T. *Narrative of the Proceedings of the Monthly Meeting of New-York*. New York: Hopper, 1843.

Hudson, David. *History of Jemima Wilkinson*. Geneva, N.Y.: S. P. Hull, 1821.

Hutchison, William R., ed. *American Protestant Thought: The Liberal Era*. New York: Harper, 1968.

———. *Errand to the World: American Protestant Thought and Foreign Missions*. Chicago: Univ. of Chicago Press, 1987.

———. *The Modernist Impulse in American Protestantism*. Durham: Duke Univ. Press, 1992.

Ingle, H. Larry. *Quakers in Conflict: The Hicksite Reformation*. Knoxville: Univ. of Tennessee Press, 1986.

Isichei, Elizabeth. *Victorian Quakers*. London: Oxford Univ. Press, 1970.

Ives, Kenneth, ed. *Black Quakers: Brief Biographies*. Chicago: Progresiv Publishr, 1991.

James, William. *The Varieties of Religious Experience*. London: Longmans, 1902.

Janney, Samuel M. *An Examination of the Causes which Led to the Separation of the Religious Society of Friends in America*. Philadelphia: T. E. Zell, 1868.

———. *History of the Religious Society of Friends*. 4 vols. Philadelphia: T. E. Zell, 1859–1867.

Jenkins, James. *Records and Recollections of James Jenkins*. Edited by J. William Frost. Lewiston, N.Y.: E. Mellen Press, 1984.

Johnson, Paul E. *A Shopkeeper's Millennium: Society and Revivals in Rochester, New York, 1815–1837*. New York: Hill and Wang, 1978.

Jones, Christiana. *American Friends in World Missions*. Richmond, Ind.: American Friends Board of Missions, 1948.

Jones, Lester M. *Quakers in Action: Recent Humanitarian and Reform Activities of American Quakers*. New York: Macmillan, 1929.

Jones, Mary Hoxie. *Swords into Ploughshares*. New York: Macmillan, 1937.

Jones, Rufus. *Haverford College: A History and an Interpretation*. New York: Macmillan, 1933.

———. *The Inner Life*. New York: Macmillan, 1916.

———. *Later Periods of Quakerism*. 2 vols. New York: Macmillan, 1921.

———. *The Luminous Trail*. New York: Macmillan, 1947.

———. *Quakers in the American Colonies*. London: Macmillan, 1911.

———. *A Service of Love in Wartime*. New York: Macmillan, 1920.

———. *Social Law in the Spiritual World*. Philadelphia: Winston, 1904.

———. *Spiritual Energies in Daily Life*. New York: Macmillan, 1922.

———. *Studies in Mystical Religion*. London: Macmillan, 1909.

———. *The Trail of Life in College*. New York: Macmillan, 1929.

————. *The Trail of Life in Middle Years*. New York: Macmillan, 1934.

Kaestle, Carl F. *The Evolution of an Urban School System: New York, 1750–1850.* Cambridge, Mass.: Harvard Univ. Press, 1973.

————. *Joseph Lancaster and the Monitorial School Movement.* New York: Teachers College Press, 1973.

Kashatus, William C. *Conflict of Conviction: A Reappraisal of Quaker Involvement in the American Revolution.* Lanham, Md.: Univ. Press of America, 1990.

Keim, Albert N. *The Politics of Conscience: The Historic Peace Churches and America at War, 1917–1955.* Scottsdale, Pa.: Herald Press, 1988.

Kelsey, Rayner W. *Friends and the Indians, 1655–1917.* Philadelphia: Associated Executive Committee on Indian Affairs, 1917.

Kennedy, Thomas C. *Hound of Conscience.* Fayetteville: Univ. of Arkansas Press, 1981.

Kenworthy, Leonard S. *Living in a Larger World: The Life of Murray S. Kenworthy.* Richmond, Ind.: Friends United Press, 1986.

Kirkbride, Thomas. *Remarks on the Construction, Organization and General Arrangements of Hospitals for the Insane.* Philadelphia: R. K. and P. G. Collins, 1847.

Kirkland, Samuel. *Journals of Samuel Kirkland.* Edited by Walter Pilkington. Clinton, N.Y.: Hamilton College, 1980.

Knapp, Samuel L. *Life of Thomas Eddy.* New York: Conner and Cooke, 1834.

Knowles, James Purdie. *Samuel A. Purdie, His Life and Letters.* Plainfield, Ind.: Publishing Association of Friends, 1908.

Kross, Jessica. *Evolution of an American Town: Newtown, New York, 1642–1775.* Philadelphia: Temple Univ. Press, 1983.

Labouchere, Rachel. *Deborah Darby of Coalbrookdale, 1754–1810.* York, England: William Sessions, 1993.

Lake Mohonk Conference on International Arbitration. *First Lake Mohonk Conference on International Arbitration.* Mohonk Lake, N.Y.: Lake Mohonk Conference, 1895.

Lake Mohonk Conference on the Friends of the Indian. *Proceedings of the Seventh Annual Meeting of the Lake Mohonk Conference of Friends of the Indian 1889.* Lake Mohonk, N.Y.: Lake Mohonk Conference, 1889.

Letter from a Friend in the Country to a Friend in the City. Philadelphia: s.n., 1825.

Letters of Paul and Amicus. Philadelphia: Joseph Rakestraw, 1823.

Levy, Barry. *Quakers and the American Family.* New York: Oxford Univ. Press, 1988.

Lewis, Evan A. *Review of the Testimony Issued by the Orthodox Seceders from . . . Westbury and Jericho Against Elias Hicks.* New York: A. Ming, Jr., 1829.

Longstreet, Stephen. *City on Two Rivers: Profiles of New York.* New York: Hawthorn Books, 1973.

Love, William. *Samson Occom and the Christian Indians of New England.* Boston: Pilgrim Press, 1899.

M'Clintock, Thomas. *Observations on the Articles Published in the Episcopal Recorder.* New York: Isaac T. Hopper, 1837.

McManus, Edgar J. *History of Negro Slavery in New York.* Syracuse, N.Y.: Syracuse Univ. Press, 1966.

Mabee, Carleton. *Sojourner Truth—Slave, Prophet, Legend.* New York: New York Univ. Press, 1993.

Marchand, C. Roland. *The American Peace Movement and Social Reform, 1898–1918.* Princeton, N.J.: Princeton Univ. Press, 1972.

Marietta, Jack D. *The Reformation of American Quakerism, 1748–1783.* Philadelphia: Univ. of Pennsylvania Press, 1984.

Martin, Isaac. *Journal of . . . Isaac Martin.* Philadelphia: William P. Gibbons, 1834.

Mekeel, Arthur J. *Quakerism and a Creed.* Philadelphia: Friends Book Store, 1936.

———. *The Relation of the Quakers to the American Revolution.* Washington, D.C.: University Press of America, 1979.

Miller, Nathan. *The Enterprise of a Free People: Aspects of Economic Development in New York State During the Canal Period, 1792–1838.* Ithaca, N.Y.: Cornell Univ. Press, 1962.

Miller, Perry. *Errand into the Wilderness.* Cambridge, Mass.: Harvard Univ. Press, 1956.

Milner, Clyde A. *Churchman and the Western Indians.* Norman: Univ. of Oklahoma Press, 1985.

Mitchell, Hobart. *We Would Not Kill.* Richmond, Ind.: Friends United Press, 1983.

Mohl, Raymond A. *Poverty in New York, 1783–1825.* New York: Oxford Univ. Press, 1971.

Moore, John M., ed. *Friends in the Delaware Valley.* Haverford, Pa.: Friends Historical Association, 1981.

Morgan, Kenneth William. *Islam: The Straight Path.* New York: Ronald Press, 1958.

———. *The Path of the Buddha.* New York: Ronald Press, 1956.

———. *Reaching for the Moon on Asian Religious Paths.* Chambersburg, Pa.: Anima Press, 1990.

———, ed. *The Religion of the Hindus.* New York: Ronald Press, 1953.

Morris, Aldon D. *The Origins of the Civil Rights Movement: Black Communities Organizing for Change.* New York: Free Press, 1984.

Mott, Edward. *Sixty Years of Gospel Ministry.* Portland, Oreg.: E. Mott, 1908.

Mott, John. *Lawfulness of War for Christians Examined.* New York: Samuel Wood, 1814.

Mott, Valentine. *Pain and Anaesthetics.* Washington, D.C.: M'Gill and Witherow, 1863.

———. *Travels in Europe and the East.* New York: Harper and Brothers, 1842.

Muste, Abraham John. *The Essays of A. J. Muste.* Edited by Nat Hentoff. Indianapolis: Bobbs-Merrill, 1967.

———. *Non-violence in an Aggressive World.* New York: Harper and Brothers, 1940.

———. *Not by Might.* New York: Harper, 1947.

Nash, George H. *The Life of Herbert Hoover.* 2 vols. New York: W. W. Norton, 1983–88.

National Service Board for Religious Objectors. *Directory of Civilian Public Services, May 1941 to March, 1947.* Washington, D.C.: National Service Board for Religious Objectors, n.d.

Nelson, Jacquelyn S. *Indiana Quakers Confront the Civil War.* Indianapolis, Ind.: Indiana Historical Society, 1991.

New York State. *New York State Census for 1845.* 2 vols. New York: Carroll and Cook, 1846.

New York State. Supreme Court. *Opinion of the Supreme Court of the State of New York, James Field, Plaintiff, versus Charles Field, Defendant.* Philadelphia: William Brown, 1833.

Newman, Daisy. *A Procession of Friends.* Richmond, Ind.: Friends United Press, 1980.

Newman, Henry Stanley. *Memories of Stanley Pumphrey.* New York: Friends Book and Tract Committee, 1883.

Niebuhr, Reinhold. *Nature and Destiny of Man.* 2 vols. New York: Scribner, 1941–43.

North, Edgerton Grant. *Seventy-Five Years of Brooklyn Friends School.* New York: Brooklyn Friends School, 1942.

O'Callaghan, E. B., ed. *Documents Relative to the Colonial History of New York.* 15 vols. Albany, N.Y.: Weed, Parsons, 1853–87.

Onderdonk, Henry. *The Annals of Hempstead, 1643 to 1832; Also, the Rise and Growth of the Society of Friends on Long Island and In New York 1657 to 1826.* Hempstead, N.Y.: Lott Van de Water, 1878.

Orr, E. W. *Quakers in Peace and War, 1920 to 1967.* Eastbourne: W. J. Offord and Sons, 1974.

Paine, Thomas. *Political Writings.* Edited by Bruce Kuklick. New York: Cambridge Univ. Press, 1989.

Painter, Levinus King. *Hill of Vision: The Story of the Quaker Movement in East Africa, 1902–1965.* Kaimosi, Kenya: East Africa Yearly Meeting of Friends, 1966.

Painter, Levinus K., and George Badgley. *Elizabeth Lawton Hazard, 1880–1968.* New York: New York Yearly Meeting, 1970.

Partington, Frederick. *The Story of Mohonk.* Fulton, N.Y.: Morrill, 1911.

Patching, Talcutt. *A Religious Convincement and Plea of Baptism and Communion of the Spirit.* Buffalo, N.Y.: H. A. Salisbury, 1822.

Patterson, David S. *Towards a Warless World: The Travail of the American Peace Movement, 1887–1914.* Bloomington, Ind.: Indiana Univ. Press, 1976.

Penn, William. *A Defense of the Duke of Buckingham, Against the Answer to His Book.* London: Printed for W.C., 1685.

———. *No Cross, No Crown.* London: s.n., 1669.

———. *William Penn on Religion and Ethics.* Edited by Hugh Barbour. Lewiston, N.Y.: E. Mellen, 1991.

———. *Works.* London: William Phillips, 1825.

Pessen, Edward. *Riches, Class and Power Before the Civil War.* Lexington, Mass.: D. C. Heath, 1973.

Philp, Mark. *Paine.* New York: Oxford Univ. Press, 1989.

Pickett, Robert S. *House of Refuge: Origins of Juvenile Reform in New York State, 1815–1857.* Syracuse, N.Y.: Syracuse Univ. Press, 1969.

Pivar, David J. *Purity Crusade: Sexual Morality and Social Crusade, 1868–1900.* New York: Greenwood, 1973.

Pointer, Richard. *Protestant Pluralism and the New York Experience.* Bloomington: Indiana Univ. Press, 1988.

Pomfret, John E. *The Province of East New Jersey, 1609–1702.* Princeton, N.J.: Princeton Univ. Press, 1962.

Post, Alfred C. *Eulogy of the late Valentine Mott, M.D., Ll.D.* New York: Bailliere, 1866.

Post, Isaac. *Voices from the Spirit World.* Rochester, N.Y.: Charles H. McDonnell, 1852.

Powell, Aaron M. *The National Purity Congress.* New York: American Purity Alliance, 1895.

———. *Personal Reminiscences of Anti-Slavery and Other Reforms and Reformers.* New York: Caulon, 1899.

Prucha, Francis Paul. *American Indian Policy in Crisis.* Norman: Univ. of Oklahoma, 1976.

Reagan, William J. *Venture in Quaker Education at Oakwood School.* Poughkeepsie, N.Y.: Oakwood School, 1968.

Reay, Barry. *Quakers and the English Revolution.* New York: St. Martin's, 1985.

Report of the Commissioners Appointed . . . the State of New York . . . 1810, to Explore the Route of an Inland Navigation from Hudson's River to Lake Ontario and Lake Erie. New York: Prior and Dunning, 1811.

A Review of Elias Hicks's Letter to Thomas Willis on the Miraculous Conception of Our Lord and Saviour Jesus Christ. Philadelphia: Printed for the Reader, 1824.

Richter, Melvin. *The Politics of Conscience: T. H. Green and His Age.* Lanham, Md.: Univ. Press of America, 1983.

Robinson, Arnold Elmo. *American Universalism.* New York: Exposition, 1970.

Robinson, Jo Ann. *Abraham Went Out: A Biography of A. J. Muste.* Philadelphia: Temple University Press, 1981.

———. *A. J. Muste, Pacifist and Prophet.* Wallingford, Pa.: Pendle Hill, 1981.

Rothman, David J. *The Discovery of the Asylum: Social Order and Disorder in the New Republic.* Boston: Little, Brown, 1971.

Routh, Martha. *Memoir of the Life, Travels and Religious Experience, of Martha Routh.* York, England: W. Alexander, 1822.

Russell, Elbert. *History of Quakerism.* New York: Macmillan, 1942.

———. *The Separation after a Century.* Philadelphia: Friends Intelligencer, 1928.

Rustin, Bayard. *Down the Line: Collected Writings of Bayard Rustin.* Chicago: Quadrangle Books, 1971.

———. *Strategies for Freedom: The Changing Patterns of Black Protest.* New York: Columbia Univ. Press, 1976.

Sands, David. *Journal of . . . David Sands.* New York: Collins and Brother, 1848.

Schlissel, Lillian, comp. *Conscience in America: A Documentary History of Conscientious Objection in America, 1757–1967.* New York: Dutton, 1968.

Schrauwers, Albert. *Awaiting the Millennium: The Children of Peace and the Village of Hope, 1812–1889.* Toronto: Univ. of Toronto Press, 1993.

Scott, Job. *Journal of the Life, Travels, and Gospel Labor of Job Scott.* New York: Isaac Collins, 1797.

Seeger, Daniel A. *Quaker Universalists: Their Ministry among Friends and in the World.* Media, Pa.: Quaker Universalist Fellowship, 1989.

Selleck, George. *Quakers in Boston.* Boston: Friends Meeting at Cambridge, 1976.

Shaw, Thomas M. *Bayard Rustin as Art Collector.* Newark, N.J.: Kean College of New Jersey, 1989.

Sheeran, Michael J. *Beyond Majority Rule: Voteless Decisions in the Religious Society of Friends.* Philadelphia: Philadelphia Yearly Meeting, 1983.

Singsen, Mary Ellen. *The Quaker Way in Old Westchester.* Scarsdale, N.Y.: Scarsdale Historical Society, 1982.

Smith, Edgar F. *John Griscom, 1774–1852, Chemist.* Philadelphia: s.n., 1925.

Smith, George L. *Religion and Trade in New Netherland: Dutch Origins and American Development.* Ithaca, N.Y.: Cornell Univ. Press, 1973.

Smith, H. P., ed. *History of Addison County, Vermont.* Syracuse, N.Y.: D. Mason, 1886.

Smith, Page. *The Shaping of America.* New York: Penguin, 1989.

Society of Friends. Albany Monthly Meeting. *Albany Friends Meeting, A Short History, 1942–72.* S.l.: s.n., 1973.

———. Five Years Meeting. *Minutes and Proceedings of the Five Years Meeting . . . 1902.* Philadelphia, 1903.

———. Five Years Meeting. *Proceedings of the Conference of Friends in America held in Indianapolis, 1897.* Philadelphia, 1898.

———. Friends General Conference. *Proceedings of Friends General Conference.* Philadelphia: The Conference, 1902.

———. Friends Union for Philanthropic Labor. *Proceedings of Friends Union for Philanthropic Labor at its Fifth Conference held in New York . . . 1888.* New York: Collies, Macy, 1888.

———. Jericho Monthly Meeting. *Testimony from the Monthly Meeting of Friends, Concerning Elias Hicks, Deceased.* New York: Isaac T. Hopper, 1830.

———. London Yearly Meeting. *Collection of Epistles from the Yearly Meeting of Friends in London.* Baltimore, Md.: Cole and Hewes, 1806.

———. Montclair Monthly Meeting. *Founding and Early History of Montclair Monthly Meeting.* S.l.: s.n., 1960.

———. New York Monthly Meeting (Hicksite). *Correspondence Between the Committee Appointed by the Monthly Meeting of Friends in the City of New York and a Committee of Those Called Orthodox . . . in relation to the property belonging to the Monthly Meeting. . . .* New York: Isaac T. Hopper, 1838.

———. New York Yearly Meeting. *Directory 1993.* New York: New York Yearly Meeting, 1993.

———. New York Yearly Meeting. *Discipline.* New York: Collins and Perkins, 1810.

———. New York Yearly Meeting (Hicksite). *Book of Discipline of the Religious Society of Friends.* New York: New York Yearly Meeting, 1950.

———. New York Yearly Meeting (Hicksite). *Discipline of the New York Yearly Meeting of the Religious Society of Friends.* New York: Caulon, 1893.

———. New York Yearly Meeting (Hicksite). *Memorials Concerning Deceased Friends.* New York: J. J. Caulon, 1889.

———. New York Yearly Meeting (Orthodox). *Constitution and Discipline for the American Yearly Meetings.* New York: Friends Book and Tract Committee, 1901.

———. New York Yearly Meeting (Orthodox). *Discipline of the Society of Friends of New-York Yearly Meeting.* New York: Samuel S. and William Wood, 1859.

———. New York Yearly Meeting. (Orthodox). *Discipline of the Society of Friends of New York Yearly Meeting.* New York: John F. Trout, 1876.

———. New York Yearly Meeting (Orthodox). *Discipline of the Society of Friends of New York Yearly Meeting.* New York: Friends Book and Tract Committee, 1890.

———. Philadelphia Yearly Meeting. *Brief Account of the Proceedings of the Committee, Appointed in the Year 1795 . . . for the Improvement and Gradual Civilization of the Indian Natives.* Philadelphia: Kimber, Conrad, 1805.

———. Richmond Conference (1887). *Proceedings, including Declaration of Christian Doctrine of the General Conference of Friends held at Richmond, Ind., U.S.A., 1887.* Richmond, Ind.: Nicholson, 1887.

Soderlund, Jean R. *Quakers and Slavery: A Divided Spirit.* Princeton, N.J.: Princeton Univ. Press, 1985.

Stephen, Caroline. *Quaker Strongholds.* London: K. Paul, Trench, Trubner, 1890.

Stewart, I. D. *History of the Freewill Baptists.* Dover, N.H.: Freewill Baptist Print., 1862.

Stone, William L. *History of New York City from the Discovery to the Present Day.* New York: Virtur and Yorston, 1872.

Tallcot, Joseph. *Memoirs.* Auburn, N.Y.: Miller, Orton and Mulligan, 1855.

Thomas, Abel C. *A Century of Universalism in Philadelphia and New York.* Philadelphia: s.n., 1872.

Thomas, David. *Travels Through the Western Country in the Summer of 1816.* Auburn, N.Y.: David Rumsey, 1819.

Thomas, Lamont D. *Paul Cuffee: Black Entrepreneur and Pan-Africanist.* Urbana: Univ. of Illinois Press, 1988.

———. *Rise to be a People: A Biography of Paul Cuffee.* Urbana: Univ. of Illinois Press, 1986.

Tolles, Frederick B. *Meeting House and Counting House.* Chapel Hill: Univ. of North Carolina Press, 1948

———. *Quakers and the Atlantic Culture.* New York: Macmillan, 1960.

Truth, Sojourner. *Narrative of Sojourner Truth.* Battle Creek, Mich.: Published for the Author, 1878.

Tuke, D. Hack. *The Insane in the United States and Canada*. 1885. Reprint. New York: Arno Press, 1973.

Updegraff, David B. *Open Letter for Interested Readers*. Philadelphia: s.n., 1880.

Van Pelt, Daniel. *Leslie's History of Greater New York*. 3 vols. New York: Arkell, 1898.

Van Wagner, Alson D. *A Short History of Oswego Monthly Meeting*. Clinton Corners, N.Y.: Bulls Head-Oswego Monthly Meeting, 1986.

Vining, Elizabeth Gray. *Friend of Life: The Biography of Rufus M. Jones*. Philadelphia: Lippincott, 1958.

Wager, Daniel E. *Our County and its People—A Descriptive Work on Oneida County, N.Y.* Boston: Boston History, 1896.

Waln, Robert. *Seven Letters to Elias Hicks*. Philadelphia: s.n., 1825.

Warren, Robert Penn. *Who Speaks for the Negro?* New York: Random House, 1965.

Weisbord, Marvin. *Some Form of Peace*. New York: Viking, 1968.

Wells, John I. *An Essay on War*. Hartford, Conn.: Hudson and Goodwin, 1808.

———. *An Essay on War*. New York: Samuel Wood, 1812.

Whittemore, Thomas. *Modern History of Universalism*. Boston: The Author, 1830.

Wilbur, Earl Morse. *A History of Unitarianism*. 2 vol. Cambridge, Mass.: Harvard Univ. Press, 1945–52.

Wilbur, John. *Letters to a Friend on Some of the Primitive Doctrines of Christianity*. London: Harvey and Denton, 1832.

———. *A Narrative and Exposition of the Late Proceedings of New England Yearly Meeting*. New York: Piercy and Reid, 1845.

Wilcox, Wilma. *Quaker Volunteer: An Experience in Palestine*. Richmond, Ind.: Friends United Press, 1977.

Wilentz, Sean. *Chants Democratic: New York City and the Rise of the American Working Class, 1788–1850*. New York: Oxford Univ. Press, 1984.

Willard, Frances E. *American Women*. New York: Mast, Crowell, and Kirkpatrick, 1897.

Williams, Walter Rollin. *These Fifty Years with Ohio Friends in China*. Damascus, Ohio: Friends Foreign Missionary Society of Ohio Yearly Meeting, 1940.

Willis, Thomas. *The Answers by Elias Hicks to the Six Queries Addressed to him . . . Contrasted with . . . the Doctrines of the Society of Friends*. New York: Mahlon Day, 1831.

Wilson, James Grant. *Memorial History of the City of New York*. 5 vols. New York: New York History, 1892–95.

Wilson, Warren H. *Quaker Hill: A Sociological Study*. New York: s.n., 1907.

Wisby, Herbert A., Jr. *Pioneer Prophetess*. Ithaca, N.Y.: Cornell Univ. Press, 1963.

Wittner, Lawrence S. *Rebels Against War: The American Peace Movement, 1933–1983*. Philadelphia: Temple Univ. Press, 1984.

Woman's Rights Convention. *Report of the First Woman's Rights Convention, Held at Seneca Falls, New York, July 19th and 20th, 1848*. Rochester, N.Y.: John Dick, 1848.

Wood, Mary S. *Social Hours with Friends*. New York: William Wood, 1867.

Wood, William H. S. *Friends of the City of New York in the Nineteenth Century.* New York: s.n., 1904.

Woodard, Luke. *Sketches of a Life of 75.* Richmond, Ind.: Nicholson, 1907.

Worrall, Arthur J. *Quakers in the Colonial Northeast.* Hanover, N.H.: Univ. Press of New England, 1980.

Wright, Conrad. *Beginnings of Unitarianism in America.* Boston: Beacon, 1955.

Articles

Bacon, Margaret Hope. "The Friends and Academic Freedom: Some Experiences and Thoughts of Henry J. Cadbury." In *Seeking the Light,* edited by J. William Frost and John M. Moore, 163–82. Wallingford, Pa.: Pendle Hill, 1986.

———. "A Widening Path: Women in Philadelphia Yearly Meeting Move Toward Equality." In *Friends in the Delaware Valley,* edited by John M. Moore, 173–99. Haverford, Pa.: Friends Historical Association, 1981.

Benson, Lewis. "That of God in Every Man—What did George Fox Mean by It?" *Quaker Religious Thought* 12 (1970): 2–24.

Bradley, A. Day. "New York Yearly Meeting at Poplar Ridge and the Primitive Friends." *Quaker History* 68 (1979): 75–82.

———. "Progressive Friends in Michigan and New York." *Quaker History* 52 (1963): 95–103.

Brinton, Howard. "Friends for Seventy Five Years." *Bulletin of the Friends Historical Association* 49 (1960): 3–20.

Brock, Peter. "The Peace Testimony in A Garden Enclosed." *Quaker History* 54 (1965): 67–80.

Bronner, Edwin B. "Quakers Labor with Jemima Wilkinson—1794." *Quaker History* 58 (1969): 41–47.

Burr, Nelson R. "The Quakers in Connecticut." *Bulletin of the Friends Historical Association* 31 (1942): 11–26.

Butler, David M. "Quaker Meeting House Architecture in America and England: Impressions and Comparisons." *Quaker History* 79 (1990): 93–104.

Cadbury, Henry J. "Hebraica and the Jews in Early Quaker Interest." In *Children of Light,* edited by Howard Brinton, 133–64. New York: Macmillan, 1938.

Cole, Alan. "The Quakers and the English Revolution." *Past and Present* 10 (1956): 39–54.

Cook, Katharine E., and A. Day Bradley. "Joseph Tallcot (1768–1853): Quaker Educator." *Yesteryears* 23 (1979): 28–33.

———. "The Young Ladies Collegiate Institute—Howland School." *Yesteryears* 20 (1977): 96–102.

Cox, John, Jr., "The Quakers in Michigan." *Michigan History* 59 (1945): 512–21.

Cox, John, Jr., and Percy Clapp. "Quakers in Rochester and Monroe County." *Rochester Historical Society Publication Fund Series,* no. 14 (1936): 97–111.

Davidson, Carlisle G. "A Profile of Hicksite Quakerism in Michigan, 1830–1860." *Quaker History* 59 (1970): 106–12.

Densmore, Christopher. "The Dilemma of Quaker Anti-Slavery: The Case of Farmington Quarterly Meeting, 1836–1860." *Quaker History* 82 (1993): 80–91.

———. "New Information on the Wilburites of New York: Discovery of the Wilburite Friends' Meeting for Sufferings Minute Book (1853–68)." *Quaker History* 72 (1983): 130–33.

———. "New York Quakers among the Brotherton, Stockbridge, Oneida, and Onondaga, 1795–1834." *Man in the Northeast* 44 (Fall 1992): 83–93.

———. "Quaker Publishing in New York State, 1784–1860." *Quaker History* 72 (1985): 39–57.

———. "The Samuel Bownas Case: Religious Toleration and the Independence of Juries in Colonial New York." *Long Island Historical Journal* 2 (1990): 177–88.

Dillon, Merton L. "Elizabeth Chandler and the Spread of Anti-Slavery Sentiment to Michigan." *Michigan History* 39 (1955): 481–94.

Evans, Joshua. "Joshua Evan's Journal." *Friends Miscellany* 10 (1837): 1–212.

Fay, Loren. "Arrivals of Friends in Scipio Monthly Meeting: From 1795 to 1828." *Yesteryears* 22 (1978): 28–33.

Freiday, Dean. "Atonement in Historical Perspective." *Quaker Religious Thought* 21 (Spring 1987): 13–32.

———. "The Early Quakers and the Doctrine of Authority," *Quaker Religious Thought* 15 (1973): 4–38.

Frost, J. William. "Our Deeds Carry Our Message," *Quaker History* 81 (1992): 3–51.

Hamm, Thomas D. "Elizabeth Leslie Rouse Wright Comstock." In *American National Biography*. New York: Oxford Univ. Press, forthcoming.

Haviland, Edith. "Reflections on Some Quaker Activities." *Michigan History* 46 (1962): 147–52.

Heale, M. J. "From City Fathers to Social Critics: Humanitarianism and Government in New York, 1790–1850." *Journal of American History* 63 (1976): 21–41.

Hewitt, Nancy A. "Feminist Friends: Agrarian Quakers and the Emergence of Woman's Rights in America." *Feminist Studies* 12 (Spring 1986): 27–49.

———. "The Fragmentation of Friends: The Consequences for Quaker Women in Antebellum America." In *Witnesses for Change: Quaker Women over Three Centuries,* edited by Elizabeth Potts Brown and Susan Mosher Stuard, 93–119. New Brunswick, N.J.: Rutgers University Press, 1989.

Hughes, Charles W., and A. Day Bradley. "The Early Quaker Meetings of Vermont." *Vermont History* 29 (1961): 153–67.

Hull, Henry. "Memoirs of the Life and Religious Labors . . . of Henry Hull." *Friends Library* 4 (1840): 236–325.

Kennedy, Thomas C. "Fighting about Peace." *Quaker History* 69 (1980): 3–22.

———. "They in the Lord who Firmly Trust." *Quaker History* 78 (1989): 87–102.

Lowe, Bernice. "Michigan Days of Sojourner Truth." *New York Folklore Quarterly* 12 (1956): 127–35.

Mack, Phyllis. "Gender and Spirituality in Early English Quakerism, 1650–1665." In *Witnesses for Change: Quaker Women over Three Centuries,* edited by Elizabeth Potts Brown and Susan Mosher Stuard, 31–63. New Brunswick, N.J.: Rutgers University Press, 1989.

McDermott, William P. "The Rev. Amanda Halstead Deyo (1838–1917): A Chrononarrative of a Preacher of Peace." *Hudson Valley Regional Review* 8 (1991): 1–23.

Marlin, Charles Lowell. "Jemima Wilkinson: Errant Quaker Divine." *Quaker History* 52 (1963): 90–94.

Masland, William M. "The History of Friends Academy." *Nassau County Historical Journal* 38 (1983): 18–35.

Mott, James. "Memoirs of James Mott." *Friends Miscellany* 9 (1837): 337–75.

———. "Observations on the Education of Children." *Friends Miscellany* 11 (1838): 1–28.

Painter, Nell Irvin. "Sojourner Truth in Life and Memory: Writing the Life of an American Exotic." *Gender and History* 2 (1990): 3–16.

Quinn, Edythe Ann. "The Hills in the Mid-nineteenth Century: The History of a Rural Afro-American Community in Westchester County, New York." *Afro-Americans in New York History and Life* 14 (July 1990): 35–50.

Routh, Martha. "Memoir of Martha Routh." *Friends Library* 12 (1848): 413–77.

Savery, William. "Journal of the Life, Travels and Religious Labours of William Savery." Compiled by Jonathan Evans. *Friends Library* 1 (1837): 327–459.

Schrauwers, Albert. "The Separation of the Children of Peace." *Quaker History* 79 (1990): 1–19.

Seeger, Daniel A. "Is Coexistance Possible? Christianity and Universalism in the Religious Society of Friends." In *Quaker Universalist Reader,* vol. 1, 85–99. Landenberg, Pa.: Quaker Universalist Fellowship, 1986.

Shiel, John B. "175 Years in One Book." *Long Island Forum* 33 (March 1970): 45–50.

Singsen, Mary Ellen. "Looking Back at the CPS Experience." *Friends Journal* 38 (January 1992): 22–24.

Stewart, Alexander M. "Sesquicentennial of Farmington, New York, 1789–1939." *Bulletin of the Friends Historical Association* 23 (1940): 37–43.

Tolles, Frederick B. "The New Light Quakers of Lynn and New Bedford." *New England Quarterly* 22 (1959): 291–319.

Van Wagner, Alson D. "Dutchess Quakers Maintain Their Testimony Against Military Preparation." *Dutchess County Historical Society Yearbook* 70 (1985): 51–58.

———. "Minutes of Meetings of New York and Ohio Yearly Meeting, Conservative, Retrieved." *Quaker History* 77 (1988): 122–23.

Weiss, Harry Bischoff. "Mahlon Day, Early New York Printer, Bookseller and Publisher of Children's Books." *Bulletin of the New York Public Library* 45 (1941): 1007–21.

Wellman, Judith. "The Seneca Falls Woman's Rights Convention: A Study in Social Networks," *Journal of Women's History* 3 (1991): 9–37.

Dissertations, Theses, and Unpublished Papers

Anscombe, Francis Charles. "The Contributions of the Quakers to the Reconstruction of the Southern States." Ph.D. diss., University of North Carolina, 1926.

Brown, Joshua. "Keeping Up to Date." Copy in Haviland Records Room, 1990.

———. "Looking For the Promised Land." Copy in Haviland Records Room, 1988.

———. "You Can't Get There from Here." Copy in Haviland Records Room, 1986.

Buscemi, Vince. "A Study in the Right Sharing of World Resources." Copy in Haviland Records Room, 1986.

Day, Lynda. "Friends in the Spirit: Blacks and Quakers on Long Island, 1789–1865." Paper presented at Conference on New York State History, Colgate Univ., June 1987.

Graf, Hildegard F. "Abolitionism and Anti-Slavery in Erie County." Master's thesis, Univ. of Buffalo, 1939.

Hale, Robert L., Jr. "Report of a Housing Project Undertaken by the Monthly Meeting of . . . Friends in Syracuse, New York, Sept. 1954 to March 1955." Copy in Haviland Records Room, n.d.

Hamm, Thomas D. "The Limits of the Peace Testimony: Hicksite Friends and the Nonresistant Movement." Copy in Haviland Records Room, 1993.

Hay, Alexander H. "The Rise of the Pastoral System in the Society of Friends, 1850–1900." Master's thesis, Haverford College, 1938.

Hill, Christopher. "George Fox and the English Revolution." Paper presented at George Fox Commemorative Conference, Univ. of Lancaster, March 25, 1991.

Johnson, Thomas P. "Quaker Activists in the Peace and Civil Rights Movements, 1955–1975: A Study of Stamford-Greenwich Friends Meeting." Earlham College, 1990.

Lutzker, Michael A. "Patrician Peace Advocates: The Lake Mohonk Conferences on International Arbitration, 1895–1916." New York State Historical Association, May 1975. Copy in Swarthmore College Peace Collection.

Mooers, Richard Earle. "Origins and Dispersion of Unitarianism in America." Master's thesis, Syracuse Univ., 1971.

Mosley, Thomas R. "History of the New York Manumission Society, 1785–1849." Ph.D. diss, New York University, 1963.

Naylor, Natalie A. "Mary Calderone, Crusader for Sex Education." Paper presented at Conference on New York State History, Seneca Falls, N.Y., June 5, 1993.

Newton, Sabron Reynolds. "Leroy Willard Reynolds." Copy in Haviland Records Room, n.d.

———. "New York Friends and the Concern About Alcohol." Copy in Haviland Records Room, n.d.

Rubin, Margery A. "The Challenge of U.S. vs. Seeger to the United States Supreme Court." Master's thesis, C.W. Post College, 1982.

Smith, John C. "Joseph Hoag, Vermont Quaker." Master's thesis, Earlham School of Religion, 1971.

Sorel Katherine. "Susan B. Anthony." Copy at Haviland Records Room, 1993.

Tucker, Leigh R. "English Quakers and World War I." Ph.D. diss, Univ. of North Carolina, 1972.

Underhill, A. "Historical Account of LeRay Friends Meeting at LeRaysville, Jefferson County, N.Y." Copy at Haviland Records Room, 1938.

Webster, Adelaide, Marjorie Banks, and Roger Riffer. "History of Syracuse Friends Meeting." Syracuse, N.Y., 1982.

Wosh, Peter J. "Bibles, Benevolence and Emerging Bureaucracy: The Persistence of the American Bible Society, 1816–1890." Ph.D. diss, New York Univ., 1988.

Index